Afghanistan, Arms and Conflict

This is the first book to provide a comprehensive assessment of small arms and security-related issues in post-9/11 Afghanistan. It includes case studies that reveal the findings of in-depth field research on hitherto neglected regions of the country, and provides a distinctive balance of thematic analysis, conceptual models and empirical research.

Exploring various facets of armed violence and measures to tackle it, the volume provides significant insight into broader issues such as the efficacy of international assistance, the 'shadow' economy, warlordism and the Taliban-led insurgency. In an effort to deconstruct and demystify Afghanistan's alleged 'gun culture,' it also explores some of the prevailing obstacles and opportunities facing the country in its transition period. In so doing, the book offers valuable lessons to the state-builders of Afghanistan as well as those of other countries and regions struggling to emerge from periods of transition.

This book will be of much interest to all students of Afghanistan, small arms, insurgency, Asian Studies and conflict studies in general.

Michael Bhatia was previously a visiting fellow at the Thomas J. Watson Institute for International Studies at Brown University, and is a doctoral candidate in the Department of Politics and International Relations at the University of Oxford. **Mark Sedra** is a Research Assistant Professor in the Department of Political Science of the University of Waterloo and a Senior Fellow at the Centre for International Governance Innovation (CIGI), also based in Waterloo, Canada.

Contemporary security studies

Afghanistan, Arms and Conflict

Armed groups, disarmament and security in a post-war society

Michael Bhatia and Mark Sedra

LONDON AND NEW YORK

First published 2008
by Routledge
2 Park Square, Milton Park, Abingdon, Oxon, OX14 4RN

Simultaneously published in the USA and Canada
by Routledge
270 Madison Ave, New York NY 10016

Routledge is an imprint of the Taylor & Francis Group, an informa business

Transferred to Digital Printing 2008

© 2008 Small Arms Survey

Typeset in Baskerville by Wearset Ltd, Boldon, Tyne and Wear

British Library Cataloguing in Publication Data
A catalogue record for this book is available from the British Library

Library of Congress Cataloging in Publication Data
A catalog record for this book has been requested

ISBN10: 0-415-45308-9 (hbk)
ISBN10: 0-415-47734-4 (pbk)
ISBN10: 0-203-92843-1 (ebk)

ISBN13: 978-0-415-45308-0 (hbk)
ISBN13: 978-0-415-47734-5 (pbk)
ISBN13: 978-0-203-92843-1 (ebk)

Contents

Figures

Maps

Tables

Boxes

About the authors

Michael Vinay Bhatia was previously a visiting fellow at the Thomas J. Watson Institute for International Studies at Brown University, and is a doctoral candidate in the Department of Politics and International Relations at the University of Oxford. He has conducted research in Afghanistan for the Overseas Development Institute, the Afghanistan Research and Evaluation Unit, the UK Department for International Development (via the International Policy Institute, King's College, London) and the Organization for Security and Co-operation in Europe.

Michael is the author of *War and Intervention: Issues for Contemporary Peace Operations* (Kumarian Press, 2003) and editor of *Terrorism and the Politics of Naming* (Routledge, 2007). He received his MSc in International Relations Research from the Department of Politics and International Relations, University of Oxford, and his BA, magna cum laude and honours, in International Relations from Brown University.

Mark Sedra is a Research Assistant Professor in the Department of Political Science of the University of Waterloo and a Senior Fellow at the Centre for International Governance Innovation (CIGI), also based in Waterloo, Canada. His research focuses on the topic of post-conflict state-building with an emphasis on the security sector. He has conducted research on a number of countries and regions, including Northern Ireland, the Middle East and the Balkans. The bulk of his research over the past five years has centred on Afghanistan, and he has published widely on security issues in Afghanistan and the Middle East. He has served as a consultant to various governments, intergovernmental organizations and non-governmental organizations (NGOs) on issues pertaining to the security and political situation in Afghanistan.

Mark received an Honours BA in Political Science and History from the University of Toronto and an MSc in International History from the London School of Economics (LSE). He is currently a PhD candidate in the Political Studies Department at the School of Oriental and African Studies (SOAS) in the University of London. His dissertation focuses on the challenges of rebuilding security structures in post-conflict societies, with Afghanistan and Iraq serving as his principal case studies.

Foreword

The United Nations-brokered peace process at the Bonn Conference in 2002 sketched a path to a stable future for a country buffeted by a quarter century of internecine war, foreign occupation and interference. Yet, after a successful initial phase during which ambitious goals were met, including the first presidential and parliamentary elections in decades, Afghanistan is again struggling with its old demons of internal strife. The Taliban are back and seriously threaten the fragile state being built in Kabul.

This book usefully focuses attention on one of the main reasons for the backsliding: the failure by the international community and the Afghan authorities to deal meaningfully with the proliferation of small arms and light weapons.

It is difficult to overestimate the influence guns have over people's lives in Afghanistan. Conflicts – be they disputes between families over marriage, intra-village battles over resources or the continued fight between insurgents and the now NATO-led Coalition – become all the more violent owing to ready stockpiles of guns and ammunition. In the political arena, warlords and local officials with guns impose their will with apparent impunity.

There have been missed opportunities to tackle this problem. The Kabul authorities were discouraged by most of their foreign supporters to engage in any meaningful reconciliation efforts. The international community ignored pressing appeals from President Hamid Karzai and the United Nations to send enough troops in 2002 to start rebuilding and disarming across the country, at a time when the Taliban had yet to regroup and the country's warlords had been decoupled from their supporters. Now the challenges are greater. International funds and attention have been diverted to Iraq, rampant corruption has cost the government support and the burgeoning opium trade is fuelling crime.

But thankfully one constant represents a source of hope to Afghan authorities as they begin to implement a legal framework to control arms proliferation: ordinary Afghans remain determined to move beyond conflict.

Containing the findings of in-depth field research, the Small Arms Survey's new book, *Afghanistan, Arms and Conflict*, provides a comprehensive and much needed assessment of small arms- and security-related issues in post-9/11 Afghanistan. It offers crucial insight for stakeholders working in Afghanistan or in other post-conflict environments where the rule of law has yet to replace the rule of the gun.

Ambassador Lakhdar Brahimi, former Special Adviser to the Secretary-General of the United Nations (2004–2005), UN Special Representative for Afghanistan (2001–2004), UN Special Envoy for Afghanistan (1997–1999), Foreign Minister of Algeria (1991–1993).

Acknowledgements

The authors of this volume recognize that any new research on Afghanistan builds on the considerable efforts of both international and Afghan scholars who have researched both the country's conflict and its people over the past 50 years. They are also grateful to numerous local and international NGOs whose representatives generously provide their insight and hospitality with visiting researchers.

Michael Bhatia would like to thank the Afghan New Beginnings Programme (ANBP), who permitted him to accompany their disarmament and demobilization teams and observe reintegration programmes throughout Afghanistan. Peter Babbington, Basil Massey, Paul Cruickshank, Steven Feller, Reuben Stewart, Samantha Perera, Sandra Langenbach and Annemarie Brolsma were particularly helpful.

Gurpawan Singh and Vikram Bhatia were especially generous during Bhatia's stay in the Hazarajat and Ghor Province. Masood Karokhel, Susanne Shmeidl and Ehsan Zahine, as well as all of the staff of the Tribal Liaison Office, facilitated his research in Paktya, Kabul and Kunduz Province. Alexander Thier, Andrew Wilder, Peter Bergen, Julie Sirrs, Haneef Atmar and Suleiman Mohammed generously introduced him to Afghanistan in August 2001. Special thanks go to Lucy Jones, Nick Downie, Christopher Freeman, Scott Braunschweig, Kate Clark, Liz Alden Wiley, Hamish Nixon, Brandy Bauer and Phil Wilkinson, who all raised Bhatia's spirits during his stays in Kabul.

Interpretation was provided by two Afghan citizens, who endured long hours and harsh living conditions. A number of other Afghan citizens graciously supported this project, most particularly those serving with the ANBP. Unfortunately, all must remain regrettably anonymous due to the sensitivity of the information provided.

Field research grants for projects that related to this book were provided by the Marshall Aid Commemoration Commission and the British Committee on Central and Inner Asia. The Watson Institute was an ideal location for the finalization of the manuscript.

The generous staff at the Library of Congress in Washington, DC, pointed out available resources and brought Bhatia's attention to books and other publications. Reference librarians Hirad Dinavari and Thomas Mann eagerly provided source material during his stay in the main reading room. The National Security Archives at George Washington University allowed him to go through boxes of uncatalogued Afghan documents. Particular thanks are owed to Mary Curry and Barbara Elias, as well as to David Corn and Steve Galster, who decades ago submitted Freedom of Information Act requests that brought these documents to public light. The Afghanistan Research and Information Center generously sent documents from their collection in Peshawar to Kabul.

This book owes its greatest debt, however, to the more than 345 Afghans who patiently allowed Michael Bhatia to interview them as to the nature of their lives, decisions and past actions. To do so, many had to overcome a range of emotions, from fear to sorrow.

Mark Sedra is grateful to the numerous officials, NGO representatives and scholars – both Afghan and international – who shared their knowledge on the small arms issue in Afghanistan. Most of these individuals were extremely open and forthcoming, providing vital information, including, in some cases, internal documents and data. As many spoke on condition of anonymity, they are not listed by name in the text, but their contributions were invaluable. Lisa Pinsley, formerly a staff member of the ANBP, deserves special mention for her generous assistance and encouragement for my research on this and other projects.

Sedra is also extremely grateful to Charles Tripp of the School of Oriental and African Studies (SOAS), his PhD supervisor, for his patience in allowing him to diverge from his PhD research to complete work on this book. Finally, Sedra extends thanks to his family for their unfailing support and encouragement.

This project benefited from an in-depth peer-review process. The authors appreciate the comments and constructive criticism offered by Antonio Giustozzi, Jonathan Goodhand, Michael Griffin, Nicolas Marsh, Dean Piedmont, Lisa Pinsley, Conrad Schetter, Chris Smith and Edwina Thompson, all of whom provided helpful comments on the original drafts. Barnett Rubin provided support and advice.

The production of this book would not have been possible without the generous financial support of the Small Arms Survey project by the governments of Switzerland, Belgium, Canada, Finland, the Netherlands, Norway, Sweden and the United Kingdom.

The Geneva-based Small Arms Survey initiated, funded and supported the research project that culminated in this publication. At the Small Arms Survey, numerous staff members helped patiently to shepherd this project through its long gestation. Particular thanks go to Christina Wille, who gave the project shape in its beginning; Diana Rodriguez, who provided invaluable support in its final stages, in particular by writing the Introduction; Jillie Luff, who produced user-friendly maps from often incongruous topographical data; and Tania Inowlocki, who supervised the publication process. Barbara Gimelli Sulashvili contributed substantially to the final form of the book by editing the manuscript. Carole Touraine provided valuable administrative support. Special thanks go to Sarah M. Hoban for her meticulous and energetic assistance in fact-checking the entire manuscript and to Tanin Bashir for his thorough look at the spelling of Afghan terms. The Small Arms Survey also extends thanks to Andrew Humphrys of Routledge for his interest in and support for the project.

About the Small Arms Survey

The Small Arms Survey is an independent research project located at the Graduate Institute of International and Development Studies in Geneva, Switzerland. Established in 1999, the project is supported by the Swiss Federal Department of Foreign Affairs, and by sustained contributions from the governments of Belgium, Canada, Finland, the Netherlands, Norway, Sweden and the United Kingdom. The Survey is also grateful for past and current project support received from the governments of Australia, Denmark, France, Germany, New Zealand and the United States, as well as from different United Nations agencies, programmes and institutes.

The objectives of the Small Arms Survey are: to be the principal source of public information on all aspects of small arms and armed violence; to serve as a resource centre for governments, policy-makers, researchers and activists; to monitor national and international initiatives (governmental and non-governmental) on small arms; to support efforts to address the effects of small arms proliferation and misuse; and to act as a clearing house for the sharing of information and the dissemination of best practices. The Survey also sponsors field research and information-gathering efforts, especially in affected states and regions. The project has an international staff with expertise in security studies, political science, law, economics, development studies and sociology, and collaborates with a network of researchers, partner institutions, non-governmental organizations and governments in more than 50 countries.

 Small Arms Survey
47 Avenue Blanc
1202 Geneva
Switzerland
tel: +41 22 908 5777
fax: +41 22 732 2738
email: sas@graduateinstitute.ch
http://www.smallarmssurvey.org

Abbreviations

ABP	Afghan Border Police
AGF/ACF	Anti-government forces/anti-Coalition forces
AIHRC	Afghan Independent Human Rights Commission
AMF	Afghan Military Force
ANA	Afghan National Army
ANBP	Afghan New Beginnings Programme
ANLF	Afghan National Liberation Front (Mullah Mohammed Nabi)
ANP	Afghan National Police
ANSO	Afghanistan NGO Security Office
APMASD	Anti-Personnel Mines and Ammunition Stockpile Destruction
AST	Ammunition Survey Team
AT&L	Acquisitions, Technology and Logistics
ATA	Afghan Transitional Authority
ATO	Ammunition Technical Officer
CIA	Central Intelligence Agency (US)
CIP	Commander Incentive Programme
CSTC-A	Combined Security Transition Command – Afghanistan
D&R	Demobilization and Reintegration Commission
DDR	Disarmament, demobilization and reintegration
DIAG	Disbandment of Illegal Armed Groups
DRA	Democratic Republic of Afghanistan
ECC	Electoral Complaints Commission
G8	Group of eight major industrial democracies
GOLIAG	Government Officials with Links to Illegal Armed Groups
HIG/HIH	*Hezb-e-Islami* Gulbuddin Hekmatyar
HIK	*Hezb-e-Islami* Khalis
HRRAC	Human Rights Research and Advocacy Consortium
HWC	Heavy Weapons Cantonment
IED	Improvised explosive devices
IOG	International Observer Group
ISAF	International Security Assistance Force

ISI	Inter-Services Intelligence (Pakistan)
JEMB	Joint Electoral Management Body
KhAD	Khadamat-e Etela'at-e Dawlati (State Information Agency) 1980–1992
MDG	Millennium Development Goals
MDU	Mobile disarmament unit
MoD	Ministry of Defence
MoI	Ministry of Interior
NAPCE	National Assembly and Provincial Council Elections
NATO	North Atlantic Treaty Organization
NDC	National Disarmament Commission
NDS	National Directorate of Security (Amaniyat)
NGO	Non-governmental organization
NIFA	National Islamic Front of Afghanistan (Pir Gailani)
NSA	National Security Archive
NWFP	Northwest Frontier Province (Pakistan)
OMC-A	Office of Military Cooperation – Afghanistan
OSC-A	Office of Security Cooperation – Afghanistan
PRD	Police Reform Directorate
PRT	Provincial Reconstruction Team
PSC	Private security company
RTC	Recruitment Training Centre
SAM	Surface-to-air missile
SCN	Supervisory Council of the North
SSR	Security sector reform
UF/NA	United Front/Northern Alliance/Council for the Defence of Afghanistan; alliance between Rabbani, Dostum and Karim Khalili
UN	United Nations
UNAMA	United Nations Assistance Mission for Afghanistan
UNDP	United Nations Development Programme
UNICEF	United Nations Children's Fund
UNMACA	United Nations Mine Action Centre for Afghanistan
UNOPS	United Nations Office of Project Services
UNPU	United Nations Protection Unit
USAID	United States Agency for International Development
USPI	US Protection and Investigation
VBIED	Vehicle-borne improvised explosive devices
WCP	Weapons collection point
WFP	World Food Programme
WHO	World Health Organization

Glossary of local terms

Arbakai, sg. (Arbakian, pl.) Tribal police, in Pashtoon communities utilized to enforce internal rules and decisions of Jirga, and to protect the community from external forces. Depending on tribe, also pronounced and spelled as *arbakee, robakee, harbakai.*

Beg/mir Local landlord, *khan* and leader.

Fedayee A term utilized in Ghazni among Shi'a militias denoting a unit of dedicated combatants, who is willing to sacrafice him/herself for the cause of religion.

Jirga 'A tribal council that has legislative and juridical authority in the name of the tribal community.' (Adamec, 2003, pp. 197–198)

Khan An honorific provided to a locally influential individual, who acquires support and power through the distribution of patronage and largesse to followers, and who ultimately serves both to influence local decisions and to arbitrate in local disputes.

Kheil Tribal sub-grouping.

Kuchi Nomad.

Loya Jirga Grand/National Council, 'highest organ of state power that Afghan rulers convened to decide matters of national importance.' (Adamec, 2003, p. 236)

Malek A centrally appointed tribal chieftain, utilized by a tribe for all engagements/interactions with the government, he is a provincial or district liaison person, not necessarily as powerful as local *khans* or other prominent individuals.

Manteqa An area of spatial cognition of various size; can refer both to the whole of Afghanistan or to a village.

Maulavi (pl. *ulama*) 'Graduate of a madrassa, college of Islamic studies;' religious cleric or teacher. The plural form more generally also designates the top class of Muslim religious officials.

Mesher Elder.

Meshrano Jirga The 102-delegate upper house of National Assembly of Afghanistan.

Mullah '[A] preacher and spiritual adviser.' (Adamec, 2003, p. 267)

Nafar-e-khas   Refers to a commander's 'special envoy,' common in strong-man militias, and utilized to recruit and enforce.

Nazm-e-khas   Means 'Special Order' and refers to either a special police unit established by former Kandahar governor Gul Agha Sherzai or (more commonly) as a commander's 'special group.'

Qawm   A unit of social cognition, denoting a group of affiliated individuals. It can refer to community, tribe, nation, sub-tribe or non-tribal solidarity or professional groups.

Qawmi mesher   The leader of a *qawm*, can be linked to performance, specific skills (military training, education) and to lineage.

Qawmi meshran   The pl. of qawmi mesher, community elders of a *qawm*, which serves as a consultative body and limits the power of *qawmi mesher.*

Sardar   Term of Persian origin referring to centrally appointed local chieftain, similar to *malek.*

Sardar-e-qawm   A less-utilized term for the leader, 'big man,' of a *qawm.*

Sayyed   Esteemed families and their descendants.

Shura   Community decision-making body constituted by elders.

Takia khana   Equivalent of the Mosque for Shi'a Muslims.

Tanzim   A political–military organization.

Wolesi Jirga   The 249-delegate lower house of the National Assembly of Afghanistan.

Woleswali   A district.

Zakat   One of the five pillars of Islam. An annual donation of 2.5–5% of some assets, income, harvest or other earning to poor people or a charity organization.

Introduction

Diana Rodriguez

The problem of small arms proliferation and misuse is not new to Afghanistan: for decades, a ready supply of arms and ammunition has allowed even the most minor of disagreements to escalate into armed conflict. Neither is the influence of guns over society unique to Afghanistan among post-conflict countries. What is striking in Afghanistan's post-Taliban era, however, is the magnitude of weapons holdings and the level of their penetration into political and economic life.

Efforts to implement a nationwide disarmament programme were introduced late and implemented slowly; they were subsequently hindered by the absence of a holistic approach to security sector reform. Long-term commitment from the government and the international community is now needed either to expand disarmament programmes or create new successor programmes. Future disarmament efforts will be complicated by the resurgence of the Taliban and other anti-government armed groups.

Afghanistan, Arms and Conflict: Armed groups, disarmament and security in a post-conflict society unpicks these specific characteristics of post-9/11 Afghanistan, providing an indispensable and comprehensive analysis of the security situation in the country. It hones in on hitherto neglected provinces to show how the motivations for acquiring and using weapons vary among regions. It also reveals that the effects of interventions aimed at demilitarizing the country are concomitantly varied.

The book looks at how power and the possession of weapons are often intertwined, though it makes clear that availability of weapons and victimization are only two determinants of influence and power. It is not only active violence, but also structural violence that underpins the so-called 'rule of the gun' in post-conflict Afghanistan. Through the threat of force, commanders and militias with weapons have insulated themselves from the checks and balances of governmental and traditional institutions; they have acquired or influenced political appointments at the district, provincial and even central government levels, and many local militias have been legalized and funded by the government, the NATO-led International Security Assistance Force (ISAF), Coalition forces and private security companies.

Estimates as to how many uncontrolled small arms and light weapons are held in Afghanistan vary from a few million to more than ten million, or up to one gun for every three men, women and children in the country. For three decades, vast weapon supplies flooded the country from opponents on either side of the Cold War, from neighbouring countries and from regional powers. While the supply of weapons in northern Pakistan and Afghanistan outstripped demand in 2005, the growth of the insurgency has increased the demand for weapons.

This widespread availability of guns is a driver of insecurity and political instability. For ordinary Afghans, security remains the number one concern, a fear that has not been dislodged by the advances made since the Bonn Agreement in 2002. These advances include the inauguration of Parliament and the initiation of the Disbandment of Illegal Armed Groups programme.

The government and international actors based in Kabul are acutely aware of security threats. But there are various interpretations of where sources of insecurity lie. In Kabul, the ISAF, Coalition forces and former members of the Northern Alliance define security in relation to the threats posed by the Taliban and other anti-government insurgents, or, more recently, by the drug trade. For the broader population, however, local security is more commonly compromised by the factional feuds, human rights abuses and predatory behaviour of commanders and former warlords. In the absence of effective national law enforcement, these combatants act with impunity.

These different viewpoints partly explain why efforts by the government and the international donor community have failed to stem small arms and light weapons proliferation.

A second explanation for the reluctance to tackle rigorously the small arms problem is the accommodationist stance taken by the Afghan authorities and external governments towards local commanders, not only in the post-conflict period, but during decades of war when weapons supplied by external governments were distributed directly or channelled through the Afghan government to local commanders. There are parallels today, since certain militias are utilizing private security company contracts, US funds and their integration into the Afghan Military Forces to consolidate local power, as illustrated in the case studies on Paktya, Kandahar and Ghor provinces. Numerous government officials are former commanders who have yet to sever their links to armed groups, a situation that both erodes the popular legitimacy of the government and stymies attempts to achieve political consensus for initiatives to reduce and control small arms.

A third explanation for failing to reduce the availability of small arms is the belief that disarming the population would lead to more, not less, insecurity, at least until the government could guarantee stability. Significant efforts have been made to restructure and arm the security forces, in particular the army, while disarmament has so far featured only as a secondary goal in the demilitarization process. Little attention was paid to weapons licensing until 2005, and progress in reforming the judicial and law enforcement bodies – vital for enforcing the new licensing regime – has been poor. Prioritizing security sector reform without parallel steps to reduce the firepower of insurgent groups and the civilian population has proved misguided. Easy access to weapons has fuelled the resurgence of warlord power, facilitated the expanding drug trade and heightened the probability of a return to civil conflict, posing one of the biggest obstacles to the ongoing security sector reform process.

The book is based on a combination of field research and reviews of existing literature, press accounts, archival material and surveys. Chapter 3 and the case studies in Part III are based on semi-structured interviews with 345 combatants in Afghanistan. The majority of interviews were conducted in 2005 and most of the interviewees were contacted through the Afghan New Beginnings Programme (ANBP). Additional interviews were conducted with the United Nations Assistance Mission for Afghanistan (UNAMA), ANBP, Afghanistan NGO Security Office, NGOs and the Coalition. Part II is primarily based on interviews conducted during three visits to Afghanistan in April and May 2005, November 2005 and June 2006. Interviews were held with more than 80 representatives of international donor missions, UN agencies, the Afghan government, international NGOs, civil society groups and private contractors.

With its meticulous retracing of the dynamics relating to small arms and light weapons, *Afghanistan, Arms and Conflict* draws valuable lessons that can be applied in Afghanistan and in other post-conflict societies. In addition to examining the role of small arms in Afghan society, it provides a theoretical model for analysing armed groups and their members, while revealing distinctions in the relationships between the state, external actors, communities, commanders and combatants. The volume also sheds light on the local impact of and responses to counter-terror and counter-narcotics initiatives. It evaluates ongoing disarmament, demilitarization, reintegration and other arms reduction efforts within the state-building process, challenging donors' assurances about the success of such programmes. The main conclusions include:

- A comprehensive disarmament process should be prioritized in the early stages of the post-conflict period. Disarmament in Afghanistan has become more difficult following the resurgence of the Taliban and other anti-government forces.
- Illegal armed groups need to be provided with realistic incentives to disarm, in particular when the government's coercive capacity is limited.
- Any effective programme to control and reduce small arms needs to be underpinned by empirical data on the extent and nature of the problem.

- The success of security sector reform (SSR) projects is directly correlated to the efficacy of disarmament activities. If there is no successful disarmament, the SSR model cannot achieve one of its main goals, namely to invest the state with a monopoly over the use of force.
- Small arms reduction and control initiatives will only be feasible with political support from the national government and the international donor community.
- Engagement by private security companies, aid agencies, the Afghan government, and Coalition and NATO forces can have the unintended consequence of increasing the political and economic influence of local armed groups and undermining community-level checks and balances.

Chapter summaries

Afghanistan, Arms and Conflict has a three-part structure, comprising a thematic part on security concerns (security, arms flows and armed groups), a second thematic part on interventions (demilitarization programmes and security sector reform) and a case study part covering six localities.

Part I: Mapping insecurity: weapons flows and armed groups in Afghanistan

Chapter 1 – Violence in Afghanistan: an overview

This chapter provides an introduction to the consequences of three decades of armed conflict and arms transfers. It reveals how the Coalition forces' concern with counter-insurgency and the reduction of poppy production stands in sharp contrast to the local population's continuing perception of insecurity. The presence of readily available small arms and ammunition, coupled with the detrimental influence of armed groups on society, threatens to render existing conflicts more violent. This chapter also provides a framework for understanding types of violence in Afghanistan, including local security concerns and the role of the state.

Chapter 2 – Small arms flows into and within Afghanistan

In analysing the historical and contemporary small arms flows into and within Afghanistan, this chapter covers the consequences of external interventions, current procurement strategies of armed groups and government forces, as well as the scale and types of weapons currently available in Afghanistan. It shows how external governments have played a critical role in sponsoring and supporting armed groups.

Chapter 3 – Armed groups in Afghanistan

Contemporary Afghanistan is home to a wide variety of armed groups, ranging from political–military parties to warlords and community militias. Recruitment motives, strategies, internal structure and the relationships between commanders and combatants differ markedly among these groups. International and national assistance to armed groups can have negative consequences unless the complex, varied and evolving nature of these groups is considered.

Part II: Addressing the small arms issue: demilitarization and security sector reform in Afghanistan

Chapter 4 – The four pillars of demilitarization in Afghanistan

This chapter explores the implications of the failure of the cornerstone programmes of demilitarization – disarmament, demobilization and reintegration (DDR) of former combatants, heavy weapons cantonment, disbandment of illegal armed groups and the anti-personnel mines and ammunition stockpile programme – to identify disarmament and small arms and light weapons reduction as a priority. The impact of demilitarization on the local security situation remains limited.

Chapter 5 – Small arms and security sector reform

This chapter examines efforts to create a legal framework to underpin small arms reduction and control efforts. It also analyses a number of laws and presidential decrees aimed at regulating firearm ownership and possession among both Afghans and international non-state actors. In the absence of far-reaching disarmament, security sector reform (SSR) – namely the transformation of the Afghan army, police and judical apparatus – has not yet led to a significant improvement of the security situation on the ground. Armed groups remain highly influential at all levels of society.

Part III: Case studies[1]

Chapter 6 – Ghor Province: all against all?

In Ghor, one of the most under-researched Afghan provinces, the authority and the legitimacy of community elders is crucial for the mobilization process. The creation of a provincial division of the Afghan Military Forces has increased the supply of weapons to the province and led to the mobilization of a new generation of combatants. This enabled commanders to increase their power to such an extent that they overpowered the elders for their own purposes, specifically to acquire combatants, prey on opposing villages and consolidate economic and political power in the province.

Chapter 7 – Paktya Province: sources of order and disorder

In Paktya Province, the influence of community elders is restricted to the mobilization of tribal police. In periods of political transition, when the elders' authority is weakened, the intervention by extra-provincial actors may produce a climate that can facilitate predation and rights abuses. In and around the capital, Gardez, for example, initial mobilization for the purpose of securing the city during a period of political transition evolved into the use of this standing force for predatory purposes. The creation of the Afghan Military Forces contributed to the legitimization of predatory commanders.

Chapter 8 – Kandahar City: the political economy of Coalition deployment

In Kandahar, where the tribes are dominated by prominent families and individuals who have been strengthened further by their commercial relationship with the Coalition, the function of tribal militias can turn quickly from self-protection into predation. The fact that private security companies hire militias is problematic, as it fortifies the commander–combatant link, prevents soldiers from going through reintegration and job retraining, and provides incentives for racketeering. Inhabitants of Kandahar City face three interwoven sources of insecurity: Taliban insurgents, intra-commander fighting or predation, and criminality.

Chapter 9 – Kunduz, Takhar and Baghlan: parties, strongmen and shifting alliances

In the three northern regions of Kunduz, Takhar and Baghlan, individuals acquire military power independently, with community elders having little influence in comparison to other areas. Mobilization takes place either by force, or for the protection of the family or village, even though economic incentives may also play a role. The creation of the Afghan Military Forces invested commanders with official status. Since the Bonn Agreement, the north has been one of the more secure areas of Afghanistan, but the predatory behaviour of commanders (many of whom acquired district and provincial government positions) has produced local vulnerabilities, including skirmishes between commanders and allegations of abuse by local commanders.

Chapter 10 – Jalalabad: the consequences of Coalition support

In the Jalalabad region, commanders embody the ideal of a strongman. They are able to utilize both elder and religious authority to mobilize combatants, and they structure their forces to ensure internal discipline. They acquire conscripts by force, though the economic incentive of a small salary in the absence of other livelihood opportunities is by far the predominant motive for combatants in this region. The newly established security institutions serve as a hiding place for commanders' militias and as a theatre for inter-factional disputes.

Chapter 11 – Hazarajat: Daykundi, Shahristan, Panjab and Syahkhak

The case of the Hazarajat shows that a broad shared ethnicity does not guarantee political unity. Locals are subject to threats from opposing commanders and to extortion and land disputes, although not to the degree common in other regions of Afghanistan, such as Baghlan, Jalalabad and Kandahar. Nevertheless, despite the high costs of infighting, the Hazara emerged from the conflict with an elite ready to play a role at the national level.

Note

1 Information on prominent individual commanders and their political affiliations in each region to be online, available at: http://www.smallarmssurvey.org/files/sas/publications/b_series5.html.

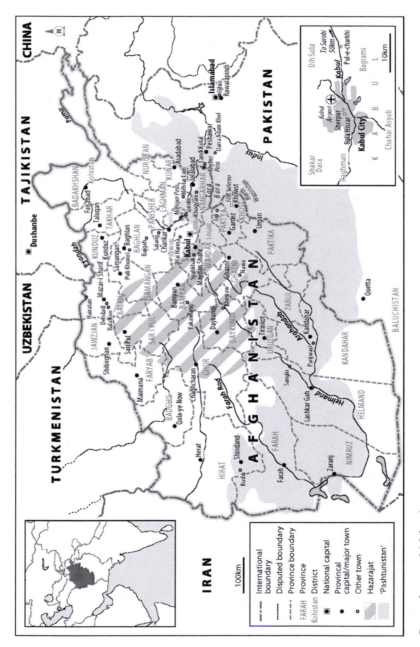

General map of Afghanistan.

Part I

Mapping insecurity

Weapons flows and armed groups in Afghanistan

1 Violence in Afghanistan
An overview

Michael Bhatia

Distressingly, 'the rule of the gun' is a term often applied to many post-conflict environments. In essence, the term refers to the continued dominance of armed groups and commanders and their influence over a broad range of sectors, from the political to the economic. While the fighting may have ended – whether as a consequence of a negotiated agreement, external intervention, war fatigue, peace-building or a changing international system – for the local population, the situation remains characterized by a high degree of insecurity. As will be demonstrated throughout this book, it is an appropriate description for Afghan politics over the past three decades.

This chapter reveals how, after three decades of armed conflict and arms transfers, security remains the primary concern of Afghans and disarmament is overwhelmingly supported by the majority of the Afghan citizenry. The chapter examines the varied domains in which insecurity is felt – chronicling both the legacy of conflict (in terms of victimization, underdevelopment, chronic deprivation and psychological trauma) and its varied dimensions. It describes the consequences of small arms proliferation and the link between small arms and the role of militias and commanders, locally and nationally.

This chapter also reveals the linkage between small arms, militias and commanders, revealing how the influence of the gun is felt far beyond direct combat, particularly in the political arena, whether in the newly established Parliament or in village politics. It concludes by engaging with three common dimensions of violence: varieties of inter-factional conflict, the role of the Afghan state and the discussion of the 'Afghan security dilemma.'

The latter two dimensions introduce the particular role of legitimacy as a prominent factor in the relationship between communities, commanders and states. The chapter shows how the absence of a state able to act as an arbiter accountable in local disputes allows the commander to acquire community legitimacy in exchange for protection. As will be demonstrated throughout this book, there is a particular need to examine the links between the different governments involved, businesses, private security companies, commanders, communities and combatants.

Afghanistan's outlook today is a mixture of hope and despair. Substantial progress has been made over the past five years:

- Emergency and Constitutional *Loya Jirgas* were convened;
- a president (2004), Parliament (2005) and provincial councils were elected;
- the 60,000-strong Afghan Military Forces were demilitarized and the Disbandment of Illegal Armed Groups (DIAG) programme was initiated;
- a locally legitimate, multi-ethnic and operationally effective Afghan National Army was created;
- roads and highways were rebuilt and schools were reopened;
- a new stable and anti-inflationary currency was promulgated.

Some prominent commanders are far weaker and less entrenched than at any point in the last 25 years. Others continue to expand their power into the economic and political realms. The conditions established under the Bonn Agreement were met with the inauguration of the Parliament, and a new Afghan Compact was signed indicating continued donor commitment in 2006. Although there are continued complaints from the Bush administration as to the lack of European burden-sharing, NATO has assumed command over Operation Enduring Freedom, with the Canadians, British and Dutch deploying substantial forces to the southwest and incurring casualties in the process (Jalali, 2006).

And yet, while the progress made since 2001 is considerable, a number of developments introduce cause for concern. Many critics point to the lack of military and financial resources provided to Afghanistan (initially considered the primary frontline of the 'war on terror'), particularly in comparison to the resources sent to Iraq. The consequences of this are threefold.

First, after several years of covert regeneration (evidence of which was dismissed throughout 2005), the revitalization of the Anti-Government Forces (AGF)[1] insurgency has graphically challenged these impressions of progress. More than 4,000 people (primarily AGF militants) died in violence in 2006 (AFP, 2006c). Spring 2006 witnessed a renewed willingness by the Taliban to engage in sizeable set-piece battles and massed attacks against Coalition and Afghan government forces, although NATO was generally viewed to have successfully rebuffed their offensive. Perhaps even more significantly, however, it decisively demonstrated the Taliban's command of the mountains and countryside in significant areas of southern and eastern Afghanistan. Moreover, the AGF felt sufficiently reconstituted so as to forego the traditional winter lull in fighting and was even able to overrun government positions in Musa Qala, Helmand in February 2007 and administer the province (imposing Shari'a law and collecting taxes) through to July 2007 (IRIN, 2007).

Second, as will be demonstrated in this chapter, questions remain as to the degree to which the positive steps detailed above are actually felt at the local level. Indeed, some individual Afghans, both in press accounts and in personal interviews, even question whether they are better off now than they were under the Taliban (Zahid, 2002a). Insecurity, whatever its sources (whether from crime, warlords, Coalition operations or the Taliban), remains the primary concern of most villagers. The Afghan National Army's (ANA) development has not been accompanied by the strengthening of the police and the judiciary, whose corruption has served to compromise the legitimacy of the emerging Afghan government and to undermine the counter-insurgency effort. While the government of Afghanistan has limited the role of commanders in the Presidential Cabinet and the Ministry of Defence, figures who maintain militias have moved to the Parliament and to positions in provincial and district administrations (Jalali, 2006; Bhatia, 2007). While these figures may provide protection to certain constituencies, they also produce vulnerability for either opposing groups or for those without connection to an armed group.

Third, the graphic increase in opium production and the inconsistent and flawed approach to both eradication and police, judiciary and local governance reform, threatens to turn Afghanistan into a narco-state. The UN Office on Drugs and Crime indicated that the area under opium cultivation reached a record 165,000 hectares in 2006 compared with 104,000 in 2005. In the southern province of Helmand, where Taliban insurgents have scaled up their attacks on Afghan government and international forces, cultivation soared 162 per cent to 69,324 hectares (Mansfield, 2006). Far from reducing the Taliban's sources of funding, the counter-narcotics campaign has increased local support for Taliban activities in the northeast and south. Moreover, appropriation of the counter-narcotics effort by local powerbrokers to consolidate their hold over land, markets, cotton, poppy and wheat produces a sense of injustice and hypocrisy among local populations (Mansfield, 2006).

The combination of a revived AGF insurgency, continued dominance of the opium economy (and its influence on national politics and institutions) and local dissatisfaction due to insecurity and underdevelopment presents a major challenge to both the international community and the Afghan government.

The consequences of small arms proliferation and conflict in Afghanistan

Since 1975, with the first failed rebellions by the political–military party Ikhwanun-ul-Musulman in the Panjsher and Charikar, Afghanistan has experienced a succession of civil wars of varying intensity. In 1978, community rebellions in Nuristan and military rebellions in Herat evolved into a decade-long sustained insurgency against the Soviet-backed Karmal and Najibullah governments. Much to the surprise of the West, the

Najibullah government was able to retain control of the government until 1992, with its collapse producing vicious inter-factional conflict around Kabul and the northeast and dividing the country into regional fiefdoms of varying size. Both through negotiations with local communities and with the support of Pakistan's government, the Taliban was able to conquer and administer as much as 90 per cent of the country, prompting the formation of the Northern Alliance between the remaining armed groups.

The deployment of American forces to Afghanistan, which, in the early phases, involved meetings between Special Forces soldiers and intelligence officials with militia commanders in Islamabad, Quetta and throughout Afghanistan, revitalized flagging militias through the provision of financial and military assistance. Elder authority was re-invoked in Kandahar by the Aliokzai, Barakzai and Popalzai *qawms*, remobilizing individuals who had left the fighting during the Taliban regime. In addition, the presence of any number of private security companies and their employment of combatants created new incentives for individuals either to retain or pick up arms.

For these reasons and due to the revitalized insurgency, the post-9/11 era in Afghanistan, while not as comparatively violent as the previous three periods, should still be viewed as a renewed period of conflict and mobilization.

Here, the consequences of small arms proliferation and conflict are examined. First, the role of small arms in the dominance of commanders and militias in local and national politics are revealed. Second, the profound human costs and legacy of more than three decades of war are reviewed. Third, the continued human impact of small arms, in terms of human rights abuses, land conflict and abuses against the humanitarian presence are reviewed.

As in perhaps no other conflict, the presence of small arms in Afghanistan is so overwhelming and easily apparent that an exploration of their significance appears almost redundant. Whether over land, water, business or marriage, conflicts between individuals, families and communities become all the more violent by the ready stockpiles of mines, explosive ordnance and guns. While the possession of weapons is the most visible way of distinguishing the power of commanders and militias, it is not the exclusive manifestation of power. Availability and victimization are only one determinant of influence and impact. The rule of the gun incorporates not only active violence but structural violence, such as the distortive effect of arms proliferation on political reconstruction and development (UNDP, 2004).

The proliferation of small arms and light weapons had significant (but by no means exclusive) consequences:

- stressing, and potentially undermining, traditional methods of conflict resolution;

- aggravating and intensifying local violence;
- empowering new elites distinct from religious and tribal institutions; (like Arabs)
- steadying the loss of a central monopoly on force in favour of regional and local militias;
- exacerbating intra-village violence;
- intensifying communal conflict throughout South Asia;
- extending the influence of commanders from the military to the economic and political dimensions;
- undermining attempts at negotiation, particularly from 1988–2001;
- strengthening extremist factions and, later, strongmen, to the detriment of traditional community elders.

The Afghan arms pipeline – the global effort to supply the warring parties, both government and non-state – has had profound regional and global reverberations. Weapons from Afghanistan and Pakistan were used by criminal agents in Karachi and Mumbai; and were later said have been utilized in Kashmir, the Philippines (Abu-Sayyaf group), Burma (anti-government forces) and Sri Lanka (Liberation Tigers of Tamir-Elam). The Abu Sayyaf group received as many as 3,000 weapons (from AKs to anti-tank rockets and landmines) in 1999.[2] Arab and other international veterans of the Afghan jihad returned home to sow disorder in Egypt, Algeria, Yemen and Saudi Arabia. The regional implications of arms proliferation remain most apparent in Pakistan. The scale of money and arms moving through the pipeline is proposed to have distorted Pakistan society. According to Attar Ansari of the *Frontier Post*,

So is it frontier or not?

> The money that flowed in has brought drugs, arms, and so much corruption that it has changed life here beyond recognition.... The lawlessness on both sides of the international border, the centuries-old smuggling networks, and the tribal loyalties that rule the trade in drugs and sophisticated arms are likely to ensure that Peshawar's frontier flavor will endure for many years to come.
>
> (quoted in Zubrzycki, 1996)

The scale and manner with which funds moved to Afghanistan considerably strengthened anti-democratic and Islamist forces within Pakistan's government. The Arab mujahideen introduced into Pakistan's borderland, Zia's appropriation of an Islamist message, Soviet/KHAD infiltration and the arms influx into Pakistan, all graphically increased internal violence in Pakistan, between Shi'a and Sunni, as well as between a number of ethnic and tribal groups (Baluch, intra-Pathan, Bihari, Sindh, etc.) (Nasir, 1987, p. 32; Hilali, 2002, pp. 299, 301, 304, 306). By 1998, there were as many as 7,000 Darra-made AKs in Karachi (Sullivan, 1998). In summer 2001, Pakistan's government was able to collect 86,757 weapons alone over a two week amnesty period, and 55,000 weapons at checkpoints, with weapons then redistributed to the police force (Terzieff, 2002). President Musharraf's attempts to limit weapons proliferation in Pakistan included a 'ban on the issuance of new gun permits and production licenses' in March 2000. Until the escalated demand that followed American intervention in Afghanistan, this induced a substantial decline in weapons production in the border areas (Terzieff, 2002).

Small arms and the rise of the 'warlord class'

Here, the impact of commanders and small arms on traditional shuras, the judiciary and prominent political events are briefly examined. To put it simply, the dilemma is not the weapons but the individuals and networks behind them. For this reason, there is a graphic need to assess both the role of the gun and the role of militias, their combined effect on local and regional politics and their broader societal impact. The legacy of small arms has emboldened commanders and militias at the expense of both government and traditional local institutions. A 'warlord-class' has arisen – which is either distinct from traditional elites or which has been able to acquire independence from other 'checks and balances' on their local and national power. While their possession of arms may be the physical manifestation of their influence, it is not, however, the exclusive expression or source of their influence.

Even after a sizeable disarmament campaign, the numbers of militia and small arms in the countryside remains significant, if not vast. Currently, the ANBP's 'warlord' database for the DIAG process includes 1,800 commanders and militias for as many as 120,000 combatants, dividing these between 'benign' self-defence militias and approximately 100 'dangerous groups' (Barron, 2005; GoA, 2006). The latter groups are then divided into three categories: 'those that pose a threat to elections (insurgents), those that pose a threat to governance (roadblock extortionists, etc.) and those involved in narcotics trafficking.' A total of 25 of these dangerous groups belong to all three categories (Barron, 2005).

An early DIAG concept paper revealed substantial conflicts over definitions (armed groups versus militias), involving a desire to legitimize two extra-government forces (the Coalition Afghan Security Force and community/tribal militias/*arbakian*) for the short term (ANBP, 2006a). One senior diplomat expressed concern that soldiers in the employ of the Coalition were 'moon-lighting' and engaging in other illegal activities.[3] The difference between illegal and permitted militias remains hazy, as does the procedure for decommissioning and disarming these militias.

The Coalition has indicated that it would be developing a DDR programme for these individuals in the future. In Paktya, this involved a cash grant of $300 and/or the potential to keep the weapon. Following the initial success of the DIAG process, largely attributed to the certification requirements for candidate registration, the continued success of the pro-

gramme is seen to be limited by the 'low government presence' in insecure and remote areas (IRIN, 2005b). Moreover, the government appears
to be forming new militias. In mid-June 2006, the Karzai government considered expanding the government's security presence in the south by utilizing community militias, as it already does in Kunar. This is believed to
involve the provision of salaries and weapons licences, with Akhundzada
of Helmand raising a militia of 500 and requesting payment of $200 per
militia member a month. For northern militias, this appears to confirm
their concerns that southern groups would be maintained and strengthened, while they themselves continue to be subject to the DIAG programme (Cameron-Moore, 2006).

These commanders have come to dominate institutions at both the
national and at the community level. Afghan society is 'ruled by the power
of armed individuals, instead of vetted democratic processes,' which has
produced a 'culture of impunity' (UNDP, 2004, pp. 53, 81). Commanders
have affected every major political event of the post-Bonn era (see Box
1.1), from the Emergency and Constitutional *Loya Jirgas* to the 2005
parliamentary elections. Not only have commanders and militias sought to
intimidate voters, during both the registration and voter phase, but they
have actively sought to crowd out other candidates for power.

Currently, the National Assembly is substantially constituted by figures
from political-military parties (Wilder, 2005). In the 2005 parliamentary
elections, candidates with jihadist credentials had a 60 per cent success
rate when running for the *Wolesi Jirga* and an 80 per cent success rate in
the provincial councils. In Kabul, half of the 33 seats were won by former
jihadists (Gall, 2005; Sedra and Middlebrook, 2005). In the Parliament's
first months, a pan-mujahideen political front asserted the privileged
place of former commanders and united to propose an amnesty bill to
avoid war crimes prosecution. Whether in Parliament or in their business
holdings, commanders also exact influence by proxy. Rather than
running themselves, relatives and other local representatives run for Parliament in place of commanders, allowing commanders to continue to
maintain militias while acquiring political influence (Giustozzi, 2005c;
McGeough, 2005).

The reform of the Ministry of Interior and Ministry of Justice continues
to be hampered by the appointment of factional commanders, linked to
extortion, kidnapping and forcible land acquisition, which continued
even after the Kabul riots of early June 2006 (Walsh, 2006a). Other
sources have argued that the Afghan police are implicated in protecting
poppy producers and traffickers (Baldauf and Bowers, 2005). As argued
by the Feinstein report, '[t]he judiciary is highly susceptible to military
and political influences at both the urban and rural levels,' while 'many
[police officers] are still loyal to their former commanders, who often
serve as the chief of police, Army officers or district or provincial authorities' (UNDP, 2004, p. 51). At the municipal and provincial level, '[y]ears

Box 1.1 The legacy of the Bonn Agreement

The Bonn Agreement, which launched the Afghan state-building project in December 2001, did not accord demilitarization a central status in the political process. It only contained a vague provision on demilitarization stipulating that

> upon the official transfer of power, all *mujahidin*, Afghan armed forces and armed groups in the country shall come under the command and control of the Interim Authority, and be reorganized according to the requirements of the new Afghan security and armed forces.
>
> (Bonn Agreement, para. V, art. 1)

The legacy of the Bonn Agreement has a deep impact on subsequent demilitarization efforts. Most significantly, the agreement contributed to the factionalization and even ethnicization of the main security institutions. The leadership faction of the Northern Alliance, the predominantly Tajik Shura-e-Nezar, was able to assume control of the Ministries of Defence and Interior as well as the National Directorate of Security intelligence agency. Shura-e-Nezar, which itself is dominated by Tajiks from the Panjshir Valley, was intent on insulating its militias from the demilitarization process and consolidating its control over the nascent security architecture as a means to militate against the reassertion of traditional Pashtun dominance over the government. Although the first post-Taliban Defence Minister, Mohammad Qasim Fahim, publicly supported the demilitarization process, he surreptitiously took steps to undermine it.

By 2006, the government had succeeded in instituting greater ethnic balance at the leadership level in the security sector. Beneath that leadership stratum remained, however, a disproportionate degree of Panjshiri Tajik influence. This has had the effect of alienating elements of the Pashtun majority population as well as other ethnic minorities, like the Uzbek and Hazara, who see the security forces as an extension of a particular Tajik political clique rather than genuinely national institutions.

The tenuousness of public trust in the security forces further eroded the potential for a comprehensive disarmament process, as many communities have been unwilling to cede responsibility for their security to a rival faction, even if it is operating under the rubric of the state.

Source: Sedra, 2007.

of 'commando administration' have deeply discredited official institutions such as courts' (UNDP, 2004, p. 84). Disturbingly, corruption is seen to be driving greater societal support for the AGF, as 'nostalgia for the ruthless rule of the Taliban is growing as the line between judges and criminals blur' (Watson, 2006).

While the role of commanders in the cabinet and the Ministry of Defence has generally been reduced, the former Minister of Interior Jalali holds that:

> over the past two years, Kabul has successfully reduced the power of warlord-governors by reassigning them away from their geographic power base, but their networks continue to influence provincial administration. Meanwhile, former factional commanders who are appointed to government positions in police and civil administration have loaded their offices with their unqualified supporters and corrupt cronies.
>
> (Jalali, 2006)

At the local level, the wide availability of weapons has shifted local power dynamics and undermined traditional methods of resolving local disputes, greatly increasing the level of violence between and within communities. Indeed, according to Giustozzi, 'the availability of guns and ammunition was one of the main factors behind the expansion of political influence in the Afghan countryside' (Giustozzi, 2000, p. 246). Accordingly, these weapons forced local communities to affiliate with the Peshawar-based political parties and ultimately further disrupted power relations by empowering those with external ties.

A commander's ascendance to local power occurs both with local consent and due to fear. According to the International Crisis Group (ICG), the commanders are increasingly the wealthiest members of the community and use this wealth to support tribal elders and 'desperately poor villages and individuals' (ICG, 2003, p. 17). Furthermore:

> Armed political groups, commanders, and warlords have strategically targeted traditional and customary justice systems (*Jirgas* and *shuras*) throughout rural Afghanistan in an attempt to control local populations. In many instances, these predatory forces have successfully positioned their loyalists within these groups, thus undermining this avenue of justice for rural Afghans – which is often the only avenue available in rural areas.
>
> (ASFIFC, 2003, p. 4)

Locally, commanders have altered the ability of community *shuras* to arbitrate local disputes, both through force and through the distribution of wealth.

The human cost of the Afghan conflict

As discussed, one of the primary (but generally neglected) legacies of the conflict is the role that small arms proliferation has played in the political and economic ascendance of new elites and a number of political parties, resulting in the emergence of a 'warlord-class.' Besides this, since 1978, the Afghan conflict inflicted massive human costs. The Soviet invasion was believed to have cost one million deaths and to have produced as many as six million refugees (Lopes Cardozo et al., 2004). The civil war killed tens of thousands and displaced another half a million (Lopes Cardozo et al., 2004). The war was believed to create as many as 200,000 widows (UNEP, 2003, p. 21).

Conflict has not only directly affected households through armed attacks, the destruction of homes and forced displacement, but it has also undermined livelihoods as well as human and community development. Warfare induced a 'complete collapse of local and national forms of governance,' which led to the unrestricted use of water wells and deforestation, in turn producing erosion, undermining livelihoods, inducing rural–urban migration and aggravating conflict between villages and nomads. Particularly in the eastern provinces (Kunar, Paktya, Nuristan, Nangarhar), communities have lost their ability to manage and preserve their forests communally, to the benefit of an alliance between commanders, 'timber barons' and regional traders (UNEP, 2003, pp. 10, 72).

The costs of the conflict on human development have been considerable. Afghanistan remains one of the most underdeveloped societies, with poor health and educational facilities and low literacy rates (69.5 per cent; 85 per cent for women), high child mortality and a low lifespan. A total of 80 per cent of the country's 6,870 schools were destroyed or damaged during the conflict (UNDP, 2004, p. 66). Another legacy of conflict is the presence of landmines, which are believed to number between 450,000 and seven million and which killed 132 and wounded 647 in the first 11 months of 2005 (USDOS, 2006b).   450K → 七百万！

In a survey conducted by the Afghan Independent Human Rights Commission (AIHRC), 69 per cent of those interviewed (of 4,151 respondents) indicated that they were the subject of serious human rights abuses over the course of the conflict. Out of 2,308 focus group participants, almost 20 per cent of those interviewed had either been a direct victim or had a family member who was a victim of torture or detention, 22 per cent (522) of these had lost a relative to violence, 13.5 per cent (312) had lost land and property, 3.7 per cent (85) had lost a family member through disappearances, 13 per cent (301) had been displaced, 9.4 per cent (218) had their homes destroyed, 5.2 per cent (121) had been orphaned or widowed and 1 per cent (25) were subject to sexual violence (AIHRC, 2005, pp. 8, 10–11, 73).

Although the Communists and Taliban were identified as those primarily responsible for violence, atrocities were common (and roughly equivalent across all periods of the violence) to all regimes. Typically, 'regime change brought renewed violations' (AIHRC, 2005, p. 11). Indeed, according to Human Rights Watch in 2000:

> throughout the war, all of the major factions have been guilty of grave breaches of international human rights law. Their warmaking is supported and perpetuated by the involvement of Afghanistan's neighbors and other states in providing weapons, ammunition, fuel, and other logistical support ... The arms provided have been directly implicated in serious violations of international humanitarian law. These include aerial bombardment of civilian targets, indiscriminate bombings, rocketing and other artillery attacks on civilian-populated areas, reprisal killings of civilians, summary execution of prisoners, rape, and torture.
>
> (HRW, 2000)[4]

The legacy of this conflict is apparent not only in terms of lives and property lost but also in the psychological consequences. The World Health Organization (WHO) estimates that 95 per cent of the Afghan population has been psychologically affected by the conflict, while 20 per cent may 'suffer ... from mental health problems' and 30 per cent 'may suffer from anxiety, depression, psychosomatic problems such as insomnia and forms of post-traumatic stress disorder' (UNDP, 2004, p. 60). A 2002 mental health status survey (with 799 respondents) by the US Center for Disease Control revealed that 62 per cent of the respondents 'reported experiencing 4 trauma events during the previous 10 years,' with deprivation (lack of food, water and shelter) considerably more prominent than bombardment or violent attack (Lopez Cardozo *et al.*, 2004).

The data revealed Afghanistan as possessing 'significantly higher prevalence for symptoms of depression, anxiety, and Post-Traumatic Stress Disorder,' with low social functioning, particularly for women (Lopes Cardozo *et al.* 2004). In eastern Afghanistan, the rate of exposure to traumatic events was particularly high, with 44 per cent of the 1,011 respondents experiencing between eight and ten traumatic events, with origins in displacement, deprivation and exposure to rocket attacks (Soviet, mujahideen) and bombardment (Coalition) (Scholte *et al.*, 2004). As is readily evident, the human consequences of the Afghan conflict have been profound. Moreover, as will be described in the following section, trauma is still being inflicted upon Afghanistan, which in part can be attributed to past and current arms flows.

The current impact of conflict and small arms

The conflict in Afghanistan is not over but ongoing. Here, the current manifestations of conflict, primarily in terms of human rights abuses, are focused upon. Even before spring 2006, all signs pointed to a security situation that was deteriorating rather than improving. For example, in the abovementioned survey, 55 per cent of respondents in Kandahar indicated an increase in crime between 2003 and 2004 while 30 per cent of those interviewed in Jalalabad and 18 per cent of those interviewed in Kandahar believed that there were more weapons in the area in 2004 than in 2003 (HRRAC, 2004, p. 20). Afghan civilians are now victims of suicide bombings, public bombings and direct assassination as a consequence of the Taliban insurgency. Others have been mistakenly targeted by Coalition forces or deliberately subjected to prolonged detainment without trial.

This conflict continues to victimize civilians and contributes to prolonged underdevelopment, hindering both the political and broader reconstruction effort. Violence has reduced access to education, particularly for girls (HRW, 2006). Indeed, more than 20 teachers were killed by the Taliban in 2006 (Walsh, 2006b). The marriage of 'wants and fears' – of local militarization and war-induced underdevelopment – is also seen in other aspects of female victimization, including 'incidents of early and forced marriages, domestic violence, kidnapping of young girls, and harassment and intimidation' (UNDP, 2004, p. 80).

Both government-affiliated and independent commanders continue to be responsible for a wide variety of human rights abuses. Even independent local commanders 'are protected and supported by powerful individuals within the central government,' with the proposition that 'money and influence are more likely to solve a crime than evidence and due process' (HRRAC, 2004, p. 6). According to UNDP:

> human rights organizations have noted extortion, harassment and violence against civilians at military and police checkpoints; the forced conscription of civilians, including under age boys; abductions; arbitrary and politically motivated arrests; and some extrajudicial killings by the police and other security forces.
>
> (UNDP, 2004, p. 83)

The 2005 US State Department Country Human Rights Report identifies a wide variety of current human rights problems, including: 'extrajudicial killings; torture; poor prison conditions; official impunity; prolonged pretrial detention; abuse of authority by regional commanders; restrictions on freedoms of press, religion, movement, and association; and violence and societal discrimination against women and minorities' (USDOS, 2006a).

Government, factional and insurgent forces use extrajudicial killings and torture. While largely committed by the AGF, government-affiliated commanders (and, in select cases, government officials) have been directly implicated in extrajudicial killings, illegal detention and the execution of political candidates (most prominently Mohammad Ramazan in

Balkh Province and Abdul Hadi in Helmand.) In Hirat, Helmand, Kabul, Faryab and Gardez, local authorities were accused of having 'routinely tortured and abused detainees' involving removing nails, burning and 'sexual humiliation and sodomy' (USDOS, 2006a).

Government agencies and commanders run private prisons in Kabul, Faryab and Mazar-e-Sharif; the AIHRC closed 36 between 2002 and 2005 (USDOS, 2006a). Illegal checkpoints are present throughout the country and are utilized by government and insurgent groups to extort money. In 2005, according to the US Department of State:

> In northern areas, commanders targeted women, especially from Pashtun families, for sexual violence. During the year, there were at least four credible reports of soldiers and commanders loyal to local warlords raping girls, boys, and women in provinces in the eastern, southeastern, and central part of the country. In one of these cases, police arrested two perpetrators, but the case remained open at year's end. A total of 21 such cases were reported.
>
> (USDOS, 2006a)

Clearly, for the individual and family without connections to political or armed conflict, the post-Bonn period still contains the potential for vulnerability and victimization.

Land disputes and property ownership are particularly affected by insecurity and weapons proliferation. The resolution of property disputes is particularly important given a series of contrasting legal codes and a long history of ethnically determined property eviction. More recently, the UN High Commissioner for Human Rights protested the apparent collusion between former Defence Minister Mohammed Fahim and Kabul's mayor in the forcible eviction of vulnerable squatters to construct a wealthy enclave for senior Afghan officials in Kabul's Sherpur district. According to the UNDP, 'some of the most common violations ... are the destruction of houses, the occupation of land and the forced selling of properties,' with the AIHRC noting 300 cases of 'arbitrary house destruction and property occupation' between June 2003 and late 2004 (UNDP, 2004, p. 83).

In an analysis of reports of the Norwegian Refugee Committee, Jo Beall and Daniel Esser show that 13 per cent of all land dispute cases in Kabul involve commanders, with an additional 16 per cent of cases involving officials, political party representatives or judges. An informant in Mazar asserted: 'So if you ask me who rules, I tell you it's the people with the guns' (Beall and Esser, 2005, pp. 39, 41).

Insecurity and arms proliferation also affect the humanitarian effort and the international community. In their daily work and life, aid professionals in Afghanistan are constantly surrounded by armed individuals (Muggah, 2004). Aid professionals have been subject to kidnapping for both criminal extortion and political agendas.

Between 2003 and 2004, there was a sharp increase in the number of violent and fatal attacks against international and local aid personnel. In the run-up to the parliamentary elections, Afghan Joint Electoral Management Body representatives were subject to repeated attacks. In July 2004, five staff members from Médecins Sans Frontières were killed in Badghis Province, prompting the withdrawal of the organization after decades of aid work there. In summer 2005, there were a number of kidnapping attempts against international aid personnel, with those responsible driven by criminal rather than political agendas.

According to Nick Downie, formerly of Afghanistan NGO Security Office, the 37 NGO fatalities against aid organizations in 2003–2004 were all close-quarter gun fatalities, within 10 metres, with the majority of these occurring as the aid professionals were en route to their project locations. In certain cases, fatalities were rumoured to be linked to a failed attempt of provincial officials to extort additional security funds from local agencies.[5]

Contrasting perceptions of threats and priorities: international and Afghan

Post-Bonn Afghanistan is characterized by sharp contrasts in the perception of security, particularly in terms of sources and priorities. There is strikingly little correlation between Afghans and the international military effort in terms of appraisals of allies, threats and enemies. Among ordinary Afghans, as will be detailed, security from all armed actors (government and insurgent) remains the predominant concern, and the disarmament programme is strongly supported (Donini, 2007, pp. 164–167). While there is a certain degree of overlap, there is also a substantial degree of exclusion and omission. Between 2001 and 2004 (prior to the completion of the ANBP programme and the reform of the Presidential Cabinet), the Coalition was preoccupied with the AGF (admittedly the core reason for its deployment), while the Afghan public focused on activities of their local commanders, who had direct impact on their daily lives. The Coalition shifted only towards a broader strategy of counter-insurgency with General Barno's selection as Coalition Force Commander.[6]

Until 2004, when the Coalition first utilized shows of force (via A-10 overflights) to induce commander compliance, the Coalition's approach towards commanders was characterized by 'strategic ambiguity – leaving factional forces to guess how far they can go before the Coalition's overwhelming military superiority is set against them' (Thier, 2003, p. 6). In 2004–2005, the international focus shifted towards reducing poppy production dramatically (after a bumper crop in 2004 proved embarrassing for the stewards of the transitional government).

The fact that the Coalition had either relied on (in 2001) or continued to employ local commanders and militias only further compromised local security. Indeed, as the March 2004 Report of the Secretary-General notes;

factional feuds, rivalries, and, increasingly, drug-related incidents continue to affect the lives of the population. The weak or corrupt provincial and district administrations, the continued rule of local
commanders, and the absence of effective national law enforcement
are more common sources of insecurity for the population than terrorist violence.

(UNSG, 2004, p. 4 (pt. 8))

A 2006 Report of the UN Secretary-General revealed how little had
changed, arguing that 'impunity of factional commanders and former
warlords has also served to undermine incremental improvements ...
Complaints of serious human rights violations committed by representatives of national security institutions, including arbitrary arrest, illegal
detention and torture are numerous' (UNSG, 2006, p. 7 (pt. 28–29)). The
combined effect of both the insurgency and factional commanders has
been to erode popular support for the central Afghan government, while
the presence of commanders with ties to armed factions in the government challenges the popular legitimacy of the government.

As stated by the Feinstein Famine project at Tufts University:

> Countrywide, rural Afghans hold views and have had experiences of
> (in)security that are very different from those of the international
> community and the Afghan government. A vast majority of areas that
> are 'High Risk/Hostile Environment' or 'Medium Risk/Uncertain
> Environment' (i.e., highly insecure and essentially off-limits or areas
> where armed escorts are required) for the United Nations and inter-
> national NGOs are often experienced as secure, with few reported
> conflicts, by the local rural populations. In contrast, regions that show
> up as 'Low Risk/Permissive Environment' (i.e., areas considered
> secure for operations) on United Nations security maps are areas
> where local populations often report high levels of conflict and are
> experiencing insecurity at the hands of armed political groups, war-
> lords, commanders and their associates, including district authorities
> and police forces.

(ASFIFC, 2003)

Populace does not experience "stability"

Threats vary considerably by region and by individual. Some villages will
be dominated by intra-village conflict. Others will be primarily affected by
the continued conflict between the Taliban insurgency and now NATO-
led Coalition. Still others remain under the dominance of local strongmen, who suppress alternative political voices and continue to extort from
local villagers and demand combatants forcibly. Some community
members feel trapped between the demands of insurgents and those of
the Coalition and government forces, while others feel more vulnerable to
criminal extortion.

Polls and surveys conducted in Afghanistan confirm these differences in perceptions of security. Positively, an ABC news poll conducted in December 2005 (with a limited random sample of 1,039 adults in 31 of Afghanistan's 34 provinces) indicated that 77 per cent of Afghans believe 'their country is headed in the right direction,' 91 per cent 'prefer the current Afghan government to the Taliban regime' and 75 per cent indicate that 'their security from crime and violence has improved as well' (Langer, 2005).

Similarly, a different poll of 2,089 Afghan adults in November/December 2005 indicated that 83 per cent of the population thought Afghanistan was 'heading in the right direction,' with 47 per cent of the population rating the security situation fair/poor in areas hit by the Taliban insurgency and 30 per cent doing so outside of those areas (PIPA, 2006). In the ABC poll, 30 per cent of all respondents indicated that 'attacks against U.S. forces can be justified.' With regard to perceptions of threat, 41 per cent cited the Taliban/AGF as the greatest threat, 28 per cent cited drug traffickers, 22 per cent warlords, 4 per cent the American forces and 2 per cent the current Afghanistan government (Langer, 2005). Both of these polls were conducted prior to the rise in violence experienced beginning in spring 2006.

Other polls, however, contradicted that positive assessment, revealing sharp differences in perceptions of security, particularly between regions and between urban and rural areas. Even the ABC poll revealed that, while 40 per cent of Afghans living in urban areas indicated that their security situation was 'very good,' only 24 per cent of those living in rural areas did so. Security remained the primary concern for 40 per cent of all Afghans, with the disarmament programme supported by 95 per cent of those interviewed (Langer, 2005).

This echoed the conclusions of a September 2004 Afghan Human Rights Consortium survey based on in-depth interviews with 763 individuals, which indicated that 65 per cent viewed disarmament as the 'most important thing to do to improve security in Afghanistan,' with this desire particularly pronounced in Mazar (87 per cent) and Hirat (73 per cent), particularly among the Uzbek and Turkmen populations of the former location (HRRAC, 2004, p. 20). In terms of current priorities, security was the predominant and overwhelming concern of most respondents (1,580 of 2000), followed by electricity (542 of 2,000), disappearances (398 of 2,000), disarmament (390 of 2,000), employment opportunities (293 of 2,000) and the rule of law (156 of 2,000) (AIHRC, 2005, p. 16).

While these reports differ considerably in terms of their views as to the chief threats and sources of insecurity, all are unanimous in showing that the primary concern of all Afghan citizens is security and that the disarmament process enjoys the vast support of the population.

Categories of local violence: dynamics and participants

The terms used in describing the actors in the Afghan conflict, particularly warlord, commanders and narco-mafias, produce absolute images that do not coincide with the complicated local dynamics surrounding commanders and violence. Afghan commanders are notoriously described as either greed-driven or as fanatics. They are alternately held to possess either intrinsic ethnic hatreds or no fixed loyalties (as particularly seen during the fighting in Kabul from 1993–1995) where allies readily became enemies and enemies became allies.

While by no means comprehensive, the following three parts of the chapter present three additional (and alternative) conceptual approaches to violent conflict in Afghanistan. The first outlines the role of the state in creating and legitimizing local militias. The second describes the 'Afghan security dilemma.' The third explores the various types of inter-factional fighting. At a basic level, all three themes add context to what is often a far too simplistic discussion of Afghan violence.

Moreover, all three serve to introduce the critical role of legitimacy in relation to local commanders and militias – whether delegated from the state or locally acquired from communities through the provision of protection. While Islam was widely proposed as a unifying force behind the jihad; in fact, the conflict between moderate and fundamentalist forces (as well as between Sufi, Shi'a and Sunni orders) revealed substantial differences in authorities, objectives and interpretations. Fundamentally, this part of the chapter also begins to answer the question of who fights whom and when.

The state and local violence

There is a long tradition of the central government utilizing community militias and strongmen for their own ends, dating back to the state-building strategies and practices of Abdur Rahman Khan (Harpviken, 1997, pp. 274–275). Even now, both the Afghan state and external governments are participants rather than arbiters in local violence, often playing critical roles in the expansion of local militias and commanders. As described earlier, commanders have captured national institutions, while the state continuously relies on local militias to make up for its lack of a monopoly on force. It often provides state licence to local forces in order to acquire greater armed support against its opponents. As will be demonstrated in Chapter 2, the state is significant not only for its provision of resources (arms and money) to armed groups but also due to its willingness to legitimize these armed groups. The generic response of every Afghan government has been to utilize, empower and legitimize local militias (Adamec, 2003, pp. 39–42; Giustozzi, 2000; Bhatia, 2007).

First, the Afghan government previously played off local inter/intra-factional disputes in order to achieve greater influence in districts and provinces and to undermine power competitors (Giustozzi, 2000). As stridently detailed by Giustozzi, the narrative trend of a 'good state' battling 'bad' regional warlords and forces of fragmentation neglects the degree to which key state ministries have been captured by commanders as well as the degree to which the state used other regional commanders to undermine competitors (as seen in the attempts to box in Ismail Khan in 2004 from Ghor, Shindand and Badghis) (Giustozzi, 2004). Rather than serve as a neutral arbiter helping to resolve local disputes and reducing the Afghan security dilemma, the state often participates in these conflicts, exacerbating local cleavages. Indeed, Hersh quotes an American official as saying: 'If Mohammed Fahim is a government minister and Ismail Khan is a warlord, you're abusing the language' (Hersh, 2004, p. 158). As will be demonstrated, historically, the line between the central government and local forces and militias has been considerably blurred. Typically, there were community militias organized around tribes and *qawms*. However, with the emergence of political–military parties and strongmen/warlords in the post-Bonn era, these militias now come from a variety of backgrounds.

Second, the state has both supported and catalysed the formation of local groups. The creation of the Afghan Military Forces during the Bonn Conference was not unique but part of a long tradition of state endorsement of local militias. A weak central government may engage with local militias in order to acquire (either active or passive) support for its authority and to increase its forces during periods of national emergency, providing in-exchange recognition (and legitimacy), resources or simply autonomy.[7]

When first established by Amir Dost Mohammed in the late 1800s, the Afghan Army was composed of a regular force of 2,000 men, supplemented by a larger reserve of *jezailchis* from the southern tribes. However, over the course of the early twentieth century, the total size of the army reached 50,000 in the 1920s and 80,000 by 1936 through compulsory enlistment, with 50 per cent of state revenue dedicated to the army (Adamec, 2003, pp. 39–42). Prior to the jihad, a number of different types of state utilization of local and tribal militias existed; this involved a series of shifting relationships between the state, the Durrani monarchy, villages and Pashtun tribes.[8]

In 1982, the Soviet-backed Karmal government began the formation of Frontier Militias in southeastern Afghanistan. As part of a broader attempt at tribal reconciliation, after 1986, the Soviet-backed Najibullah government sponsored local self-defence forces, providing salaries, food coupons and weapons for use against transiting groups. Only one of these (Dostum's Jawzjani militias) was a mobile, cross-provincial and centrally deployed militia (Adamec, 2003, p. 199; Giustozzi, 2000, p. 222). The

others were localized and, in some cases, neutral between the various
parties.

With the Taliban's collapse, the Northern Alliance was formally integrated into the government through the creation of the eight corps Afghan
Military Forces (AMF), with the Bonn Agreement demanding that:

> Upon the official transfer of power, all mujahideen, Afghan armed
> forces and armed groups in the country shall come under the
> command and control of the Interim Authority, and be reorganized
> according to the requirements of the new Afghan security and armed
> forces.
>
> (globalsecurity.org)

By creating the AMF and integrating militias into the MoD, the government provided local commanders and strongmen with the legitimacy that
many had been sorely missing.

Given the above, the role and impact of the Afghan state with respect
to sponsoring, legitimizing and empowering militias should not be
understated. While the Afghan Army continues to expand (and is scheduled to reach 70,000 by the end of 2007/2009), local militias will likely
continue to be utilized by the Afghan government, the Coalition,
UNAMA and private security companies in order to ensure their short-
term security.

The AMF legitimized many commanders and private militias by means
of association with the state (Bhatia, 2007). By providing formal titles to
these commanders as well as a poorly monitored monthly stipend to each
soldier, the state enabled commanders to reinvigorate decrepit local militias. In turn, the continuation of predatory activities by these very militias
weakened the government's legitimacy in the eyes of a population thirst-
ing for enhanced security and justice and tired of 'rule by the gun.' Again,
the sanction and badge of government legitimacy – one of the government's few areas of power – was sold too cheaply.

Moreover, foreign military contingents in the Coalition and ISAF continue to endow national commanders with legitimacy through association.
This trend of legitimizing local militias continues while the DIAG programme is under way. An early DIAG concept paper excluded local tribal
militias (e.g., the Paktya arbakian) and those Afghan militias employed by
the Coalition (the Afghan Security Forces) from being designated illegal
armed groups (GoA, 2006).

Beyond their employment by the Coalition, other militias are able to
continue to exist through their reconstitution as private security companies (PSCs). As proposed by Poulton, 'many warlords will try to convert
their armies into private military companies' (Poulton, 2004, p. 23).
Certain PSCs, most prominently Louis Berger Associates and US Police
Investigation, pursue a policy of co-option, i.e., to pay off the commanders

on their route in order to ensure the security of their construction project (see also Chapter 5).

The Afghan 'security dilemma'

The Afghan 'security dilemma' is a product of the fact that the forces used to protect a community easily become involved in offensive operations against neighbouring communities (Lake and Rothchild, 1996; globalsecurity.org; Rubin 2003). Others define the Afghan security dilemma as consisting of 'the privatization of security and a pervasive military mentality in the country' (UNDP, 2004, p. 52). These definitions speak to a similar dynamic whereby commanders acquire local power, no matter the services they may provide to local communities. The measures taken to protect a community threaten other communities, villages and populations. As a consequence, a cycle of counter-mobilization and retribution is established.

According to Giustozzi, following the Soviet withdrawal and collapse of the Najibullah government, the countryside experienced intense insecurity due to massive weapons proliferation, the disintegration of state control in the countryside and the resistance parties' inability to create an interim government:

> The ability to offer protection (against the government or the opposition, against rival clans, against bandits) became the driving factor in local politics. Armed groups sprang up everywhere, and at least in the south, south-east and south-west of the country practically every village got at least one. Weapons were in heavy demand, but isolated villages could get a sufficient supply without linking up to some external power, which could be a mujahideen party, the state itself or some middleman who in turn enjoyed privileged access to one of these sources. A better guarantee of protection could often be obtained by joining a large conglomeration of villages, headed either by a renowned and powerful mujahideen leader or by a government militia leader or some independent 'warlord.'
>
> (Giustozzi, 2000, p. 247)

Yet, while commanders provide security and protection to their communities and enable the community to become involved in national-level armed disputes, they also pose a threat to neighbouring villages and induce counter-mobilization. Commanders are able to utilize grievances to acquire combatants and then to use these combatants for their own ends. Many commanders can best be described as engaging in 'moonlighting.'

While generally viewed to be 'predatory and parasitic,' warlords may acquire local military legitimacy and 'are not necessarily worse predators

than states themselves, not only because they may provide a few social services and infrastructure, but most of all ... security from external threats'
(Giustozzi, 2005a). State views of and actions towards the alternate legitimacy sources described above have alternated between tolerance, appropriation and enforcement.

While filling a critical need for the community (either in providing protection or responding to grievances) or for external actors (in providing
local partner militia for the Afghan government, PSCs or international
forces (the Soviets, ISAF and the Coalition)), the commander is further
empowered to utilize the militia for his own private ends. The latter can
range from the consolidation of *qawm*, village, district or provincial power
to predatory activities, whether against a neighbouring community or by
establishing checkpoints. At a certain level, checkpoints may well be an
informal type of taxation, though acquired not through a community levy
from the *shura* but at the barrel of a gun and with the constant potential
for excessive theft and other abuses (Giustozzi, 2004, pp. 5–6).

Box 1.2 The UN Protection Unit: the formalization of party militias

With its fixed installations and road missions vulnerable to attack,
UNAMA and its affiliated agencies are required to acquire armed
forces for their protection. Indeed, since 2001, the UN has lost a substantial number of local and international field staff in Afghanistan
and has had its offices in Herat raided and its staff terrorized.
However, as occurred in Somalia, while few would doubt this imperative, the manner in which the UN contracts local armed forces may
cause detriment to the mission's overall and long-term objectives. As
will be described in this box, this may well be the case with the UN
Protection Unit.

The UN Protection Unit (UNPU) was created (*circa* 2004) by the
Ministry of Interior in order to provide armed guards to UN compounds, road missions and to the Mobile Disarmament Units
(MDUs) of the ANBP. These forces are available at the request of
the regional UN Office and are currently present in Herat and
Kabul. Originally, there were 100–120 UNPU soldiers in Herat. Two
to four UNPU staff are stationed at each UN office and a provincial
UNPU Quick Reaction Force exists for use during crises and outside
of the provincial centre. In Jalalabad, the UNPU was not accepted by
the UN Security Management Team and Area Management Team,
although the regional UN security official asserted that the UNPU
strength is such that, 'on an operational level [the UNPU] provides
a degree of flexibility to train people up to higher standards.'[9]

UNPU members receive $150 per month and an additional $7 for
every day spent on road missions, which is distributed directly from
UNAMA to prevent commander fraud. The soldiers are not locally

recruited but centrally deployed from Kabul. Some soldiers only received training from Afghan police, while others went through a formal Regional Training Centre programme. Of the seven UNPU members interviewed in Herat and around Kabul, the vast majority were first recruited by the Jamiat or Ittihad party before the age of 18, as was generally the case for approximately one-half to one-third of the combatants interviewed in Afghanistan. As a whole, those combatants interviewed were polite and disciplined in the execution of their responsibilities. When on field deployment, the UNPU combatants revealed a pervasive sense of entitlement to high wages and to other comforts.

Combatant profiles

The combatants generally began fighting and joined a Jamiat commander during either the waning years of the Najibullah regime or the early years of the civil war (1990–1992) or in the campaign against the Taliban (2000). With regard to primary incentives for initial mobilization, three cited economic incentives and two proposed protection and local defence, with one other group citing belonging and two other groups citing belonging and ideology (a product of youth group training.) Following the Taliban withdrawal, two of the combatants served with the Jamiat contingent at Kabul airport. Two of those interviewed formerly belonged to Mullah Nasim (former Jamiat armoured brigade in Panjshir/Takhar, now an MoD official), who directed his soldiers to disarm without participating in the DDR process.[10]

Of those interviewed, three were previously members of a youth group in a Jamiat-run school, provided with educational texts produced by the Jamiat printing press (specifically religious and military texts, including *Dowran-e-Jihad* and a pamphlet by Abdullah Azam on 'The Jihad period in the Panjshir'), and participated in organized military exercises. The effect of participation in the youth group is evident from the following account:

> [This training was] so important for us. After we understood what was the real life, and [learned] to never be scared of heavy weapons. We became more brave, [and] to not be scared about anything. We learned that we must help people, and not to steal from people. We learned these good ways from youth groups and from magazines. We learned not to be scared of anything.[11]

Youth groups were used to create combatants for the future and also to supplement a commander's militia when the Panjshir came under threat, as occurred in 2000 with the Taliban's offensive. A Panjshiri UNPU member recalled: 'From the beginning they put my hand on the Koran, and I said for the rest of my life I would be in Jamiat; so I will stay with them.'[12]

Problems surrounding the UNPU
The troubled history of the UNPU's leadership. The force is recruited by and under the direction of General Din Mohammed Jurat, a Jamiat commander accused of running private jails and of involvement in kidnapping and the violent suppression of the protests at Kabul University in 2002.[13]

The use of the UNPU by commanders to remove combatants from DDR. Although all of the UNPU soldiers interviewed belonged to Division 1 of the Panjshir, none of them participated in the ANBP DDR process with their corps. One combatant recalls: 'I don't need to be DDRed, as I am working as police.'[14] As a location for non-DDRed combatants, the UNPU is thus similar to the Afghanistan Highway Police and the Kandahar PSCs.

The resulting maintenance of the commander–combatant patronage link. As a consequence of their avoidance of DDR and their continued dependence on a Jamiat commander for employment, the commander continues to act as a source of patronage, and the symbolic link between commanders and combatant is never severed.

The dominance of Jamiat party cadres within the UNPU. The UNPU is largely organized around former Jamiat party cadres. The UNPU was not autonomously recruited and trained but was instead constituted by combatants who had previously belonged to Jamiat militias. These combatants were able to join the UNPU through either their direct contact with General Jurat or through their commander's or fellow combatants' (friends') affiliation with him. However, the majority of combatants were primarily socialized within the party and do not hold primary obedience to a particular local commander and community. Most of these combatants previously belonged to Jamiat youth groups.

This is a basic, if poorly acknowledged, trade-off. In certain examples, a community can establish procedures and mechanisms to prevent a commander from mobilizing combatants utilizing the community's name. Similarly, individuals, during periods of socially sanctioned warfare (anti-Soviet and, for some communities, anti-Taliban), can choose to join groups outside of their communities in order to ensure that their decision to mobilize will not play into the hands of local power brokers. However, it is relatively rare for individuals to recognize the tension between the relief of grievance (vengeance, local protection, etc.) and its appropriation by local commanders in order to pursue alternative forms of fighting and mobilization.

Still driven by grievance to fight against the Taliban, one combatant from Daykundi migrated out of his home province and joined another armed group in Syahkhak to ensure that he would not become entangled in local fighting due to his affiliation with a commander. Explaining this, he argued:

> If I took the weapon in my own village, afterwards we would have con-flict in our village. If I selected a commander from our place, he could tell me to do things against other people, to recruit people by force, so I wanted to avoid this, and joined a commander from outside.[15]

The line between protection and predation thus becomes a matter of perspective. As long as commanders meet the immediate needs of the community, they are then able to utilize those same forces for their own entrepreneurial purposes. A local security dilemma emerges, with each community threatened by their neighbours but largely unaware of the manner in which their own activities and commanders appear as similarly threatening.

Inter-factional fighting: parties and communities

The broad one-dimensional frames used to describe the conflict neglect the disputes that occurred between and within the parties. Moreover, as has become evident during the civil war, the dividing lines of ideology and ethnicity do not predetermine alliances or national alignments. Each period of conflict in Afghanistan is characterized by disputes and conflicts between more than two parties; this challenges easy descriptions of the conflict. For example, in an interview in 1988 (the year before the Soviet withdrawal), the eminent Afghan anthropologist, archaeologist and histo-rian, Louis Dupree, argued that 'a number of civil wars have been occur-ring simultaneously: mujahideen versus the Kabul regime; Khalq versus Parcham; Babrak Parchamis versus Najib Parchamis'; and, further, includ-ing the conflicts between the Shi'a parties in the Hazarajat and the mujahideen factions throughout Afghanistan (AIC, 1989a).

During the jihad, there were three different forms of infighting: community versus community, party versus party and party versus community/tribe. The latter two conflicts were present prior to the Soviet invasion, both between Communist and Islamist groups. However, prior to the jihad, community versus community fighting is viewed to be con-strained and limited. One consequence of the arms pipeline was to increase greatly the violence involved in these disputes, undermining the typical mechanisms for resolution. Describing violence in the Pashtun bor-derland, Bazzi asserts that 'the [Afghan] guerrilla war changed the scale of conflict in the tribal belt. Instead of using knives and pistols, tribal chiefs now settle scores with machine guns and rocket launchers' (Bazzi, 2001).

Between communities, conceptual obligations to jihad did not overcome local cleavages and conflicts. Pre-existing conflicts (between tribes, personalities or villages) shaped the affiliation of local communities (whether in terms of their choice between different *tanzims* or between the government and the mujahideen). As described in the case-study chapters, communities distinguish between legitimate (and conceivably) limited violence and unbounded conflict. As described previously, while provided with community legitimacy due to their protection of the community, commanders are then able to utilize standing forces (as was demonstrated by the Gardez Tajiks and in Ghor) in order to engage and moonlight in entrepreneurial violence.

With regard to inter-party conflict, each group sought to acquire dominance over all similarly ideologically oriented groups. In order either to expand their base of support or secure transport routes, *tanzims* sought to eliminate power competitors. Jamiat pushed from the Panjshir into the Andarabad valley and eliminated Hezb-e-Islami influence there. Hezb-e-Islami expelled the Wahhabit Dawa'at party from Asadabad and Kunar. The Iranian-backed Pasdaran and Nasr parties expelled the traditional Shura-e-Ittifaq from Bamyan to Ghazni in the Hazarajat. This also involved the crowding out and elimination of non-religious, nationalist resistance organizations, such as the Sitami Milli (Shahrani, 1984, pp. 44–45; Dorronsoro, 2005, pp. 212–213). The existence of a broad variety of donors further permitted fragmentation. At times, party objectives were more important than the broader success of the jihad against the Soviets.

Finally, party versus tribal/community conflict was particularly prominent in the south. Hezb-e-Islami actively sought to appropriate tribal bodies in their favour, assassinating both those tribal leaders seen to obstruct this attempt (as occurred with the Ahmadzai and Mangal) and also other civil society figures (e.g., the journalist Sayyed Majrooh) who challenged the activities of the *tanzims* and their appropriation of the jihad. As revealed in the Kandahar chapter, the Kandahar *shura* consistently sought to resist the migration of eastern parties to the province in order to preserve their autonomy and independence.

Parties can take punitive actions against communities, particularly when the latter prevented the transit of mujahideen forces through a locality due to a desire to preserve a local community for fear of government retribution. Parties would then punish a community for not assisting their operations. Outside armed groups took steps to undermine the compromises made by local communities with the governments – punishing those that did not permit mujahideen to attack from their area (which would be seen to invite reprisals).

While this was first evident during the jihad, communities in the south face a similar challenge today, whereby the AGF enforce their ability to transit through villages (and punish those who either refuse or are seen to cooperate with the government) (IRIN, 2007).

Conclusion

Unfortunately, the spectre of warfare will not be leaving the Afghan landscape anytime soon. This chapter demonstrated both the real consequences of conflict and arms proliferation, while also exploring issues of priorities, past victimization and demands for justice. It introduced many dynamics, including:

- The importance of non-military manifestations of armed group power, particularly in terms of officials with armed groups' continued role in provincial and national government bodies and their use of military power to gain economic power. The weak development of national institutions further facilitates their capture by local commanders.
- The critical role of the state and external governments in contributing to both weapons proliferation and the expansion and maintenance of militias. The government, and, at times, the Coalition, are better understood as participants in local insecurity than as neutral guarantors of local security. By virtue of providing funds, licence and endorsement, both the Afghan and external governments become implicated in local violence and disputes.
- The vast scale of victimization, occurring during all periods of the conflict, as well as the psychological consequences of both war and deprivation.
- The differences between international (whether held by aid workers or military forces) and local perceptions of security.
- The role of arms proliferation in undermining traditional mechanisms. Certain commanders utilize local insecurity to fortify their positions. Only a few communities have been able to retain the community checks and balances that restrain commanders.
- Given the above, an exclusive focus on small arms proliferation (whether in terms of the continued arms trade or continued possession/stockpiling) would neglect the broader role and influence of armed groups in Afghanistan.

Notes

1 The AGF (a name given by the Coalition, with the insurgents also known as Anti-Coalition Forces or as the neo-Taliban) is a loose Coalition of Hezb-e-Islami party members, former Taliban, new recruits and local tribal members, with the insurgency making some steps towards establishing a series of unified regional commands.
2 *Manila Philippine Daily Inquirer*, 2001; *AFP*, 1999; *New York Times*, 1998.

3 Interview with donor-nation diplomat, May 2004.

4 The AIHRC report further indicated that: 'Almost two thirds (63 per cent) of the respondents felt that the conflict in Afghanistan was not primarily ethnic in nature, but that ethnicity was manipulated and used by commanders (and external powers, including Iran and Pakistan)' (AIHRC, 2005, p. 11).

5 Data based on review of ANSO database of security incidents. Interview with Nick Downie, ANSO, 30 January 2005.

6 Observation based on research on security sector reform and interviews with international and Afghan security officials conducted in Afghanistan in 2004.

7 Historically, with the emergence of European states, there was a long tradition of the state co-opting non-state armed actors (warlords, bandits, privateers and outlaws) by providing them with official title and integrating them into emerging national armed forces (Tilly, 1985, p. 173).

8 *Hasht-nafari* (eight persons): 'A system of recruitment imposed on the frontier tribes by which they were to provide one able-bodied man out of eight,' which was introduced in 1896, resurrected in 1922 and that was largely utilized in periods of national emergencies. Present among the Durrani tribes of Kandahar (as well as among the Hazaras and Uzbeks under Murad Beg prior to the expansion of the Afghan state), under the *jagir*, the state provided 'an allotment of land that was tax-exempt but required its holder to provide a number of troops and arms.' Among the Waziri and Mahsud tribes, the khasadar was a tribal militia supplementing the regular Afghan army, usually under the direct command of provincial governors or district chiefs and utilized as border guards. Among the southeastern Ghilzais, the tribal *lashkars* could produce as many as 20,000–100,000 short-term combatants for use against a foreign invader, although they were generally viewed to be undisciplined and temperamental (Adamec, 2003, pp. 154, 197, 220, 237).

9 Interview with UN Security official, Jalalabad, June 2005.

10 UNPU members also previously belonged to: Jamiat (Commander Pana'a (killed during civil war), Commander Husseini, Mirza Rahim), Ittihad (Commander Sher Alam).

11 Combatant #126, Chaghcharan, Ghor, April 2005.

12 Combatant #126, Chaghcharan, Ghor, April 2005.

13 Samander, 2003; Jurat was the former head of a 5,000 person Public Security Office and was accused by Karzai of being involved in the death of the former Minister of Aviation (Abdul Rahman) at Kabul Airport, as well as in the violent repression of a demonstration at Kabul University. Reports were obtained by Human Rights Watch of Jurat's involvement in the maintenance of private prisons and arbitrary detentions for extortion and torture (HRW, 2003, fn. 28–31).

14 Combatant #136, Herat, April 2005.

15 Combatant #309, Siakhak, Wardak, June 2005.

2   Small arms flows into and within Afghanistan

Michael Bhatia

Although Afghanistan is also home to massive stockpiles of heavy weapons and munitions (from battle tanks to SCUD rockets), small arms are particularly significant in terms of their dominant combat role and their local political impact. According to Tarzi:

> heavy weapons are not the weapon of choice for local or regional militias. Since early 2002, only once have warlords used main battle tanks against each other. Even antigovernment forces such as the neo-Taliban do not rely on heavy weaponry. The power of warlords, regional commanders, and others in control of armed groups outside the government is determined by the number of fighting men and the availability of small arms.
>
> (Tarzi, 2005)

Substantial problems exist in determining the precise number of small arms and light weapons in Afghanistan. Estimates vary considerably and range between 500,000/two million and ten million.[1] The ammunition and munitions survey conducted by the Afghanistan New Beginnings Programme (ANBP) led to the identification of more than 100,000 metric tons of ammunition in various stockpiles; with 600 Kamaz trucks of ammunition in Mazar-e-Sharif and 5,000 metric tons located in Herat (IRIN, 2005a). In neighbouring Pakistan, 'according to Interior Ministry records and Small Arms Survey in 2002, there are 18 million illegal weapons ... while licensed arms holders number 2 million plus' (Khan, 2003). A former head of the Inter-Services Intelligence (ISI) indicated that as many as three million new Kalashnikovs were available in Pakistan's weapon stores as of 1993 (Smith, 1993, p. 8; Giustozzi, 2000, p. 245).

Given the above, complete disarmament will not be achieved in the near term in Afghanistan. Weapons proliferation and local weapons availability will be a characteristic of Afghan life for years to come. Combined with its porous borders, Afghanistan's geographic position between four major weapons manufacturers (Russia, India, China and Pakistan) guarantees the availability of arms to parties thus inclined.

amazing!

Afghanistan currently lacks a domestic arms manufacturing industry – content to import its weapons from the vast number of producers available over its borders. The Peshawar border market is home both to craft arms manufacturers and to arms markets. Local Afghan cottage producers are crowded out by the well-developed national and craft arms manufacturers in Pakistan's Northwest Frontier Province (NWFP).[2] In Darra Adam Kheil alone – the most famous of the NWFP's gun-producing towns – there are believed to be 3,500 gunsmiths working in 900 factories, with 150 gun shops (Khan, 2003; *Daily Times*, 2006). The local gunsmiths can produce everything from imitation Kalashnikovs and .227mm/8mm assault rifles to anti-aircraft guns (Stobdan, 1997, p. 252). Refugee repatriation could lead Afghans skilled in the production of weapons to return to Afghanistan and set up shop there.

Pakistan's border markets have weapons available for purchase from four sources and periods of the Afghan conflict: first, those weapons *1. 1980's* diverted from the 1980s era Afghan pipeline, which supplied arms to the *2. FSU stocks* mujahideen through Pakistan by their Arab and Western government supporters; second, weapons captured from Soviet outposts and stockpiles in *3. NWFP stocks* Afghanistan; third, weapons manufactured in the border areas; and, *4. Miscellaneous* finally, small numbers of 'miscellaneous weapons' with diverse origins (*Nation*, 1994). During the 1980s, a substantial portion of the weapons supplied to Afghanistan through Pakistan was diverted to other parts of South Asia, with Afghan combatants on both sides often transporting captured weapons back to Pakistan in order to sell them on the frontier weapons markets. This continued during both the civil war and the Taliban regime, and even now. With the conclusion of DDR and the initiation of DIAG, there was a considerable danger of Afghanistan becoming an exporter of weapons, as commanders and combatants sought to profit from the sale of excess stocks both internally and externally rather than submit their weapons under government control.

This chapter is divided into three. The first part offers a historical review of arms and military assistance both to the Afghan government and to non-state armed groups from 1973 until 2005. Table 2.a.2 in the Appendix to this chapter describes both the value of and type of arms delivered by year. Table 2.a.1 (also in the Appendix) provides a list of weapons types found in Afghanistan. This part of the chapter also details the implications of the manner in which weapons were delivered to Afghanistan, revealing the significance of internal weapons transfers, particularly in terms of the acquisition of government stockpiles and transfers between parties. The second part outlines both the illicit transfer of weapons in contemporary Afghanistan, and the type of weapons found in insurgent weapons caches and utilized by Afghan anti-government forces (AGF) forces. The third part seeks to contextualize sources of support for armed groups, examining the comparative significance of government funding versus internal political economy and commercial purchases, challenging some of the core assumptions regarding the role of internal political economy in arms acquisitions and combatant mobilization.

With the Coalition unwilling to release data as to the scale of caches captured, collected and destroyed during its search and seizure operations, data as to the scale of small arms in Afghanistan is limited and confined to those stockpiles identified and collected by the ANBP. Therefore, the methodology used in this chapter produces qualitative rather than precise quantitative results.

Historical flow of small arms to Afghanistan, 1973–2005

The Afghan arms pipeline – the global effort to supply both the mujahideen forces and the Democratic Republic of Afghanistan (DRA) government – was potentially the most significant arms conduit of the past two decades, both in scale and type of weapons supplied. Since 2001, both the arms trade and the Afghan conflict have had a profound seismic effect on global politics and security. What was a 'forgotten war' – a conflict existing in the shadows of a post-Cold War globalizing world during the 1990s – became connected with a terrorist attack that targeted all of the critical symbols of American supremacy. A review of the historical flow of small arms to Afghanistan reveals:

- the overwhelming significance of covert/overt external government transfers in supporting both the Afghan government and the anti-government forces;
- the primacy of donation over commercial purchase (particularly until the Taliban era);
- the importance of the pattern of external government distribution of weapons to Afghan parties, redistribution within Afghanistan due to tactical victories, and attempts by interim governments to consolidate arms holdings;
- the increased sophistication of government donations;
- external involvement in training both the government and non-state armed groups in unconventional warfare and urban sabotage and the use of Afghanistan as a training camp for global insurgents after 1992.

The historical distribution of small arms can be differentiated between periods of distribution, consolidation and redistribution. A period of distribution is characterized by the influx of weapons into Afghanistan from the outside; a period of redistribution involves the acquisition of internal stocks by an opposing party; and a period of consolidation reveals an attempt by an emerging central government to 'de-weaponize' society through a disarmament campaign.[3] Each period is characterized by distribution, as there has been a constant flow of weapons into Afghanistan via external governments over the past three decades. Political transitions, as

Table 2.1 Periods of weapons distribution, redistribution and consolidation

Period	Characteristic
1973–1981	Distribution and redistribution
	Mujahideen capture of arms stockpiles
1981–1989	Distribution
	Graphic increase in supplies and ammunition
1989–1992	Consolidation and distribution
	USSR distribution to GoA
1992–1996	Redistribution and distribution
	New commercial purchases/donation
1996–2001	Consolidation and distribution
	Continued supply to UF
2001–2006	Distribution, redistribution and consolidation
	DDR and DIAG programmes carried out by the ANBP and the GoA

occurred in 1989–1992 and in 2001–2002, are often accompanied by the broad and uncontrolled dissemination and redistribution of weapons to emerging power figures.

The availability of weapons in Afghanistan can be incompletely inferred by the tracking of weapons prices relative to demand. Unfortunately, no single source has monitored the price of Kalashnikovs in Pakistan over the entire course of the conflict. Table 2.2 provides a historical breakdown of the price of a Russian or Chinese Kalashnikov in Pakistan beginning in 1980. Data was largely gathered from reports and news articles on the Pakistani border markets, and so are approximate rather than authoritative. The data reveals the graphic reduction in the price of a Kalashnikov, potentially revealing how supply has far outstripped demand. From a peak price of $2,500–3,500 in 1982 (which is logically coherent given the scale of the rebellion and the underdevelopment of the arms pipeline), the price of a Kalashnikov reached an all-time low of $308 in 2000 until rebounding to $500 in 2005. The most dramatic price collapse occurred in 1989, when the AK price fell from 30,000 to 17,000 Pakistan rupees (Kartha, 1999, p. 64). Prices for Pakistani replicates are between one-half to one-quarter of the price of original Soviet and Chinese models. The return of conflict and the rise of the AGF insurgency are generally viewed to be contributing to a rise in weapons prices.

While Kalashnikov-type weapons are prevalent in Afghanistan, depending on the type of opponent and form of warfare, different weapons are considerably more desirable at different times; and with individuals receiving different weapons depending on their status in the armed group. Certainly, the Kalikov and the Krinkov were accorded the greatest significance during the Soviet period (Isby, 1989, p. 112). The commander and his bodyguards will carry light machine guns (PPSH) or modified 5.45 AKZSU, while the standard soldiers would carry either AKs or Lee Enfields, depending on the type of armed group and the soldier's

Table 2.2 Evolution of Kalashnikov prices in
Pakistan (Russian or Chinese origin)

1980	$1,500
1982	$2,500–3,500
1985	$1,200
1987	$750
1988	$1,363
1989	$794
1990	$694
1991	$458
1993	$576
1998	$320
2000	$308
2001	$400
2002	$346
2005	$500

Sources: AIC, 1991b, pp. 41–42; Smith, 1993; Kartha, 1999, p. 64; Adamec, 2003, p. 39; Galster, 1990, p. 129; Sullivan, 1998; Bazzi, 2001; Interviews with Afghan and international officials for current prices. Pakistan rupees to dollar conversions found online, available at: intl.econ.cuhk.edu.hk/exchange_rate_regime/index.php?cid=22 (accessed 16 August 2007).

standing within it. Community militias are generally under-resourced in comparison to political–military parties. Over all periods of the conflict, there has also been considerable geographical variation in the scale of resources available to armed groups.

As seen throughout this chapter, there was no shortage of parties vying for international support in Afghanistan, both during the jihad period and the civil war. Nor was there any shortage of international parties (state, Islamic and Western charities) willing to provide assistance. The significance of this external assistance cannot be understated. Cordesman and Wagner highlight the significance of this external assistance:

> The most important changes affecting the Mujahideen's military capabilities came from the outside and consisted primarily of the sanctuaries and support provided by Pakistan and Iran and the weapons and funds provided by the West and the Gulf states. It was this support that allowed the Mujahideen to steadily improve their weaponry and military capability.
>
> (Cordesman and Wagner, 1991, p. 23)

External states could choose among a variety of ethnic groups and differently ideologically oriented parties, with considerable differences as to their ideal post-conflict end states. The decision as to who to support was then based on a mix of the donor government's geo-political interests and ideological affinities and goals.

Islamabad favoured Islamic fundamentalist parties over any nationalist or traditional organization, partly in order to avoid a resurgence of Pashtun nationalism (Dorronsoro, 2005, p. 145). Teheran altered its party preferences considerably over the course of the conflict, offering support to a broad range of organizations early in the jihad, then focusing on militant Shi'a organizations (to the decline of the traditional *Shura*), and, ultimately, by the late 1980s and early 1990s, extending its support to the broader Supervisory Council of the North (SCN) and anti-Taliban resistance (Hilali, 2002; Griffin, 2001, p. 111).

With regard to American assistance, considerable tensions existed within the Reagan administration as to the ends of Afghan policy between 'dealers' and 'bleeders,' over whether the primary goal was to achieve as immediate a Soviet withdrawal as possible or to utilize Afghanistan as a method of inflicting as great a human and material cost on Soviet forces as possible (Cordovez and Harrison, 1995, p. 31). At no point did the West believe that it would be possible to defeat the Soviet forces militarily, seeking to prolong the insurgency without provoking a Soviet attack on Pakistan. This consequently shaped both the scale and type of weapons procured for the mujahideen. Concurrently, this also served to prolong the conflict. According to Cordovez and Harrison:

> the United States did its best to prevent the emergence of a U.N. role, actively working to replace Pakistani leaders who sought an Afghan peace settlement with others who were ready for a Pakistani role as a conduit for aid to the Afghan resistance.
>
> (Cordovez and Harrison, 1995, Preface)

The Soviet invasion and the Afghan arms pipeline, 1973–1989

The period from 1979 until 1988 was marked by the distribution of weapons to factions by their sponsors (either the government of Afghanistan and its local militias or the mujahideen *tanzims*.) Arms supplied during this period remain the primary source of weapons in Afghanistan. All parties to the conflict utilized stockpiles created during this period over the following decades.

Ambushes for spoils were the primary source of weapons in the early years of the jihad.[4] Tactical victory resulted in the acquisition of greater weapons stores by the conquering party – potentially greatly enhancing a group's capabilities and providing a far broader mix of weapons than initially available. Captured ammunition critically replenished dwindling supplies. For example, the capture of the DRA garrison in Alingar provided the local mujahideen forces with 80 heavy weapons and 1,200 small arms to include a: '76 mm mountain gun, one 76 mm field gun, some ZGU-1 heavy machine guns, a 107 mm mortar, several DShK heavy machine guns, and some 82 mm mortars' (Jalali and Grau, 1994, p. 121). Defections from DRA units, which were negotiated via tribal intermediaries or tribal linkages, provided additional sources of weapons (Jalali and Grau 1994 pp. 172–173).' Furthermore, 'Soviet conscripts would sell fuel, ammunition, weapons, batteries and military equipment for hashish, food and Afghan money' (Jalali and Grau, 1994, p. 370).

Weapons captured by mujahideen in Afghanistan were then sold on the Pakistani market, and the funds were used to support families residing in Pakistan's refugee camps. Captured weapons were distributed as follows: 'all heavy weapons and 1/5 of the loot from an ambush or raid went to the commander. The other 4/5 was divided among the mujahideen combatants' (Jalali and Grau, 1994, pp. 22, 65, 172–173, 370).

Beginning in 1956, the Afghan military received a substantial amount of training and military equipment from the Soviet Union. President Daoud attempted to lessen Afghan reliance on Soviet assistance between 1975 and the Khalqi coup in 1978. Pakistan first provided weapons to mujahideen parties in 1973, supplying weapons to Shi'as and to Islamist parties in order to execute a rebellion against the Daoud government. An ISI 'Afghan Cell' was established by President Bhutto, which trained 5,000 Islamists in guerrilla war. The 1975 revolt, however, was a failure, with 60 of the 150 commanders killed inside Afghanistan (Bradsher, 1999, pp. 17–18).

Prior to the Soviet invasion, with a series of rebellions in Nuristan, the Hazarajat and Herat, and, with a number of military contingents defecting with their weapons, local communities were able to acquire government weapons stocks. During this period, before the formalization of the weapons pipeline, Oman became a prominent 'pick-up point' for Afghan armed groups, with weapons then entering Afghanistan via Baluchistan (Galster, 1990, p. 121). Shortly thereafter, Saudi Arabia and China began providing Soviet and Chinese-made weapons to the various parties, with the US establishing the 'arms pipeline' in 1980.

The US initially provided $30 million, but its assistance ultimately grew to over $630 million per year from 1986–1990. Aside from the provision of UK Blowpipe and ultimately US Stinger SAMs (surface-to-air missiles), all weapons were of Soviet, Chinese, Italian, Pakistani or Indian manufacture, in an attempt to hide US covert assistance. Both Pakistan and Egypt used weapons purchases and deliveries as opportunities to modernize their own military stockpiles. Total US and Saudi Arabian assistance between 1979 and 1991 was from $6–8 billion and ultimately delivered more than 400,000 Chinese Type-56/59 Kalashnikov-type weapons, 100,000 Indian .303 rifles and 100 million rounds of ammunition (see Table 2.a.1 in the Appendix for sources and data).

In 1984, Saudi Arabia agreed to match all US contributions, depositing these funds directly into a shared Swiss Bank account, with private donors providing direct financial assistance to the parties. According to the head of Pakistan's ISI, whether provided by governments or by private individuals, 'Arab money ... saved the system,' particularly in terms of paying for transport costs (Yousaf and Adkin, 1992, p. 106). Charitable networks were established, and 5,000 Arab volunteers came to participate in the fighting. According to Salamat Ali, 'Arab revolutionary groups ... established offices, arms dumps and training camps' and were allegedly linked to the 'local underworld and foreign intelligence agencies' (Ali, 1991b, p. 23). *Zakat* donations were provided as cash rather than in-kind, which lowered the mujahideen's reception of criticism from Western groups on human rights and humanitarian issues (Ali, 1991c, p. 24). The aid response to the refugee influx established the trend of utilizing Islamic charities as fronts for propaganda and fundraising (Gunaratna, 2001, p. 2).

*Training was an important part of external military assistance, from the USSR's initiation of Afghan Army training in the 1950s (and the decision by the United States to forego military engagement) to Pakistan's early support of contra-state armed groups as early as 1973. After the Soviet invasion, military training camps were established inside Afghanistan for Islamist insurgencies and for Al-Qaeda.

Pakistani training camps expanded, from two camps capable of training 200 trainees in 1983, to the training of 1,000 per month in 1984, to 19,400 ultimately able to complete a training course in 1986 alone. In the end, approximately 80,000 mujahideen were trained in a variety of skills, from basic infantry to sabotage and demolition and SAM operations (Yousaf and Adkin, 1992, p. 117). Mujahideen teams were trained in urban terrorism and became practiced in the construction of improvised explosives.[5]

In its primary, but not exclusive, manifestation, the 'arms pipeline' involved the delivery of weapons by third party governments sympathetic to the mujahideen's cause, the delivery of these weapons to Pakistan government officials at Karachi for transfer to Ojhiri and Peshawar and the distribution of weapons to the parties. A 1986 document obtained by the National Security Archive (NSA) reveals one model for covert arms transfers to Afghanistan. In this model, the head of GeoMiliTech Consultants Corporation and of the anti-communist US Council for World Freedom (which was affiliated with the Committee for a Free Afghanistan) offers the CIA Director the company's services in arranging third party arms transfers to Afghanistan, Nicaragua, Angola, Ethiopia and Cambodia, with the primary goal of evading increased Congressional restrictions on covert arms transfers (GeoMiliTech, 1986).

As described in Figure 2.1, a three-way trade was proposed, whereby Israel received 'credits towards the purchase of High Technology from the US' Israel then transferred these weapons to China, and China delivered Soviet-style weaponry of similar value to a trading company for transfer to the identified armed group or 'freedom fighters.' Weapons available

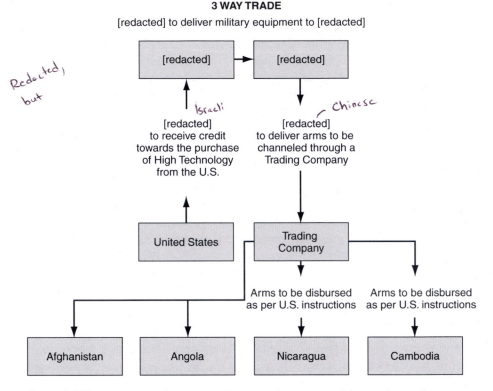

3 WAY TRADE

[redacted] to deliver military equipment to [redacted]

Figure 2.1 Three-way trade to supply armed groups with weapons (source: GeoMiliTech, 1986).

included SA-7s, AKMS, RPG-7, 12.7 mm and 14.5 mm machine guns, RPKs, mortars and plastic high explosives. While this was a proposal rather than a full order, this does reveal one model of arms sourcing employed during the Reagan administration (GeoMiliTech, 1986).

The ISI was responsible for allocating weapons among the seven mujahideen parties (HIH, HIK, Jamiat, NIFA, Ittihad, ANLF and Harakat-ul-Nabi). The ISI's head during the mujahideen period argued that the ISI's decision was largely based on 'maximum combat effectiveness,' although others contend that the ISI favoured fundamentalist parties due to their fear of Pashtun nationalism (Yousaf and Adkin, 1992, p. 103). A total of 80 per cent of material was given to the parties, with 20 per cent reserved for specific operations.

The CIA was seen to favour supporting commanders instead of political parties. According to Yousaf, '[i]n 1987 the broad percentages allocated to the Parties were Hekmatyar 18–20 per cent, Rabbani 18–19 per cent, Sayaf 17–18 per cent, Khalis 13–15 per cent, Nabi 13–15 per cent, Gailani 10–11 per cent, and Mujaddadi trailing with 3–5 per cent' (Yousaf and

Adkin, 1992, p. 105).[6] Hezb-e-Islami was the only organization that 'owned' its weapons. Weapons were given to mujahideen for their combat operations and then returned to a central stockpile afterwards. The Hezb-e-Islami Khalis commander Abdul Haq attempted a similar programme, whereby weapons were not the property of commanders but the property of the party, with little success.

There was limited oversight and accounting as to the status of weapons upon their arrival in either Rawalapindi or Karachi, with Smith arguing that, 'in all likelihood, arms were siphoned off at every point of the pipeline,' and other observers placing the amount of diversion as high as 70 per cent of the shipments (Smith, 1993, p. 8; Cordesman and Wagner, 1991, p. 20). Transit within Afghanistan led to additional seepage, with local commanders enacting a 10 per cent tax on all goods moving through their territory (Jalali and Grau, 1994, p. 403).

Substantial portions of these weapons were believed to have been deliberately leaked out and to have ended up in Kashmir and India. The diversion of weapons is believed to have increased substantially the intensity of armed conflict throughout India and Pakistan. According to Human Rights Watch (1994):

> Large numbers of pipeline weapons have made their way into the hands of Sikh and Kashmiri militants. Evidence suggests that the militants obtain the weapons in several ways: directly from members of Pakistan's intelligence and military establishment, particularly the ISI, from the arms bazaars in Pakistan's Northwest Frontier Province, and from former Afghan fighters.[7]

Upon receipt of weapons, commanders would sell supplied weapons (from the ISI) in order to acquire needed weapons and other supplies. The 1988 explosion at Pakistan's weapons dump in Ojhiri (near Rawalapindi) ended the potential for any final accounting as to the precise scale of seepage from the Pakistani arms pipeline (Smith, 1993, pp. 8–9).

Mujahideen logistics focused on maintaining ammunition resupply and medical evacuation. The Soviet strategy of depopulation, as well as the graphic increase in international assistance, led to the creation of massive supply depots and forward supply points, particularly in the Tora Bora mountain areas between Nangarhar and Paktya Province (Jalali and Grau, 1994, pp. 125–125, 267).

As early as 1982, there were considerable discrepancies in the variety of weaponry that mujahideen groups possessed. Some held a broad range of weapons, from AKs to RPGs and mines (Fullerton, 1981, p. 26). The most developed possessed mortars, mines, a range of both heavy and light machine guns and a broad range of automatic and standoff weapons. Other groups, as of 1983, still only possessed older bolt-action rifles (Lee

Enfields and G3s) and only a small selection of Kalashnikovs (Jalali and Grau, 1994, p. 251).

For example, Commander Tsarenwal Sher Habib of Paghman reported that his forces contained some 800 mujahideen, possessing 'ZGU-1s, DShKs, many RPG-7s, PK machine guns, 82 mm mortars, 82 mm and 75 mm recoilless rifles, machine guns, and a number of .303 bolt-action Lee Enfield rifles' (Jalali and Grau, 1994, p. 244). While generally disparaged due to its age, the .303 Lee Enfield had double the range of the AK and was able to penetrate a Soviet flak jacket (Jalali and Grau, 1994, p. 245).

Over the course of the 1980s, the mujahideen received increasingly sophisticated weapons, including mortars, anti-tank missiles and SAMs. Until then, the mujahideen were exclusively limited to engage with Soviet forces within 300–400 metres, which was the 'maximum effective range' of their weapons (Cordesman and Wagner, 1991, p. 144). The acquisition of sniper rifles and heavy machine guns extended their range to 800 metres, which was then followed by a broader array of 'standoff' weapons such as SAMs, mortars and other munitions.

At the same time, the Soviet forces were acquiring more advanced forms of common Soviet weapons, including modified versions of the RPG (RPG-18 and RPG-22, with the RPG-16, RPO, RPO-A or AGS-17 grenade launcher replacing the RPG-7) (Shaw and Spencer, 2003, p. 183). The RPG quickly became the most significant weapon – useful against both armour and helicopters and described as a 'great equalizer and a great weapon in an ambush' (Jalali and Grau, 1994, p. 66). It was in Afghanistan that non-state groups mastered the art of utilizing RPGs against helicopters, whereby a $100 rocket is able to ground a $1 million piece of machinery, which has posed a challenge to Coalition forces in Somalia, Iraq and Afghanistan.

A major transition occurred in terms of both training and supply in the mid-1980s, with the creation of mujahideen mortar and SAM teams by the CIA–ISA partnership. Moreover, the CIA recognized the necessity to increase the supply of ammunition dramatically, upon recalculating the mujahideen needs for sustaining operations (Crile, 2003, pp. 300–301). Beginning in 1984 and completed by 1988, various mujahideen forces had acquired a range of weapons, from tanks and lightly armoured transports to a range of crew-served (76 mm, 122 mm D-30 howitzers, 107 mm/122 mm multiple rocket launchers, 51 mm/60 mm/82 mm mortars, 40 GAI-BOI 200 AA guns, 12.7 mm/14.5 mm AA guns) and small arms (AGS-17 30 mm grenade launchers, RPG-7, SPG-9). The acquisition of 107 mm/122 mm Multiple Rocket Launchers, as well as 82 mm mortars, allowed for symbolic, standoff, long-range and harassment attacks (Isby, 1989, pp. 109–110; Jalali and Grau, 1994, p. 400).

The Soviet withdrawal, the Najibullah government's collapse and civil war, 1992–1995

The Soviet withdrawal accelerated rather than reduced military assistance to both the government and the mujahideen parties. While the US committed to reducing its weapons deliveries to the parties and focused on supporting specific commanders, the Saudis compensated with the delivery of Iraqi heavy weapons, which were viewed to 'only stiffen the hardliners resolve to fight rather than negotiate' and that consequently affected both the formation of a mujahideen alliance and the attempts to form a unity government with the Najibullah regime (Ali, 1991a, p. 28). Internally, the Najibullah government's attempt to disarm local factions (pursuing consolidation through a process of reconciliation) was matched with its arming of local tribal militias.

American assistance declined by 60 per cent after the Jalalabad offensive and ended completely in 1991. For the Soviet Union:

> arms deliveries ... were so massive that, in absolute terms, the volume of exports in these three years (1989 through 1991) exceeded the amount of Soviet exports in the whole preceding period of military-technical cooperation with Afghanistan, beginning in 1955.
>
> (Kenzhetaev, 2007)

As described by Cordesman and Wagner, 'the USSR ... provided an airlift of 25 to 40 IL-76 aircraft per day to the [D]RA' as well as billions in financial assistance, which 'gave the RA much the same firepower advantage against the mujahideen that the Soviets had had before their withdrawal' (Cordesman and Wagner, 1991, pp. 97–98).

The 1992 collapse of the Najibullah government and the capture of garrison weapons stockpiles allowed internal commanders to acquire further autonomy from the Peshawar party representatives. The capture of the garrison in Gardez provides an example of the scale of material kept in the provinces: 6,000 Kalashnikovs; 129 tanks with 3,500 rounds; 70 howitzers with 4,000 rounds; 15 BM-21 rocket systems with 2,000 rounds; four BM-15s; eight Oragan rockets; 380 rocket launchers; 300 PKs; 30 ZU 23 mm; 20 AGS grenade launchers; 70 APCs; 15 BMPs; eight ZSU-23s and 2,500 assorted other weapons (AIC, 1992a, pp. 24–25).

The Uzbek commander and Junbish party leader Abdul Rashid Dostum acquired the stocks of the Dehdadi military base in Balkh Province, which allegedly included as many as 240,000 light weapons (AIC, 1992b, p. 31). For a brief period, the capture of these stocks led to a decline in demand from abroad and a decline in the price of many weapons (see Table 2.2), as commanders and combatants were able to acquire all that was required within Afghanistan (AIC, 1991a, pp. 38–42). Inter-factional Coalitions – which had formed to conduct the offensives on Khost and Gardez –

quickly collapsed into bickering over the distribution of the captured stockpiles.

During the civil war, the armed factions continued to receive military assistance from neighbouring states and regional powers (Saudi Arabia provided $150 million, and additional donations came from Iran, Uzbekistan and Pakistan), while also purchasing ex-Soviet stocks on a commercial basis from Ukraine, Belarus, Uzbekistan and Tajikistan (see Table 2.a.2). Beginning with the civil war, and particularly in Nangarhar and Takhar provinces, training camps migrated from the Pakistan border areas to Afghanistan. Afghanistan began to provide small cadres of combatants for other conflicts, most prominently in Azerbaijan, Tajikistan and Chechnya.[8]

The Taliban's rise and the anti-Taliban alliance

The rise of the Taliban ended the factional infighting in Kabul, with a rough alliance (Supervisory Council of the North/United Front/Northern Alliance) forming between formerly bitter allies and with all parties receiving aid from neighbouring powers and involved in the commercial purchase of weapons from global traffickers. The Taliban both acquired weapons from stockpiles (whether by force or through negotiation) from commanders and received extensive training as well as material, financial and diplomatic assistance from Pakistan. The Taliban's public mythology stressed weapons acquisition through stockpiles in order to assert their exclusively indigenous origins.[9]

The Taliban's emergence in 1994 – and capture of Kabul in 1996 – inaugurated a period of substantial arms consolidation. The Taliban disarmed those areas under their control, with these disarmament campaigns inducing public unrest. Anecdotally, the campaign was founded on the belief that each Afghan household possessed a weapon. Families were thus required to surrender a weapon or a substantial cash substitute. If the family was unable to provide either, a male family member was then subject to a jail term.

Upon gaining control of Kabul in 1996, the Taliban established a security commission in order to disarm the city by issuing weapons permits and banning walkie-talkies and tinted automobile glass (Radio Afghanistan Network, 1996a). The seizures revealed the scale of weapons available in Kabul prior to the Taliban's arrival. A cache uncovered in 1996 contained 11 light and heavy weapons (including one Goryunov), 15 boxes of Kalashnikov ammunition, 300 hand grenades, eight boxes of PK ammunition, mines and 20 BM-12 rockets. Other caches discovered included flame-throwers, mortars and DShks. Stockpiles acquired outside of Kabul were even more substantial (Radio Afghanistan, 1996a, b, c).

In Khost, beyond a range of manned artillery and recoilless rifles as well as other small arms, the Taliban acquired 105 Kalashnikovs; four

DShKs; 26 ten-round box magazine rifles; 14 RPG rocket launchers; one recoilless gun; 47 medium-range 82 mm mortars; one mountain 125 mm artillery; 21 recoilless 82 mm artillery; 16 recoilless 75 mm artillery; 2 Blow-pipe rockets; 10,128 boxes of Kalashnikov ammunition; 350 boxes of PK ammunition; 28 boxes of recoilless gun ammunition; 783 boxes of Brno ammunition; 11,416 boxes DShK ammunition; 14,036 boxes of ZK-1 ammunition; 303 boxes of PK ammunition; 1,900 shells for medium-range rocket launchers; seven RPG-2 rockets; 5,442 shells for recoilless guns (Radio Afghanistan, 1996d).

The Russian arms trafficker, Victor Bout, provided heavy weapons and small arms to both sides of the conflict, via Albania and the United Arab Emirates (van Niekerk and Verloy, 2002). Initiating formal transfer in 1997, Turkmenistan supplied the Taliban with AKM 7.62 mm ammunition, as well as fuel and engine lubricants (Orazmukhamedov, 2002). The Taliban sold captured weapons from Baghlan, Kunduz and Mazar on the Pakistani market, even while conducting offensive operations against the Northern Alliance (Shinwari, 2002).

An arms embargo was imposed on the Taliban regime by the United Nations Security Council in December 2000, although the Northern Alliance forces were excluded from this embargo. Prior to September 11, in a 2001 attempt to reduce small arms proliferation within its own borders, the government of Pakistan entered into negotiations with representatives from the Taliban, HIH and HIK, in order to facilitate the disarmament of the Afghan settlements and refugee camps in Pakistan's NWFP (*News*, 2001). During the ensuing raids, for example, 'the Khyber Rifles officials recovered ten Kalashnikovs, one single barrel gun, one stane gun, two pistols, about 5,000 cartridges and 83 magazines' (*Frontier Post*, 1997). This crackdown induced the sale of arms to the UF forces, with tribal arms dealers in the NWFP selling weapons to UF agents in Kunar, to include mortars, SAMs, RPGs and anti-aircraft guns (*KHAAR*, 2001).

During the Taliban era, Tajik officials regularly uncovered arms caches on the Afghan border, apparently more for the personal defensive use of drug smugglers than indicating any substantial overlap between the arms and narcotic trade. In February 1996, a small boat caught crossing the Panj river contained an AK, an RPG, a collection of hand grenades and 90 kg of drugs (*ITAR-TASS*, 1996). In March 2001, Tajik border guards discovered 'tens of firearms, including a Kalashnikov assault rifle with spare cartridges, up to 20 hand grenades, over 4,000 rounds of ammunition and 18 kg of marijuana' (*ITAR-TASS*, 2001). In the late 1990s, drug traffickers typically moved with RPGs, AKs and hand grenades. Thus, as interdiction efforts increased, both on the Iranian border and in Central Asia, drug traffickers also increased their armament.

The alternatives to massive expenditure on weaponry both by donors and by the various factions were illustrated by Secretary of State Madeleine Albright in 1998:

Consider that the warring parties in Afghanistan recently spent USD 200 million on weapons over a three-year period. For the same money, they could have built 400 rural hospitals to give health care to families who have never had it; or educated 200,000 Afghan young people from kindergarten through high school.

(Lumpe, 1999)

Transparent and covert weapons flows after 9/11

Following 9/11, the Coalition supplied commanders with money and material, with the Taliban first abandoning substantial weapons stockpiles and then reinitiating the focused purchase of standoff weapons in the Pakistani border regions. As the US initiated Operation Enduring Freedom, weapons were again purchased on the regional arms market for shipment into Afghanistan, inducing a structural change in Pakistan's weapons industry, as well as a sharp increase in the price of both ammunition and arms. This was partly fuelled by the million-dollar pay-offs provided to Northern Alliance commanders as inducements for organizing operations and/or for successful operations, although the funds were also utilized for the payment of wages, the bribery of opposing Taliban commanders and for personal accumulation of wealth (Hersh, 2004, pp. 142–143). General Dostum utilized the American payments to purchase assault rifles, mortars, grenade launchers, anti-tank weapons, mines and other supplies in Uzbekistan (Kenzhetaev, 2007).

In 2002, the United States and other European countries, such as France and Germany, began purchasing weapons and ammunition from the government-run Pakistan Ordnance Factories for use in Afghanistan and Iraq (ul Haque 2004). Shortages of ammunition in Afghanistan led to a graphic increase in the price of ammunition and weapons in neighbouring Pakistan. The price of a Chinese or Russian AK increased from 16,000 rupees to 18,000 rupees, and the price of ammunition also increased (see Table 2.2) (Shinwari, 2002). Scarcity, as well as the Pakistan government's attempt to nationalize the industry, prompted protests in some quarters and the belief that this was part of a 'conspiracy to disarm the Pakhtoons' (Paracha, 2002).

The wide availability – but generally poor quality (some combatants indicated that the weapons became unusable after one clip) and undesirability – of craft-produced Kalashnikovs was utilized by some commanders to attempt to manipulate DDR (see Chapter 4). As once observed and as reported, 'Afghan commanders have been known to buy up cheap Kalashnikovs in the area, smuggling them back over the porous frontier, and handing them in to officials in return for compensation' (*Daily Times*, 2006).

The ANBP prohibited Dera-made weapons for DDR and thus prevented commanders from buying knock-offs from Pakistan, handing them in and either trading or selling their high-grade weapons instead.[10] Although the quality of the weapons varied greatly, the ANBP appears to have successfully managed this problem.

More recently, there are reports that;

> the Pentagon is investigating purchasing weapons for the Afghan Army from the Russian Federation, with the goal of completely refitting the Afghan Army. Pentagon chiefs have asked arms suppliers for a quote on a vast amount of ordnance, including more than 78 million rounds of AK47 (the well-known Kalashnikov submachine gun) ammunition, 100,000 rocket-propelled grenades and 12,000 tank shells.
>
> (MosNews.com, 2006)

In conclusion, there appear to be two rearmament initiatives in Afghanistan, with the Coalition both purchasing and redistributing weapons to its local Afghan militias (predominantly in 2002), and with external donors now trying to source mass quantities of weaponry for the central government, the Afghan National Army (ANA) and the Afghan National Police (ANP) via Russia and other Eastern European governments. In 2003, Albania donated 600 AKs and 10,000 units of ammunition. Bulgaria donated a collection of AKs, machine guns, mortars and ammunition. Pakistan donated 5,000 submachine guns. In January 2007, the United States announced that it would provide the ANA with 12,000 weapons as well as other military equipment.

Contemporary flows of small arms: illicit and insurgent

The previous analysis of the (still continuing) flow of weapons revealed historical increases in both scale and advancement of weapons supplied to the parties to the Afghan conflict. In seeking to provide the new Afghan government with a physical monopoly on force to match its monopoly on legitimate force, the United States, Eastern European and South Asian governments are supplying the emerging national security bodies with weapons and ammunition.

The distinction between government and non-state and between licit and illicit arms possession was only recently established in Afghanistan. In July 2004, a Presidential Decree was released stipulating punishment for maintaining armed groups outside of the MoD, remobilizing demobilized groups and for retaining weapons from the arms collection programme. In 2005, the government defined illegal armed groups as 'quasi military groups of armed men who are not officially recognized as part of the recognized Afghan military forces. They are outside the chain of command and control of central government.' Having discussed the history of covert and overt military transfers to both state and non-state actors previously in the chapter, here, the illicit market in small arms, focusing first on trade and then on the AGF insurgency is examined.

Currently, there is no single arms market in contemporary Afghanistan. In the border regions, the AGF appears to be making focused purchases of new weapons, specifically seeking standoff weapons (e.g., sniper rifles). With DIAG/ANBP having removed significant weapons from the Afghan countryside, communities may now seek to rearm and commanders may justify their purchase of new weapons with the re-emergence of the Taliban and the absence of security.

Current arms stockpiles have their origins in one of multiple periods of weapons supplies, stretching back not only to the 1970s, but in some cases to the century before. The ANBP's DDR programme, the DIAG programme and the Coalition/NATO's own disarmament efforts all deal with these residual stockpiles. While the ANBP has been primarily involved in collecting, destroying and centralizing all weapons (for future use by the ANA) (see Chapter 4), the Coalition has been involved both in the procurement of new weapons and the redistribution of collected weapons.

Contemporary illicit arms trade

There are two dimensions to contemporary arms availability in Afghanistan: markets and internal availability. Until 2002, Afghanistan had been a net importer of weapons. While there continue to be weapons flows (largely specialized and small-scale) into Afghanistan, Afghanistan may now either become an exporter or serve as a transit route for weapons from Central Asia to Pakistan. Weapons prices are reported to have increased both in Afghanistan and in Pakistan since 2005, as communities and commanders are reportedly rearming in anticipation of the continued growth of the AGF insurgency. 'Weapons prices in northern Afghanistan – a region where warlords still hold sway – have more than doubled in the past few months, signaling a setback for disarmament efforts,' with communities reportedly stockpiling in anticipation of a Taliban comeback (Morarjee, 2006).

As early as 2002, soon-to-be-disarmed soldiers began selling their weapons on the local market, with one report indicating that: 'Northern Alliance soldiers have become players in one of the world's biggest and most unregulated weapons markets, perpetuating the region's war machine' (Buchbinder, 2002). One armed smuggler is quoted as saying:

> We mostly buy the arms from soldiers who are not paid their salaries. We then take them through Logar and Wardak provinces to the border towns of Pakistan, like Miranshah, Wana and Bannu, where we sell them to tribal people for a high price.
>
> (IWPR, 2002)

I think these prices reflect local
demand in face of Coalition vs. Ins.
In '05 was Ghor even contested?

Afghanistan: small arms flows   55

Table 2.3 Comparative arms prices in Afghanistan in US$ (2005)

Weapon type	Ghor	Kabul	Jalalabad
Ammunition (5.45 mm)	.2–.4/round	n/a	500–600 for 1,000 rounds.
Ammunition (7.62 mm)	.1–.6/round	20 for a case of 100	300 for 1,000 rounds
Kalashnikov (Pakistani)	40–120	n/a	150
Kalashnikov (Russian)	40–240	400	150–600
Kalashnikov (Chinese)	40–100	600	150–600
AK-74/AKZU/AKZSUKalikov (5.45 mm)(AKZU)	80–260	n/a	600–1,200
Markov pistol	100–500	n/a	300–400
Krinkov (AK with grenade launcher)	n/a	800–1,000	n/a
TT	100–300	n/a	300–400
PK (heavy machine gun)	60–160	n/a	800
RPG	40–140	300	100–150
RPG rocket	High availability/ low use	300	Cheap
Russian AK short barrelled in Pakistan	n/a	n/a	300–400

Source: Interviews with local arms traders by Afghan and international security officials.

The same report indicated a substantial difference between internal and external weapons prices, with soldiers selling their weapons for 5,000 Pakistani rupees and those weapons valued at 18,000 Pakistani rupees on the Pakistani black market (IWPR, 2002). The 'war on terrorism' has also led to the introduction of new types of weapons into Pakistan's border markets, including US M-4/M-16 carbines, MP-5s and Israeli automatic pistols. These were either stolen from US forces or part of consignments to the US Afghan allies. Accordingly, one Nangarhar commander sold 300 M-16 rifles in Landi Kotal, with M-16s now selling for 180,000 rupees each in Darra (Ali, 2002).

A series of interviews with both international and national security officials in Kunduz, Kandahar, Ghor, Paktya and Jalalabad revealed that, currently, there is no one weapons market in Afghanistan. The circulation of weapons characterizes the southern border with Pakistan. Commanders and combatants sell their weapons stocks in Afghanistan. These weapons are transported to Pakistan, from where they are either returned to Afghanistan (in potentially modified form, e.g., short-barrelled) or used as substitutes for other weapons.

The Tajik border region around Kunduz serves as a transit point for relatively small amounts of specialized and rare light weapons from the Russian Federation. Tajik weapons are supplied through Maimana and the western part of the country through Ghor Province. They are then used by the AGF and narcotics traffickers in northern Uruzgan or for ship-ment to Pakistan. Both Kandahar and Jalalabad are currently facing an ammunition shortage, which has limited the ability of local private secur-ity companies (PSCs) to source ammunition on the local market.

As a whole, there is limited evidence of any substantial intermingling of the arms and narcotics trade. Only small poppy traders are also trafficking in weapons. Narcotics traffickers are, however, believed to carry arms to secure narcotics shipments from local policemen and officials. Massive convoys (as large as 60 vehicles long) of well-armed Afghan drug smug-glers regularly cross through Iran and are believed to have killed as many as 3,000 Iranian police officers over the past decade. As of March 2005, Austria was providing 2,000 armour-piercing sniper rifles to the Iranian government, with the UK providing 250 night vision goggles and 50 body armour vests for use against the smugglers (AP, 2005a). Particularly on Afghanistan's northern and Iranian borders, narcotics smugglers employ substantial armament, including night vision goggles and RPGs, so that they are prepared to fight with border forces for hours, if need be (ESGER, 1996).

Small arms and the insurgency

As described in Chapter 1, the current insurgents are more accurately described through the Coalition's use of the phrase 'Anti-Coalition Forces or Anti-Government Forces,' than via the more popular term 'neo-Taliban.' While possessing general agreement in terms of their goal of avoiding and countering government power and the Coalition presence, these groups differ considerably both as to the extent and nature of their orientation and are a conglomeration of Al-Qaeda, core Taliban, other Afghan militant groups, disaffected tribal members and narco-traffickers.

For example, Friel holds that an unholy alliance between the Taliban and drug smugglers emerged due to local ties and opportunism, with drug smugglers supporting the Taliban with arms, vehicles and cash in order to acquire protection. Accordingly, 'analysts say drug barons are fuelling instability, backing the Taliban and other militant groups, to keep the police and the government out of their areas, allowing them to grow more' (Friel, 2006). The AGF also supposedly acquires funds through the taxation of the local poppy trade and both external and local donations (Grau, 2004, p. 42).

In spring 2006, the Taliban unified their internal command structure under Jalaluddin Haqqani and supplied both funds and arms stockpiles, as well as fighters trained in Iraq, for guerrilla warfare (Shahzad, 2006b). Bergen argues that there are approximately 2,000 Al-Qaeda fighters oper-ating in small training camps in Pakistan. He describes how the Taliban 'have increasingly identified as part of the global jihadist movement, [so that] their rhetoric [is] full of references to Iraq and Palestine in a manner that mirrors bin Laden's public statements' (Bergen, 2007). The Taliban also apply tactics previously unseen in Afghanistan, including suicide bombings and beheadings (Bergen, 2007).

Unofficial estimates indicate that approximately 1,700–2,000 Taliban militants have been killed since 2005 (CPIC, 2006b). The March 2006 report of the UN Secretary-General notes that the number of suicide bombings has increased from five from 2002–2004 to 17 in 2005 and 11 as of February 2006, with each attack costing twice as many lives (UNSG, 2006, p. 10 (pt. 40, 42)). During 2005, according to a report in the *Christian Science Monitor*, the number of roadside bombings increased by 40 per cent, with these bombings then accompanied by ambushes by insurgents employing small arms (Baldauf and Khan, 2005).

In both the eastern and southern provinces, AGF insurgents are reportedly earning approximately $140 per month, with unemployment and drought further driving mobilization (Franco, 2007; Rubin, 2007). As discussed in Chapter 3 and the case study chapters of this book, elder and community authority played a particularly important role in mobilizing combatants during the jihad and the post-9/11 period. Currently, there is little evidence that communities are willing to mandate their members directly to fight against the Coalition. Any evidence to the contrary would constitute a disturbing development. Communities in areas under AGF control generally acquiesce to, rather than endorse, their presence. According to Shahzad, in Kunar and Nuristan, 'local support, after being neutral for some time, is now in favor of the Taliban and Al-Qaeda, which have comfortable places to hide and carry out random attacks at their convenience' (Shahzad, 2006a). However, the AGF are again presenting themselves as an 'alternative to corruption and incompetence,' seeking to acquire support due to dissatisfaction with the speed of recovery and the penetration of the security forces by commanders and corrupt officials (Franco, 2007).

In early summer 2005, after a peaceful winter, the insurgency appeared to be on its last legs. A year later, insurgency activity accelerated in southern Afghanistan, particularly in the provinces of Uruzgan, Zabul, Kandahar and Paktika. Initially, the Coalition attributed this to its own heightened activity. Others link this to the insurgency's perception that the deploying NATO forces are casualty-averse.[11]

Notably, the movement returned to mass attacks (no longer singularly on government outpost forces but also on Coalition forces), while continuing to assassinate prominent Pashtun tribal and religious leaders who cooperated with the government. Previously, the AGF generally operated in smaller groups of 25–40 fighters. In 2005, the AGF primarily attacked poorly manned and undersupplied government outposts; in contrast, in spring and summer 2006, the AGF again displayed a willingness to go up against large Coalition units. The general failure of these missions for the Taliban – the Coalition was able to inflict substantial casualties on any Taliban force – still constituted a symbolic success. The AGF was able to demonstrate to the southern population that it had returned to contest the Karzai government forcibly.

Meanwhile, having deployed some 80,000 federal troops to the tribal areas and having established approximately 762 guard posts on the border (120 at the border to Afghanistan), Pakistan's approach to the AGF insurgency has produced controversy in its relationship with both Afghanistan and the United States, particularly its decision to negotiate a truce with tribal elders in North Waziristan and its tolerance of the Taliban's open presence in Quetta (Jawad, 2005).

Between March 2004 and September 2005, Pakistan killed 353 militants, including 175 foreigners from Uzbekistan, Tajikistan, Turkmenistan, Chechnya and parts of the Arab world (Jawad, 2005). However, according to Rashid, the government of Pakistan is divided in its approach towards the AGF. While the regular Pakistan army units continue to engage with insurgent groups on the frontier (to an unsatisfactory degree for the governments of Afghanistan and the United States), elements within the ISI 'allow the Taliban [AGF] to raise money, buy arms and recruit fighters' (Rashid, 2006). Rubin argues that the ISI is 'continuing to actively support the Taliban leadership' (Rubin, 2007).

There are two primary dimensions to the use of small arms by the AGF insurgency: their use and modification of munitions for the distant targeting of government officials and Coalition forces and their return to direct combat against Coalition forces. In its current manifestation, the Taliban/AGF insurgency is utilizing pre-existing caches, establishing new caches and acquiring new weapons from Pakistan. Both the Coalition and ISAF remain concerned as to the potential use of Stingers (delivered by the US in the 1980s) against their aircraft. Although these are largely considered inoperable due to the short lifespan of their battery packs, the CIA is still offering $150,000–200,000 for each missile and captured a cache of 30 Stingers in 2002 (AFP, 2006a).

The vast munitions available in Afghanistan allow the AGF to target both government and Coalition forces via roadside and suicide bombings. The availability and import of small arms, combined with the small size of both government security forces and of the NATO/Coalition presence, allows the AGF to maintain a 'balance of fear' over districts and villages. The attested availability of SAMs presents a (yet unrealized) threat to civilian, government and Coalition aircraft. Coalition operations against insurgent groups in Kandahar and Helmand Province in spring and summer 2006 led to the discovery of numerous weapons stockpiles. These are no longer the residue of weapons from the previous conflict but were newly created specifically in order to build a logistics network for operations against the government and Coalition.

In September 2005, Pakistan captured a major AGF/Al-Qaeda weapons cache in North Waziristan, with the cache under the direction of Sirajuddin Haqqani, the son of the prominent Hezb-e-Islami Khalis commander and Zadran tribal leader Jalaluddin Haqqani (Jawad, 2005). At the base, which was composed of 18 compounds and a madrassa, Pakistan discovered 15 truckloads of ammunition, as well as anti-aircraft guns, rockets, improvised explosive devices (IED), communication equipment and military fatigues (Jawad, 2005).

In direct combat, the insurgents now employ mortars, sniper rifles and other standoff weapons to great effect, utilizing their knowledge of the terrain and the lack of either a permanent government or Coalition presence in most southern districts to move with little obstruction. In the eastern provinces (led by Hekmatyar loyalist Kashmir Khan), an AGF unit will operate with AK-47s (or Kalashnikov-type weapons), AK-74s (Kalakovs), sniper rifles, RPGs and DShKs (Franco, 2007). During the fighting in September 2006 in Panjwayi district in Kandahar Province, the AGF expended 400,000 rounds of ammunition, 2,000 RPGs and 1,000 mortars (Rashid, 2007).

While the DIAG process is focused on commanders that are not a part of the Taliban, the Coalition is largely concerned with those commanders, communities, combatants and caches that are linked to the Taliban and anti-Coalition forces or are present in the Coalition's southern area of operation. The detonation of improperly stored ammunition and other munitions had cost lives in both Baghlan and Parwan (*Xinhua*, 2006b). The location of weapons caches is a primary objective of Coalition search operations in Afghan villages. The provision of intelligence as to the location of caches (whether of the Taliban or local warlords) can be seen to indicate consent and support for both the Coalition and the government.

As such, an increase in cache seizures is an indicator of success. In 2005, according to the Coalition, there was a 25 per cent increase in the number of caches seized (CPIC, 2005e). One Coalition officer explained that 'finding these caches is important to security ... because these discoveries enable security forces to reduce the means that anti-Coalition militia can use to target security forces and intimidate the Afghan people' (*Defenselink*, 2004a). While the Coalition supports the DIAG programme by collecting weapons from local commanders, in the past it has not followed the ANBP procedure of surrendering weapons to the organization for cataloguing and for centralization in the Pul-e-charkhi supply depot (CPIC, 2006a). The Coalition is suspected of disseminating/redistributing these weapons among its local militias. Moreover, there is some indication that, although the ANBP refuses to provide cash incentives for the location and surrender of weapons caches, the Coalition continues to do so (IRIN, 2005a).

There is a considerable difference between home stockpiles (maintained for either protection, for future sale or for participation in the insurgency), commander stockpiles and those maintained or newly formed by armed factions.[12] Home stockpiles will typically involve an older mix of light weapons and explosives. Commanders' stockpiles will contain a broad range of material accumulated over the course of the conflict of variable quality and current value. Newly initiated stockpiles and caches will contain ammunition, small arms, communications equipment and munitions/bomb-making material. Munitions (rockets, mines and artillery shells) are now utilized and modified for use in IEDs or in vehicle-borne improvised explosive devices (VBIED) rather than for conventional delivery. One of the most significant recent discoveries was 1 ton of bullets in March 2006 near Herat (*Pajhwok*, 2006b).

Contextualizing sources of support: the state, external governments and internal political economy

The academic debate on the primary causes and motives behind contemporary wars – which was characterized as greed versus grievance – has placed considerable emphasis on the role of domestically raised funds in allowing combatants to retain soldiers, purchase arms and motivate combatants to join commanders (Berdal and Keen, 1997; Berdal and Malone, 2000). The concluding part of this chapter demonstrates and comparatively assesses the significance of both arms and funds in supporting armed groups, assessing the comparative role of state sponsorship versus internal political economy in Afghanistan. This chapter reveals that external governments, and not internal resources, were the most significant sources of funding and small arms in Afghanistan, serving as a form of 'start-up' capital that led to the emergence of an Afghan warlord class.

Resources permit the acquisition and maintenance of weapons and combatants. Yet, particularly over the past decade, internally generated resources have been given far more attention than external government donations. External governments have provided the bulk of financial and in-kind assistance to parties, however. Still, while, in total, foreign assistance has been the most significant source of arms and funds, the significance varies by both period and specific armed actor. Moreover, while external governments provide mainly material resources, the internal government has proven willing to provide symbolic resources to local groups, particularly title and legitimacy. This is of importance, as combatant interviews revealed that, in terms of mobilizing combatants, non-economic assets can be considerably more significant (see Chapter 3). The provision of entitlements and material incentives is neither the exclusive nor the dominant motive in the relationship between commanders and combatants.

As described earlier, captured stockpiles played a prominent role in the public mythologies of both the Taliban and the mujahideen, permitting them to present themselves as popular movements in line with the public descriptions of their early rebellions with fists, knives and antique weaponry only. A war of words exists in Afghanistan over precisely these issues. Most armed movements have sought to distance themselves both from external government support and from involvement in trafficking, while accusing their competitors of being either directly involved in the narcotics trade or of being sponsored by Iran and Pakistan.

As mentioned earlier, the most common approach to the relationship between commanders and combatants is the economic model (Özerdem, 2002). Accordingly, grievance is a rhetorical tool for armed movements, masking the primary economic motives of commanders and combatants. Here, the challenge of peace involves allowing commanders to consolidate their economic gains and profit through peace rather than through warfare. In Afghanistan, commanders have acquired funds from the following sources:

- direct provision of funds and arms by external governments;
- sale of captured weapons;
- manipulation of humanitarian aid and development projects;[13]
- control and leasing of lapis lazuli and coal production (Jamiat in Baghlan and Badakhshan) (AIC, 1991a);
- taxation of any imported or exported good via official/unofficial checkpoint (poppy, dried fruit, timber, tin, carpets and consumer goods under the Afghan Transit Trade Agreement);
- direct involvement in and potential domination/taxation of agricultural production (poppy, wheat, cotton) (e.g., the Akhunzadas in Helmand) (AIC, 1991a; Mansfield and Pain, 2005);
- control over gas fields in northern Afghanistan (Junbish-e-Milli);
- land confiscation (both private and public and also of displaced families) (e.g., Hai Hanna/Sherpur in Kabul, Mazar, Kandahar) (Alden Wily, 2004).

The scale of financial assistance to the armed groups over the past two decades is nearly unprecedented, whether provided by external donors or the government of Afghanistan itself. The decision to fund militias failed to take account of the fact that 'once armed and funded, commanders can become economically self-sufficient by gaining control of customs posts, bazaars, and opium trafficking routes' (Rubin, 2003, p. 1). And, thus, beyond these subsidies, armed groups were also able to acquire local resources, whether by taxing the local population or commodities within or in transit through a locale.

As demonstrated in Table 2.a.1, the amount of internally raised funds pales in comparison to the scale and importance of funding and resources provided by external governments. External funds, however, have operated as a form of 'start-up capital,' allowing commanders to expand their control over local businesses and primary commodities. Generally, internally raised funds can only sustain basic membership and maintain a basic level of combatants, typically drawn from immediate family or close kin groups. As in the 'Afghan security dilemma,' while commanders provide a basic level of protection to a local community, they also maintain a 'balance of fear' over local populations, and predate neighbouring populations and other village members.

Customs revenues were viewed to be particularly significant for the Taliban (which collected $75 million from cross-border trade between Pakistan and Afghanistan in 1997 alone as part of the Afghanistan Transit Trade Agreement) as well as for Ismail Khan in Herat and Dostum at the Hairatan border point with Uzbekistan. Each region has a different set of resources that feed warlord economics: opium in the southeast and northeast, lapis lazuli in Badakhshan, construction and land in Kabul, smuggling and hashish in Jaji, wood in Khost/Wardak/Nuristan and the control of factories (cement) in the Salang (Bhatia and Goodhand, 2003, pp. 71–77).

Commanders, either directly part of or protected by the government and police, are also confiscating public land, as has occurred throughout Kabul (Sherpur, Hai Hanna, etc.) (Foley, 2004, p. 18). Moreover, the relative peace of the Coalition presence has allowed commanders to diversify their economic portfolios further, from black/grey area economic activity towards legal economic activity (construction, import/export, service provision, etc.), acquiring further resources by converting their militias into private security companies.[14] Segments of the diplomatic community and the military intervention appear willing to tolerate this expansion and employ these militias, perhaps under the logic that this would divert their attention from military action and towards economic profit and a peace dividend. These commanders and their subordinates have adapted their activities according to what is permissible under the security umbrella.

Similarly, there is considerable debate over the significance of poppy/narcotics in financing the activities of both warlords and terrorists. The opium economy is described as a particularly prominent source of financial support, producing accusations of narco-terror, narco-mafias and narco-commanders. Poppy production in Afghanistan increased significantly during the 1980s, which can be attributed to the lack of a strong central government, the involvement of commanders and successful eradication efforts in Turkey, Iran and Pakistan.

According to a 2003 estimate, the Taliban and their allies derived more than $150 million in revenue from drugs (Chouvy, 2004, p. 8). For example, Grau argues that the majority of funds provided to the Taliban are now locally acquired via the drug trade, with 'maintaining the drug trade often justify[ing] guerrilla activity' (Grau, 2004). Yet, much of the discussion collapses the various forms of involvement into a singular accusation. Instead, it is necessary to determine the scale of involvement of each group and distinguish between direct involvement, poppy-driven violence and the taxation of the trade.

Beyond the pursuit of wealth, it is necessary to qualify the various descriptions of a war economy. First, a focus simply on economic resources neglects other types of resources that can produce similar ends – namely, authority and legitimacy (Edwards, 1986). It is thus necessary to place resources and economic activities in context. These resources can be discussed in terms of traditional or familial authority (whether derived from religion or tribal position), wealth or education. Economic resources are but one asset for maintaining influence. Of course, a select few may simply seek to pursue the accumulation of wealth.

Second, most commanders seek to convert wealth into influence and power, whether at the local or the national level. With regard to land, a commander will distribute land to his soldier in order to consolidate his political power (Beall and Esser, 2005, pp. 12, 38–39). To a degree, military power is required to acquire, protect and sustain economic gain. Generally, however, the function of wealth is its conversion into influence, largely through patronage, displays of power and the provision of services. Wealth must be seen primarily in terms of its role in maintaining ties of loyalty with others. The continuance of these systems (linked to specific militias, parties or *tanzims*), and their penetration of district/provincial/national government offices and ministries, as well as of the police and the army, substantially extends the reach and influence of the commander. The goal is less to have a standing 'active' force than to maintain a network of connections and potential combatants. Indeed, 'commanders can mobilize a much larger number of troops than what they normally maintain in active service; however, they must pay them for the period in which they are mobilized' (Giustozzi and Sedra, 2004, p. 13).

└ referring to surge capacity

Conclusion

This chapter has outlined the historical and contemporary nature of arms flows into and out of Afghanistan. It firmly demonstrates that external governments, particularly when placed in historical context, have played a critical role in sponsoring and supporting armed groups, considerably more so than internally generated resources. The chapter revealed the comparative insignificance of external commercial purchases of small arms in comparison with the internal market. In Afghanistan, the West is less confronting the endemic dysfunctions of a society and its population than the consequences of great and regional power competition. States are strongly culpable for the destruction of Afghanistan, its evolution into a haven for terrorist organizations and militant Islam and other insurgent groups, as well as for the destabilization of Pakistan and parts of South Asia.

The Soviet strategy of rural depopulation desolated the countryside, while its provision of financial and material support to the Najibullah government after their withdrawal undermined attempts to resolve the conflict peacefully. And similarly, both the US and its partners in Pakistan pursued strategies that further undermined the Afghan society's foundations. The nature of the Western, Pakistani and Arab response to the Soviet invasion favoured the emergence of Islamist militancy and radicalism, both regionally and throughout much of the Middle East, as well as the rise of sectarian violence in Pakistan and the Taliban in Afghanistan.

Ultimately, in terms of scale and timing of weapons delivered and the parties supported, regional and major powers neglected the context in their pursuit of their primary ends, showing little concern for 'blowback.' Even now, immediate priorities have consistently ignored and even undermined long-term stability and sustainable security. Programmes for human rights, democracy and security sector reform in post-Taliban Afghanistan were complicated by the US partnership with the various parties belonging to the United Front.

Afghanistan has entered a period of consolidation, with the various disarmament programmes having consolidated and acquired substantial amounts of weapons stocks. However, the spectre of redistribution looms large, as the government raises the idea of rearming local tribal militias. There is an additional danger of Afghanistan becoming an exporter of weapons, even though the government's and the Taliban's rearming efforts and import of weapons has deferred this prediction somewhat into the future.

The scale of weapons available in northern Pakistan and Afghanistan far outstrips demand. Substantial shortages are attested and anecdotally evident only in ammunition. Vast stores of unsecured munitions (mines, mortars, artillery shells and rockets) are readily adapted for use as IEDs, with construction methods now imported from Iraq. New stockpiles are being created for use by the insurgency. Meanwhile, since the mid-1990s, narcotics traffickers have utilized the weapons market to acquire substantive firepower for their protection, violently challenging under-resourced interdiction authorities. Both European states and the Chinese are now supplying the Iranians with night vision goggles and ballistic vests in order to match the capabilities of narco-traffickers.

Chapter 4, as well as the case studies chapters, will reveal the role of arms and resources (particularly when provided through governments) in undermining the relationship between commanders and communities, as well as in inducing a local change in community militias towards becoming local strongmen.

Appendix

Table 2.a.1 Weapons found in Afghanistan

Name	Source	Use	Range/qualities/Afghan nicknames
7.65 mm Tokarev	USSR	Semi-automatic pistol	40 m
9 mm Markov	USSR	Semi-automatic pistol	40 m
7.62 mm PPSH-41	USSR	Submachine (selective fire) gun	200 m
.303 Lee Enfield	UK/India/Pakistan	Bolt-action rifle	'11 shooters'; 800 m
G3/USM1917 Springfield	US	Bolt-action rifle	
7.62 mm M1891/30 Mosin Nagant	USSR/China	Bolt-action rifle	'5 shooters'; 400–800 m, 2,000 m
7.62 mm SKS	USSR/China	Semi-automatic	'Carbines,' 400 m
M26	Czechoslovakia	Light machine gun	'20 shooter'
7.62 mm G3	Iran	Automatic rifle	
7.62 mm AK-47/AKM/Type-56	USSR/China/Pakistan	Selective fire automatic rifle	400 m
5.45/5.56 mm AK-74/AKS-74	USSR	Selective fire automatic rifle	'Kalikov'; 600 m
5.45 mm AKSU-74	USSR	Short-barrelled automatic rifle	Short-barrelled AK
5.45 mm AK-74 w/40 mm GP-25/30	USSR	Rifle-mounted grenade launcher	'Krinkov'; both air burst and anti-personnel rounds; 400 m
222 Kalakov	Bulgaria/Czechoslovakia	Automatic rifle	New variant on Soviet-model
7.62 mm Dragunov	USSR	Sniper rifle	800 m
7.62 mm ZB 36	Czechoslovakia	Light machine gun	
7.62 mm RPK	USSR	Selective fire light machine gun	800 m
7.62 mm PK	USSR	Light machine gun	'100 shooters'; 800 m
7.62 mm RPD	China	Light machine gun	'Sadtaka'; 800 m
7.62 mm RP-46	USSR	Light machine gun	800 m
7.62 mm SGM-49 Coryunov Grinov	USSR	Light machine gun	1,000–2,500 m
12.7 mm DshK-38	USSR	Heavy machine gun	Use in anti-aircraft
	USSR/Pakistan	Heavy machine gun	'Dashika'; used for both mountain warfare and air defence (with AA mount); range of 1,000 m
M053 12.7 mm HMG	Czechoslovakia	Heavy machine gun	Used for ground and air defence
30 mm AGS-17	USSR	Selective fire grenade launcher	1,700 m

Table 2.a.1 Weapons found in Afghanistan (*continued*)

Name	Source	Use	Range/qualities/Afghan nicknames
RPG-7	USSR	Rocket launcher	Shaped charge rocket; 300–1,700 m
RPG-18	USSR	Rocket launcher	1,700 m; anti-tank weapon, 66 mm shaped charge rocket; 135 m; copy of the USM72A2 LAW
RPO-A	USSR	Rocket flamethrower	1,700 m
Milan		Anti-tank missile launchers	
73 mm SPG-9	USSR	Recoilless rifle	1,300–4,500 m
82 mm	USSR	Recoilless rifle	400–4,500 m
82 mm B-10	USSR	Multiple rocket launcher	Multiple varieties, from BM-1 to BM-12/63 – these varieties are man-portable
107 mm/122 mm Saqar	China/Egypt	Multiple rocket launcher	8,000–10,800 m
60 mm Mortar	China	Mortar	
M-1937 82 mm Mortar	USSR	Mortar	3 km
M-43 120 mm Mortar	USSR/Spain	Mortar	5,700 m
M-38 107 mm Mortar	USSR	Mortar	5,150–6,300 m; both light and heavy rounds; transported on pack animal
SA-7 Grail	USSR	SAM	3,200 m
Blowpipe	UK	SAM	Man-guided missile
Stinger	US	SAM	Heat-seeking 'fire and forget'; 1,000–8,000 m
14.5 mm KPV ZGU/ZPU/ZSU	USSR	Air-defence weapons	'Zigroiat'; 5,000–8,000 m; multiple varieties of air-defence weapons, used in mountains, against air assets, and for mountain fighting; single, double and quadruple barrel varieties.

Sources: Jalali and Grau, 1994, pp. 407–414; Cordesman and Wagner, 1991; USDoD, 2001, pp. A-1–A-24; Ali, 2002; Isby, 1989, p. 112.

Annex 2.a.2 Arms transfers to Afghanistan, value and type, 1978–2002

Date	Value and type of military assistance (weapons/training)
1956–1978	*Value/training*: USSR supports creation of 100,000-man Afghan Army, provides $1.25 million in military aid and trains 3,725 Afghan military personnel.
1973	*Training*: Pakistan initiates training of Afghans against President Daoud (as a consequence of his Pashtunistan policy); trains 5,000 insurgents both to unified Jamiat-e-Islami (Massoud, Hekmatyar, Rabbani) and to Hazaras.
1975	President Daoud initiates military cooperation training with Iran, Egypt, India and reduces USSR influence.
1979	Afghan army size compromised/weakened by succession of desertions and mutinies (Hirat, Jalalabad, Bala Hissar, Kabul). *Value*: Saudi Arabia provides $1–2 million to Jamiat and HIH. *Material*: June: arrival of first freighter of Soviet-made weapons to Pakistan for supply to rebels. July: Libya initiates military assistance to rebels. China initiates commercial arms supply to Pakistan for rebels (small arms, mortars, recoilless rifles, RPGs, SA-7s).
1980	*Value*: US FY aid: $30 million; USSR FY aid: $332 million; Saudi Arabia: $24–30 million. *Weapons*: Egypt contracted to provide AK-47s, SAM-7s, SAMs and anti-tank grenades; China provides SAM-7s, AK74, RPGs, RPK, RPD. SAMs include: UK Redeye, Egyptian Sakr, Igla, Strela. Iran provides M-1/G-3 rifles, anti-tank weapons and heavy machine guns to HIH, lending additional support to Harakat and Shi'a groups (1980–1982).
1981	*Value*: US FY aid: $50 million; USSR FY aid: $372 million; Saudi Arabia donates $15–39 million to Ittihad.
1982	US decision to expand substantively quantity/quality of military assistance to the mujahideen. USSR FY aid: $203 million.
1983	*Value*: US FY aid: $80 million; USSR FY aid: $96 million. Iran ends provision of assistance to Peshawar Sunni parties, focuses exclusively on Shi'a parties, and sends military advisers to the Hazarajat. *Training*: Pakistan trains 80,000 mujahideen between 1983 and 1987 (Kartha, 1999, p. 88).
1984	*Value*: US FY aid: $120 million; USSR FY aid: $176 million. Commitment by US/Saudi Arabia to place $500 million for military assistance into Swiss Bank Account.
1985	*Value*: US FY aid: $250 million (supplementary funding for anti-aircraft e.g. Swiss Oerlikon gun, UK Blowpipe); USSR FY aid: $81 million; Saudi Arabia matching grant: $250 million. Bulgaria (1983–1985): $20 in small arms. US Congress proposes transfer of $10 million of DoD excess stock to Afghan rebels. *Weapon*: RPG-18; purchase of 40 Oerlikon guns for $50 million.
1986	*Value*: US FY aid: $470 million; Saudi Arabia matching grant: $470 million; USSR FY aid: 374 million. US initiates military training for Afghan rebels in Pakistan. Iran offers financial incentives to spur recruitment to radical Shi'a parties.

Annex 2.a.2 (continued)

Date	Value and type of military assistance (weapons/training)
	Weapon: 900–1,000 Stingers arrived between 1986 and 1987; 200–300 missing; 340 fired.
1987	*Value:* US FY aid: $630 million; USSR FY aid: 473 million; Saudi Arabia matching grant: $630 million.
	Congressional allegations that 70% of supplies diverted in Afghan arms pipeline and of disappearance of $309 million and diversion to ISI and Nicaraguan rebels.
1988	*Value:* US FY aid: $630 million; USSR FY aid: 846 million; Saudi Arabia matching grant: $630 million.
	Material: Despite transport difficulties, US provides TOW anti-tank weapons prior to Soviet withdrawal.
	Blast in Ojhiri, Pakistan, destroys $80–200 million worth of weapons.
	Saudi Arabia sends 500 youths for training in Sada camp, Pakistan.
1989	*Value:* US FY aid: $630 million; USSR FY aid: $2.216 billion; Saudi Arabia matching grant: $630 million.
1990	*Value:* US FY: 60% decrease (after failure of Jalalabad offensive); Saudi Arabia provides $435 million + $100 million from Saudi/Kuwait royalty; USSR FY aid: $2.201 billion.
	Material: HIH receives 700 trucks of ammunition from Pakistan, also supplies from Libya and Iraq.
	Outflow of weapons from Afghanistan to other parts of South Asia.
	USSR initiates delivery of new AK; Czech 12.7 HMG.
1991	*Value:* Additional $500 million from government of Saudi Arabia and Kuwait; $30 million of HW transferred from Iraq to Afghanistan; USSR FY aid: $1.344 billion.
	Material: Provision of financial and material assistance directly to local commanders rather than through the Peshawar party representatives.
	Saudi Arabia (via US) transfers captured heavy weapons (rockets, APCs, 155 mm guns, etc.) from Iraq to Afghanistan.
	Ultimately, at the conclusion of US assistance, the mujahideen received $6–8 billion of material assistance involving: 400,000 rifles (Chinese type 56/59 AK-47), SAMs, Italian anti-personnel mines, 100,000 .303 Indian rifles, 60,000 old rifles and 8,000 light machine guns from Turkey, and 100 million rounds of ammunition, of which 30 million were from the Pakistan Ordnance Factory). Total of 80,000 mujahideen trained in Pakistan; 5,000 Arab mujahideen trained by governments and Islamic charities were sent to Afghanistan.
1992	Commanders capture and distribute Najibullah government's weapons stocks.
1993	*Value:* Saudi Arabia provides $150 million to Jamiat/government of Afghanistan between 1993 and 1994; 'unidentified' NATO country provides $5–10 million in commercial weapons to government of Afghanistan.
1994	*Material:* Taliban capture Hezb-e-Islami arms cache in Kandahar Province (October) and other parts of Afghanistan.
	Uzbekistan commences arms shipments to General Dostum: 'significant part' of $180 million between 1994 and 1997.

Annex 2.a.2 (continued)

Date	Value and type of military assistance (weapons/training)
1995	*Material*: Capture of Tatarstan Aviation Company airliner (via Albania/Sharjah organized by Victor Bout) by Taliban with 3.4 million AK-47 rounds. Capture of Belarussian airliner by Kazakh government with 35 tons of grenades. Arms supplied by Uzbekistan, Tajikistan, Russia and Iran to Jamiat and Ittihad, HW and Junbish. Southern commanders (Helmand, Kandahar, Logar, Paktya) hand over arms caches to Taliban. *Training*: 1995–2000: Pakistan's ISI deploys advisers to assist in planning/execution of Taliban offensives on Hirat, Kabul and other areas. Rishkor military garrison (near Kabul) utilized for training Arab (8–15,000) and Pakistani volunteers.
1996	*Material*: Russia initiates arms transfers to Northern Alliance: largely heavy weapons, grenades and rockets via Tajikistan. Iran initiates commercial arms transfers to the Northern Alliance: RPG-7s, F-1 hand grenades, HW ammunition, 7.62 mm rifle ammunition; also provides Iranian military advisers to Northern Alliance units in Mazar-e-Sharif and Bamyan.
1997	*Material*: Iranian shipment to Northern Alliance in Mazar: 122 mm shells; 120 mm mortar bombs; 7.62 mm ammunition.
1998	*Material*: Interception of 16 Iranian railway cars in Kyrgyzstan: 700 metric tons of weapons (both heavy weapons and RPG-7, F-1 hand grenades and 7.62 mm rifle ammunition). *Value*: 1995–1998: Afghan factions spend $200 million on new arms.
1999	Seizure of arms shipment in NWFP: 23 small arms, 11 bombs, 73 grenades, 1,000 rounds of ammunition.
2000	Russian commercial (India-funded) arms transfers to Northern Alliance include: 10 Igla-1 SAMS, Russian Mi-17 helicopters. Discovery of arms cache on Tajik border: 50 small arms, 40 land mines, 600 kg of opium.
2001	Autumn 2001: Russian commercial arms shipment to Northern Alliance worth $35–40 million of heavy weapons (40–50 tanks and 100 APCs/BMPs); also mortars and rocket systems. Discovery of arms cache on Tajik border: 1 AK-47, 20 grenades, 4,000 rounds of ammunition, 18 kg of marijuana. April/May: 30 trucks were crossing Afghan–Pakistan border, with some carrying RPGs and other munitions.
November 2001	Coalition forces provide millions in funds, and air and helicopter drops of small arms (AK, ammunition) to commanders in Jawzjan, Samangan and Ghor. Taliban abandon arms caches in Loya Paktya and other areas during retreat, recaptured by local commanders.
2003	Albania donates 600 AK-47s, 10,000 units of ammunition and various quantities of both mortars and machine guns. Bulgaria donates 900 grenades, 400 AKs, 8 other machine guns, 300 mortar rounds, 8 mortars, 27 RPGs and 120,000 units of small arms ammunition. Pakistan donates 10,000 mortar rounds, 180 mortars, 75 RPG launchers and 5,000 submachine guns.

Annex 2.a.2 continued

Date	Value and type of military assistance (weapons/training)
2007	US donates 800 military vehicles and more than 12,000 weapons to the ANA; Hungary – 20,500 assault rifles and 150,000 rounds of ammunition; Slovenia – 10,000 machine guns, 2 million rounds of ammunition; Bulgaria – 50 mortars, 500 binoculars, 21.6 million rounds of ammunition; Croatia – 1,000 machine guns, 300,000 rounds of ammunition; Czech Republic – 20,640 machine guns; Estonia – 4,000 machine guns, 4 to 6 million rounds of ammunition; Greece – 300 machine guns; Latvia – 337 rocket propelled grenades, 8 mortars, approx. 13,000 various arms, approx. 9 million rounds ammunition; Lithuania – 3.7 million rounds of ammunition; Montenegro – 1,600 machine guns, 250,000 rounds of ammunition; Poland – 110 Armoured Personnel Carriers, 4 million rounds ammunition; Turkey – 2,200 rounds of 155 mm ammunition.

Source: Table drawn from: Harpviken, 1997, p. 280; NISAT; Kartha, 1999, pp. 61–62, 66–68, 77, 82; Bradsher, 1999, p. 17; Rubin, 1995, p. 22, 30; Lumpe, 1999; Kenzhetaev, 2007; Galster, 1990, pp. 58, 62, 79, 81, 85, 96, 101, 115, 118, 119, 129, 138, 140, 144, 146, 149, 159, 160, 163, 165, 167, 186, 190; HRW, 2001, pp. 23–48; Yousaf and Adkin, 1992, p. 117; NATO, 2007.

Note
The table discloses various forms of military assistance (monetary, in-kind, training), both donation and commercial purchases, sent to Afghanistan since 1956. A variety of other weapons types (largely European and American) are available, albeit in far smaller quantities.

Notes

1 Musah and Thompson, 1999, pp. 38, 96, and Small Arms Survey, 2003, as cited online, available at: research.ryerson.ca/SAFER-Net/regions/Asia/ Afg_ AT03.html (accessed 1 June 2006).
2 Previously, in the late nineteenth century, the Afghan Amir Sher Ali established domestic production of small arms in Afghanistan with small-scale production of ammunition for the Snider rifle. This was accelerated under the reign of Amir Abdur Rahman Khan who sought to attain autonomy from British weapons supplies via the creation of the *mashin-khana* factories.
3 The first attempt to disarm the Afghan population by the government occurred during the reign of Amir Aminullah and was an attempt to acquire those weapons distributed either by the previous regimes or by the British.
4 'The most successful mujahideen ambushes organized the ambush into a heavy weapons support group, flank security groups, an assault group, and a logistics support/spoils removal group' (Jalali and Grau, 1994, p. 67).
5 'Many Afghans are inveterate tinkerers and they preferred to make their own anti-tank mines from unexploded ordnance and other antitank mines' (Jalali and Grau, 1994, p. 138).
6

Eighty per cent of all arms and ammunition was allocated to the Parties for onward distribution. Commanders had to belong to a Party in order to get weapons, the only exception being when they came for training for special operations, but, even though they were then given the weapons direct, they came from their Parties' allocation. Our American allies favoured giving arms direct to Commanders.

> (Yousaf and Adkin, 1992, pp. 103–104)

7

> Advanced weapons, many of them originally from the Afghan pipeline, were used frequently by Sikh militants directly in the perpetration of abuses, and allowed them, in violation of international norms, to instill terror deliberately in the general population. The influx of automatic rifles, in particular, made it easier for Sikh militants to kill greater numbers of civilians by opening fire on crowds of people. Kashmiri militants have also used advanced weapons in the course of attacks on civilians, through far less frequently than Sikh militants. It is also likely that the Kashmiri militant arsenal has contributed to their ability to instill terror in the civilian population, particularly local Hindus, tens of thousands of whom have fled the Kashmir valley.

> (HRW, 1994)

8 Gunaratna, 2001, p. 1; Combatant No. 340, Jalalabad, July 2005.

9 Davis questions the Taliban 'mythology' surrounding the capture of the Spin Boldak arms depot: 'the purported seizure of the dump established a strong case for the Taliban's subsequent campaign being conducted without their depending on external sources, and also provided a thick smoke screen behind which such supplies might flow' (Davis, 1998, p. 46).

10 The author witnessed an attempt to submit a Dera-Kalashnikov during a disarmament ceremony in Hai Hanna, Kabul in July 2004. The weapons were rejected by the ANBP. In violation of the rules, however, the commander kept the weapons, even though he had brought them to the ceremony.

11 Discussion with ex-Department of Defense official, Washington, DC, June 2005.

12 An analysis of the contents of recently discovered weapons caches to be online, available at: smallarmssurvey.org/files/sas/publications/b_series5.html.

13 Accounts of this were encountered in interviews with local combatants and international aid representatives in Kabul, Ghor, Bamiyan and southeastern Afghanistan. As recalled by one combatant from Uruzgan, for 'most NGOs, when they help, it goes to the commanders not to the people.' (Combatant #125, Ghor, April 2005).

14 Lister and Pain, 2004; Poulton, 2004, p. 23; interview with Shahmahmood Miakheil, Deputy Minister of Interior, February 2005.

3   Armed groups in Afghanistan

Michael Bhatia

According to the International Institute for Strategic Studies projections, as many as 262,000 Afghans served with the government (whether as part of the Soviet-backed army or in local militias) (IISS, 1988). Mujahideen forces totalled some 339,000 at the peak of the conflict in 1991 (IISS, 1992). Around 50,000 combatants were believed to belong to the Taliban (IISS, 2001). In 2005, the 60,000-strong Afghan Military Forces were disbanded, and the Disarmament of Illegal Armed Groups (DIAG) programme was initiated. Currently, the Afghan New Beginnings Project's 'warlord' database for the DIAG process includes 1,800 commanders and militias for as many as 120,000 combatants, dividing these between 'benign' self-defence militias and approximately 100 'dangerous groups' (Barron, 2005; GoA, 2006).

As described in Chapter 1, armed factions play a significant role in all areas of Afghan society, from politics to the economy. An exclusive focus on arms proliferation and on the arms trade may be misleading. The main threat largely resides in the maintenance of the threat of violence, and the expansion of commanders into business and political positions of district, provincial and national prominence. A primary way in which local power is expressed in the regions is through influence over the choice of district and provincial officials, which may prevent the deployment of new, centrally nominated individuals. Thus, military resources matter less for their immediate combat potential than for their symbolic power to display strength and potential violence, as revealed in Faryab, Ghor and Hirat. Therefore, given the constancy of supply, it is necessary to examine factors that shape demand and use of small arms and light weapons.

Afghan armed groups are often conglomerated under broad terms, such as warlords and mujahideen. Terms such as warlord, commander and strongman are infused with ideas as to their fundamentally predatory nature and potential for unchecked violence. However, while the past 20 years has witnessed the rise of a 'warlord class,' often at the cost of both existing elites and traditional community leaders, there is no single type of armed movement or militia present in Afghanistan. There is an immediate need to disaggregate armed groups as well as to differentiate between types of armed groups and types of combatants in order to move beyond stereotypes of armed groups as either fanatics or plunderers. The diverse nature of the mujahideen was previously recognized by William Maley in 1998:

> the vocabulary of Islamic resistance embraced a remarkably diverse range of politico-religious forces, varying from the intensely ideological to the avowedly rustic. The Afghan resistance, collectively known by the title Mujahideen (meaning 'Warriors in the Way of God'), ranged from 'parties' (*tanzims*) with headquarters outside Afghanistan to forces organised on a regional basis, to scattered groups of fighters with local interests and agendas whose attachment to the wider resistance was dictated by a need for access to weaponry, but whose tactics resembled those of seasonal tribal warfare and whose ideological affinity with the parties they nominally represented was potentially quite tenuous.
>
> (Maley, 1998/2001, p. 9)

So to demonstrate further the variety of armed groups in Afghanistan, this chapter develops a typology of armed groups in Afghanistan, examining the role of small arms in relation to the government, political–military parties, leaders/elites, local communities and group members.[1]

The goal of this chapter is to develop a broader theoretical framework by which to analyse newly encountered groups, allowing the reader to place an armed group within this spectrum. Information was drawn from the substantial existing literature on Afghanistan and from combatants' interviews throughout Afghanistan.

Three 'ideal types' of Afghan armed groups are identified: political–military organizations (known in Afghanistan as *tanzims*); community militias (including the *arbakian* tribal police); and warlords and strongmen (whether operating at a regional or village level). Table 3.a.1 in the Appendix of this chapter provides an in-depth outline of different political–military parties in Afghanistan (including communist groups and the various Shi'a parties), identifying these according to their primary area of operation, type of armed group, peak membership, prominent members and specific features. In the post-Bonn period – aside from the ANA and those sections of the ANP recruited and trained independently of *tanzim* or personal networks – the majority of security bodies (whether now decommissioned Afghan Military Forces contingent, Coalition militia or PSC) are likely to be linked to one of these three types of groups. Each of the ideal types involves a different balance between elites, communities, political–military parties and individual followers. Critical considerations include:

- the structure of armed groups (the relationship between the core of a group and the periphery),

- sources of authority and legitimacy,
- mobilization structures (how combatants are recruited and maintained),[2]
- their relationship with local communities,
- the distribution and ownership of weapons,
- types and range of activities,
- political economy.

Most armed groups are hybrids and occupy some space between these ideal types, combining various features of various ideal types.

The chapter also differentiates between the varied motives driving and sustaining combatant mobilization. In the literature of the 1990s, individual motivation was seen a primary vehicle for exploring ongoing wars, from descriptions of anarchy at the beginning of the decade to the prevalence of greed and economic agendas by the end of it. Thus far, conventional wisdom and press accounts tend to aggregate armed groups and soldiers under a series of broad terms, such as mujahideen, Taliban and warlords. Only a select group of authors, however, have revealed the different types of armed groups and configurations.[3] No authors have explicitly examined the relationship between different types of armed groups and the different factors that shape individuals' motives. The models established in this chapter – describing both the forms of armed groups and factors influencing combatant decisions – will then be applied to reveal the shifting relationships between the state, political–military parties, strongmen, communities and combatants in the various case-study chapters.

This research on Afghanistan reveals a multiplicity of motives during each period of conflict and also within locations. It proposes that a different set of categories is required in order to understand better variations in combatant motives, identifying the importance of the individual's primary unit of affiliation (individual, family, community, commander, political–military party) and position in the armed group (general member, *nazm-e-khas* has (commander's special group), bodyguard, relative or ideologically trained cadre).

The previous chapter has demonstrated the critical role of the state and external governments in providing both resources and legitimacy to local armed groups. External military assistance serves as a form of 'start-up capital,' through which commanders are eventually able to expand their power into the political and economic realm. It also showed how the state was a participant in local violence and how commanders can perform local security functions while also contributing to a local 'security dilemma' that induces counter-mobilization by neighbouring villages. A commander may acquire legitimacy by protecting the community in times of crisis while also utilizing his standing relationship with soldiers to engage in entrepreneurial violence against neighbouring villages.

The focus on material resources neglects, however, the critical role of legitimacy and charisma as resources utilized by commanders in shaping combatant decisions. Discussing armed groups only in terms of their predatory and contra-state functions fails to assess their composition, evolution and varied membership.

Certainly, exclusive criminal groups and gangs exist. However, as demonstrated by Hobsbawm, there is a danger that the local governance functions of these groups will be dismissed by focusing exclusively on their criminal role (Hobsbawm, 1969/2000; Bhatia, 2005). As is particularly evident in relation to narcotics, conceptions of criminal and illicit activity vary considerably both between and within states. Criminal activity and banditry can be a sign of revolt and state resistance, particularly if the state is considered compromised. At the same time, criminal organizations and networks between criminal agents can be closely tied to other forms of solidarity. Moreover, the Afghan national security institutions (particularly the police) have been heavily implicated in local criminal activity.

State + Criminal Structures overlap

Typology of armed groups

Ideal types of Afghan armed groups

Previously, armed movements have been differentiated in terms of the tension between modern and traditional 'primitive' armed groups – Dorronsoro describes political–military parties as bureaucratic organizations (Harpviken, 1997; Roy, 1986, pp. 9, 81–83, 110–113; Dorronsoro, 2005, pp. 137–169). In this book, a clear divide is made between those commanders linked to (and drawing their power from) specific communities or solidarity groups (*qawms*) and those that draw their power from specific political parties. At the national level, those commanders and leaders that have achieved prominence are best identified as either emerging from within political–military parties or as strongmen–warlords. Each ideal type of armed groups differs as to the degree of segmentation within the movement, its goal and objectives and the constitution of the movement, as well as in terms of internal weapons ownership and distribution.

Community militias are largely egalitarian, with each individual owning his own weapons and with most combatants possessing similar weapons. Community militias focus on protecting their local community and enforcing internal norms and community decisions, although, in certain locations, smaller contingents will threaten neighbouring communities and engage in district disputes and predation outside local boundaries. The power of community militia and commanders is limited by the community of elders.

In contrast, strongmen and warlords have acquired substantial independence from community checks and balances and community restrictions over their uses of force, although these strongmen may consult the *qawmi meshran* (community of elders) in order to acquire legitimacy. The relatives, close affiliates and internal enforcers (bodyguards and *nazm-e-khas* has) are provided with rare expensive weapons (AK variations such as the Krinkov and Kalikov). Commanders possess substantial standing stockpiles of diverse weapons (either accumulated over time or through the capture of government stocks). Other combatants are typically required to purchase and bring their own weapons. Local strongmen will be substantially internally oriented, employing their *nazm-e-khas* to assure their continued dominance.

Political–military parties, in contrast, focus on capturing the state and are more likely to control their weapons and be organized around a conventional military model, dividing their soldiers by speciality as well as incorporating heavy weapons. Although they may be affiliated with community militias or strongmen, these parties are ideologically oriented and delocalized.

As will be detailed in the second part of the chapter, each ideal type can bring to bear (utilize) a different collection of assets to recruit and sustain combatants. Charisma (whether organized around traditional, religious or military capability) plays a role in all three types of armed groups, particularly with the creation of a cult of personality around commanders, complete with murals, posters and other expressions of loyalty and devotion (Bhatia, 2007; Azoy, 2003). Different forms of charisma, however, are aligned with each different ideal type: patronage and tribal authority to community militias and military performance to warlords and strongmen (Giustozzi, 2005a).

Each of these three ideal types plays a different role (and requires different strategies) in the reconstitution of state authority and administration in 'collapsed states.' While community militias and provincial *shuras* (consultative bodies) are successful at addressing certain issues (protection against external attack, short-term security, etc.), these groups can fall prey to influence meddling and are generally not successful at governing localities beyond the provision of a basic level of protection and conflict resolution due to the absence of a broader consensus beyond stabilization. These militias tend to prefer the reconstitution of central authority by conducting a consultative process (*loya jirga* or national *shura*) with community and tribal elders to select a central leadership and create a power-sharing government.

Strongmen and warlords are typically able to establish a monopoly of force within their locality and may even create an effective administrative structure and provide basic social services. For example, Ismail Khan administered Herat City and the outlying areas, and Dostum was able to develop a proto-government in Jawzjan and Balkh Province during the civil war. However, these strongmen face dilemmas of institutionalization, as well as a shifting relationship with the central government, competition from neighbouring commanders and weaknesses inherent in their dependence on maintaining allies by distributing patronage.

Table 3.1 Ideal types of Afghan armed groups

Type of armed group	Source of authority	Composition	Activities	Weapons ownership	Internal weapons distribution	Examples
Political–military party	Organization and indoctrination, charisma	Detribalized, delocalized and ideologically oriented	Contest for national power or regional autonomy	Party stockpiles with central distribution	Tactical units oriented towards external enemy, mix of heavy weapons, infantry, specialized units	Hezb-e-Islami Gulbuddin Hekmatyar
Warlords and strongmen	Charisma, force and patronage	Both community members and other de-localized elites	Contest for regional, provincial or local power and autonomy	Individually owned weapons and commander stockpiles	Relatives, close affiliates and nazm-e-khas given 'special' weapons for predation and internal enforcement	Regional: Ismail Khan Local: Abdul Salaam Reza (Ghor)
Community militia	Tradition and charisma	Local community members	Local protection and predation; autonomy	Individually owned weapons	All combatants possess similar weapons	Paktya *arbakian*

Ideologically oriented, political–military parties provide both a delocalizing ideology and a platform for escaping local politics. Positively, in pursuit of legitimacy and local consent, political–military parties may seek to extend their influence – and counter their lack of community links and traditional authority – through the provision of services including: education, training, health and the arbitration of disputes. Thus, Massood sought to develop a proto-state in the Panjshir, although his political–military organization supported and consulted with community elders and the local *ulema* (religious scholars). In contrast, Hekmatyar's Hezb-e-Islami controlled but never administered territory. His proto-army was both detribalized and deterritorialized. A *tanzim*'s ability to achieve either regional or national power is lessened by the presence of other political–military groups, necessitating either the forceful elimination of competitors or the creation of a broad Coalition.

The evolving, umbrella and hybrid character of most Afghan armed groups

In truth, few groups belong exclusively to any one category, with most armed groups best characterized as hybrids, combining elements of each type. Indeed, the aggregation of these groups under a singular title neglects the substantial differences in the composition and orientation of armed groups between villages, groups and regions. These leaders or groups, most particularly the large political–military parties (e.g., Jamiat, the Taliban) and the prominent warlords (such as Dostum and Sayyaf), are often the peak of a broad network of affiliated militias and groups, serving as umbrella movements and leaders of a larger network of independent local strongmen and regional affiliates.[4]

A political–military party may be founded upon a core supported by a series of community militias, with the party employing ideological and organizational strategies to reduce local affiliation and increase party support (e.g., the activities of Jamiat-e-Islami in the Panjshir valley) (Roy, 1989a, pp. 56–57; Nojumi, 2002, pp. 92–93).

Strongmen can either possess their own party (*tanzim*) or simply be nominally allied with a party in order to attain resources. Strongmen may seek to institutionalize and transfer their power by creating permanent institutions and transforming into a political–military party. Other strongmen may refrain from institution building and continue to rely on a personalized style of rule in fear of losing power or due to their limited territorial ambitions. As revealed in the Ghor case study, these strongmen can also emerge out of the remnants of community militias, leveraging both these external resources and local breakdown in order to overturn traditional elites and traditional checks and balances on internal power.

Similarly, for community militias (as seen with Commander Daoud Jaji in Paktya) affiliation with political–military parties is largely coincidental and based on either broader traditional links (belief in the charismatic religious authority of the Sufi Pirs Gailani and Mojaddedi) and the availability of resources and in response to the alliances of neighbouring villages (particularly if there is a pattern of previous enmity and disputes).

Most of the prominent warlords and strongmen discussed do not fulfil the ideal type of a perfectly controlled and hierarchical network of subcommanders and combatants. Considerable differences exist between the core of a group and its peripheral affiliates, whether the latter are allied communities, commanders or combatants. A core group of armed men and political structures in one location only expands through a network of affiliates. The more loosely allied and peripheral to the central figure or party, the more autonomous is the local militia in determining its own activities and the more likely it is that the group will switch sides in response to particular conditions.

Over the course of a conflict and in a post-conflict phase, an armed group may evolve into a different form, whether deliberately or as a consequence of local conditions. Some of the factors that may spark a transition include:

- the provision of resources and support by external actors (whether from the central government or external governments, as well as from diasporas, private security companies and trans-national non-state actors);
- the consequences of conflict (mass community displacement and the destruction of established patterns, e.g., Soviet destruction of rural Afghanistan);
- the response to a shift in the national political environment (democratization, civil war, etc.).

The role of external resources in potentially sparking this transformation was problematized by a United States Agency for International

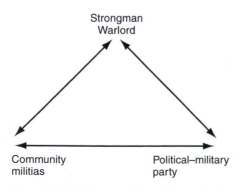

Figure 3.1 Shifting position of armed groups in relation to the ideal types.

Table 3.2 Evolution of armed groups in Afghanistan

Evolution in relation to the ideal types	Examples
Community militias → political–military party	Jamiat
Strongman → political–military party	Junbish
Community militia → strongman	Ghor and Kandahar militias
Political–military party → strongman	Ittihad (an umbrella movement)

Development (USAID) official, who noted: 'we can turn a legitimate governor into a warlord by playing into his network, and by making him independent of the central government.'[5] It is thus necessary to understand both the aspirations of an armed group and the other factors that will shape its transformation into a new form, in particular the impact of assistance and resource provision. The remainder of this part of the chapter will provide a closer look at these three ideal types.

Political–military parties[6]

Emerging in Kabul in the early 1960s – with the formation of the Jawanan-e-Moselman (Muslim Youth) at Kabul University in 1968, the Jamiat-e-Islami in 1972 and the steady emergence of competing communist and Maoist groups (Khalq, Parcham, Shola-e-Jawid) – political parties (*tanzims*) appealed to those educated elites lacking a foothold in local or tribal political structures, ultimately penetrating high schools and military academies. Ahmed Shah Massoud (the Jamiat military commander of the Panjshir valley), Gulbuddin Hekmatyar (the head of the Hezb-e-Islami) and Burhanuddin Rabbani (the head of the Jamiat-e-Islami) all emerged within this structure, achieving prominence at least partly due to the imprisonment of the senior leadership and traditional religious figures by President Daoud in 1974.

Even without a substantial membership outside of Kabul, through its presence within military units in the capital and the Presidential Guard, the Khalq party was able to execute a coup against the Daoud government. Thus, a small political party was able to capture the central government – illustrating the potential impact of these groups. Since then, only the Taliban were able to realize a similar degree of control over an administration of Afghanistan.

With the collapse of the Najibullah government, all *tanzims* (but particularly Jamiat and the Taliban) absorbed former Afghan government military personnel. The Taliban significantly benefited both from advisers from Pakistan's army as well as through its absorption of government military personnel and ex-Khalqis. Indeed, rather than being dispersed (although ethnic identity often predetermined future employment), the Ministry of Defence has revealed a remarkable degree of continuity in its staffing system.

With the Khalqi coup and the Soviet invasion, according to Harpviken, 'neither of the existing tribal or religious forms of organization was able to generate the organizational coherence for larger-scale organization' required to defeat the Soviet forces (Harpviken, 1997, p. 277). Instead, the Islamist *tanzims*, who had developed advanced organizational abilities since the 1970s, graphically expanded as a consequence of the Soviet invasion and the Khalqi government's brutal response to local rebellions (in Nuristan, Hazarajat and Hirat) and were able to channel local grievances towards their own party objectives. According to Giustozzi, as many as one-third of the 6,000 armed groups in Afghanistan had no major affiliation with political–military parties (*tanzims*) during the jihad (Giustozzi, 2000, p. 242). Generally, *tanzims* were almost exclusively dominant in the provinces surrounding Kabul (Kunar, Nangarhar, Wardak, Logar, Parwan, Panjsher, Kunduz and Taluqan), with their importance declining significantly the further westward one moved. In these regions, commanders, and their ability to mobilize individuals, were based largely on their previous tribal or *qawm* connection, although, in certain cases, this was seen to be linked to their military performance and charisma.

The *tanzims* have previously been divided into moderate and traditionalist, fundamentalist, communist and nationalist (Roy, 1986). Moderate and fundamentalist religious *tanzims* are present among both the Shi'a and Sunni groups. Generally, moderate groups are founded upon the pre-conflict religious, community and local-based (*qawm*) order. Their goal is generally restorative. In contrast, the fundamentalist religious *tanzims* are descendants of the political Islam that evolved in Pakistan and Egypt in the 1950s or preceded the Iranian Revolution in 1979.

A political–military party can be further divided between internal commanders and external, diaspora-based political leadership.[7] Arms and other entitlements were provided through the external representatives of the seven *tanzims* in Peshawar, which produced considerable tension between the external representations and internal commanders over the distribution of resources (Clapham, 1985, p. 169). Following the Soviet withdrawal, the balance between the external leadership in Peshawar and the internal commanders shifted decisively in favour of the latter, with greater coordination between commanders within Afghanistan (Shahrani, 1984, pp. 34–35).

Prior to the Soviet invasion, major political–military parties emerged either among educated groups without a strong concept of ethnicity (Tajiks) or among urbanized and detribalized Pashtuns. After 1992, political–military parties were increasingly organized around a singular ethnicity (Giustozzi, 2005a). Yet, ethnic differences and inter-ethnic conflict was a consequence and not a cause of the war.[8] Instead, the core units of armed groups belonged to a shared ethnic base, with alliances then formed with other groups – some of which were permanent while others were expedient.

An overemphasis on a party's Peshawar manifestation neglected the manner in which each party was constituted within Afghanistan. As discussed in terms of the hybrid, umbrella and evolving character of armed groups, there is a considerable difference between the declared existence of a party and the degree to which it conforms to the ideal type of a political–military party. Only Hezb-e-Islami closely fits the ideal type of a political–military party. Hezb-e-Islami was essentially a delocalized movement, although it did have a support base near the Tajik border in Kunduz Province and was able to consolidate further its base in Kunar. Most of the parties – particularly the National Islamic Front of Pakistan (NIFA), Afghan National Liberation Front (ANLF) and Harakat – mobilized combatants through tribal *khans* or the *qawmi meshran* according to a 'patrimonial model' (Dorronsoro, 2005, p. 150). As a consequence, they operated more as networks and franchises – providing resources to a series of local affiliates demanding little in return – and maintained small secretariats and party structures. *Tanzims,* such as NIFA and Harakat, never sought to create a corporal identity beyond the identification of their members with the charismatic religious authority. As such, they do not fulfil the classical example of a political–military party. Junbish continues to develop national party programmes, although it remains largely constituted by either Dostum's own patronage structure or through affiliation with a series of other commanders.

Jamiat in the Panjsher is an example of a political–military party and community militia hybrid. Figure 3.2 reveals the division between community militias and central party organs (Roy, 1989a, pp. 56–57; Nojumi, 2002, pp. 92–93). Within the Panjshir, Jamiat employed a multidimensional programme. Rather than opposing community and patrimonial leadership structures, Jamiat harnessed them to create local militias and recruit combatants, while also building party-oriented armed groups. Beginning in 1975 in the Panjshir, Jamiat negotiated with existing local community militias while also encouraging the further formation and enlargement of these militias. Outside of the Panjshir valley, the Jamiat party was allied with either local strongmen or community militias. In the mid-1980s, Massoud created mujahideen manoeuvre units of 120 individuals, which were 'paid a salary and able to fight anywhere in the north,' described by Isby as the 'first true Resistance manoeuvre units' (Isby, 1989, p. 37). However, particularly in the neighbouring valleys of the Salang, this could lead to disputes over the selection and deployment of commanders to villages. Describing the tension between community militias and Jamiat in the Panjsher, one commander in the Salang recalls:

> [Commander] Arab was selected from Panjsher. He didn't know the people and people didn't know him. People selected Hussein [a commander from the community], and removed Arab because he did not understand the people ... We only knew the party because they gave

the weapon to us. When we took the weapon, we knew from which party we took the weapon.[9]

Similarly, in other areas, such as Kunar, Kandahar and Paktya, tensions emerged between a strict political military party (Hezb-e-Islami) and local communities and tribes.

Political–military parties are particularly significant for their creation and utilization of youth movements, which have had a profound impact on the Afghan security environment, from the Islamist and communist student parties that formed in Kabul University before the war to the use of the party schools in refugee camps and madrassas as key recruiting points. For political–military parties, the young were considered particularly attractive combatants because of their openness to ideological indoctrination.

However, the familial or community foundations of many militias also led many adolescents to join and become involved in combat. The Hezb-e-Islami contingent in Laghman involved a group of 13 to 18 year old combatants known as the 'bull terriers' (Jalali and Grau, 1994, p. 121). As the core mujahideen leadership continues to age, some of these parties are attempting to increase their support among youth in a search for new constituencies. With 8,000 former child soldiers, thousands of war-affected children, 44.6 per cent of the population under the age of 15 (median age

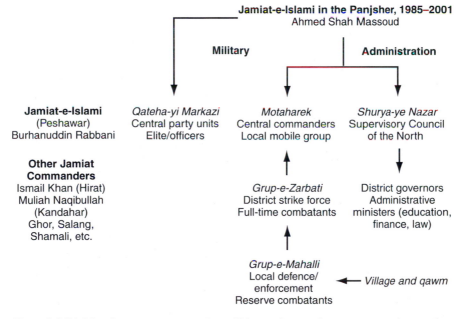

Figure 3.2 Division between community militias and central party organs (example of Jamiat).

of 17.6) and a male literacy rate of 43.1 per cent, there appears to be ample potential for the further expansion of these groups (UNICEF, 2004; CIA, 2007).

Political–military parties, most prominently Hizb-e-Wahdat, Junbish-e-Milli, Jamiat-e-Islami and Hezb-e-Islami, have developed a broad platform of programmes and institutions – from youth groups to party-run schools (whether in Afghanistan or in Pakistan's refugee camps) – in order to institutionalize a broader programme and engender greater loyalty to the party among younger members outside of communal links. For Junbish, this has accelerated, as Dostum has broadened his political activities in an attempt to create a new generation of party loyalists and acquire political legitimacy beyond Afghanistan's northwest corners.[10]

The military components of youth groups vary considerably, with Jamiat providing youth groups with military training throughout the 1990s, while Junbish focuses exclusively on political mobilization. However, during the presidential elections, the Junbish youth group was implicated in protests in Faryab and Samangan and actively engaged in rock throwing, agitation and propaganda, partly with the goal of inducing a harsh response from the government security services.[11] Thus, although Junbish's youth groups are not provided with small arms training, these groups are utilized to perform political duties and undertake violent action.

Warlords and strongmen

Currently, a factionalized government with only haphazard penetration into the provinces and districts is countered by warlords and commanders with a vertically integrated network of support and diverse sources of funding and arms. Not only do they have local movements and a diverse range of connections to local groups as well as representatives within district, provincial and national government, but they also have a broad range of regional supporters and diverse international linkages (business, diplomatic, etc.). A dominant characteristic of strongmen–warlords is their autonomy from the state and their combination of both local and international connections (Jackson, 2003).

There are two different forms of warlords–strongmen in Afghanistan, largely categorized in terms of the scale of their control and their position in terms of traditional structures. National and regional warlords control provinces and parties – such as Dostum and Ismail Khan. However, the vast majority of strongmen operate at the local level, within provinces or districts or between a collection of villages. They are significant for having transcended local barriers and checks and balances and for the fact that these checks have yet to reassert themselves.

As seen in Figure 3.3, a strongman should be assessed not only in terms of his military resources but also in terms of his diplomatic, religious and

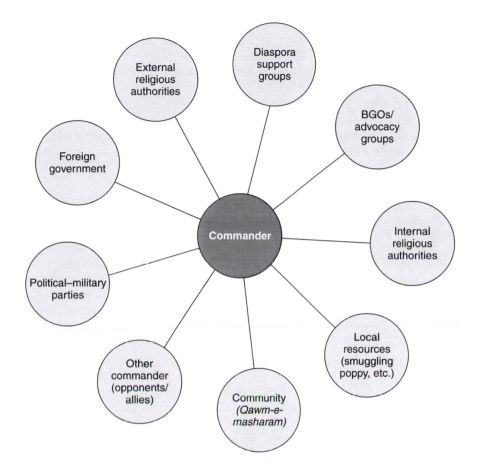

Figure 3.3 Strongmen and their network of resources.

community/tribal assets. For example, both Gul Agha Sherzai and Rashid Dostum hired lobbyists as their representatives to the US Congress, with the latter also maintaining strong diplomatic links to the Uzbek government as well as to other governments (facilitated no doubt by the numerous consulates (e.g., Iran, India, Pakistan, Uzbekistan) present in Mazar-e-Sharif (Grass and Mullins, 2003). Some individuals have been able to carve out a position autonomous from local communities and other political–military parties, particularly after 1989, when the CIA provided assistance directly to internal commanders (rather than via the Peshawar party offices) and weapons stockpiles were captured from the collapsing central government (Dorronsoro, 2005, p. 229).

In Afghanistan, strongmen–warlords can be differentiated in terms of their origins, scope of objectives and source of authority. Strongmen–

warlords come from a mix of different origins: localized and delocalized; emerging from community militias or without these local ties. Strongmen are either disaffiliated from the local community elders or have been able to determine the membership of this body such that it does not interfere with their activities. Delocalized strongmen generally achieved prominence due to organizational and military proficiency, most prominently Dostum and Ismail Khan (Giustozzi, 2005b, p. 10).

Strongmen–warlords pursue different ends. Some seek to create national movements; others simply wish to consolidate their hold over districts. Dostum and Junbish provide an example of a provincial strongman seeking to play a greater role in Kabul; in contrast, Ismail Khan appears focused on maintaining his power in the West. While they may aspire to establish a political–military party, they are still in the process of doing so. Over an extended period, and in the absence of a state, the warlord can potentially emerge as a 'proto-statebuilder,' providing services and protecting communities and utilizing this as a base upon which to acquire central power (Bhatia and Goodhand, 2003).

In many ways, the strongman seeks to reference symbolically (but in fact far transcends) the role of the traditional tribal *khan* as an arbiter of local disputes and distributor of resources. The traditional tribal *khan* seeks to acquire authority through the distribution of resources, the maintenance of a sizeable retinue of loyalists and the ability to arbitrate disputes (Anderson, 1983). For Ismail Khan, Dostum and Sayyaf, these traditional roles are further supplemented by their role in securing their communities (while persecuting others) and securing the interests of their ethnic minorities from competing regional groups or in the national government. Yet, as Maley argues, the traditional *khan* and *maleks* 'act as mediators rather than as commanders' (Maley, 1987, p. 709). In reality, while he may position himself as a contemporary manifestation of the traditional *khan*, the contemporary strongman (or warlord) holds far greater power and has been able to restrict or reduce the traditional checks on his power.

While the major armed leaders (Dostum, Rabbani, Hekmatyar, Sayyaf, Ismail Khan, etc.) are perceived as widely known with community and tribal links (delocalized), the vast majority of strongmen have local ties and primarily operate at the provincial, district or sub-district level. Within a *qawm*, there will be powerful figures, whether tribal leaders, *maulavis*, *khans* or *maleks*. A commander's ability to become a strongman involves the (deliberate or inadvertent) weakening of the *jirga* and community of elders. As demonstrated by Abdul Salaam of Ghor Province, the relationship between commanders and the communities that select them is in transition. While commanders may initially be selected at the behest and control of the broader *shura* (composed of elders, *maulavis* and *mullahs*), over time, the commander can accumulate enough power so as to dictate the composition of the *qawmi meshran* and thus remove any checks on his power. He then becomes a 'commander for life.'

"Commander Tenure"

According to one combatant, 'When the community first selected him [Abdul Salaam], the elders and the religious people were more powerful. Now the commander is more powerful: he can change the community, but the community cannot change Commander Abdul Salaam.'[12]

The community of elders (*qawmi meshran*) and other traditional authorities either become irrelevant or constituted by individuals selected by the commanders. The delivery of money and other resources from external groups allows them to gain further autonomy.

Figure 3.4 shows one potential structure for a local strongman's forces. A commander is surrounded by bodyguards drawn from his extended family then by a special group (*nazm-e-khas*) utilized both for self-protection and for predation and then by a broader force drawn from community members. There will be a difference in roles and responsibilities between these different levels. The outer ring will be a reserve force used for the defence of their locality and only rarely against neighbouring villages. The two inner rings will serve not only to protect the commander but also to maintain internal order (as enforcers), forcibly recruit soldiers, confiscate land and undertake other forms of predation against both their own and neighbouring villages.

As is particularly evident in Ghor, Daykundi and Kunduz, the *nazm-e-khas* are used to policing the actions of the other foot soldiers and recruits drawn from the community. As described by one combatant from Ghor, who began fighting in the early 1980s against the Karmal government:

> We stayed by force, because we couldn't stay in our home peacefully. If I didn't go they came by force and they would take my cows, money, and everything in my home. They would hurt us and put us in prison. From the time of Karmal until the time of Karzai, this was by force. A big commander has a special force [*nazm-e-khas*] to control his own soldiers, also to bring new soldiers from families. If they told us to fight, we were fighting – sometimes with each other, sometimes with other nations. In the beginning, the community selected me. When the commander became more powerful/rich, he never listened or respected the old people from the community.[13]

In Ghor and other areas, these different levels of membership also correlated to a different distribution of weapons. A political–military party or another professional military force (see the ANP Rapid Reaction Force in Daykundi and the Afghan Stability Force in Paktya) will be arranged according to its best tactical use against an opponent and structure its small unit to include: one RPG, one RPG assistant, one Pk/heavy machine gun and then a body of common soldiers equipped with AK-47s. In contrast, a local strongman structures his forces in order to achieve inner discipline and control over a community. The inner core of bodyguards and *nazm-e-khas* will receive the newest, most exclusive and generally

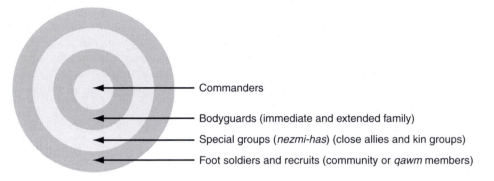

Figure 3.4 Power structures around strongmen (model).

deadliest weapons – RPGs, pistols and small-barrelled AKs – and will have
access to a constant supply of ammunition. The outer ring of foot soldiers
and recruits will generally be provided with limited (or perhaps exclusively campaign) ammunition and with older AKs of limited quality. Problematically, the *nazm-e-khas* and the bodyguards were frequently kept aloof
from the ANBP programme by their commanders and are conceptually
the focus of the DIAG programme.

Community militias

Many of the armed groups in Afghanistan are best described as community militias. Indeed, one of the dominant early interpretations of the
Afghan conflict was that of a tribal revolt, with the conflict described as
being between a modernizing state versus landowners and tribal *khans*
manipulating religion (Shahrani, 1984, p. 33). Community militias are
seen to pursue essentially limited violence of a seasonal nature, with otherwise employed community members as fighters. The tribal police
(*arbakian*) are a small standing force, characterized by monthly or yearly
rotations, surrounded by a broader reserve force.

Certain communities have weaker traditions of community checks on
individual power. To an extent, this correlates with certain ethnic groups.
For example, the Hazara and Uzbeks are proposed to possess substantially
weaker community egalitarian traditions, with a longer tradition of consolidation in the hands of local landowners (*begs* or *mirs*) (HRRAC, 2003, p.
55). As described above, there is a continued danger of these community
militias evolving into strongmen-controlled militias, with the weakening of
community checks on the commander's use of force and community combatants.

Among members of community-oriented militias, two common Dari-
Pashto terms repeatedly appeared: *manteqa* and *qawm*. *Manteqa* is a 'unit of

spatial cognition' of varying geographical size depending on the community.[14] *Qawm* is a unit of political and community cognition, which can denote clan, solidarity group, profession, nation, tribe or sub-tribe. Described as 'elastic,'

> literally translated as 'people,' 'nation,' 'tribe,' 'sect,' 'group of followers,' the term qaum is common among various ethnic groups in Afghanistan.... Overwhelmingly used as a mark of distinction vis-à-vis outsiders, it designates solidarity groups of varying sizes. According to context, that is, according to the social/spatial distance between the informant and the questioner, it may be employed to describe multiple levels of local organization. Thus the term qaum can emphasize the mutual support afforded by kinship units of different sizes, referring 'to the whole segmentary descent groups extending upwards from the nuclear family to the ethnic totality...' Among groups with little emphasis on agnatic or genealogical relationships, qaum may assume a wider sociological meaning, signifying any solidarity group or 'aggregation of dependents.'
>
> (Noelle, 1997, p. 107)

Roy translates qawm as 'solidarity group,' and refers to it as the 'lowest common denominator of group affiliations in Afghanistan,' which refers to 'any segment of society bound by solidarity ties, whether it be an extended family, clan, occupational group or village' (Roy, 1989b, p. 71).

The term exists not only among Pashtuns but is also used by Tajik and Hazaras. Among Tajiks, this was evident in Ghor Province and in the Kabul suburb of Sorkh-e-Parsa. In this chapter, *qawm* will interchangeably refer to either nation or tribe, using the former when referring to non-Pashtun groups and the latter when referring to Pashtuns. Each nation is further divided into sub-groups, with tribes further divided into a series of *kheils*.

In its ideal egalitarian form, the *qawm* is managed by a community of elders (the *qawmi meshran*) who select a leader (the *qawmi mesher*). In this case, a commander can either be the *qawmi mesher* (the head of the community) or the *sardar-e-qawm* (a 'big man' in the community) or even the *kalan-e-qawm* (the honoured man from the community). Depending on the community, there are differences between whether the community or elder authority (asserted through a meeting of the *qawmi meshran*, *shura* or *jirga*) is utilized to mobilize individuals only for community protection and the local security or whether it can also recommend and demand participation in a certain political–military party and involvement in external violence and national emergencies (e.g., the anti-Soviet resistance).

The community determines when it is acceptable to be involved in the selection of combatants and utilize the name of the community. Local leadership does not come from the centre but from the community. Those locals given authority positions by the central government are viewed with suspicion. Indeed, according to Shahrani:

> local leadership in rural Afghanistan is based on voluntary, participatory, and often dyadic ties of mutual confidence and trust between leaders and followers. Local leaders often do not have official connections, and they emerge by gaining the support of individuals in their communities. They maintain their legitimacy by mediating among disputants within a community, safeguarding local interests against outside interference (including that of the local government), and defending such interests militarily when required.
>
> (Shahrani, 1984, p. 51)

According to Olivier Roy:

> A traditional leader is someone who has been able to establish a personal patron–client relationship, at the expense of a real political party structure. He is not a feudal lord, but uses his influence to protect and promote the interests of his own segmentary group, thus enhancing his own status in terms of wealth and prestige.
>
> (Roy, 1989b, p. 71)

Under these circumstances, the *khan* does not operate as a strongman. Instead, in its traditional and pre-conflict form, his influence is both limited by the community and based upon opinion. As argued by Noelle:

> They have to prove their leadership qualities continuously by offering protection to their followers in times of conflict or material need. On the basis of their reputation as powerful men and exemplary Pashtuns they are able to act as 'opinion leaders' on the village level and thus shape the process of decision making. But given the egalitarian structure of Khost society it would be unthinkable for a khan/Malik to act against the will of his tribesmen. Functioning as the spokesman of his group, he represents its collective authority but is not set apart from his fellow tribesmen otherwise. The Pashtun concept that each man is sovereign precludes concentration of power. Tribal councils are attended by all men of the community and decisions are made strictly on the basis of consensus.
>
> (Noelle, 1997, pp. 151–152)

To varying degrees, his continued position as a commander requires the consent of elders and the community, which serves to restrict the commander's activities. While they will still distribute patronage, the purpose is not dominance but continued support and prominence, which considerably differs from the power acquired by the strongmen–warlords described above.[15]

In order to redress grievances and access resources, or in order to extend their activities, communities may need to ally with external actors. During periods of national crisis, a community militia may also consciously spread out its members to different *tanzims* in order to protect itself and secure greater resources, as occurred in both Kandahar and areas of Wardak Province. According to Dorronsoro, 'in some instances the qawm may support more than one commander, the better to protect itself from political events' (Dorronsoro, 2005, p. 111).

The arrival of a national conflict will either play into local disputes or induce local unity (against an external invader). As described by Rubin:

> If a prominent leader of one organization belonged to a particular qawm, members of that qawm tended to join that group ... And a leader might join a different party from those of his local social rivals ... This pattern of micro-segmentation by qawm, encouraged by the system of distribution of weapons, explained much of the fragmentation of affiliation at the local level.
>
> (Rubin, 1996, p. 202)

Community militias and commanders either received support from external parties or were sponsored by the state (most prominently by the Najibullah government after 1986). In exchange for those resources, communities then had either to lose or negotiate their autonomy from the party. Tensions emerged between community militias and parties. As described above, in some cases, this gradually led to the weakening of the internal community, which was further exacerbated by rural displacement induced by the Soviet strategy of 'rubbleization' (the destruction of the Afghan rural economy). The provision of resources allowed the emergence of new elites, the consolidation of power by certain individuals and the formation of new power dynamics.

Community militias, in their ideal form as embodied by the Paktya *arbakian*, play a critical local security role. This has been recognized by ISAF, the government of Afghanistan and the Ministry of Defence in their exclusion of community militias from the DIAG programme. Yet, there is a danger that this label is applied to a broader number of militias than would meet the criteria identified here. Moreover, when considering employing or utilizing these local militias, both international and national initiatives and programmes need to be evaluated in terms of whether these actions will transform community militias into strongman militias.

Community-militia commanders are endowed with local legitimacy due to their foundation in traditional *qawm*-based decision-making bodies (*jirgas* or *qawmi meshran*). Those communities that retain the most intact local decision-making bodies (which have not been captured by the

Combat Involuntary

commanders) are best able to restrain the commander's activities. For those with senior tribal positions, this will involve a decline of their ability to invoke tribal authority to mobilize individuals. Yet, three decades of conflict allowed commanders to accrue even greater power, offsetting the influence of the community of elders that had initially selected them. Further evidence as to the continued power of commanders is evident in the following account by an Alekozai Pashtun from Kandahar:

> These people from the qawm can get everything, can quickly collect a lot of people, but officially they don't have militia. The reason people join is the question of the qawm – he talks with the nation and after an hour he can collect 1000 people. Many people are tired and don't want to go, but still people are scared of these people. Many people cannot trust them anymore … For me, the money's not important, he's the person from our nation, he told me to come and I came.[16]

Indeed, the potential for these combatants to be able to reject future mobilization appears limited. In a more hopeful account, another combatant in Daykundi noted that his participation with the commander in the future would be limited: 'If there was an attack, I would participate in fighting, but otherwise not. I will participate in legal fighting and not in illegal fighting, in defence of this country I will fight.'[17]

The individual and combatant mobilization in Afghanistan

When occurring between Pashtun community/tribal units, the traditional source (and driving motive) of intra-village/ *qawm* conflict in Afghanistan is described as *zar, zan, zamin* (gold, women, land) (Dupree, 1980, pp. 210–211). These are collectively held objectives, and while this may indicate the areas of dispute, they do not help us understand the factors that shape an individual's decision to join in the fighting, both locally and when broader national issues are involved. In these traditional cases, conflict occurs between roughly equivalent political entities (villages, tribes, *qawms*, etc.). As noted, over the course of the long conflict, two additional (though not necessarily new) types of armed groups have emerged (political–military parties and strongmen). Current conflict dynamics differ from those that marked the early phases of the Afghan conflict (from 1978–1982).[18] War induces profound social change, challenging and uprooting existing social orders. The conflict since 1978 represents a breach rather than a continuance from past patterns and traditions of warfare.

In this part of the chapter, the factors shaping an individual's decision to join an armed group in Afghanistan are examined. Exploring individual motives will help explain factors shaping the persistence of militias and the challenges involved in achieving sustainable demobilization. A

Zar, Zan, Zamin

common problem recurring in the study of both motives and armed groups is the view of all combatants as similarly motivated, be it for greed, grievance, forced conscription or fanaticism. Instead, one of the major outcomes of the present research on the Afghan combatant is that individual motives will vary by period, location, position of the combatant and type of armed group.

Each of the three ideal types of armed groups will involve a different mix of combatants. Each possesses different resources for recruiting individuals and can appeal to different motives for combatant mobilization. A strongman utilizes force and incentives; a party can ideologically indoctrinate combatants through educational programmes; and a community and tribe utilizes respect for local elder and community authority. Individuals also hold different motives depending on their place within a movement. It is thus necessary to distinguish between commanders, elite members and followers. Elites play key organizational roles and have access to exclusive resources.

Motivational sequences exist, whereby either mobilization only occurs as a consequence of a cascade of motives or the individual's motives change over time due both to changes in the political–military environment or the activities and resources of the unit. The reasons for joining an armed group will often differ from the reasons for remaining in the group and sustaining membership. This relates to the fact that motives can be further differentiated between intrinsic versus extrinsic motives: namely, those present prior to recruitment versus those provided by the armed group to the individual (Newsome, 2003). Given the absence of correlation in motives according to period of conflict and location, it is necessary to examine other factors that may predict and determine why certain motives occur.

Here, an attempt is made to outline and create a nuanced model for assessing Afghan combatant mobilization by exploring type of motive, units of affiliation, type of combatant and type and proximity of fighting.

Types of motive

The question of 'why do people fight' first emerged in nineteenth century studies of crowd violence, to be reinvigorated in the 1960s in an attempt to develop a mathematical function able to determine the likelihood of individual participation in an insurgency, rebellion and revolution. The latter approach views the government and other armed groups as competing for individual support, with the individual rationally assessing the relative utility of joining either side. Based on a review of a wide range of theoretical and secondary source literature on war and collective violence, from rational choice theory to military sociology, revolutionary war doctrine and theories of ethnic violence, potential motives for combatant mobilization can include:

- ideology
- material entitlements and incentives
- grievance and revenge
- primary group belonging and affiliation
- authority and obedience
- coercion and enforcement
- protection and defence
- adventure
- habit.

In the Afghan context, group belonging for friendship and adventure is a fairly rare motive, only observed with select number of combatants in Kandahar and Hirat.[19]

Material incentives are a broad category encompassing substantial profit, simple survival and also entitlements, whether this involves access to education (a common motive among communist officers) or the ability to receive a ration card (a common motive for Afghan refugees).[20]

Authority is divided according to the primary figure demanding obedience: family head of household, a community elder, a religious leader, a charismatic leader or a political–military party. Obedience is linked both to the perceived legitimacy of the authority figure and potentially to issues of socialization and ideology (to the individual's position in relation to existing or newly emerging social institutions).

A perception of the legitimacy of the demand for mobilization (both in terms of the legitimacy of the actor (commander) and the legitimacy of the type of mobilization) will shape the type of motive identified by the combatant. This is most immediately evident in a combatant's description of force versus authority. If the combatant views the authority figure (whether tribal elder, religious figure or family member) to be legitimate, then the demand for mobilization is rarely attributed to force. Of course, a type of compulsion is present within obedience to authority. Although unlikely to lead to forced conscription or overt punishment (destruction of house, etc.), a failure to obey a community elder, a family member or a religious figure will produce social alienation.

For others, their position as combatants is due to their victimization by the conflict. Pre-existing conflict is a structural condition that creates conditions favouring the perpetuation or prolongment of conflict, by reducing livelihoods and inducing individuals to affiliate with armed groups for protection. As described in Chapter 1, greed and predation by one group produces a counter-response among the victims: mobilization for protection.

Mobilization does not need to be based on a complete understanding of the environment. Combatants occasionally offer incomplete or limited information as to the nature of the conflict, their opponent or their party affiliation prior to joining an armed group. As one Jamiat member from a community militia recalled: 'We were so small that we don't know why they [the commanders] chose [to join Jamiat]. Ghulam went to Pakistan and made the choice, perhaps because of weapons, but we do not know why.'[21] In many cases, others involved in inter-factional fighting, the civil war or fighting against a neighbour indicated that they did not know the origin or reasons for the dispute.[22]

This further emphasizes the distinction between the broader objectives of an armed group and commander versus the motives of the combatants that belong to the group. The Afghan wars since 1978 have been labelled according to a number of broad frames: nationalist rebellion, jihad and inter-ethnic civil war. However, the relevance of these broad frames to the individual motives of combatants may be extremely limited, depending on the primary unit/level of affiliation, the proximity of conflict and the type of combatant.

Units of affiliation

A unit of affiliation is best described as the primary actor towards which the individual directs his primary attention, loyalty and obedience (Apter, 1997, p. 2). While the core relationship in combatant mobilization is that between commanders and individual members, three additional components can shape an individual's decision to become a combatant: political–military parties, commanders, communities and families. Any of these four groups or actors can play a prominent role, with the dominance of a level depending on the context and the individual. These levels will coalesce in different ways depending on the region, period and the individual combatant. It is thus necessary to determine what the primary unit of affiliation is for each individual. Understanding how the relationship between commanders, political–military parties, communities, families and individuals shifts in particular contexts is critical to the understanding of the security situation in Afghanistan. The importance of those different levels varies both between and within communities, by period of conflict and also depending on the type of mobilization. For example, a detribalized refugee camp dweller in Pakistan isolated from his community members and studying at a party school will be shaped more by political–military organizations than by his community.

Individual combatants

As idealized in utilitarian and rational choice approaches to combatant mobilization (proposing a *homo economicus*), an individual founds his/her decision on the direct opportunities and expected costs of joining an armed group. In this model, an individual's decision is not mediated by family or community factors but is singularly based on the interaction between the commander/party and the individual. Both the environment

and the resources a commander is able to offer determine whether mobilization is attractive. Upon mobilization, combatants do not wholly belong
to their commanders for use at the latter's whim. Instead, as best displayed
in Jalalabad, combatants may 'shop around' to find the commander that
provides the best incentives and least trying working conditions or who
best conforms to their ideology or other needs.

As described by a combatant interviewed in Maidan Wardak, 'people
made independent choices based on which group gave more money. We
were not told by a commander, but made an independent decision.'[23]
Combatants also retain concepts of legitimate and illegitimate mobilization. This is evident in descriptions of mobilization that cite obedience
to authority rather than force. In many cases encountered in Afghanistan,
however, an individual's decision to join an armed group will be shaped
by his community and family. In certain cases, the combatant has the
option of joining one of several commanders. His basis for selecting a
commander will be his *qawm*, with the fear that a decision to join a commander will make their families vulnerable. A combatant will choose
another commander if he is involved in a dispute with his local *qawm*-
based commander.

Family

The family influences whether an individual becomes a combatant as well
as what group he chooses to serve with. While the role of the family is by
no means clear, the ultimate objective is the maintenance and survival of
the family unit. Traditionally, according to Dupree, 'the extended family
currently serves as the major economic and social unit in Afghanistan' as
characterized by 'residential unity' in either village or compound
(Dupree, 1980, p. 189). The family unit is less mutually consensual than
hierarchical, with the paternal figure making decisions as to the best distribution of a family's resources.

Under family authority, a lead family member (whether uncle, grandfather, father or elder brother) deploys the individual in order to meet a
collective need. The individual is following family authority in the pursuit
of a collective end. Family selection occurs when a son is chosen to
become a soldier by a family elder (grandfather, father, uncle, elder
brother) in order to fulfil either a familial obligation or to safeguard the
family's interests.[24]

This can occur in cases of community selection – in which the
community of elders stipulates that one family member must join a
community militia – or in reaction to local insecurity.[25] In the first case,
the family is fulfilling a community obligation. In the second, it is seeking
to manage risk and its vulnerability to attack by any of the parties to the
conflict. Some families – particularly in those areas that contain multiple
commanders from different factions (whether government or non-state),

fall between two strongholds or are in areas transited by different groups – consciously spread their family members to different groups, in order to reduce their exposure to repression, recrimination and predatory action.

Monsutti describes the primacy of risk management among Hazara kin groups, arguing that:

> the fact that members of the same kinship group have opposing political allegiances does not prevent the continuation of strong ties of solidarity. Indeed, members of the group see such diversification as a kind of guarantee in the event of a worsening of the security situation. As one Hazara friend put it with reference to himself and his brothers, 'whichever faction gets the upper hand, one of us will be part of it.' At the same time, the mere fact of kinship does not always entail mutual support or cooperation. Behavior must therefore be contextualized if it is to be properly understood.
>
> (Monsutti, 2005, p. 240)

Although the family unit and individual members may have specific ideological affinities, the primary goal behind decision making is survival. Individuals are thus 'strategically deployed' to different groups. While commonly described in field anecdotes, this practice appears to be confined to frontline or mixed areas.

In situations of extreme scarcity and deprivation, individuals may be sent to armed movements simply for their individual survival and sustenance, in order to reduce their demand on scarce family resources. This may also involve a family rotation system, in which a family has decided to provide one son to the jihad and will send one son at a time, while the remaining sons engage in economic activity. When a brother returns, another will have to go.[26] In a family with multiple brothers, familial risk management may include sending a son abroad in order to raise funds (for survival, for marriage or to start a business venture) by working as a wage labourer in Iran or in Pakistan, although this involves a degree of risk due to the substantial cost of arranging the move (Stiger and Monsutti, 2005, p. 5).

Finally, family members may be required to join a family elder who is a commander and who creates an armed group. Or, if he decides independently to participate in a conflict, a combatant may prefer to join a group composed of relatives and family members (Jalali and Grau, 1994, p. 84).

Community

With community militias – or when a strongman has acquired control of collective decision-making bodies – the selection of combatants by community elders was previously known as the *lashkar* system (Edwards, 1984). Herein, the community of elders (*qawmi meshran*) or the local *mullah* (religious adviser) nominate a combatant, requiring a certain number of individuals to join from either an extended family or a collection of families. The legitimacy of these community authorities will shape whether the combatant describes mobilization as being characterized by obedience to authority or by force. A community militia generally relies on an individual's previous intrinsic position within the community and his general obedience to existing religious and elder authorities.

Aside from core family members and relatives, the economic incentives available to community militia members will be limited. The general weakness (and absence of a previous tradition) of community militias in the northeast provinces of Baghlan and Kunduz may be one reason for the high incidence of accounts of force in those provinces. In contrast, the previous history of these structures in Paktya (as well as communities restriction of selection only for the protection of the community) may account for the absence of accounts of forced conscription.

Political–military party

To a greater extent than the other ideal types (strongmen and community militias), political–military units are able to shape their combatants through education and indoctrination. Political–military parties, including the Taliban, also benefited from recruitment in the refugee camps. There, removed from community structures and the restrictions that these structures typically involve, the parties were able to indoctrinate combatants more successfully and acquire greater loyalty to their cause. Many parties (Junbish, Hezb-e-Islami, Jamiat-e-Islami) developed a network of high schools, mobile propaganda units and youth groups. As such, these parties were able to 'get them young,' shaping their conceptions and converting short-term mobilization into long-term loyalty. Hezb-e-Islami used these party schools to create an Army of Sacrifice (Lashkar-e-Isar), which numbered as many as 5,000–6,000 by 1992.[27]

Commander

Independently, a commander will have to rely on either forced conscription or the provision of incentives in order to attract combatants. However, a commander can substantially increase the likelihood that his request for mobilization will be obeyed (and lower the 'cost' of recruiting combatants) by increasing his ties to other community authorities, whether elders, religious figures or critical family members. In addition, a commander can become a unit of primary affiliation either through his dominant position in the family and the community or independently through a patronage structure and forced conscription.

As will be shown in the Kandahar case study, a commander's possession of multiple lines of authority will enhance his ability to mobilize combatants. Given the role of different forms of authority, a particularly potent authority figure is able to integrate multiple overlapping forms of authority. Elder authority becomes all the more executable when supported by both local and national religious authorities (both the village *mullah/maulavi* and a prominent national leader (Gailani, Mojaddedi)) as well as by the support of the leading family member. The presence/incorporation of *mullahs* and other religious figures into an armed group further prevents a combatant from questioning ends or mobilization.

Proximity of conflict and scale of mobilization

Motives and the importance of particular units of affiliation will also shift depending on the proximity of violence to an individual's home. Traditionally, in Afghanistan, anthropologists have identified a series of ascending loyalties. The primary units of affiliation are partly related to the sources of threat. As described by Dupree, 'vertically, an Afghan kin-system stretching from nuclear family to nation can be described' (Dupree, 1980, p. 183). Similarly, for Goodson:

> the most prevalent pattern throughout Afghan history, however, is one of short-term alliances between even traditional enemies in the face of a common external threat.... When the threat is eliminated or sufficiently reduced, there is a return to regular patterns of traditional warfare.
>
> (Goodson, 2001, p. 26)

Echoing this, according to Maley:

> deep-rooted culturally determined sources of identity, such as ethnicity and tribe, have formed the bases for distinctive patterns of political action. On the other hand, ephemeral political groupings, what one might loosely call coalitions, can emerge in response to particular political circumstances. The superficial pluralism within the Afghan population has thus tended to mask an underlying propensity to act concertedly in the face of generalized threat.
>
> (Maley, 1991, p. 115)

The nature of the opponent will induce certain units of affiliation to become more important. For example, an 'ideal type' community militia will only invoke elder authority for the protection of the community. As discovered during interviews with combatants, some *qawms* demanded participation in the jihad, while others simply endorsed it without directly selecting combatants. Figure 3.5 illustrates this approach.

The individual's autonomy in determining the type of violence he can engage in increases with the distance from the community. An attack on a

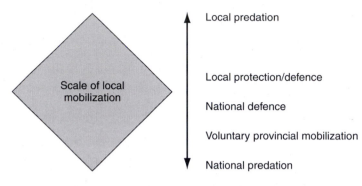

Figure 3.5 Proximity of conflict and scale of mobilization.

community will produce mass mobilization, requiring many community members to participate. Outside of the community, new opportunities emerge, providing incentives for combatant mobilization as a member of a government or independent security body. A combatant can then join the government forces in order to enhance his social mobility (ANA/ANP) or join a PSC for the purpose of employment. As discovered in Paktya Province, this will be facilitated through familial ties and networks via family members who are already established or working for these security institutions.

This can also include involvement in national or extra-local predation (such as the looting of major regional cities or the fighting in Kabul). For example, in Paktya, local defence and security would best be displayed by the *arbakian*; a smaller number would be expected to participate in offensive actions against a neighbour. While individuals can also freely choose to join government police forces, PSCs or the Coalition outside of the community, others can also choose to participate in national predation.

Type of combatant

As described earlier, it is necessary to distinguish between types of combatants, particularly between commanders, elites and followers. These different individuals or groups will have different tasks and derive different benefits and costs from participation. Child combatants can be a primary example of differentiated combatants, who, over the period of their involvement, will shift from cooking, tea-making and portering, eventually taking on a formal combat role by 'picking up the gun.' In certain cases, they will sleep in different locations and carry different weapons at different ages, later graduating to become full combatants. Herein, they undergo a broad period of socialization into the armed group, moving from non-combatant to combatant functions over time.[28]

In their ideal form, aside from the combatant, community militias are largely homogeneous. In contrast, both political–military parties and strongmen have varied units. Within strongmen armed groups, the critical role of extended family members and other affiliates (*nazm-e-khas* or *nafar-e-khas*) in enforcing in-group cohesion produces segmented motivation within the group. A serious split exists between the motives/activities of the bodyguards/ *nazm-e-khas* versus those of the other followers. A political–military party will mix permanent party members (largely removed from community dynamics and deployed from either refugee camps or a neighbouring safe haven) with foreign combatants and local militias. Political–military parties either utilize individuals that have already become delocalized (removed from local authority structures) or employ practices (indoctrination and ideological training) that shift an individual's loyalty from the community to the party or the strongman. Political–military parties will also possess elite units. Some of the Shi'a Hazara and Sayyed militias of Ghazni had special ideological branches known as the *fedayee*, which received special training. One of the combatants interviewed, recruited at the age of 14 in 1980, notes that a *fedayee* unit was created by the commander and received special military and religious instruction.[29]

Conclusion

This chapter has provided a framework for analysing newly encountered armed groups in Afghanistan as well as for assessing the information presented in the following case-study chapter. The primary conclusion concerns the need to take a broad view and variable approach to the armed groups, rather than subsuming all under a singular category, excavating the broad descriptions of Afghan militias. Depending on the province, any number of different types of armed groups may be present. This analysis emphasizes the need to differentiate between types of armed groups and forms of combatants, identifying those that threaten local security and engage in predation versus those that are primarily involved for the protection of their communities and at the behest of community elders. Individual participation in violence will vary considerably depending on the proximity and form of violence, the perceived legitimacy of mobilization, individual level of affiliation and position in an armed group. This chapter also raised and identified a neglected aspect of militias, revealing the critical role and functions of the *nazm-e-khas* in predation and local enforcement.

The discussion of the political economy of the Afghan war tends to focus on privately or independently raised funds through either primary commodity resource extraction or the taxation of trade. However, as revealed in the previous chapter, detailing the scale of arms flows into Afghanistan, the primary source of resources has been external governments, with the Afghan government both distributing these weapons and also legitimizing local commanders by providing title and legitimacy. The state is not distinct from these local armed groups but is directly involved and often implicated in local violence and factional conflicts. The government's reliance on local militias and provision of funds, arms and title increased throughout the 1980s (Giustozzi, 2000, 2004).

The previous chapter illustrated the significance of external funding and resource provision in supplying and supporting armed groups. The primary policy prescription of this chapter regards the necessity of assessing the way in which engagement (by PSCs, aid agencies, the Afghan government, Coalition and NATO forces) can spark a transformation in local armed groups and potentially undermine community-level checks and balances. International and national engagement and assistance can promote negative transitions in armed groups, unless the evolving nature of these armed groups is considered. This will be further demonstrated in the case studies on Paktya, Kandahar and Ghor Province. Certain militias there have utilized the PSC contracts, American funds and their integration into the AMF to consolidate local power.

Appendix

Annex 3.a.1 List of political–military parties

				Sunni political–military parties in Afghanistan, 1978–2005			
Name	Prominent members	Form	Composition	Special features	Ideological orientation	Geographical distribution	Parliamentary representation
Hezb-e-Islami (HIG/HIH) (2001).	Hekmatyar, Zirdad, Kashmir Khan.	Political–military party.	Detribalized, educated Pashtuns with substantial Arab support and Iranian backing until 2002. Some Uzbek affiliates in the northeast.	Youth groups; schools; propaganda; external diplomatic representatives.	Political Islamist; Fundamentalist.	Kunar (Asadabad); Kunduz (Imam Sahib); Takhar; Badakhshan; Laghman; Logar.	12–40 members in *Wolesi Jirga* (lower house of National Assembly) (now pro-government).
Ittihad-e-Islami.	Sayyaf, Dr. Ibrahim, Mir Alam.	Political–military party → strongman.	Paghman-area Pashtuns with some other affiliated commanders; substantial Arab support (15,000).	None.	Political Islamist.	Paghman and Kabul Provinces; small affiliated commanders in Paktya.	Tanzim Dawat-e-Islami-e-Afghanistan; 7 members in *wolesi jirga* (including Sayyaf).
Jamiat-e-Islami (JI).	Massoud, Rabbani, Fahim, Mansour, Mohammed Atta.	Community militias → political–military party.	Community links, state-trained *ulama*; now fragmented among different factions and Tajik groups. Tajik, Pashtun and Aimaq membership	Administrative structure in the Panjsher; youth groups; propaganda; diplomatic representatives.	Political Islamist.	Badakhshan, Balkh and Panjsher Provinces with affiliated commanders in Ghor, Hirat and Kandahar.	Jamiat represented in Parliament by 10 members, with 25 affiliate members through Hezb-e-Afghanistan Naween of Qanouni and 12 affiliate members through Nahzat-e-

Annex 3.a.1 (continued)

Name	Prominent members	Form	Composition	Special features	Ideological orientation	Geographical distribution	Parliamentary representation
Ma'az-e-Milli (NIFA).	Pir Sayed Gailani.	Charismatic religious authority with community militias.	(40,000–60,000 as of 2001). Sufi traditional Pashtun; nationalist; Western-educated Pashtuns; tribal *khans*.	None.	Traditionalist monarchist with local *khan* and individual support.	Paktya, Kandahar	Milli of Wali Massood and Mohammed Atta. 10 representatives in *Wolesi jirga*.
Harakat-e-Inqilab-e-Islami (1980–1992).	Mullah Mohammed Nabi Mohammadi (deceased).	Charismatic religious authority with community militias.	Sufi traditional Pashtun; some Uzbeks and previously some Tajiks (25,000).	Publications.	Traditionalist, anti-monarchist; *ulema*, dissenting members joined Taliban and HIK.	Kandahar, southern Afghanistan, Logar/Loya Paktya.	n/a.
Taliban (Pre-2001).	Mullah Omar, Maulvi Mohammad Rabbani, Maulvi Ahsan Ullah, Maulvi Abbas, Maulvi Mohamad, Maulvi Bor Jan, Maulvi Mohammad Hussain.	Political–military party with strongmen and militia affiliates.	Core as detribalized Pashtun (6–30,000 with additional 70,000 affiliated combatants via commanders).	Complex administrative apparatus.	Political Islamist.	Zabul, Uruzgan, southern Kandahar, Khost, Paktia, Paktika, Ghazni, Helmand, Logar, Wardak.	6–8 members in *woolesi jirga*, including Sayed Muhammed Gulabzoi (Khost), Abdul Salam Rocketi (Zabol) and Mohammad Islam Mohammadi.
Hezb-e-Islami (HIK).	Maulavi Khalis;	Political–military party	Charismatic Maulavi with Zadran/	Affiliation with AQ-Taliban	Political Islamist.	Zadran districts of Loya Paktya,	n/a

Party	Leaders	Type	Support base	Role in government	Ideology	Geographic area	Current status
	Jalaluddin Haqqani, Adbul Haq, Haji Qadir, Hazrat Ali, Amin Wardak.	with community militias.	Khogyiani tribal following.	since 1995, facilitated access to Jalalabad.		Jalalabad, Kunar.	
Jabh-e-Nijat-i-Milli (ANLF).	Sibghatollah Mojaddedi.	Charismatic religious authority with community militias.	Sufi traditional Pashtun.	None.	Traditionalist and pro-monarchist.	Pashtun areas.	Jabha-e-Nijat-e-Milli with 5 members in *wolesi jirga*; Mojaddedi heads the *Meshrano Jirga*.

Communist-affiliated political-military parties, 1978–1992

Party	Leaders	Type	Support base	Role in government	Ideology	Geographic area	Current status
Khalq.	Nur Mohammed Taraki; Hafizullah Amin; Shahmawaz Tanai.	Political–military party.	Led government from 1978–1979; military officer corps (particularly armour and air force) and Sarandoy gendarmerie.	Government from 1978–1979; ministerial infiltration and military support; propaganda.	Communist.	Rural provincial centres.	Former members of Khalq and Parcham factions have been elected to the *Wolesi Jirga*, numbers n/a.
Parcham (later Watan party).	Babrak Karmal, Mohammad Najibullah; Dostum.	Political–military party with community militias.	Kabul University; military officer corps; KHAD militias.	Government from 1979 until 1992.	Communist.	Urban areas and provincial centres.	
Junbish-e-Milli.	Abdur Rashid Dostum, General Farid Mazdak (later Jamiat),	Strongman ? political–military party.	Uzbek and Ismaili, some Pashtun and Turkmen; now fragmented among different factions.	Youth and women's groups (training and education centres);	Communist affiliate until 1992; Secular-ethnic post-1992.	Jawzjan, Balkh, Faryab, Kunduz, Samangan, Sar-e-Pul and Takhar.	20 representatives in *Wolesi Jirga*.

Annex 3.a.1 (continued)

Name	Prominent members	Form	Composition	Special features	Ideological orientation	Geographical distribution	Parliamentary representation
	Mahmood Baryali, Najim-ud-Din, Nabi Azmi (later Jamiat), Asif Dilawar, Abdul Fatah, Nur Mohammad Kohnaward, Nasim Mehdi, Sayed Noorullah.		Militia in 1980s was 3–4,000, expanded to 160,000.	propaganda; diplomatic representatives and congressional lobbying.			

Shi'a political–military parties (1978–2001)[a]

Name	Prominent members	Form	Composition	Special features	Ideological orientation	Geographical distribution	Parliamentary representation
Hizb-e Wahdat (1988–).	Abdul Ali Mazari, Mohammad Mohaqeq, Karim Khalili, Akbari, Ansari.	Alliance of 10 parties.	First a party and later an umbrella movement of Hazara and other Shi'a groups, now fragmented between traditional (Khalili) and radical 'Iranian' group (Akbari).	Diverse propaganda, arms and numerous newspapers; diplomatic representation; youth groups.	Mixed, though primarily moderate Islam and Hazara nationalism; mix of Imami, Iranian-backed and traditional Shi'a parties, links to local khans and community militias.	Mazar-area, Bamyan; Daykundi, northern Ghazni, northern Wardak, Kabul, Hirat.	Represented by numerous parties in Wolesi Jirga, with 25 aligned with pro-opposition and 5 pro-government.

Party	Leaders	Type	Composition	Ideology	Activities/Administration	Regions	Seats
Shura-ye Inqelab-e Ittifaq Islami (1979–).	Sayyed Ali Beheshti, Sayyed Muhammed Jagran Mujahedi/Sayed Jaghor Mujahed, Ayatollah Hussain Nasiri.	Alliance party with community militias.	Alliance of traditional (mirs/sayyeds), secular and Islamist Hazaras (1,000 staff, 2,000 soldiers).	Traditionalist.	Central administration (schools, justice, culture), taxation, central army and diplomatic representations.	Panjab, Waras, Bamyan, Quetta, Ghazni, Balkh.	
Sazman-e-Nasr (1979–1983).	Muhammad Montazeri, Mehdi Hashemi, Mazari and Khalili (prior to HW).	Political–military party with community militias.	Iranian-trained sayyids, educated and Islamist Hazaras (1,500 staff, 4,000 troops; later 50,000 soldiers).	Political Islamist and Hazara nationalism (strong Iranian support).	Central administration as of 1984, publication, joint council.	Bamyan, Waras, Ghor, Wardak, Shahristan, Yakawlang, Parwan, Ghazni, Balkh and Kabul.	
Pasdaran-e-Jihad/Sepah-e-Pasdaran (1979).[b]	Shaikh Sayyed Mohammed Akbari (Qizilbash).	Political–military party with strongmen/community militias.	Educated and Islamist Hazaras (1,500 staff, 4,000 soldiers).	Political Islamist (Iranian support); allied to Jamiat during civil war, with Taliban after 1998.	None.	Daykundi, Ghor, Helmand, Bamyan, Ghazni, Parwan.	7 Akbari affiliates in Wolesi Jirga.
Harakat-e Islami.	Shaikh Asif Mohseni Kandahari, Muhammad Anwari.	Political–military party.	(Non-Hazara), Qizilbash, Shi'ite Khan, clerical, educated youth (200 staff, 3,000 soldiers; later 20,000 soldiers at peak).	Anti-Iran (did not join Hizb-i-Wahdat), conservative.	Publications.	Kandahar, Kabul, Mazar, Hirat, Samangan.	

Annex 3.a.1 (continued)

Name	Prominent members	Form	Special features	Composition	Ideological orientation	Geographical distribution	Parliamentary representation
Sazman-e Fallah-e-Islami.	Mo'llim Babab Qarabaghi.	n/a.	n/a.	n/a.	n/a.	Ghazni.	
Sazman-e Mujahidin-e-Mustazaffin.	Engineer Hashemi.	Political–military party.	n/a.	Educated, joint council, sizeable Shi'a non-Hazara membership.	Islamist, anti-nationalist.	Bamyan, Ghazni, Ghor.	
Hizbollah.	Qari Ahmad Ghordarwazi (Qari Yakdasta); Sheikh Wusuqi.	Political–military party.	n/a.	Largely Shi'a, non-Hazara membership (1,000 staff, 2,000 soldiers; later 4,000 soldiers).	Political Islamist, Iranian support.	Hirat, Ghor, Helmand.	

Sources: Dorronsoro, 2005, p. 151; Rubin, 1996, pp. 208–209; Adamec, 2003, pp. 199, 214–215, 337; Ahmad, 2000, p. 70; Yusufzai, 2000, pp. 95, 97; Christensen, 1988, pp. 12–13; Wilder, 2005, p. 5; Katzman, 2006, pp. 4–5.

Notes
a Dorronsoro, 2005, p. 151; Mousavi, 1998, pp. 247–249; Rubin, 1996, pp. 191–192, 222–223; Sarabi, 2005, pp. 49–55, 81; Canfield, 2004; Wilder, 2005, p. 5. All staffing figures are drawn from: Emadi, 1997, pp. 378–379.
b Akbari is believed to have changed the name of the Pasdaran to Sepah-e-Mohammad in Iran and to Safi Sahaba in Pakistan.

Notes

1 For the first attempts to develop a typology of armed groups, see: Dorronsoro, 2005, p. 151; Roy, 1986.
2 Within this chapter, a combatant is seen to be a broad category incorporating any individual who bears arms. This can include both permanent and temporary combatants, members of formal government security bodies and informal groupings. As such, it is a category distinct from soldier, which in both conception and strict definition, applies to either government forces or to those of an armed movement.
3 See, for example: Roy, 1986; Rubin, 1996; Harpviken, 1997; Dorronsoro, 2005.
4 Categorization was provided via written correspondence with Dr. Antonio Giustozzi, Autumn 2006.
5 Interview with USAID official, February 2005.
6 For an overview over the Afghan political–military parties, see Table 3.a.1.
7 The senior leadership of the Peshawar-7 were all *ulema* (Islamic intellectuals and scholars), although with substantively different interpretations of Islamic doctrine.
8 'The origin of the war is not ethnic, and the solution will not be ethnic, but the conduct of the war is ethnic, which has had corrosive effects on the potential for national reconstruction' (Rubin *et al.*, 2001, pp. 8–9); 'Ethnicisation was therefore an unintended and counter-productive result of regionalization, rather than a strategy of mobilisation' (Dorronsoro, 2005, p. 258).
9 Combatant #64, Salang, April 2005.
10 Information gathered in Kunduz in May 2004 and in Mazar-e-Sharif as an OSCE Electoral Expert during the presidential elections, September–October 2004.
11 Information gathered in Mazar-e-Sharif as an OSCE Electoral Expert during the presidential elections, September–October 2004.
12 Combatant #112, Chaghcharan, Ghor, May 2005.
13 Combatant #117, Chaghcharan, Ghor, May 2005.
14 'At a simple level it connotes "place," where the place can be composed of one of a variety of components' (Allan, 2001, p. 554).
15 One commander (of 50 people) describes his role in the following manner:

> It was good friendship, they had to want from their own heart. It is not easy to become a commander. I was a little bit rich, so I could give these people some food or a place to stay, but other people cannot do the same thing.
> (Combatant #273, Kandahar, June 2005)

16 Combatant #269, Kandahar, June 2005.
17 Combatant #18, Shahristan, July 2004.
18 This is reminiscent of Mats Utas' description of the Liberian civil war:

> What initially was seen as a revolution in which the people in Nimba County (Nimbadians), in particular, fought with sticks and cutlasses, was eventually transformed into a war of terror where young people started fighting each other. The violence did not so much serve political ends, but aimed at the protection of one's family, and at accessing sources of power and wealth. Political leaders with their own private interests started making their appearance fighting over the control of mineral-rich areas and logging concessions.
> (Utas, 2005, p. 55)

19 Combatant #277, Kandahar, June 2005.
20 Combatant #179, Sayed Karam, Paktya, May 2005.
21 Combatant #272, Kandahar, June 2005.

22 Combatant #108, Chaghcharan, Ghor, June 2005.
23 Combatant # 67, Maidan Wardak, April 2005.
24 For example, Combatant #98 and #99, Chaghcharan, Ghor, June 2005.
25 Combatant #145, Paktya, June 2005.
26 Combatant #179, Sayed Karam, Paktya, May 2005.
27 'Their education in *Hizb* schools had taught them loyalty to revolutionary Islam, to the party, and to its leader' (Rubin, 1996, p. 252).
28 While some individuals recruited as children alluded to sexual abuse, none mentioned the forced committing of atrocity, as seen among West and East African armed groups. Combatant # 54/61/157 Kabul, April/June 2005; Combatant #93/123/124, Ghor, June 2005; Combatant #338, Jalalabad, July 2005.
29 Combatant #301/305, Ghazni, June 2005.

Part II

Addressing the small arms issue

Demilitarization and security sector reform in Afghanistan

Introduction

Mark Sedra

Demilitarization is one of the cornerstones of the Afghan peace-building project. After 23 years of civil war and internecine strife, it is the key to removing the culture of impunity that prevails in Afghan society, to replace the rule of the gun with the rule of law. The process features four pillars: the disarmament, demobilization and reintegration (DDR) of the formal militias associated with the government; the disbandment of illegal armed groups (DIAG); the cantonment of heavy weapons and the collection and destruction of anti-personnel mines and ammunition stockpiles. Although each pillar of the process has a disarmament element, little consideration has been accorded to the establishment of a countrywide small arms and light weapons collection programme. In light of the fact that estimates of the number of uncontrolled small arms in the country range from 1.5 to 10 million, such a process would seem to be a prerequisite for sustainable peace and security (Small Arms Survey, 2003, p. 74; Pirseyedi, 2000, p. 13). The flagship of the demilitarization process, the DDR programme, treated the collection of small arms as a secondary and largely symbolic objective. Disarmament has a more central role in the DIAG programme but is perceived as a means to achieve the programme's central goal, the disbandment of informal militias, rather than as an end in itself.

The Bonn Agreement, which launched the Afghan state-building project in December 2001, did not accord demilitarization a central status in the political process. It only contained a vague provision on demilitarization stipulating that 'upon the official transfer of power, all *mujahideen*, Afghan armed forces and armed groups in the country shall come under the command and control of the Interim Authority, and be reorganized according to the requirements of the new Afghan security and armed forces' (Bonn Agreement, 2001, para. V, art. 1). The conspicuous absence of any explicit reference to disarmament, a concession to the Northern Alliance commanders who would not countenance the notion, missed a seminal opportunity to tie the country's main power brokers to the project. While the successor to the Bonn Agreement, the Afghanistan Compact, signed at a donor conference held in London on 31 January to

1 February 2006, includes a succinct provision calling for the disbandment of illegal armed groups, it still does not explicitly address the small arms issue.

Despite the conspicuous absence of the small arms issue in the formal political process, few would deny the need to address it in some fashion in order to achieve long-term peace and stability. In the Afghan government's Millennium Development Goals (MDG) Report, sponsored by UNDP, target 21 reads: 'reduce the misuse of weapons and reduce the proportion of illegally held weapons' (Islamic Republic of Afghanistan, 2005a, p. 108). The inclusion of the issue as one of the report's 25 targets testifies to the importance ascribed to it by segments of the Afghan government and donor community, but few steps have been taken to realize it on the ground and there is no succinct timetable to do so.

In many ways, it is the pervasive nature of the problem that has deterred international and local actors from addressing it in a meaningful and systematic manner. The notion of the Afghan 'gun culture,' perceived to be inextricably interwoven into the fabric of Afghan society, has served as a powerful psychological obstacle to any considerations of a comprehensive, countrywide weapons collection and control programme. Complete disarmament is held as a goal that can only be pursued once security and political conditions in the country have reached a high level of stability. According to the MDG report, 'in a fragile environment, characterised by partial disarmament and low public confidence in the institutions of the state as they undergo reform, it will be impractical to aim for complete disarmament.' In fact, during such times of 'rapid change, forcible disarmament of commanders and other powerful individuals may lead to increased insecurity' (Islamic Republic of Afghanistan, 2005a, p. 108).

Conversely, the widespread presence of the gun in Afghan society has been a driver of insecurity and political instability. Leaving commanders armed grants them a veto over the state-building process and raises the stakes and risk of political disputes. It has allowed them to carve out space in the illicit economy, most notably the opium trade, which has spurred state corruption and hindered growth in the formal economy. This has allowed commanders and armed groups to bolster their patronage networks, which extend deep into the central state, and consolidate their power, insulating them from pressure to disarm. This shows that disarmament is an indispensable element of peace-building and stabilization activities in the immediate aftermath of violent conflict. A comprehensive disarmament process may take years to reach fruition, but it should be launched in the early stages of the post-conflict period, something that did not happen in Afghanistan.

In parallel to efforts to address the legacy of war and past weapons proliferation in Afghanistan, the government, under the auspices of the internationally supported security sector reform (SSR) programme, has endeavoured to develop a coherent weapons procurement policy and endow its security forces with the tools needed to secure one of the central prerequisites for statehood, a monopoly over the use of coercive force. Paradoxically, despite the glut of weapons circulating in private hands in Afghanistan, shortfalls in lethal equipment continue to present one of the paramount obstacles to the development of the fledgling security forces.

In 2005–2006, the DDR and DIAG programmes began to serve as a significant source of light and heavy weapons for the Afghan National Army and Police. However, the low volume and variable quality of the weapons transfers, a by-product of the secondary status accorded to small arms collection in the DDR and DIAG programmes, forced the government to look outside its borders to meet its equipment requirements, primarily through donations and purchases of surplus weapons brokered by the principal donors supporting the police and military reform processes, the United States and Germany.[1]

The procurement process has not only revealed the need to develop new procurement structures and procedures but to undertake an assessment of the equipment needs of the security forces, measured against their individual mandates and budgetary constraints. It has also stimulated thinking and action on associated issues such as stockpile management, maintenance and security, as well as the establishment of a legal framework for weapons possession and ownership.

Despite steps undertaken to collect small arms and light weapons under the auspices of the four-pillar demilitarization process and the government's incipient efforts to design an effective weapons procurement and control regime, political will continues to be a major obstacle to action. Although President Karzai has issued numerous public statements and presidential decrees decrying illegal weapons ownership, his government, comprising numerous former commanders that have retained arms stockpiles and links to illegally armed groups, has not shown the requisite capacity or political will to fulfil his edicts.

The international donor community has been unwilling to press the government to accelerate current demilitarization efforts or expand their scope out of fear that it could catalyse a disruption in the prevailing political and security equilibrium. This is particularly true of the largest donor in the country, the United States, which, from the outset of the process, showed little interest in demilitarization. After the dust had settled from the military operation to unseat the Taliban, the United States perceived that disarming the country was not only unfeasible but also contrary to US interests. The war on terror, rather than notions of nation building, drove US policy and demanded alliances with armed Afghan commanders, some of which had a tenuous and even hostile relationship with the central state. As US appreciation of the importance of the Afghan nation-building project in countering Taliban and Al-Qaeda influence in the country increased, so too did its engagement in the demilitarization process. However, reluctance remains to consider plans to approach the wider problem of illegal small arms possession, seen as unachievable and even counterproductive in the present security and political environment.

Afghan government and donor reticence to confront the small arms issue is out of step with Afghan public opinion. A survey conducted in Afghanistan in September 2004 by the Human Rights Research and Advocacy Consortium (HRRAC), a group of seven Afghan and six international organizations, found that 65 per cent of the respondents viewed disarmament as the single most important action for improving security in the country. The survey report, entitled *Take the Guns Away: Afghan Voices on Security and Elections*, testified to the high level of public support a comprehensive weapons collection programme could receive in Afghanistan if advanced under the right conditions, notably alongside the provision of security and improvements in the economic climate (HRRAC, 2004). As Hafizullah, an Afghan civilian, stated in an interview with the *Institute for War and Peace Reporting* in November 2004, 'all these militia forces are thieves, and we have to be armed because we are afraid of them ... When the arms are collected from the militia commanders and their supporters, I will be the first to turn my weapons in to the government' (Ibrahimi, 2004). This public will for disarmament and weapons control represents a window of opportunity that the Afghan government and international community have yet to exploit.

This is not to say that if a country-wide weapons control and collection programme had been implemented in 2002 it would not have encountered major obstacles. Rather, this part of the book will argue that entry points existed to begin a dialogue and lay the legal and institutional foundations to address this issue over the medium to long term. It is important to recall the political and security environment in Afghanistan in 2002. The Taliban had been defeated and had yet to regroup; the country's warlords had yet to re-establish their mini-fiefdoms in the periphery or ensconce themselves in government institutions; the security situation was stable; and regional actors, notably, Pakistan and Iran, were largely quiescent, waiting to determine the durability of the international commitment to the country before re-engaging in proxy competition. Coupled with a palpable public fatigue with war, there was political space to introduce ideas of large-scale disarmament.

If we contrast this situation with the conditions prevalent in Afghanistan in 2008, where a Taliban-led insurgency has reached unprecedented levels of intensity; where regional warlords control large swathes of territory and have 'colonized' segments of the government and security apparatus; where the insurgency, terrorism, general criminality and the drug trade have created a level of insecurity that has prompted many Afghans to speak nostalgically of the stability provided by the Taliban and where regional actors have resumed proxy competition, one can starkly see the opportunity that was missed. Afghans remain steadfast in their determination to move beyond conflict, but even this support for peace-building efforts is beginning to falter due to the failure of the state-building process to deliver genuine change.

Exploiting the window of opportunity that existed in 2002 would have required the convergence of a constellation of factors. First, wide donor buy-in for the concept would have been needed at the outset of the state-building process. Support from the Coalition would have been crucial in this regard, as the potential threat of force would have served as a powerful motivation for commanders to disarm. International pressure could also have been employed to ensure the inclusion of a clearer and more robust provision on demilitarization in the Bonn Agreement.

Second, President Karzai would have had to emerge as a champion of the process during the period of the Afghan Interim Administration, building domestic Coalitions in favour of the process, spearheading efforts to establish legal instruments to frame it and developing government capacity to advance it. The actual collection of weapons could have happened at a later stage, once these foundational steps were taken and parallel progress was made to reform the security sector. Considering the historical challenges of consensus building in Afghanistan and the fractious nature of internal politics, it is understandable that the government and international community were reticent to take on such a divisive issue; however, this was rooted to a miscalculation of the strength of the principal commanders or warlords during this period. The demonstration effect of confronting certain recalcitrant commanders during this formative stage in the country's political transition might have facilitated a more ambitious demilitarization programme. The accommodationist approach that the government adopted, with the connivance of the international community, has, by contrast, undermined government leverage to advance demilitarization activities.

Part II of the book is divided into two chapters. Chapter 4 will deconstruct and assess the impact of the four pillars of the demilitarization process – the disarmament, demobilization and reintegration (DDR), heavy weapons cantonment (HWC), Disbandment of Illegal Armed Groups (DIAG) and Anti-Personnel Mine and Ammunition Stockpile Destruction (APMASD) programmes. It will show that, across the process, particularly in its two core pillars – DDR and DIAG – the imperative of small arms collection and control has been viewed as secondary in importance, a means to achieve the breakdown of military formations and the severing of patronage links between commanders and militiamen, rather than an end in itself. It tends to treat the dilemma of small arms proliferation as a symptom of a broader problem of military mobilization rather than a dilemma in its own right. Accordingly, it presupposes that the decommissioning of formal units and the disbandment of informal ones will inevitably lead to a reduction in demand and use of small arms and light weapons, a diagnosis that has proven spurious in the case of Afghanistan. On the contrary, the widespread presence of small arms, even after the completion of demilitarization programmes, has enabled an anti-government insurgency gradually to gain momentum, fuelled the resurgence of warlord power and facilitated the exponential rise of the drug trade. The presence of small arms is not itself a cause of conflict but provides an enabling environment for insecurity and heightens the probability that political grievances will degenerate into violence.

Chapter 5 will examine the issue of small arms in the context of the Afghan security sector and the ongoing process to reform it. It will examine efforts to create a legal framework to underpin small arms reduction and control efforts and analyse a number of laws and presidential decrees that have been promulgated to regulate firearm ownership and possession amongst both Afghans and international non-state actors. It concludes that, while these legal instruments are adequately designed, the lack of political will amongst the government to apply them uniformly across the country – not just against their factional rivals – coupled with the lack of capacity amongst both the judicial and law enforcement apparatuses to enforce them has made them largely irrelevant.

Chapter 5 will focus on statutory and non-statutory security actors and examine how they procure and use small arms and light weapons. In the case of the statutory security actors, efforts of the Ministry of Defence and Ministry of Interior, with support from the donor community, to meet the legitimate equipment needs of the Afghan National Army (ANA) and Afghan National Police (ANP) through both external donations and transfers from the demilitarization process will be critiqued. The chapter will also highlight the problem of weapons leakage and mismanagement in the security forces, particularly in the police, where weapons are often treated as personal rather than duty weapons. As for the non-statutory security actors, methods by which they procure arms, most notably through the illicit weapons market, will be explored. One of the overarching conclusions of the chapter is that efforts to reform the Afghan security sector have been hampered by the failure to address the issue of small arms and light weapons.

Note

1 Interview with adviser to the Defence Minister, Kabul, 18 May 2005.

4 The four pillars of demilitarization in Afghanistan

Mark Sedra

Pillar 1 – Disarmament, demobilization and reintegration (DDR) of former combatants

On 22 February 2003, President Hamid Karzai stated that 'achieving DDR answers the deepest aspirations of the Afghan people, who are eager to move away from war and violence toward a peaceful, safe and civil society' (Karzai, 2003). President Karzai was speaking at a conference organized in Tokyo by the government of Japan to provide a forum for the Afghan government to present its plans to reform the security sector. Japan assumed a prominent role in the process after accepting the status of lead donor for DDR in spring 2002 at a G8 security donor meeting held in Geneva. At the Tokyo conference – attended by more than 30 donor countries, the European Union and 12 international organizations – the Afghan New Beginnings Programme (ANBP) was first introduced, a DDR project to be implemented by the United Nations Development Programme (UNDP) on behalf of the Afghan government.

The programme was designed to work with Afghan government ministries in the development and implementation of policies approved by the Afghan government's four Defence Commissions, appointed by President Karzai in January 2003. They included the National Disarmament Commission, established to oversee the collection and storage of weapons; the Demobilization and Reintegration (D&R) Commission, created to direct the demobilization and reintegration of former combatants; the Officer Recruiting and Training Commission, intended to develop the strategy and methodology for the recruitment and training of commissioned and non-commissioned officers; and the Soldier Recruiting and Training Commission, meant to oversee the recruitment of soldiers for the Afghan National Army (ANA). The commissions were created for the dual purpose of asserting Afghan ownership of the DDR process and coordinating the multiplicity of actors involved in it.

The National Disarmament Commission

The primary purpose of the National Disarmament Commission (NDC) was to approve the final version of the disarmament plan developed through discussions with the Afghan Ministry of Defence (MoD) and the ANBP and provide some oversight of its implementation. From its inception, however, the commission sought to expand its mandate, positioning itself as the main implementing actor for the process and launching its own disarmament initiative before the ANBP was able to assert itself as the focal point for the process. It represented an attempt to pre-empt the nascent ANBP to impose an Afghan solution to the small arms crisis. These efforts could be characterized as *ad hoc*, factionalized and opaque. The failure of the commission's programme and its inability to assume its designated role ultimately led to its dissolution.

Deputy Defence Minister, General Atiqullah Baryalai, was appointed as the head of the NDC. Its stated goal was to collect 'a million weapons and pieces of military equipment' (Wali, 2002). A collection programme was launched in five northern provinces in 2002: Badakhshan, Takhar, Kunduz, Parwan and Kapisa. The programme targeted the Afghan Military Force (AMF), the assemblage of militias that came to power in the wake of the Taliban's collapse, the bulk of which were affiliated with the Northern Alliance. According to the Afghan government, 50,000 pieces of military equipment were collected during the operation, including 100 mortars, 130 armoured vehicles and 40 tanks. The commission affirmed that the weapons would be stored temporarily in local facilities until they could be transferred to a national depot in Kabul (Wali, 2002).

Following the northern disarmament drive, General Sher Mohammad Karimi, a member of the NDC, affirmed that 'the collection process will be applied all over Afghanistan in the next six months' (Wali, 2002). Additional weaponry was collected in subsequent months, but it is not clear how much. The programme also sought to register weapons possessed by the AMF, recording their serial numbers. By the end of 2002, the programme had registered 126,051 weapons in the possession of 248 AMF formations (Islamic Republic of Afghanistan, 2006a, Annex A, p. 1).

While the stated results of the programme were impressive, little documentation was released by the NDC or the Defence Ministry to substantiate them. A great deal of ambiguity surrounds the process and its results. In the weeks following its conclusion in the summer of 2002, many of the men who submitted weapons claimed that they had not received compensation that they were promised, and allegations circulated that guns collected were circulated to other militia groupings rather than being transferred to Ministry of Defence depots.

Such concerns would later prompt Presidential Decree 31, issued on 6 February 2005, which recognized that 'considerable weapons and ammunition were cantoned by different government authorities ... but they have not provided sufficient information ... to the D&R Commission and other responsible parties of the MoD' (Presidential Decree No. 31, 7 February 2005). The decree ordered the Ministry of Defence and Ministry of Interior 'to hand over all weapons, ammunitions, vehicles and technical fighting tools which have been collected outside of the DDR process and have not been registered based on official documents by concerned authorities to the Demobilization and Reintegration (D&R) Commission' (Presidential Decree No. 31, 2005). In the light of continued government shortfalls in firearms, it is clear that despite the promulgation of Presidential Decree 31, a significant proportion of the weaponry collected never found its way into government depots.

Questions regarding the impact of NDC disarmament programming coupled with its perceived factional orientation and dysfunctional mode of operation stimulated trenchant criticism of the body by members of the government and international community. While the mere establishment of the commission can be perceived as an expression of political will to address the small arms problem, in effect it was an attempt by factional actors in the Ministry of Defence to consolidate their control over the country's military assets. Accordingly, the initiative had the potential to exacerbate inter-factional tension and insecurity rather than ameliorate it.

The approval of the ANBP's DDR plan on 8 October 2003 provided the government with an opportunity to dissolve the commission. It was subsumed into the Office of Strategy and Policy within the Ministry of Defence. In fact, by early 2005, only the D&R Commission continued to function, with the Officer and Soldier Recruiting and Training Commissions having been dissolved and similarly integrated into the Ministry of Defence. In the absence of a government body that could oversee the disarmament component of the demilitarization process, the scope of the D&R Commission was broadened to encompass this role; however, it did not develop the requisite capacity to assume it competently.

The NDC episode reflects both the problem of ownership that marred the disarmament process from its inception and the peripheral status accorded to the issue. After the dissolution of the NDC, the DDR process would become an internationally driven enterprise. The ambivalence of the highly factionalized and politicized Ministry of Defence towards the process in its early stages deprived it of a robust government partner, creating an ownership gap. The Ministry was playing a double game, supporting the process publicly in order to appease donors and ensure the uninterrupted supply of donor aid and assistance, while seeking to insulate Shura-e Nezar allied units and militias from the process. In effect, it was seeking to buttress its dominant military position in the country, militating against any prospective Taliban comeback.

The failure of the international community to address this ownership gap in a meaningful way demonstrated on one hand its lack of trust in Afghan actors to elevate national over factional interests, and, on the other, the low priority it accorded the issue. As one senior figure in the D&R Commission stated in February 2006, the international community missed a 'critical moment' to advance the disarmament process due to its own perception of the intractability of the small arms problem in Afghanistan.[1] The belief that a large-scale effort to remove the gun from Afghan society would provoke a violent reaction and unravel the peace informed their approach towards the small arms issue. Disarmament would subsequently become only a symbolic aspect of the formal DDR process and small arms control was an issue left pending for an unspecified time in the future. What this interpretation of Afghan history and society missed, according to the commission representative, was the widespread public revulsion for the rule of the gun and culture of impunity that had emerged in Afghanistan after three decades of war.

The Afghan New Beginnings Programme

The limited disarmament component of the ANBP reflects the timidity with which the international community has approached the issue of disarmament.

On 6 April 2003, the Afghan Transitional Authority (ATA) and UNDP signed an agreement that officially launched the Afghan New Beginnings Programme. It was a voluntary programme focusing solely on active units of the AMF. The programme set the following objective:

> To decommission formations and units up to a total of 100,000 officers and soldiers and in the process to collect, store and deactivate weapons currently in their possession in order to be able to reconstruct the Afghan National Army (ANA) and return those not required to civilian life.
>
> (quoted in Sedra, 2004a, p. 3)

While disarmament was explicitly mentioned as a central goal in the programme's blueprint, in practice, it was treated as a peripheral aspect. The two underlying goals of the process were: 'to break the historic patriarchal chain of command existing between the former commanders and their men; and to provide the demobilised personnel with the ability to become economically independent' (ANBP, 2006a, p. 3). In contrast to the expectations of many local and international observers and diverging from the DDR experience in other settings, the programme 'was never mandated to disarm the population per se or provide direct employment but to assist AMF military personnel to transition from military into civilian occupations' (ANBP, 2006a, p. 3).

The Afghan government and ANBP initially estimated that there were 100,000 combatants eligible to enter the DDR process. This figure represented a compromise with the Afghan Ministry of Defence, which initially claimed that there were more than 250,000 AMF soldiers on duty, and the United Nations Assistance Mission for Afghanistan (UNAMA), which asserted that there were only 45,000–50,000 ex-combatants (ICG, 2005, p. 3). After 13 months of operation, the ANBP lowered its operational target to approximately 60,000, concluding that a large proportion of the AMF personnel on the payroll of the Ministry of Defence were in fact 'ghost soldiers.' No comprehensive needs assessment on the scale and nature of the problem was conducted to inform the programme's design, leaving ANBP officials reliant on force figures provided by the Afghan Ministry of Defence. The problem was that the Ministry and the AMF commanders under its authority had an interest in overstating the number of troops under their command, as they could claim more resources from the central government to feed, house and remunerate them.

Further complicating efforts to arrive at a reliable figure for the number of ex-combatants in Afghanistan was the seasonal or part-time nature of soldiering. Rather than a standing force, the AMF was an assemblage of irregular militias mobilized by commanders on an *ad hoc* basis. Most Afghan combatants served only part of the year in a militia, dedicating the remainder of their time to civilian professions, such as agriculture or wage labour work (Özerdem, 2002, p. 971). After the fall of the Taliban, a large number of ex-combatants spontaneously demobilized and returned to their communities, making it difficult to identify them and their specific needs (ICG, 2005, p. 2).

Moreover, the programme lacked an accurate picture of the weapons holdings of AMF personnel, permitting widespread concealment of arms. While some superficial efforts were undertaken to determine AMF troop levels in the country, virtually no research was undertaken to gauge the number of weapons in their possession. Afghan commanders had become skilled during the civil war at hiding their arms stocks, often in underground caches or unmarked urban dwellings; however, the absence of concerted ANBP or government pressure to divulge their numbers and locations did not necessitate significant obfuscation.

Colletta, Kostner and Wiederhofer argue that a successful DDR programme requires 'careful preparation based on rapid assessments of the opportunity structure and a profiling of ex-combatants ... according to their characteristics, needs, and desired way of earning a livelihood (mode of subsistence)' (Colletta *et al.*, 2004, p. 171). Designing a DDR strategy requires the mapping of militia groups, surveying their composition and structure; the profiling of both soldiers and commanders, with an assessment of their skills and needs,[2] and analysis of the numbers and types of weapons in circulation. Without good data for planning purposes, the programme will be ill-equipped to respond to the needs of ex-combatants and the wider security environment or adapt to changing conditions (Kingma, 2002, p. 183).

This would be a good appraisal of the Afghan DDR process in its initial stages. Nowhere was the lack of a needs assessment more apparent than in the disarmament component of the process, where the programme operated with crude and outdated estimates of the number of arms in the possession of the AMF. Afghanistan's 2005 MDG report indicated that the government was considering launching a 'community-level survey of weapons ownership.' This would certainly resolve the small arms information gap, but the report was unclear about how, when and under what conditions the survey would be conducted (Islamic Republic of Afghanistan, 2005a, p. 108).

The three-year $142 million (see Table 4.1) DDR programme was implemented from a central office located in Kabul and eight regional offices in Kunduz, Kabul/Parwan, Gardez, Mazar-e-Sharif, Kandahar, Bamyan, Jalalabad and Hirat. At its apex, the programme consisted primarily of Afghan staff – approximately 700 – with up to 70 international advisers. The disarmament and demobilization phase came to a conclusion in July 2005 and the reintegration phase one year later in June 2006 (Sedra, 2004a, p. 3).

The ANBP's operational plan (see Figures 4.1 and 4.2) called for individual AMF units to submit a list of their personnel to a Ministry of Defence Operational Group. Once the names on the list were verified as legitimate candidates by a Regional Verification Committee composed of seven respected public figures drawn from each DDR target area, the listed soldiers and officers could enter the programme.

The minimum requirements for entry into the programme were eight months of military service, plus the submission of an operational weapon to an MDU, a 20-member team that collected arms and initiated demobilization.[3] Weapons constructed locally or in the Pakistani weapons workshops that dot the border with Afghanistan were categorized as unserviceable and rejected. This prerequisite for entry into the programme was largely symbolic, intended to demonstrate the firm commitment of the individual soldier to peace. The programme did not contain

Table 4.1 ANBP funding breakdown

Donor	Contribution (US$)
Japan	91 million
UK	19 million
Canada	16 million
USA	9 million
Netherlands	4 million
European Commission	1.9 million
Norway	0.8 million
Switzerland	0.5 million
Total	142.2 million

Source: ANBP, 2006a, p. 5.

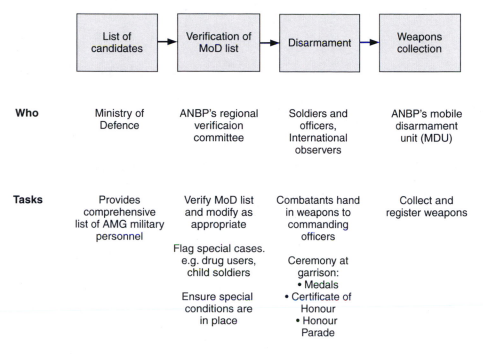

Figure 4.1 The disarmament process (source: ANBP website, online, available at: undpanbp.org/ (accessed 1 December 2007)).

any mechanism to verify that individual soldiers or commanders were submitting all of their weapons stocks, nor to compel them to do so.

Alternatively, the programme accepted the submission of heavy weapons[4] by groups of ex-combatants according to a predetermined formula establishing the number of soldiers that would be required to operate a specific heavy weapon system. For instance, four soldiers could enter the programme in exchange for the submission of a T-54 tank, while five were deemed sufficient to constitute the crew of a ZSU 23-4 anti-aircraft gun (ICG, 2005, p. 3).

Once submitted, small arms and light weapons were engraved with an alpha-numeric code for future identification. Information on the make, model and serial number of each weapon was linked to the data of each ex-soldier and stored in a database at the central ANBP office in Kabul. The weapons were subsequently transferred to the ANA Central Corps Depot, situated at the Pul-e-charkhi military complex in Kabul, where they were stored under a dual key system, one held by the Ministry of Defence and the other by the International Observer Group (IOG), a body of international monitors created to provide external oversight of the process until they could be handed over to the ANA.

MoD operational   Verification   MDU   Regional office   Civilian
      group

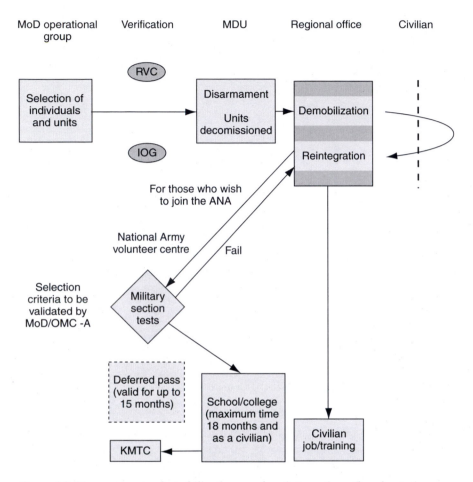

Figure 4.2 Disarmament, demobilization and reintegration flowchart (source: ANBP website, online, available at: undpanbp.org/ (accessed 1 December 2007)).

Notes
KMTC refers to the Kabul Military Training Centre, the US-run facility responsible for training the new Afghan National Army (ANA). OMC-A refers to the Office of Military Cooperation–Afghanistan, the Coalition body established to oversee US support to the ANA and Afghan MoD.

After weapons collection in a particular area was completed, ex-soldiers were directed to the ANBP regional office for demobilization. There, ex-combatants were briefed on the programme and assigned to a case worker who interviewed them to determine their aspirations, skill sets, desires, experience and education. This information was registered in an ANBP database, along with each ex-combatant's fingerprints, photo, unique identification number, weapon barcode, personal history and career goals. Identification cards were subsequently issued to each ex-combatant. After taking an oath pledging not to bear arms again, the ex-combatant was awarded a medal for distinguished service and a certificate of honourable discharge. Finally, he was given a severance package consisting of clothes and food.[5] Originally, a cash payment of $200 was provided to each ex-combatant who submitted a weapon, but this measure was discontinued following the pilot phase due to reports that commanders were systematically intimidating soldiers for part or all of the cash grant (Sedra, 2004a, pp. 3–7).

During the interview at the demobilization centre, the case worker presented a list of employment or educational options for the ex-combatant compiled on the basis of his profile. The ex-combatants were advised to return to the facility following a period of two weeks to select a reintegration option. Ex-combatants were offered a choice of several reintegration packages devised by the ANBP in cooperation with the Afghan government and international partner organizations. If no immediate opportunities could be identified for ex-soldiers, or if the agricultural package could not begin for seasonal reasons, the ANBP would offer temporary wage labour positions until suitable options could be made available (Sedra, 2004a, pp. 3–7). Ex-combatants could opt to join the Afghan National Army (ANA) if they were within the age range of 18–28, passed a standard physical and had no criminal record (Afghan Ministry of Defence, 2006). The fact that only 2.42 per cent of the ex-combatants that received reintegration assistance (1,389) entered the ANA was largely because the majority exceeded the age range for entry. The average age of ex-combatants entering the programme was 27.[6]

The pilot phase of the programme, designed to test its feasibility, began on 24 October 2003 in five regions: Kunduz, Gardez, Mazar-e-Sharif, Kandahar and Kabul. Initially scheduled to begin on 22 June 2003, the programme was delayed on several occasions due to the reluctance of the Ministry of Defence to undertake structural reforms, a prerequisite set by the Japanese for the release of their committed funds. Limited personnel changes implemented by the Ministry in September 2003, resulting in 22 new senior appointments, while falling short of expectations, was deemed sufficient to move ahead with the process (Sedra, 2004a, p. 14).

The pilot phase revealed that the design of the programme was not in line with prevailing conditions on the ground. Commanders wilfully and systematically manipulated the process. For instance, in Kunduz, local commanders submitted only their least loyal and competent troops – 'dead wood' as one ANBP official termed it – and handed over weapons that were barely serviceable.[7] Such incidents were indicative of a trend witnessed across the pilot sites, highlighting the programme's lack of capacity to engage commanders effectively (Sedra, 2004a, p. 9). The programme incorrectly assumed that the link between commanders and their militiamen could be severed solely through the provision of incentives to militiamen. It underestimated the strength of the commander patronage networks and the legitimacy many of these figures enjoyed in their home communities. It became clear that they would not fade away as the programme gained momentum and would obstruct it if they were not adequately engaged.

The main phase of the programme began in May 2004 targeting all regions of the country. It proceeded at a deliberate pace during its first three months of operation, primarily as a result of commander obstructionism and insecurity. AMF commanders appointed by the central government to civilian posts, such as provincial governors or police chiefs, were particularly adept at manipulating or circumventing the DDR process. They regularly exploited their positions to shift former militiamen into police units under their authority (ICG, 2005, p. 6).[8] Such manoeuvres enabled commanders to maintain the integrity of their patronage networks and insulate their economic interests. This trend was particularly apparent in the highway police – which has since been disbanded – where four of the six regimental commanders were former AMF or National Directorate of Security (NDS) commanders in 2005, two of whom openly transferred militiamen into their regiments (ICG, 2005, p. 7).

Commanders characteristically only submitted a fraction of their weapons holdings to the process, the minimum required to certify their participation. There are reports of commanders providing their militiamen with their least functional weapons for submission, those that meet the minimum criteria of serviceability for entry into the programme, while concealing their most up-to-date equipment in arms caches, often below ground. It is conceivable that an effort to engage commanders more effectively early in the process, coupled with the introduction of credible disincentives for non-compliance, would have assured greater commander cooperation with the process.

There are indications of significant fraud during the DDR process. A common method observed was the falsification of ANBP identification cards, which permitted individuals who failed to meet the basic prerequisites for entry into the programme to benefit from its reintegration packages (Rossi and Giustozzi, 2006, p. 5).[9] According to a UNAMA report, 80 per cent of the participants in the central highlands region failed to meet the basic criterion for entry into the programme, eight months of military service (Dennys, 2005, p. 4). Consistent with trends during the pilot phase, commanders manipulated the process in particular regions, arbitrarily choosing candidates for entry into the programme and pilfering reintegration assistance (Dennys, 2005, p. 4; Rossi and Giustozzi, 2006, p. 4).[10] Moreover, Rossi and Giustozzi note 'a clear regional bias in the distribution of the benefits of DDR,' as two regions, both of which under the control of a single Northern Alliance faction – Shura-e-Nezar – accounted for 56 per cent of all militiamen who entered the process (Rossi and Giustozzi, 2006, p. 5).

In an attempt to resolve the dilemma of commander obstructionism, the ANBP launched a Commander Incentive Programme (CIP) in the autumn of 2004. The central component of the scheme was a financial redundancy package, which provided commanders with a $550–650 monthly cash stipend for a two-year period in exchange for their cooperation with the ANBP. For commanders unlikely to be enticed by financial incentives alone, opportunities for travel and training overseas (primarily in Japan), and the prospect of a government posting were offered to suitable candidates as determined by the government and ANBP.[11] The two-year $5 million programme, funded by Japan, targeted 550 militia commanders across the country, 460 of whom had entered the programme by June 2006.[12] The redundancy payments will continue until June 2007 with the entire programme wrapping up in September 2007.[13]

The DDR process only began to achieve tangible results in the autumn of 2004 due to two factors. First, the Political Parties Law promulgated on 18 October 2003 provided a powerful incentive for armed factions with political ambitions to comply with the process (ICG, 2005, p. 6). It prohibits political parties from having 'military organizations or affiliations with armed forces,' a principle also enshrined in the constitution, and allows for the dissolution of parties that transgress the statute (Political Parties Law, art. 6, no. 5, online, available at: afghan-web.com/politics/parties_law.html (accessed 4 December 2007)). Intent on registering candidates in time for the October 2004 presidential elections, factional groups such as the Uzbek-dominated Junbish-e-Milli, led by Rashid Dostum, and the mainly Tajik Jamiat-e-Islami, led by former President Burhanuddin Rabbani, sought to demonstrate their support for the DDR process by demobilizing elements of their militias. The increased level of cooperation exhibited by all the main factional groups, although short of full compliance, was a product of their political ambitions and determination to avoid complications in the registration process (ICG, 2005, p. 6). Second, in the run-up to the October 2004 presidential elections, the US deepened its engagement in the process, applying pressure on recalcitrant commanders to comply. This largely took the form of political pressure on commanders allied to the government. The shift in the US approach, which had previously been characterized by ambivalence and even obstructionism, was calculated to boost President Karzai's electoral fortunes and address deteriorating security conditions. Early in the process the US expressed reservations about the programme being applied in areas of the south and east where Afghan militias were supporting Coalition forces to combat the Taliban.[14] They did so despite the fact that many of those same proxy militias opposed the extension of central state authority in their regional strongholds.

The disarmament and demobilization phase of the process formally came to an end on 7 July 2005, resulting in the demobilization of 63,380 ex-combatants and the collection of 57,629 light and medium weapons (see Box 4.1). The programme also resulted in the 'de-financing' of 100,000 soldiers – denoting the formal removal of soldiers, both 'real' and 'ghost,' from the state payroll – resulting in savings of $120 million per annum in state expenditures (ANBP, 2006a, p. 2). These figures prompted many observers and DDR practitioners to refer to the programme as an unqualified success.[15] In the light of the challenges faced by the programme, its accomplishments are surely impressive; however, they belie the reality that many militia networks have remained intact. Moreover, it would be premature to deliver a final verdict on the programme until the impact of its reintegration component is adequately assessed.

Box 4.1 DDR achievements at a glance[16]

A total of:

- 63,380 former officers and soldiers of the AMF disarmed and demobilized
- 259 units decommissioned
- 53,415 ex-combatants have benefited of the reintegration option[17]
- 57,629 light and medium weapons collected.

Source: ANBP, 2006a, p. 4.

The fundamental goal of DDR was to break down military formations permanently, severing the patronage-based links between commanders and their militiamen. Reintegration programming – which included vocational training, small business support and agricultural packages[18] – may have provided the basic tools for former combatants to re-enter civilian life; however, it is unclear whether the entry points in the civilian economy will exist for them to exploit those tools over the medium and long term. With economic activity in many areas of the country still stagnant and unemployment hovering in the vicinity of 25–30 per cent, ex-combatants could be forced back into previous patterns of mobilization (UNDP, 2004, p. 57).

Until viable alternative livelihoods can be provided in the civilian economy, ex-combatants will remain vulnerable to commander power and patronage. The ready availability of illegal weapons across the country may provide a means for ex-combatants to return back into military life. Just as illegal weapons provided an 'entry ticket' to the DDR programme, they also provide readmission into the militias, a tool to roll back the reintegration process.

While on the surface the DDR programme may have formally decommissioned 259 AMF units, the informal networks that bind those units together are merely dormant and can be reconstituted by commanders at will. Disrupting the integrity of the militias will remain an impossible task as long as commanders have access to money garnered from the illicit economy; guns withheld from the demilitarization process and purchased anew on the black market; and militiamen who lack long-term employment prospects in the licit economy.

As the preceding analysis shows, disarmament represented a marginal aspect of the DDR programme. In fact, at one stage, the Japanese government considered the notion of removing the disarmament component from the process altogether. Such thinking was based on the rationale that the security environment was not conducive for disarmament and that allowing ex-combatants to retain their arms for self-defence would remove any impediment to their demobilization and reintegration. Although this notion was eventually dismissed, few would characterize the ANBP as a disarmament programme (Rossi and Giustozzi, 2006, p. 5).

By the time of the reintegration phase's conclusion in June 2006, 56,365 ex-combatants had benefited from reintegration packages, which were typically nine months in duration. However, significant criticism has been raised over the efficacy of reintegration programming (Rossi and Giustozzi, 2006; Dennys, 2005). A focal point of attention was the consultation phase of the process, in which ANBP case workers steered ex-combatants toward particular reintegration options. This crucial step was taken without the aid of a formal labour market survey.[19] Although ex-combatants were responsible for choosing their reintegration option, several observers saw case workers placing undue pressure on ex-combatants to select particular reintegration packages.[20] Ex-combatants were often steered to reintegration options due to considerations of programme availability and administrative expediency rather than on sound analysis of market gaps and needs in a specific region (Dennys, 2005, p. 4).

In an effort to gauge the impact of the reintegration process, the ANBP launched a Client Evaluation Survey of 5,000 programme beneficiaries who had received at least six to nine months of reintegration assistance. The survey results were extremely positive: 93 per cent of respondents were satisfied with the reintegration assistance that they received, and 90 per cent were still employed.[21] What the survey did not illustrate was the sustainability of this situation, i.e., the resilience of the ex-combatants to natural fluctuations in the economy. Would ex-combatants be able to endure the inevitable burst of the international aid bubble, which has provided a steady stream of labour-intensive aid projects? To ensure that Afghan ex-combatants will not fall back into previous patterns of military mobilization, they require, among other things, continuous long-term support from a permanent government body. Recognizing this reality, plans have been introduced to build the capacity of key ministries, such as the Ministries of Labour and Social Affairs and Agriculture, to 'deliver reintegration services over the long-term' to former combatants (ANBP, 2006a, p. 2). One such plan envisages the integration of some of the structures of the ANBP into a special branch of the Ministry of Labour and Social Affairs.[22]

While the Client Evaluation Survey sought to measure the impact of the reintegration component of the programme, little consideration has been given to examining the effects of its disarmament counterpart. To assess the impact of disarmament, a prospective monitoring and evaluation system could use indicators such as: levels of gun ownership; rates of violent crime involving firearms; and price levels of firearms in the legal and black markets.

Pillar 2 – Heavy weapons cantonment (HWC)

The sight of heavy weapons, ranging from tanks to SCUD missiles, most in a state of disrepair, was common in Afghanistan until the Taliban's fall. The collapse of the communist and Taliban regimes led to the distribution of military equipment to numerous factional groups across the country. Direct imports from external state and non-state patrons coupled with weapons captured in military operations were another source of heavy weapons. While once greatly valued both militarily and financially, such weapons are increasingly viewed as redundant in the contemporary strategic environment in Afghanistan, where international military forces, notably air power, have neutralized any conventional military threat to the state, and stealth and agility are the new strategic imperatives. Moreover, most non-state actors lack the expertise or resources to maintain heavy weapons. Accordingly, Afghan commanders have displayed an increased willingness to relinquish their heavy weapons.

The notion of heavy weapons cantonment (HWC) in Afghanistan first emerged in 2003 in the northern province of Balkh in response to rising tensions between the two principal government-affiliated militia groups in the region, Jamiat-e-Islami led by General Atta Mohammad and Junbish-e-Milli, headed by Rashid Dostum. Armed confrontations between the two groups, which featured the deployment of tanks on several occasions, resulted in the deaths of numerous combatants by early October 2004. A ceasefire agreement between the opposing parties, brokered by UNAMA, the former Afghan Interior Minister, Ali Jalali and the British Ambassador Ron Nash, paved the way for the merger of the Jamiat-controlled 7th Corps and the Junbish-controlled 8th Corps of the AMF and the collection of their heavy weapons. The British Provincial Reconstruction Team (PRT) in Mazar-e-Sharif surveyed the weapons holdings of each group and, after obfuscation and delays by the two factions, collected and cantoned the majority of the weapons in two sites west of the city. Both groups withheld some arms from the process, but the initiative nonetheless set an important precedent (ICG, 2005, pp. 9–10).

In January 2004, the NATO-led International Security Assistance Force (ISAF) reached an agreement with the Afghan Defence Ministry to remove all heavy weapons from Kabul to three sites immediately outside the city,[23] fulfilling one of the provisions of the Bonn Agreement which called for the demilitarization of the capital (Bonn Agreement, 2001, Annex 1, No. 4). The programme reached its fruition in September 2004, completing the transfer of all heavy weapons outside the city. The ISAF initiative created momentum that led to the acceleration of ANBP efforts to canton heavy weapons on a countrywide level. Although formal responsibility for the collection of heavy weapons was conferred on the ANBP in 2003 it was the entry of ISAF in the process in early 2004 that gave it the momentum needed to achieve tangible results.

The countrywide HWC programme, funded by the United States, Canada and NATO, was formally launched by a presidential decree issued on 27 March 2004 calling for the cantonment of all AMF heavy weaponry by the Defence Ministry, with ANBP assistance (ICG, 2005, p. 9). A subsequent presidential decree issued on 7 September 2004 declared all heavy weapons to be the exclusive property of the state (Presidential Decree No. 69, 7 September 2004).

The programme was shaped by a national survey conducted in the summer of 2004 that identified 5,606 heavy weapons in circulation. The weapons were recorded and categorized according to weapons type – including armoured personnel carriers, artillery, anti-tank weapons, main battle tanks, mortars and surface-to-air missiles (Post-Conflict Reforms Website, 2006). The survey classified 1,604 of the weapons as operational, 2,600 as repairable and the remaining 1,402 as wrecks (ANBP, 2004).

Four weapons collection teams were formed to collect the operational and repairable weapons and transport them to one of 15 regional cantonment sites protected by the ANA.[24] The teams were responsible for locating the weapons, negotiating with commanders to secure their release and transporting them to secure sites. In the summer of 2004, the Coalition and ISAF lent their support to the process, helping the ANBP meet the immense logistical challenges posed by the programme.

The weapons systems cantoned were rendered inoperative through the removal of key components, such as the weapon's breechblock or fuel pump, by the ANBP's main implementing partner, the HALO Trust. Accordingly, even if the cantonment sites are compromised, the weapons cannot be used. Nonetheless, regular inspections by Afghan and international observers are undertaken to ensure that the weapons are secure. Serviceable spare parts garnered from the process are transported and held at the Pul-e-charkhi weapons depot in Kabul.[25]

As of June 2006, 12,248 heavy weapons had been collected and cantoned (see Table 4.2), far exceeding the number identified by the national survey (ANBP, 2006a, p. 10). This discrepancy can be attributed to two factors. First, the ANBP conceded that the scope of the initial survey was limited in that it relied on cooperation from local actors and

Table 4.2 Breakdown of heavy weapons cantoned

Weapon type	Number cantoned
Anti aircraft guns	4,322
Armoured personnel carrier	437
Artillery guns	1,147
Anti tank weapons	1,501
Main battle tanks	633
Multi-barrel rocket launchers	1,329
Mortars	2,821
Other heavy weapons	58
Total	12,248

Source: ANBP, 2006a, p. 10.

could only identify weapons that were 'found or known, and accessible' not those that were deliberately concealed (ICG, 2005, p. 10).

Second, there is a growing realization among commanders that the international military presence in the country, particularly US air power, has made heavy weapons redundant. Storing and maintaining heavy weaponry is no longer perceived by commanders as a cost-effective means to advance their interests (ICG, 2005, pp. 10–11). In the absence of all-out war, lightly equipped and highly mobile militia units provide the better means to advance factional interests. Small arms are easy to use, maintain, conceal and transport, ideal for engagement in the illicit economy or to wage an asymmetric conflict against international military actors. For the most part, heavy weapons in the hands of non-state actors are outdated, only partially functioning and costly to maintain. Where commanders have resisted the process, such as in the Panjsher valley, it is predominantly due to the symbolism of the disarmament act and the growing perception among some ethnic factions, including the Panjsheri Tajiks, that the process is targeting them disproportionately.[26]

While the HWC programme has benefited from the change in attitudes towards the utility of heavy weapons, the increased emphasis on maintaining the integrity of militia groups has, as a surrogate, placed new pressure on the DDR programme and its successor, the DIAG process.

Pillar 3 – Disbandment of Illegal Armed Groups (DIAG)

A glaring shortcoming of the mandate of the DDR programme was its singular focus on officers and soldiers within the formal structure of the AMF, ignoring informal militia groups. Afghanistan's illegal armed groups range from tribal self-defence forces to criminal gangs (ICG, 2005, pp. 11–12). The Afghan government defines an illegal armed group as: 'a group of five or more armed individuals operating outside the law, drawing its cohesion from (a) loyalty to the commander, (b) receipt of material benefits, (c) impunity enjoyed by members, [and] (d) shared ethnic or social background' (Islamic Republic of Afghanistan, 2006a, p. 2).

The failure to target these groups from the outset of the process allowed them to solidify their power bases and consolidate their control over vital sources of revenue, such as the drug trade. Moreover, as the DIAG strategy affirms;

> several groups who entered the AMF and were formally demobilized through the DDR programme retained in many cases their core staff and a substantial amount of light weapons ... [and] a number of commanders retained control of armed groups through their position as governors, chiefs of police and other local official positions.
>
> (Islamic Republic of Afghanistan, 2006a, p. 1)

Both the groups excluded from the DDR mandate and those that did fall under its remit but were able to circumvent the process, present a major obstacle to the consolidation of security and good governance. The threat these groups pose to the state is multifaceted: they collect illegal taxes, obstructing government revenue collection; they are involved in the illegal exploitation of natural resources – oil, gas, coal and gemstones – and, in some cases, have assumed control over state-owned industries; they subvert reform processes and intimidate local government officials and security forces; and they drive the illegal economy, most notably the drug trade (Islamic Republic of Afghanistan, 2006a, Annex A, p. 4). The power that these groups wield stems from their monopolization of the means of violence in their regional strongholds. Their access to guns has enabled them to insulate their interests, carve out mini-fiefdoms and curtail the expansion of government authority into the periphery. This made a further round of disarmament necessary.

The legal foundation for a process to confront illegally armed groups in the country was set in July 2004 with the promulgation of Presidential Decree 50, which designated all armed groups outside of the AMF illegal and called for their disbandment (Presidential Decree No. 50, 14 July 2006). In February 2005, as the formal DDR programme entered its final phase, the ANBP was authorized and funded with a grant from the Canadian government to begin planning a programme to disband illegal armed groups. A planning cell was established within the ANBP to collect intelligence and, in conjunction with the Afghan government and a range of international stakeholders, to devise an approach to address the problem.

The planning cell estimated that there were 1,870 illegal militia groups in the country comprising roughly 129,000 militiamen.[27] The government has conservatively estimated that these groups possess approximately 336,000 small arms and light weapons, 56,000 of which are believed to have been surreptitiously concealed from the DDR process by the AMF. The actual number is likely to be much higher considering the scale of previous arms transfers into the country and the size of illegal weapons caches uncovered by Coalition, ISAF and government security forces since 2001.

The ANBP built a database of information on illegal armed groups from a variety of sources, including the NATO-led ISAF, the Coalition, the Ministry of Interior, the Ministry of Defence, the National Directorate of Security (NDS) and UNAMA. The groups were sorted according to their threat level, which was assessed on the basis of the threat they pose to good governance, to the National Assembly and Provincial Council Elections, and to counter-narcotics operations. In each category, a group is assigned a threat rating on a scale of zero to three, with three denoting a high level of threat. A total of 25 groups were deemed high risk in all three categories.[28]

Whereas disarmament represented merely a symbolic step in the DDR process, it occupies a more central role in the DIAG programme. Nonetheless, disarmament is still held as a means to break down illegal militias, rather than an end in itself. The programme has diverged from the incentives approach of the DDR programme, approaching the problem of illegal armed groups as a law enforcement issue. While development incentives are provided to communities where commanders comply with the process, direct incentives are not provided to militiamen submitting their arms. Force is supposed to be used to disarm groups that do not voluntarily comply.

While the DDR process was an internationally driven process, the DIAG programme is government led (see Figure 4.3). The D&R Commission has assumed the dual role of DIAG Steering Committee[29] and high-level policy lead for the process, giving it strategic direction and coordinating the various actors engaged in it at the political level. The Commission reports to the Security Coordination Forum,[30] a national level coordination committee chaired by the President.

Under the DIAG Steering Committee is another consultative body, the DIAG Forum, responsible for coordinating DIAG activities at the operational level. Its institutional composition is identical to that of the DIAG Steering Committee but, whereas the Steering Committee is a ministerial- and ambassadorial-level body, the forum assembles its deputies and provides direction to the Joint Secretariat, the central implementing body for the programme.

The Joint Secretariat collects and collates data, engages in public information activities and supports operational planning and implementation by serving as a node connecting the DIAG Forum with the DIAG Provincial Committees, which are responsible for grassroots implementation. The ANBP provides technical assistance and expertise to the Joint Secretariat, which also comprises working level representatives from the

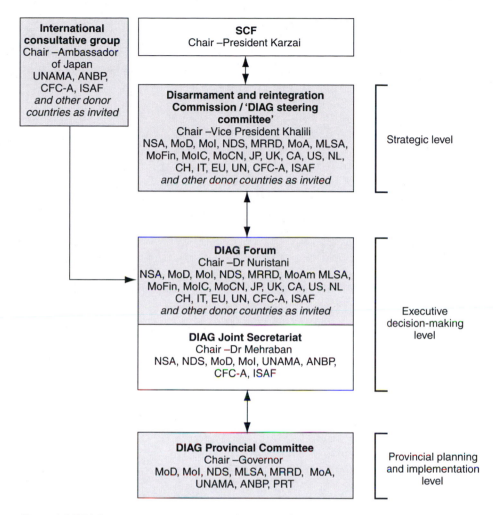

Figure 4.3 DIAG management structure (source: Islamic Republic of Afghanistan, 2006a, p. 6).

DIAG Steering Committee, the Office of the National Security Council, the National Directorate of Security (NDS), the Ministry of Defence, the Ministry of Interior, UNAMA, Combined Forces Command–Afghanistan, the ANBP and ISAF.

The DIAG Provincial Committees are chaired by the provincial governor and comprise the deputy governor, the chief of police, the provincial NDS director, the provincial department heads of the Ministries of Defence, Labour and Social Affairs, Rural Rehabilitation and Development and Agriculture and representatives of the ANBP, UNAMA and the

Provincial Reconstruction Team (where they exist).[31] While the DIAG process is centrally planned, it is implemented by local actors spearheaded by the Provincial Committees. The DIAG process is flexible, allowing the Provincial Committees to develop individual regional implementation plans, in line with the overall parameters of the process and in consultation with the DIAG Forum and Joint Secretariat (Islamic Republic of Afghanistan, 2006a, p. 5).

The programme aims to disarm and disband 'all identifiable illegal armed groups' by the end of 2007 (Islamic Republic of Afghanistan, 2006a, p. 7). Its estimated cost is $11 million with a $35 million fund earmarked for community development projects, the bulk of the funding coming from the Government of Japan.[32] The DIAG programme has been staggered in three stages: the National Assembly and Provincial Council Elections (NAPCE) stage, the Government Officials with Links to Illegal Armed Groups (GOLIAG) stage and the main stage (Islamic Republic of Afghanistan, 2006a, pp. 2–4).

The National Assembly and Provincial Council Elections (NAPCE) stage

The NAPCE stage involved the targeting of commanders who had entered as candidates in the legislative elections. Just as the presidential elections gave the ANBP more traction to disarm AMF commanders with political ambitions, it was envisaged that the legislative elections would provide the DIAG programme with comparable leverage. Afghanistan's electoral law is very clear on the issue of commanders engaging in the democratic process, prohibiting 'anyone who commands or belongs to an unofficial military force or armed group from becoming a candidate' (Islamic Republic of Afghanistan, 2005e, Art. 15, No. 3).

Prior to the polls, a list of 1,108 candidates with potential links to armed groups – out of the roughly 6,000 contesting the polls – was compiled by the Joint Secretariat and passed to the independent Electoral Complaints Commission (ECC), formed to adjudicate all electoral complaints and challenges. Candidates were only listed if they were identified by more than two sources on the Joint Secretariat, one of which had to be Afghan. From this list, the ECC provisionally disqualified 207 candidates pending their compliance with the directive to disarm (ANBP, 2006a, p. 12).

This led to the submission of 4,857 weapons from 124 candidates (ANBP, 2006a, p. 12). Despite a brazen failure to comply among the remaining candidates, the ECC, under pressure from the government and international community, chose to exclude only 34 candidates from the ballot for links to armed groups (ICG, 2006, p. 4). The Afghan Independent Human Rights Commission (AIHRC) would affirm in the aftermath of the election that more than 80 per cent of the winning candidates in the provinces and 60 per cent in Kabul maintained ties to armed groups (IRIN, 2005b).

The laissez-faire approach to the vetting process was driven by concerns that armed power brokers barred from the elections would oppose the central government, undermining the fragile network of disparate groups that President Karzai had constructed. The international community was complicit in this accommodationist approach, opposing any step that could jeopardize the landmark event and exacerbate insecurity and instability (Sedra and Middlebrook, 2005). Even its marginal successes must be qualified, as few of the commanders that did engage with the process are believed to have fully complied, only submitting samples of their weapons stocks. The NAPCE stage represented a significant missed opportunity to jump-start the nascent DIAG process.

The government and international community squandered rare leverage to advance the DIAG programme and sent a signal to non-state actors that the government was not serious about disarmament. A more forceful and rigorous application of the vetting procedures would have had a powerful demonstration effect, compelling armed actors with political ambition to buy into the demilitarization project.

The Government Officials with Links to Illegal Armed Groups (GOLIAG) stage

The GOLIAG stage was a product of the growing awareness that a significant number of government officials in Afghanistan maintained links to illegally armed groups. In September 2005, the Joint Secretariat compiled a list of 600 government officials with suspected links to armed groups for internal consultation and deliberation. As with the NAPCE stage, the process can only move forward after agreement on a specific candidate is reached by one Afghan and one international member of the Joint Secretariat.[33]

In the first round of the process, a consensus could only be reached on 28 of the officials listed. Each of the officials was given 30 days' notice to disarm voluntarily any associated armed elements. After the expiry of this period, a two-month[34] window of negotiation was opened to compel the actor to disarm. Failure to comply at the end of this period is supposed to result in immediate dismissal. However, of the 28 actors identified during the first round, only five were dismissed and one was killed in an unrelated incident by the end of the negotiation phase. The remaining 22 failed to comply yet retained their positions.[35]

The second round of the process identified 13 additional officials from the list of 600. After the completion of the voluntary compliance period in early April 2005, eight had partially or fully complied, submitting 1,080 weapons (Islamic Republic of Afghanistan, 2006a, p. 10). Notionally, those that have not complied face sanction or removal from their positions;

however, that would require the support of the central government minister or provincial governor to whom they report, which has rarely been forthcoming. The majority of the figures targeted for the process have been employed by the Ministry of Interior. Despite being a key stakeholder in the DIAG process, the Ministry has resisted efforts to remove targeted officials. Even when it has complied with the process, the Ministry has tended to shift officials to different positions rather then remove them outright. By June 2006, eight officials in the Ministry of Interior had been earmarked by the Joint Secretariat for dismissal, but the Ministry had only agreed to the removal of three by the end of the month.[36]

The GOLIAG stage has demonstrated how deeply entrenched patronage networks are in the Afghan government and society. The process has proven singularly unsuccessful in deconstructing those patronage links, not only between commanders and their militiamen but between commanders and their superiors ensconced in the government.

The main stage

A pilot project for the main stage of the DIAG process was launched in late May 2005, shortly after the ratification of the DIAG project concept document by the government on 15 May 2005. The pilot project targeted low risk groups in three areas: Laghman, Maimana and Nangarhar. The modest results of the pilot project informed the design of the strategy paper for the process, released in January 2006, which proposes breaking down the disarmament exercise into three phases: Voluntary Compliance, Negotiated Compliance and Enforced Compliance (see Table 4.3) (Islamic Republic of Afghanistan, 2006a).

The first phase involves the fostering of conditions conducive to voluntary compliance. Compliance is defined as the submission of 70 per cent of the estimated weapons of the illegally armed group being targeted (Islamic Republic of Afghanistan, 2005b). However, it is important to note that, unlike the DDR programme, there is no prescription that the weapons submitted meet a certain standard of functionality. Ex-combatants are informed of their legal obligations to disarm and provided with a 30-day amnesty period to comply.

Community and religious leaders are used as intermediaries to encourage commanders to cooperate with the process. The prospect of community development incentives in exchange for disarmament is introduced to local communities as a means to place pressure on militiamen and their commanders. Provincial Community Development Teams are used to coordinate and oversee the implementation of mutually agreed development projects in communities that meet the DIAG programme's criteria for compliance (Islamic Republic of Afghanistan, 2005d).

While many observers have likened the DIAG programme to a weapons-for-development scheme, such as that pioneered in Gramsch,

Table 4.3 The three phases of the DIAG process

	Phase 1 *Voluntary compliance*	Phase 2 *Negotiated compliance*	Phase 3 *Enforced compliance*
Political levers	Public information campaign Presidential decree Law on weapons	Public information reinforcement Negotiation at national level Use political parties Negotiation at provincial level Negotiation at local level Legal deadline	Public information residual Law enforcement Shame list Forcible compliance/removal
Cultural levers	Influence via *shuras*/elders	Negotiation by *shuras*/elders Influence through *jirga*	
Religious levers	Influence via fatwa/mosque	Negotiation by fatwa Influence through mosques	
Economic levers	Influence via access to incentive programmes	Influence via access to incentive programmes Programme deadline	Denied access to all development programmes

Source: Islamic Republic of Afghanistan, 2005f.

Albania, the Afghan government has sought to dispel this notion. The 'Guidelines for DIAG Development Activities' clearly state that 'development projects shall not be considered as direct incentives to, or rewards for, disarmament, but may serve as a motivation for the community (*shuras*,[37] leaders) to persuade the illegal armed group to disarm and disband' (Islamic Republic for Afghanistan, 2005c). The government is keen to avoid incentivizing the illegal possession of arms, opting instead to emphasize the obligation of armed groups to disarm under state law.

Phase two comes into effect when the designated period for voluntary compliance has expired. It involves multi-track negotiation at the national and provincial levels as well as through local actors such as village *mullahs* and local *shuras*. Public information efforts are intensified with a focus on the implications of non-compliance, most notably the denial of access to community development funds.

When the negotiation window expires, the enforcement phase comes into effect. The mandate for enforcing the process falls to the Ministry of Interior and the Afghan National Police. Political mechanisms such as 'shame lists' may also be used to induce compliance. In extreme circumstances, the Afghan National Army and international security forces could be called in to assist. All development opportunities associated with the process are withdrawn during this phase.

ANBP mobile disarmament teams collect weaponry from illegally armed groups and transport them to Weapons Collection Points (WCPs) that have been established in every province. The WCPs are guarded by the ANA and are supervised by ANBP Weapons Collection Teams (Islamic Republic of Afghanistan, 2005d). Receipts are provided to groups that submit weapons. The receipt is particularly important, as numerous cases have emerged of NDS and Ministry of Interior personnel fraudulently confiscating arms under the name of the programme. The arms seized in these unsanctioned operations have characteristically been sold or distributed to militia allies. Such incidents have been reported to the government, but no action has been taken.[38] All officially collected weapons are subsequently transferred from the WCPs to the main weapons depot in Kabul.

The main phase of the process was launched on 1 May 2006 in Kapisa Province. It proceeds in stages, addressing a set number of provinces in each stage. Along with Kapisa, the provinces of Farah, Hirat, Laghman and Takhar were targeted in the first stage. In each province, the programme will begin by targeting what have been deemed to be the 'top four illegally armed groups,' those who pose the highest risk according to the programme's threat level matrix. In Kapisa, 38 commanders were issued notices at the launch of the process, instructing them to submit their weapons within the standard 30-day period. By the end of the 30-day voluntary period in Kapisa, only seven weapons had been submitted, exposing serious problems in the structure of the programme.[39]

As of June 2006, the DIAG process had engaged 1,275 illegally armed groups, resulting in the collection of 24,182 weapons. These weapons were predominantly collected during the NAPCE stage of the process and through ongoing *ad hoc* voluntary weapons submissions. Only 40 per cent of the weapons collected have been categorized as usable, a product of the programme's failure to insist on the submission of serviceable firearms. Illegal armed groups are giving the perception of cooperation by merely dumping their unserviceable equipment, concealing their best weaponry either for use or for sale on the illicit weapons market. Furthermore, the wholesale lack of compliance witnessed during the first phase of the process revealed the inability of the programme to engage commanders effectively. The same problem was experienced during the early stages of the DDR programme and resulted in the establishment of the Commander Incentive Programme. However, the unwillingness of the government and principal donors to provide individualized incentives to soldiers and commanders transgressing the weapons law prevented the establishment of a similar initiative under the auspices of the DIAG programme. One official of the Joint Secretariat said 'DIAG nearly died' due to the disappointing early results of the main stage.[40]

The initial stages of the DIAG process – the NAPCE, GOLIAG and main stages – have failed to achieve their goals due in large part to a lack of political will among the government. At the second Tokyo conference on the 'Consolidation of Peace in Afghanistan,' held on 5 July 2006, President Karzai reiterated the government's 'strong commitment to stand firm on DIAG and accomplish it at any cost despite the difficulties and challenges lying ahead' (Government of Japan, 2006). In this government statement, as in so many others regarding the demilitarization process, rhetoric has not matched reality.

The most conspicuous example of the tenuous nature of the government's commitment to the process relates to the GOLIAG stage. High profile government ministries, even those directly involved in the DIAG process, have obstructed and even subverted it. The executive branch, rather then championing the concept across the government, pressuring government officials up to the level of ministers to comply, has sought to provide protection for government officials targeted by the DIAG process.

Besides simple subterfuge and graft, one of the primary means by which commanders have been able to evade the process has been through their ties with officials in the central government. Government officials up to the level of minister maintain links with armed groups across the country, often based on ethnic or political ties, providing them with political cover. Drug mafia networks that extend into the government have also enabled militias involved in the trade to circumvent the process. The massive profits accrued from the trade by numerous high-ranking officials have provided a powerful incentive to shield drug traffickers and their foot soldiers. They are protecting what is for many government officials their most lucrative source of income.

According to one official of the Joint Secretariat, the body was instructed by the government not to pursue government officials at the governor or cabinet level.[41] The names of several cabinet ministers, governors and parliamentarians appear on the list of the top ten illegally armed groups in the country, as compiled by the Joint Secretariat. Until serious effort is made to persuade these figures to disarm, the process may remain paralysed. According to a senior ANBP official, the programme's first mistake was its failure to target the 30 highest profile commanders in the country at its outset. If it had done so, 'the rest would have rolled over.'[42] However, such an approach ran contrary to the accommodationist approach of President Karzai and the United States; it risked unravelling the fragile coalition of commanders and power brokers that they had constructed.

Countervailing logic affirms that this fragile coalition, while assuring a degree of stability in the short term, has hindered the state-building process. The power of many of the commanders or warlords that the government appeases is overstated. For instance, the removal of Fahim, viewed as the most powerful warlord in the country, as Defence Minister in 2004 did not trigger the *coup d'état* that many had predicted. Similarly, the transfer of Ismail Khan from the governor's post in his regional stronghold of Hirat to a ministerial post in Kabul only aroused a minor anti-government outburst. These incidents showed that the government has more scope for action against regional commanders, some of whom could be described as 'paper tigers,' than it has used.

As time has passed and these commanders have consolidated their positions, the scope for action has decreased. Many of the commanders who could have been sidelined in 2002–2003 with relative ease now require the threat or even the use of force in order to be contained. The dichotomy between accommodationism and instability advanced by the Karzai administration is a false one. Quite to the contrary, the government will only be able to assure the long-term stability of the country by confronting warlords and commanders who challenge the sovereignty of the government.

While support for the DIAG process within the executive branch has been tepid, it has verged on collapse in Parliament. In late May 2006, the upper house of Parliament, the *Meshrano Jirga*, unexpectedly approved a resolution calling for the temporary halt of the DIAG process, on the grounds that the adverse security environment demanded that Afghans be allowed to maintain their weapons for self-defence. This is perhaps unsurprising considering the high proportion of members of Parliament with links to armed elements.[43]

Nonetheless, for the DIAG process to recover from its significant early setbacks, President Karzai must not only convince the international donor community of the government's resolve and dedication to realizing the goals of the process, he must also impress upon his own government the need to adopt these goals. The donor reaction to the intra-governmental divisions over the DIAG programme has been muted. This can be attributed to an unwillingness to place undue pressure on President Karzai and to avert the perception that the programme is being imposed externally. Unlike the DDR programme, which was undertaken under the auspices of the ANBP, the DIAG programme was intended to be fully government owned and directed, with only technical support from the donor community.

The unwillingness of the government and international community to attach credible incentives to the programme has also contributed to its inertia. Given that many of the high-threat groups targeted by the DIAG process are alienated from the communities in which they reside and are deeply immersed in the profitable illicit economy, it is unlikely that the promise of community development projects will be sufficient to secure their cooperation. One former commander from Faryab Province called the programme 'completely unfair' in an interview with the *Institute for War and Peace Reporting*. In an indication that the non-incentivized approach of the DIAG process may not be feasible, he went on to say that 'if the time for using weapons is gone, at least we can sell them. That would be better than giving them to the government for free' (Ibrahimi, 2006b).

It is clear that the government may have to consider providing targeted incentives to groups to secure their engagement with the process. Of course, such an incentive framework will only have perverse effects if it is not buttressed by credible and robust disincentives in the form of security force coercion. Even on this score, it is unlikely that the government has the capacity and political will to disarm uncooperative groups forcibly. Despite non-compliance by targeted groups during all stages of the process, the government, as of June 2006, had yet to employ force as dictated by the programme.

Achieving the goals of the DIAG process must involve serious efforts to crack down on corruption and factionalization in the government. Sidelining the commanders in the periphery can only be achieved by either removing or reforming their backers ensconced in the central government in Kabul. To make real headway on demilitarization, the government will have to confront some high profile officials deeply entrenched in the post-Taliban political order, jettisoning the accommodationist posture that has sustained the administration since the fall of the Taliban. The government can only embark on this path with the unwavering support of the international donor community, who have themselves directly and indirectly supported leaders with links to armed elements and the illicit economy. The small arms problem in Afghanistan is inherently political and necessitates a political solution.

The belief that illegal militias can be compelled to disarm voluntarily without incentives or coerced to comply by a police force that is still under-resourced, poorly trained and under-equipped reflects the unrealistic nature of the programme's design. Perhaps most worrying is that the programme appeared to miss the clear lessons of the DDR programme, which showed the need for more incentives, not less – particularly directed at commanders – and recognized the limitations of the government's coercive capacity. As one Western official stated in June 2006, 'DIAG was designed in isolation from reality.'[44]

Pillar 4 – Anti-Personnel Mines and Ammunition Stockpile Destruction project (APMASD)

While much of the focus of the demilitarization process has been on small arms, light weapons and heavy weapons, it is believed that Afghanistan possesses one of the largest open stockpiles of ammunition in the world. Although some ammunition was collected under the auspices of the NDC's abortive disarmament initiative, the ANBP did not systematically collect ammunition. Limited amounts of ammunition have also been collected by the DIAG programme but only on an *ad hoc* basis. The government and international community were slow to take steps to address the ammunition dilemma. This stemmed partly from the difficulty of situating the issue within the wider demilitarization process. It does not neatly fall under the remit of the DDR, DIAG, HWC or Mine Action programmes.

In November 2004, a survey was conducted to gain a more precise picture of the problem. The Preparatory Assistance project, funded by the government of Canada, estimated that there may be approximately 100,000 metric tons of ammunition in the country, a large proportion of which had either been abandoned or left unguarded (ANBP, 2006a, p. 7). Ammunition caches, which litter the country, provide a ready source of explosive material for insurgent and terrorist groups that can be utilized to construct improvised explosive devices (IEDs), perhaps the most pervasive weapon utilized against Afghan and international military forces.[45]

Ammunition that has been exposed to the elements for a significant amount of time poses a significant risk to civilians who may come into contact with it. The accidental explosion of an illegal munitions store in Bajgah, Baghlan Province in May 2005, killing 28 and wounding 70, acutely demonstrated the volatility of some of the aging munitions caches in the country (ANBP, 2006a, p. 7). This incident also provided a glimpse of how commanders have been able to evade the DDR process. The owner of the weapons, Jalal Bajgah, had ostensibly disarmed under the DDR programme, but, as the incident demonstrated, withheld a significant amount of weapons from the process. The munitions included artillery and tank shells, as well as rocket-propelled grenades and smaller ammunition (BBC Online, 2005).

The massive scale of ammunition proliferation, coupled with the unique demands of disposal and destruction, justify a dedicated programme. The security and public health risk unguarded ammunition poses is comparable to that of landmines and should be treated with equal urgency. Therefore, in late 2004, the decision was made to establish a stand-alone ammunition programme, with links to mine action activities, under the auspices of the ANBP.

A memorandum of understanding between the Ministry of Defence and the UNDP establishing the APMASD programme was signed in December 2004, but a nationwide programme did not formally commence until July 2005. Although the Ministry of Defence was designated as the lead agency for the project, the ANBP gradually became the de facto lead, due in large part to a lack of capacity within the Ministry. A unit was established within the ANBP to advance the process, with regional operations directed out of the eight ANBP regional offices. The project was earmarked to last for two years at a cost of $16 million, with Canada, the UK, the European Commission and UNDP being the main financial contributors (see Table 4.4).[46]

Programme operations are supported by two implementing partners, DynCorp International (sub-contracted to UXB International) and the HALO Trust, which are primarily responsible for ammunition disposal. The UN Mine Action Centre for Afghanistan (UNMACA) is also a partner organization in the programme. UNMACA had originally planned to undertake its own survey of mine stocks in the country in conjunction with the Afghan government's Department of Disaster Preparedness and Relief, to ensure that Afghanistan met its obligations as a state party to the Ottawa Convention, also known as the Convention on the Prohibition of the Use, Stockpiling, Production and Transfer of Anti-Personnel Mines and on Their Destruction, endorsed on 1 March 2003.[47] Article seven of the treaty obligated the government to destroy all stocks of mines within four years or by February 2007. However, instead it partnered with the APMASD programme to carry out the survey (ANBP, 2006a, p. 8).[48]

Demonstrating the massive amounts of mines still stockpiled in informal caches across the country, in late March 2006, more than 80 tons of TNT and over 15,000 anti-personnel and anti-vehicle landmines, detonators and other hazardous explosives were discovered in five antiquated bunkers near Shibirghan of Jawzjan Province. The cache, one of the largest found in Afghanistan over the past four years, was discovered by a

Table 4.4 APMASD funding breakdown (as of June 2006)

Donor	Commitment (US$)
Canada	5.1 million
United Kingdom	3 million
European Commission	1.8 million
UNDP	0.5 million

Source: ANBP, 2006a, p. 8.

contractor with UXB International attached to the APMASD project. NATO subsequently assumed control over the site with the intent of destroying the materials (United States Department of State, 2006b).

With the bulk of the ammunition in the country unstable, unprotected and hidden – in many cases abandoned in dated weapons caches – the principal imperative of the programme is detection and destruction rather than negotiated or incentivized collection. The programme is more akin to demining activities than the DDR, DIAG and HWC programmes, hence their amalgamation in APMASD. However, one principal difference remains between the landmine and ammunition collection initiatives: ammunition programming is partially intended to gather usable ammunition for government use while the landmine programme is solely dedicated to its destruction.

The APMASD programme consists of nine Ammunition Survey Teams (ASTs), which were originally mandated to assess the scale of the problem. However, their mandate soon expanded to include 'the destruction of anti-personnel mines and dangerous ammunition as well as the consolidation of disparate concentrations of ammunition' (ANBP, 2006b). Each team comprises an international adviser, a Ministry of Defence official and a representative from one of the implementing organizations. The ASTs use various sources of intelligence to locate caches of landmines and ammunition, including the National Directorate of Security (NDS), the Ministry of Interior, ANBP regional offices, the Coalition, the PRTs and ISAF.

The standard operating procedure for the ASTs can be summarized as follows: survey, segregation, transportation and destruction. Once an AST surveys a particular area and locates a cache, it proceeds to remove the material from its enclosure and segregate usable ammunition from material deemed to be unsafe. Ammunition is categorized as usable if it is packaged and earmarked for collection by the Ministry of Defence. Prior to the launch of the programme, the Ministry of Defence compiled a list of its ammunition requirements. All ammunition that does not meet the criteria is destroyed. Usable ammunition is transported to one of 12 Ministry of Defence protected consolidation points.[49]

As of July 2006, the programme had surveyed 1,057 ammunition and mine caches across the country, amounting to 31,820 mt. As the programme utilizes the 100,000 mt. estimated figure as its operational target, it is approaching the one-third mark in the process. From the caches surveyed, the programme had destroyed 6,798 tons of ammunition; 187,887 anti-personnel landmines and 11,604 anti-tank landmines by June 2006 (ANBP, 2006a, p. 8).

While the Ministry of Defence is responsible for site security at the ammunition consolidation points, numerous weapon and ammunition caches discovered by the government across the country remain unprotected. To fill this void in the interim, a new security force was created with the support of Combined Security Transition Command Afghanistan (CSTC-A)[50] – the Coalition body responsible for overseeing Coalition assistance to the Afghan security sector reform process – called the Afghan Guard Force.

Under the umbrella of the Ministry of Defence, the Afghan Guard Force comprises 3,500 soldiers (265 officers and 3,235 guards). In addition to protecting ammunition depots, it is also responsible for guarding installations, property and land of the Ministry of Defence. The Afghan Guard Force primarily consists of demobilized AMF soldiers who live in close proximity to the sites that they are mandated to protect. In many cases, they are stationed at the same posts that they occupied while serving in the AMF; they have merely been 're-hatted.'[51]

Two weeks of training are provided to Afghan Guard Force officers and one week to the rank-and-file by the CSTC-A, with oversight from the Ministry of Defence and the ANBP. The training for the guards covers weapons management, security standards, uniforms and administration. Only officers of the Afghan Guard Force are provided with weapons, primarily Kalashnikov assault rifles and 9 mm pistols yielded by the DDR programme. In October 2005, 400 Kalashnikovs and ammunition were delivered to the Afghan Guard Force, fulfilling their lethal equipment requirements. The Afghan Guard Force is only an interim measure, meant to fill a manpower gap until the APMASD project can be completed and the ANA reaches a critical mass in which it could assume all site protection responsibilities.[52]

The CSTC-A, with the support of the ANBP, has undertaken the refurbishment of two National Ammunition Depots located at Khairabad and Chimtallah, both in the immediate environs of Kabul, and four regional Ammunition Supply Points situated at the four ANA regional corps commands, in Kandahar, Gardez, Mazar-e-Sharif and Hirat. An AST was deployed to the Khairabad depot in April 2006 to support the refurbishment process. Among the accomplishments of the process by September 2006 was the rearrangement of 50 of the facility's 54 ammunition bunkers, the sorting of 10,000 tons of ammunition and the destruction of 1,400 tons of unserviceable ammunition. Ongoing activities of the programme include the completion of an inventory for the depot and the replacement of all bunker doors. The project is also funding the construction of 22 ammunition bunkers at the Central Corps Command at Pul-e-charkhi military base. Construction was completed in 2006.

In spite of these efforts to create the infrastructure to hold and safeguard ammunition stocks, insufficient attention has been paid to developing permanent human capacity to manage it.[53] In an attempt to address this gap, three ammunition trainers were hired by the ANBP and seconded to the CSTC-A's ANA Ammunition School to train ANA personnel. The pilot programme, a seven-month programme of instruction for 14 prospective Ammunition Technical Officers (ATOs), began on 11 May

2006. It covered explosive theory and ordnance in possession of the ANA, ammunition storage and movement, ammunition inspection and repair, ammunition management and inspectorate duties, and ammunition disposal. Exceptional graduates from the pilot course were subsequently trained to teach at the school. The pilot course ended in mid-December 2006 and will be followed by a second course for 20–30 students. Originally based at Pul-e-charkhi, the school – authorized by Ministry of Defence Decree 4–5 on Ammunition and Explosives Operations in Support of the Afghan Military – was shifted to the Khairabad depot in September 2006 where a new teaching facility was unveiled (ANBP, 2006b).

The establishment of the ANA Ammunition School and ATO course is an important step, but it is clear that a significant infusion of resources will be required to meet the minimum international standards for stockpile management. While the Afghan Guard Force may provide an acceptable short-term solution to address a glaring security gap, long-term technical expertise must be developed to ensure that the massive amounts of ordnance being collected and procured are handled safely and securely.

Civil society engagement in demilitarization

At the second Tokyo Conference on the Consolidation of Peace in Afghanistan, convened in July 2006 to take stock of the achievements of the demilitarization process and look to the future, the participants recognized that civil society has a crucial role to play in creating an Afghanistan 'where power resides with accountable and democratically elected representatives and in ensuring the rule of law' (Government of Japan, 2006). In Afghanistan, civil society groups form a vital medium between the centre and the periphery, through which rural communities can project their needs and concerns to the central state, and the state can, in turn, build bridges to those communities and adapt political and development processes to local realities.

Civil society groups formed the backbone of the reintegration component of the DDR programme and will similarly have a central role in delivering community development incentives under the auspices of the DIAG programme.[54] However, they have shied away from engagement in the related issue of disarmament. Security issues have tended to be viewed as the purview of the state and international donors, off-limits to civil society. When they have ventured into the security arena, they have characteristically been confined to 'soft' security issues, such as the reintegration of ex-combatants and human rights advocacy. However, over the past year, a number of civil society groups have begun to deviate from this trend, touching on 'hard' security issues, such as disarmament and the reform of the police. In light of the reticence of the government and international community to consider the idea of a comprehensive small arms reduction and control campaign, it may be up to civil society to initiate the debate. In the summer of 2006, an international NGO, Oxfam, sought to do exactly that.

On 26 June 2006, Oxfam held a seminar in Kabul that brought together representatives from 13 Afghan and international civil society organizations to address the small arms issue. The meeting sought both to provide a forum for civil society groups to explore the role they could play in mitigating the threat posed by small arms and light weapons and to 'assess opportunities for civil society to collaborate and organise policy responses regarding small arms' (Oxfam, 2006b). The seminar particip- ants recognized that the DDR and DIAG programmes 'had not been suc- cessful' and that 'their impact on security was minimal' (Oxfam, 2006b). They confirmed a trend of 'rearmament and remilitarisation both of mili- tias and even amongst civil society' in response to escalating levels of inse- curity and political uncertainty. In spite of these conditions, the participants affirmed the importance of addressing the small arms issue with some urgency, as 'the window of opportunity for dealing with small arms in Afghanistan may be closing sooner rather than later' (Oxfam, 2006b).

The conference was intended to serve as a launching pad for an Oxfam-funded project to empower Afghan civil society actors 'to engage the Government and donors on the issue of small arms' (Oxfam, 2006c). While the project is tiny in the context of the broader demilitarization effort – its budget is £2,000 ($3,600) – it represents a necessary initial step, albeit late, in generating a societal dialogue on the issue. Its long-term goals are to re-examine and deconstruct the notion of the Afghan 'gun culture' and compel the government and donors to take steps to address 'the root causes of small arms proliferation' (Oxfam, 2006c). By chan- nelling domestic perceptions on the issue into a coherent advocacy cam- paign and raising awareness among government and international actors of the intricacies of the problem, civil society actors could spur govern- ment and donor stakeholders into action.[55]

The failure of donor and civil society actors to launch an initiative of this type earlier, coupled with the minute level of funding dedicated to it, reflects the surprising absence of dialogue on small arms issues among international actors working in the country. This can be attributed to, as already mentioned, an unwillingness to challenge a perceived 'gun culture,' which is seen as an unalienable element of Afghan society. Just as the ANBP treated disarmament as a symbolic element of the DDR process, international and local civil society actors have prioritized what are seen as more manageable issues in the areas of development or social protection. International NGOs could have taken a more active role in promoting civil society engagement in the small arms issue, lobbying donors, for example, to fund initiatives of the type launched by Oxfam, at an earlier stage and on a greater scale.

Perhaps a more fundamental obstacle to civil society engagement in the small arms issue relates to the state-centric focus of international donors. The bulk of donor assistance has been channelled to strengthening state institutions rather than empowering civil society actors. Moreover, the Afghan state has tended to view civil society actors as competitors for international assistance rather than as partners in the reconstruction process, a perception that the international donor community has done little to assuage. As a result, the government and donor community have failed to exploit opportunities for collaboration between the government and civil society around issues like small arms, where there is clear scope for complementarity.

Lessons learnt and major findings

A number of lessons can be drawn from the analysis of the demilitarization process about the implementation of small arms reduction and control processes in post-conflict environments. First, the failure to identify disarmament and small arms proliferation as a priority in the initial stages of the post-Taliban period hindered subsequent disarmament efforts. It missed a seminal opportunity to advance the process at a time when public support for the measure was high, the security situation was relatively stable and regional warlords and spoilers had yet to regroup and entrench themselves. The Afghan government and international actors have always perceived the notion of complete disarmament as a distant goal that can only be achieved under ideal security and political conditions.

Accordingly, the disarmament measures that have been implemented in the context of the demilitarization process have had a very limited and symbolic character, whose main purpose was to facilitate and validate the decommissioning of militia units. The Afghan experience demonstrates the importance of addressing small arms issues and disarmament from an early stage of the post-conflict period. This does not necessarily entail the immediate launch of a community weapons collection programme; rather, it should involve efforts to gauge the extent of the problem, sensitize the public of the dangers it poses and develop the political consensus needed to address it.

Second, the lack of empirical data on the extent and nature of the small arms dilemma has marred efforts to devise effective programmes to confront it. Neither the DDR nor DIAG programmes launched a survey of the small arms situation prior to developing their strategic plans. Collecting data on this issue presents a major challenge and would invariably lack precision, but even a basic survey of the issue would have greatly aided planning and implementation. The two programmes have operated without adequate knowledge of the scale of the small arms problem, both in terms of militia holdings of weapons and those in the hands of private citizens. By contrast, surveys of heavy weapons and ammunition were conducted to guide both the HWC and APMASD programmes. While imperfect, the surveys imbued the two programmes with a degree of structure and direction lacking in the disarmament component of the DDR and DIAG programmes. It is clear that one of the first steps that must be undertaken by any prospective DDR programme is to develop as detailed a picture as possible of the small arms problem. This can be carried out through comprehensive village-based survey work, including family profiling, the cataloguing of arms cache discoveries and weapons seizures and the monitoring of weapons markets.

Third, perhaps more than anything else, it is the absence of political support for the project amongst the Afghan government to advance small arms reduction and control initiatives that has accounted for the inertia of the process. Numerous government officials are former commanders, many of whom have utilized their political offices to insulate their own militias and those of their allies. The DIAG programme has recognized this problem, seeking to target government officials with links to armed groups; however, in a demonstration of the great reach of commander patronage networks into the government, it has had only a marginal impact. Moreover, the determination of President Karzai and donors like the US to appease prominent commanders in the interest of short-term stability has militated against overt confrontations over commander recalcitrance.

Disarmament is innately a political issue. Before a small arms programme will be feasible in the Afghan context, or any other for that matter, a political consensus must be struck amongst the main factional groupings within the government on the need for disarmament and the approach to be taken. This consensus can only be achieved with the provision of a tailored mix of incentives and disincentives from donors, coupled with efforts to provide an adequate security buffer for the process in the form of a countrywide international peace support mission. Both of these prerequisites have been lacking in the Afghan context – the absence of donor disincentives being particularly conspicuous.

Strong parallels can be drawn between the approach of the Afghan government and international donor community towards the disarmament issue and its position on transitional justice. The government has officially recognized the importance of the transitional justice process – investigating and trying the vast number of class-A human rights abusers from the various stages of the 23-year civil war – as a precondition for national reconciliation. However, as in the case of disarmament, only symbolic steps have been taken to advance the process due to the belief that disturbing the status quo would trigger the disintegration of the prevailing balance of power and a return to internecine conflict.

Many potential targets of a prospective transitional justice campaign, almost all of which are commanders with links to armed groups, are influential members of the government who have used their positions to obstruct the process. The discourse often employed by government representatives and international stakeholders to justify the reticence to address past crimes is almost identical to that used to rationalize reservations against the establishment of a comprehensive countrywide disarmament programme. Neither the security nor political environment is perceived as conducive for such a process; it is believed that only in the long term when a high degree of security has been achieved and the political process has matured can it be advanced. In essence, it is not the right time.

Human rights activists in Afghanistan would respond to such logic by stating the importance of confronting abusers during the formative stages of the political process as a means to consolidate the peace, build the legitimacy of the new political dispensation and sideline potential spoilers before they could embed themselves in the political order, points that can also be employed to argue the merits of confronting armed commanders early in the post-conflict period.

Transitional justice like disarmament symbolizes a break with violence and impunity and a commitment to the rule of law. Failing to address these issues merely demonstrates to the population the government's ambivalence to change. The striking similarity between government approaches to transitional justice and disarmament in Afghanistan aptly illustrate the fundamentally political nature of the problem. The government's political approach, one of short-term accommodationism, is incompatible with the long-term peace-building outlook needed to undertake an ambitious disarmament or transitional justice process.

Lastly, even if a political consensus is achieved among the main factional groupings engaged in the political process on the imperative of disarmament, spoilers will inevitably resist the process. Accordingly, the state requires coercive mechanisms to compel recalcitrant actors to comply. This can take the form of either international or local security forces. However, in the Afghan context, neither has exhibited the capacity or will to fulfil this role. The NATO-led ISAF lacked the countrywide military presence to support the demilitarization process and the mandate of the US-led Coalition was limited to combating Al-Qaeda and the Taliban. As for Afghan security structures, the slow pace of SSR deprived the government of the ability to erect a security buffer for the process and fill the security vacuum that will inevitably emerge following disarmament.

Notes

1 Interview with senior member of D&R Commission in Cambridge, UK, 27 February 2006.
2 This would entail the compilation of detailed demographic information on combatants including their age, number of dependents, education, literacy, skills, assets, rank, number of years in service, involvement in the shadow economy, aspirations for future employment, and training needs (Özerdem, 2002, p. 970).

3 Rossi and Giustozzi quote a UNAMA official as saying that 36 per cent of all weapons collected were deemed unserviceable, the bulk constructed in Pakistani workshops straddling the border with Afghanistan (Rossi and Giustozzi, 2006, p. 4).

4 Heavy weapons were defined by the Afghan Ministry of Defence as being of 14.5 mm calibre or heavier and crew served (ANBP, 2006a, p. 9).

5 Interview with senior ANBP official in Kabul, 3 June 2004.

6 Interview with senior ANBP official in Kabul, 30 April 2005.

7 Interview with senior ANBP official in Kabul, 3 June 2004.

8 Interview with senior ANBP official in Kabul, 30 April 2005.

9 Interview with senior ANBP official in Kabul, 13 June 2006.

10 Interview with International Organization for Migration (IOM) Consultant in Kabul, 5 May 2005.

11 Interview with ANBP Special Adviser in Kabul, 29 April 2005.

12 Interview with senior ANBP official in Kabul, 13 June 2006.

13 Interview with senior ANBP official in Kabul, 13 June 2006.

14 Interview with Senior ANBP official in Kabul, 2 December 2003.

15 Interview with senior ANBP official in Kabul, 13 June 2006.

16 It is important to note that specialized programmes have been established to provide support to the dependents of ex-combatants and to demobilize and reintegrate underage combatants. As of June 2006, 24,536 women connected to the ex-combatant community were enrolled in an ANBP sponsored programme offering education and income generation opportunities in development projects. Also the World Food Programme (WFP) has initiated a programme to prioritize 4,455 women from the ex-combatant community for inclusion in WFP programmes from 2006–2010 (ANBP, 2006a, p. 5). UNICEF implemented a $10 million demobilization and reintegration programme targeting 8,000 child soldiers identified across the country (Chrobok, 2005).

17 A total of 2,759 ex-combatants chose a reintegration option, but subsequently dropped out of the programme. Also, 5,899 former officers will continue to receive reintegration support, which will likely include a severance scheme, beyond the completion of the DDR programme as a part of a separate joint initiative of the ANBP and Ministry of Defence (ANBP, 2006a, p. 4).

18 The majority of ex-combatants chose the agricultural option (41.9 per cent) with small business support (24.6 per cent) and vocational training (15.5 per cent) the other most popular options. The reintegration programme cost approximately $1,200 per ex-combatant, with $700 being directly expended on reintegration packages and the remaining $500 absorbed by overhead costs (ANBP, 2006a, p. 5); interview with Richard Scarth, USAID DDR Programme Manager, Kabul, 24 May 2005.

19 Interview with Richard Scarth, USAID DDR Programme Manager, Kabul, 24 May 2005.

20 Interview with International Organization for Migration Consultant in Kabul, 5 May 2005; interview with Richard Scarth, USAID DDR Programme Manager in Kabul, 24 May 2005.

21 Interview with senior ANBP official in Kabul, 13 June 2006.

22 Interview with senior Japanese Embassy official in Kabul, 12 May 2005.

23 These sites were located at Hussain Kot to the north, Band-i Qargah to the west, and Rishkhor to the south.

24 The site locations are as follows: Gardez, Hirat, Jalalabad, Kabul (six), Kandahar, Kunduz (four), Mazar (Post-Conflict Reforms Website, 2006).

25 Interview with senior ANBP official in Kabul, 30 April 2005.

26 The Panjsher valley was the last region to be subjected to the programme, where it experienced resistance from commanders and militiamen. By August

2005, the programme had collected 129 weapons, including 20 SCUD missiles in the valley.

27 Interview with ANBP official in Kabul, 23 May 2005.
28 Interview with ANBP official in Kabul, 23 May 2005.
29 The members of the committee include: the National Security Adviser, Ministry of Defence, Ministry of Interior, National Directorate of Security, Ministry of Rural Rehabilitation and Development, Ministry of Agriculture, Ministry of Labour and Social Affairs, Ministry of Finance, Ministry of Commerce and Industries, Ministry of Counter Narcotics, Japan, the United Kingdom, Canada, United States, the Netherlands, Switzerland, Italy, EU, UNAMA, ANBP, the Coalition and ISAF (Islamic Republic of Afghanistan, 2006a, p. 6).
30 It is also known as the National Security Coordination Forum.
31 The Provincial Reconstruction Teams (PRTs) are small units of soldiers, military civil affairs officers and civilian government representatives mandated to provide a security umbrella for reconstruction activities, carry out small-scale development projects, support security sector reform and serve as a link with the central government at key locations across the country (see Sedra, 2004b).
32 Japan's contribution to the $35 million DIAG development fund has largely been channelled through Afghan development initiatives, such as the National Area Based Development Programme and the National Solidarity Programme, which are engaged in the provision of DIAG community development projects. Other donors to the DIAG process include: the United Kingdom, Switzerland, the Netherlands, UNDP and Denmark.
33 This formula was altered prior to the launch of the second round of the GOLIAG stage in spring 2006. To make the process more flexible, it was decided that the assent of two Afghan actors would be sufficient to move ahead with the process (interview with official of the DIAG Joint Secretariat in Kabul, 24 June 2006).
34 The voluntary period was originally one month in duration but was extended to two months in the summer of 2006 in response to the poor early results of the programme.
35 Interview with official of the DIAG Joint Secretariat in Kabul, 24 June 2006.
36 Interview with official from the DIAG Joint Secretariat in Kabul, 24 June 2006.
37 A *shura* can be described as a village council.
38 Interview with official from the DIAG Joint Secretariat in Kabul, 14 November 2005.
39 Interview with official from the DIAG Joint Secretariat in Kabul, 24 June 2006.
40 Interview with official from the DIAG Joint Secretariat in Kabul, 24 June 2006.
41 Interview with official from the DIAG Joint Secretariat in Kabul, 24 June 2006.
42 Interview with senior ANBP official in Kabul, 13 June 2006.
43 Interview with senior UNAMA official in Kabul, 17 June 2006.
44 Interview with Western donor official in Kabul, 24 June 2006.
45 According to one Western diplomat, the escalating problem of IEDs has prompted the Coalition to introduce a buy-back scheme that pays sums up to $1,500 for the submission of an IED. As numerous money-for-guns schemes have demonstrated, this could have the perverse effect of triggering increased production of IEDs as a means to secure the submission fee. This phenomenon was demonstrated in Afghanistan in two ways. First, the cash grant distributed to ex-combatants as a part of the DDR process for the submission of a functioning weapon was discontinued due to the widespread prevalence of fraud and the intimidation of ex-combatants by commanders to secure the money. Second, a UK-funded counter-narcotics programme launched in 2002, which awarded farmers cash incentives for the eradication of their poppy crops, was discontinued in 2003 after it was discovered that it had contributed to an

expansion rather than a reduction in production. Interview with private security contractor in Kabul, 14 May 2005; interview with Western donor official in Kabul, 18 June 2006.

46 The US State Department's Explosive Remnant of War programme has also provided in-kind support.

47 Afghanistan is one of the most mine-affected countries in the world. Estimates affirm that, since 1979, more than 200,000 Afghans have been killed or injured by landmines and unexploded ordnance and an average of 80 continue to be killed on a monthly basis, the bulk of which are civilians. By mid-2005, mine action programmes had succeeded in removing 2.8 million explosive devices clearing 320 million square miles of land. However, it is estimated that 815 million square miles remain to be cleared (Oxfam, 2006a, p. 10).

48 Interview with ANBP official in Kabul, 13 May 2005.

49 Interview with ANBP official in Kabul, 13 May 2005.

50 This Coalition body has been known by three different names since its formation in 2002. In July 2005, the Coalition's Office of Military Cooperation – Afghanistan (OMC-A), the body established to coordinate US and Coalition support to the military reform process, was renamed the Office of Security Cooperation – Afghanistan (OSC-A) after it assumed the mandate to support the police as well. The name of the office was again changed in May 2006 to the Combined Security Transition Command – Afghanistan (CSTC-A).

51 Interview with CSTC-A official in Kabul, 16 May 2005.

52 Interview with CSTC-A official in Kabul, 16 May 2005.

53 Interview with ANBP official in Kabul, 13 May 2005.

54 Among the NGOs that played a key role in the reintegration process were the Agency for Rehabilitation and Energy Conservation in Afghanistan, the Helping Afghan Farmers Organization, Afghan Technical Consultants and the Welfare Association for Development of Afghanistan (see ANBP website online, available at: undpanbp.org/ (accessed 4 December 2007)).

55 Interview with Oxfam Policy and Advocacy Adviser in Kabul, 25 June 2006.

5 Small arms and security sector reform

Mark Sedra

Experience from recent post-conflict reconstruction processes shows that the success of a security sector reform (SSR) project is directly correlated to the efficacy of disarmament activities. If there is no successful disarmament, the SSR model cannot achieve one of its main underlying goals, investing the state with a monopoly over the use of coercive force. The inverse is also accurate, as small arms reduction and control programmes will be hard-pressed to succeed until people feel secure, have confidence that the security forces are competent and acting in their interest and have legal recourse if their rights are violated. Most donors engaged in SSR activities recognize the need to integrate disarmament and weapons control activities into the SSR agenda in post-conflict countries. However, as the Afghan case demonstrates, theory often fails to translate into practice.

The failure to exploit synergies between SSR and small arms programming cannot only limit progress in peace building but can become a source of instability. Ineffective, repressive or corrupt security sectors can increase demand for guns and, conversely, small arms proliferation can lead to the breakdown of state order and the militarization of security structures. Both phenomena can be detected in the Afghan case.

The Afghan government's 2005 *Millennium Development Goals* report explicitly recognizes the inextricable link between disarmament and SSR and the importance of both enterprises in advancing security and stability. However, it tends to view disarmament as a distant or ancillary goal to be achieved only after meaningful reforms have been enacted in the security sector. The report argues that 'large scale civilian disarmament, without the strengthening and reform of the police and justice systems, is likely to be both difficult and may also increase peoples' vulnerability and perception of mistrust of the state.' It goes on to state that 'the registration and regulation of small arms may be a more viable option' when reforms in the security sector have reached a more advanced stage (Islamic Republic of Afghanistan, 2005a, p. 105). The report seemingly ignores the reciprocal importance of disarmament in facilitating SSR, an omission clearly perceptible in the approach taken by the Afghan government and international donor community towards the SSR and demilitarization processes.

The implementation of the SSR process in Afghanistan has been encumbered by the absence of parallel steps to address the issue of small arms proliferation, one of the principal drivers of insecurity. It is the persistence of insecurity, in the form of a resurgent Taliban-led insurgency, warlordism and general criminality – all facilitated by the widespread availability of small arms – that has stood as the most profound obstacle to SSR. The SSR model, a process of institutional reform, is ill suited to succeed in contexts facing high levels of insecurity and political instability. Accordingly, initiatives to control and collect the principal instrument of violence in the Afghan context – small arms and light weapons – will help to mitigate such conditions and facilitate reform.

At a G8 conference on Afghanistan held in Geneva in the spring of 2002, a donor support framework for the Afghan security sector reform (SSR) process was created. It divided the process into five pillars, assigning a 'lead donor' to each – military reform (US); police reform (Germany); judicial reform (Italy); the disarmament, demobilization and reintegration of former combatants (Japan); and counter-narcotics (UK) (Sedra, 2006).

SSR is inherently a holistic process balancing the imperative of enhancing the operational effectiveness of the security forces with the need to ensure democratic civilian control of the sector and embed modern international standards and principles. However, the persistence of insecurity, driven by a resilient Taliban-led insurgency and the re-emergence of the phenomenon of warlordism, upset this equilibrium, imbuing the process with a 'hard' security orientation. Training and equipping the country's security forces – the Afghan National Army (ANA) and Afghan National Police (ANP) – overshadowed the 'soft' elements of the process, most notably the entrenchment of norms of democratic accountability and the advancement of reforms in the judiciary.

In the absence of a robust countrywide peace support mission capable of providing the necessary security buffer to advance the reconstruction process and extend the government's authority into the periphery, efforts to prepare the Afghan security forces to fulfil their role as the ultimate security guarantor for the country were accelerated. One of the central elements of the train and equip process has been the provision of lethal equipment. In spite of the focus on rapidly enhancing the operational capacity of the security forces, both the ANA and ANP have faced debilitating shortfalls in equipment, notably firearms.

Box 5.1 Legal framework of firearms possession and use

After the fall of the Taliban, Afghanistan's laws regulating firearm
possession were convoluted, poorly understood and rarely enforced.
Consistent with the wider judicial reform process, efforts to rationalize legal statutes regarding small arms and light weapons were characterized by inertia during the first two years of the reconstruction
process. In spite of the importance of endowing the disarmament
and weapons control process with a solid legal foundation, little
consideration was accorded to reforms of the existing weapons laws
until 2004. In that year, President Karzai issued an important Presidential Decree that endowed the demilitarization process with the
political authority that it required. The decree, issued on 14 July
2004, recognized disarmament as 'one of the substantial conditions
of the restoration of law, provision of a permanent peace, improvement of the economic situation, safeguarding of human rights and
ruling on the basis of people's will' (Presidential Decree No. 50, 14
July 2004).

    The strongly worded decree was a response to the slow early pace
of the DDR process engendered by rampant commander obstructionism and Ministry of Defence obstinacy. The donor community,
led by the Japanese government, had placed increasing pressure on
Karzai to take a hard line on the issue.[1] The decree would go on to
threaten 'the severest punishment for any actors who attempted to
circumvent the process and maintain armed groups' (Presidential
Decree No. 50, 14 July 2004). The decree seemingly marked the
emergence of a new level of political will among the Karzai government to advance the flagging process; however, it still lacked a
coherent legal framework to draw upon or an effective security
apparatus to enable implementation.

The law on fire weapons, ammunitions and explosive materials
The Law of Fire Weapons, Ammunitions and Explosive Materials,
which came into force on 24 June 2005, provides the demilitarization process with the legal basis it was lacking. It firmly establishes
that 'the government has sovereignty over those fire weapons,
ammunitions and explosive materials which are existing in this
country' and affirms that 'other persons and authorities without
legal permission have no right to produce, import, export, gain, use
and keep them' (Law of Fire Weapons, Ammunitions and Explosive
Materials, ch. 1, art. 4, online, available at: diag.gov.af/mDoc.htm
(accessed 4 December 2007)). The law outlines a licensing and registration system for the acquisition, possession and sale of small arms,
to be managed and overseen by the Ministry of Interior. It stipulates

that a weapons licence must feature a photo of the licensee and list the weapon's serial number.[2]

While the law places strict conditions on firearm ownership, it recognizes that to protect their lives and property 'individuals and non-governmental bodies can gain non-hunting fire weapons and ammunitions,' a concession to a significant constituency of disarmament sceptics (ch. 2, art. 7). As such, it tacitly recognizes the prevailing gun culture and the difficulty of completely removing the gun from Afghan society amidst rising levels of insecurity. Failure to register a weapon will result in fines commensurate to the value of the weapon and associated ammunition, confiscation and legal prosecution (ch. 3, art. 10). The weapons licensing programme will draw on citizen information collected under the auspices of the electoral registration process; the electoral registration cards represent the country's only reliable form of national identification.

The application of the weapons registration system will enable the collection of data on weapons possession in the country, developing a better understanding of the shifting patterns of weapons ownership and use. The government has proposed monitoring two indicators to gauge its progress in reducing the availability of guns: the proportion of firearms licensed and the statistical rates of gun crime as a share of overall reported crime (Islamic Republic of Afghanistan, 2005a, p. 106). However, it has not identified any specific benchmarks or milestones to be achieved in either of these areas.

The law on private security companies
Another legal statute that seeks to regulate gun ownership of the private security industry was developed concurrently. Since 2001, the number of private security companies (PSCs), primarily international, operating in Afghanistan has risen exponentially. Both Afghan and international law lack mechanisms to regulate the activities and behaviour of these firms. PSCs both surreptitiously import weapons, circumventing Afghan customs duties and import regulations, and illegally purchase arms on the black market.

In 2005 the government began to develop legislation that would curb such actions through the establishment of a comprehensive registration system. A draft of the Law on Private Security Organizations, produced in late 2005, would require PSCs, individual contractors and any associated armed personnel to acquire permits to operate and to carry firearms.

Annual fees would be levied for registration, ranging from $10,000 for a PSC to $250 for an individual guard (Draft Law on Private Security Organizations, ch. 2, art. 6). Contractors could also

be required to submit fingerprints, photographs and detailed personal information upon application for a licence, including a cur-
riculum vitae detailing the five previous years of employment
experience (ch. 3, art. 8 and 9). Following background checks
undertaken by the Ministry of Interior, the contractor would be
issued an identification card that includes the serial number of their
duty weapon; contractors are required to possess the card at all
times. If an individual is apprehended without an identification card,
he or she could face monetary fines ranging from $500 to $2,500,
have their firearm seized and possibly have their registration revoked
(ch. 4, art. 12).

The draft law calls for the establishment of a commission to hear
complaints about individual contractors or companies. In the event
that complaints directed against a specific company or contractor
are deemed valid, the commission has the authority to take a
number of punitive measures, including the revocation of the individual's licence (ch. 5). In all cases, contractors are subject to
Afghan law and would be prosecuted for any criminal offences
arising out of their use of firearms in Afghanistan. The PSC law was
expected to be finalized and come into force by the end of 2006,
however, by early 2007 it was still under consideration.

The development of the PSC law, while vital to regulate the
behaviour of security contractors, cannot be seen as a substitute for
greater donor and private sector vigilance in monitoring the PSCs.
Donors have not taken sufficient responsibility in providing oversight of the PSCs whom they have contracted. Anecdotes of private
security contractors offending Afghan cultural sensitivities or utilizing excessive force are common, creating tremendous resentment
among ordinary Afghans, not solely directed at those firms involved
but the international agencies that contract them and the wider
international community.[3] In the short term, pressure from donors
will have a greater impact in altering PSC behaviour than nascent
government legislation that lacks mechanisms for enforcement.

The promulgation of the weapons law and the drafting of the PSC
law were intended to give a boost to the nascent DIAG programme.
However, the weapons law has not been adequately disseminated
across the capital, let alone the country, and the PSC law had, by
early 2007, yet to come into force. Furthermore, the Ministry of Interior has yet to demonstrate the capacity or political will to enforce
them. As the 2005 MDG Country Report states, 'encouraging those
who currently own weapons to apply for licenses, and identifying and
punishing those who fail to comply with the new law will be a
resource-intensive process' (Islamic Republic of Afghanistan, 2005a,
p. 108). As of early 2006, the Afghan National Police lacked the

means to carry out basic policing functions, thus the enforcement of a countrywide registration system seemed beyond its capability. Targeted international support to the Ministry of Interior, enabling it 'to process applications, document the licensing process and maintain records,' will be required to ensure the consistent application of the law (Islamic Republic of Afghanistan, 2005a, p. 108).

Perhaps one of the most imposing obstacles to the enforcement of the weapons law has been the slow pace of police and judicial reform in the country. Until judicial and police reforms are accelerated and expanded outside the capital and some major urban hubs, the weapons laws, however well designed, will be unenforceable (Sedra, 2006).

Statutory security forces

The military

By early 2006, the achievements of the military reform pillar far outstripped the other pillars of the SSR process. The centrepiece of the pillar, the Afghan National Army (ANA), had reached a strength of approximately 36,000 troops of a designated force ceiling of 70,000 by November 2006. Although the force still requires Coalition support to conduct complex operations, by all accounts it has performed well during its initial deployments, demonstrating a high degree of effectiveness and professionalism. As the Afghan National Military Strategy affirms, over the long term, the 'ANA will assume its traditional role as ultimate guardian of the independence and freedom, national interests, and the defender of the territorial integrity [and] national sovereignty' of Afghanistan, denoting a conventional military posture vis-à-vis external threats (Afghanistan Ministry of Defence, 2004, pp. 4–7).

The presence of Coalition and ISAF forces in the country mitigates the conventional military threat posed by Afghanistan's neighbours, primarily Iran and Pakistan, allowing the country's military to face inward, adopting a domestic focus. Accordingly, the primary goal of the force in the short term is 'to counter the internal threats,' namely the 'Taliban and Armed Extremist Groups along the border areas,' illegally armed groups, and the narcotics trade (Afghanistan Ministry of Defence, 2004, pp. 4–7).

US weapons procurement plans for the ANA have reflected this domestic focus, fostering a flexible and mobile force capable of waging a counter-insurgency campaign. This obviates the need for heavy armour, such as tanks and artillery, and calls for quick reaction units equipped with appropriate transportation assets. The Coalition's CSTC-A is responsible for equipping the ANA and initially opted to provide it with Russian- and Eastern European-made equipment, either salvaged from domestic sources or donated. This approach was adopted on the basis of two factors. First, the Afghans were most familiar with such equipment as the majority of the weaponry used by the former Afghan army and the country's plethora of militia groupings was Soviet in origin. Second, several Coalition countries from the former Soviet Union expressed a willingness to donate equipment to the ANA (USGAO, 2005, p. 16).

In spite of the US procurement programme, the ANA continued to face acute equipment shortfalls in 2006. This can be attributed to the lower than expected transfers of serviceable weapons from the DDR process and the inadequacy of a significant proportion of the equipment donated by foreign states, which were assessed to be 'worn out, defective, or incompatible with other equipment' (USGAO, 2005, p. 16). Another factor that slowed down the procurement of equipment involved the internal organization of OMC-A, the forerunner of the CSTC-A, which was understaffed, lacked training in defence security assistance procedures and was unable to preserve institutional memory due to rigid rotation schedules (USGAO, 2005, p. 15).

In line with the US procurement strategy, the bulk of the weapons and ammunition donated to the ANA up until the summer of 2006 emanated from former Eastern Bloc countries such as Romania, Bulgaria, Albania, Slovenia, Croatia and the Ukraine (see Table 5.1).[4] Endorsing this approach, NATO urged its member states, particularly the new members from Eastern Europe, to expand their contributions. However, in July 2006, the US shifted its strategy, announcing the donation of $2 billion worth of US-made military equipment to the ANA.[5] The equipment package was reported to include 2,500 Humvees, tens of thousands of M-16 assault rifles and 20,000 sets of bullet-proof helmets and flak jackets (Tran, 2006). The change was stimulated by two factors: the variable quality of the Eastern European donations and persistent Afghan exhortations for US equipment, notably M-16 assault rifles. The donation was intended to ensure that the US met its target of filling 80 per cent of the ANA's equipment requirements by the end of 2006.

Creating a rational, transparent and accountable procurement system is a vital element of the SSR process and small arms control efforts. The CSTC-A has supported the strengthening of a Department for Acquisitions, Technology and Logistics (AT&L) within the Ministry of Defence, one of whose functions is to procure small arms and light weapons. It is responsible for ensuring that official weapons imports into the country are commensurate to the legitimate equipment needs of the security forces in terms of scale and content, thereby militating against the leakage of equipment into the hands of non-state actors, the expansion of security force capacity beyond their mandate and the misappropriation of scarce funding.

While the AT&L Department is still undergoing reform and receiving US mentoring, it has demonstrated increasing competency and assertive-

Table 5.1 Selection of weapons donations to the ANA (as of June 2006)

Country	Weapons donated
Bosnia-Herzegovina	• machine guns (4,500) • howitzers (400), 7.62 mm calibre ammunition (1,000,000)
Albania	• AK-47 (600), ammunition (100,000) • PKM machine guns (27), ammunition (25,000) • 82 mm mortars (8), ammunition (256) • 60 mm mortars (27), ammunition (256)
United States	• M-16 assault rifles (tens of thousands), ammunition (n/a)
Germany	• 9 mm Walther P-1 pistols (10,000), ammunition (n/a)
Pakistan	• 82 mm mortars (180), ammunition (10,000) • RPG-7 (75), ammunition (750) • MP5 sub-machine gun (5,000), ammunition (50,000)
Bulgaria	• AK-47 (400), ammunition (120,000) • PKM machine guns (8) • 82 mm mortars (8), ammunition (1,150) • 72 mm SPG-9 (12), ammunition (1,400) • grenades (900)
Romania	• AK-47 (1,000) • PKM machine guns (8) • RPG-7 (15), ammunition (90) • 82 mm mortars (8) • Assorted ammunition (n/a)
Slovenia	• AK-47 (900), ammunition (1,800,000) • 60 mm mortars (81), ammunition (4,800) • 82 mm mortars (8) • RPG-7 (26), ammunition (138)
Ukraine	• AK-47 (600), ammunition (1,000,000) • PKM machine guns (27), ammunition (300,000) • 73 mm SPG-9 (12), ammunition (500)
Croatia	• AK-47 ammunition (2,000,000) • 73 mm SPG-9 (12), ammunition (10,000) • RPG-7 ammunition (10,000)

Sources: Oxfam, 2006a, pp. 15–16; Tran, 2006; Lowery, 2006; Iqbal, 2003; *Xinhua*, 2005; US Department of State website: online, available at: state.gov/p/sca/rls/18035.htm (accessed 4 December 2007); interview with adviser to the Defence Minister, Kabul, 18 May 2005; interview with CSTC-A official in Kabul, 16 May 2005.

Note
This is not an exhaustive list. It details donations and purchases for which public information is available.

ness. In February 2006, it rejected, under Coalition supervision, some donations, including a Romanian offer of T55 tanks, on the basis that they were inconsistent with the force's profile and equipment requirements. The ANA possesses an abundance of Soviet-era tanks and artillery, and such heavy equipment is incompatible with the focus on constructing a lightly equipped mobile force geared to guerrilla and counter-insurgency warfare. The capacity of the AT&L is growing, but it lacks the funds and capacity to oversee large acquisitions. All the major arms purchases and donations for the ANA are still overseen by the CSTC-A, with minimal Afghan input. Furthermore, the department still lacks the capacity to fulfil another of its primary functions, assuring end-user accountability of all distributed weapons.

Weapons transfers from the DDR and DIAG programmes failed to meet the expectations of the CSTC-A and the Ministry of Defence. By the conclusion of the DDR programme in July 2006, the total number of weapons transferred by the ANBP to the Ministry of Defence was 21,780 (ANBP, 2006a, p. 4) (see Table 5.2 for breakdown of weapons transfers as of November 2005). It is hoped that the ongoing DIAG programme will inflate these figures, which were far lower than originally envisaged. The heavy weapons cantonment programme has handed over 530 pieces of weaponry to the government, primarily consisting of artillery, anti-aircraft and anti-tank systems as well as mortars (Post-Conflict Reforms Website, 2006).

When weapons are transferred to the central weapons collection point at Pul-e-charkhi, they are inspected by a team consisting of Coalition and Afghan Ministry of Defence weapons specialists. The team determines whether a weapon is serviceable, repairable or unserviceable. Unserviceable weapons are cannibalized for usable parts, both for weapons repairs and to construct new weapons.

Table 5.2 Serviceable light and heavy weapons transferred to Ministry of Defence (as of November 2005)

Weapons type	Number transferred
AK-47 assault rifle	17,144
PKM machine gun	663
RPK machine gun	780
RPG-7 rocket-propelled grenade	1,879
82 mm mortar	276
60 mm mortar	14
82 mm recoil	40
75 mm recoil	20
ZEGO (AA Gun)	35
SPG-9 rifle	79
122 mm D-30	46
Tank RE	4
DShK machine gun	13
Total	20,993

Source: Interview with ANBP official in Kabul, 9 November 2005.

The police

While the United States chose to build the ANA from the ground up, breaking completely with previous structures and practices, the government of Germany opted to reform existing police structures and personnel. The police consist largely of former militiamen who are illiterate, paid an inadequate wage, loyal to regional commanders rather than the Ministry of Interior and work in squalid institutional conditions, lacking basic equipment to fulfil their duties.

The German Police Project successfully reopened the Kabul Police Academy in 2002, which catered to officers and non-commissioned officers, but its failure to target rank-and-file patrolmen limited the impact of its assistance. To ameliorate this situation, the United States entered the police reform process in 2003, rapidly becoming the largest donor.

The US programme accelerated the pace of training through the establishment of eight police training centres across the country, providing entry-level training to all 62,000 officers of the ANP by the end of 2005. However, only 30,395 of those officers were judged by the CSTC-A to be ready to assume their duties by June 2006, on the basis of three criteria: the level of training received, unit staffing levels and equipment status (US Department of State and US Department of Defense, 2006, p. 15). Even this figure overestimates the capability of the ANP, which has been shown to be largely ineffective in countering crime, terrorism and general insecurity and continues to be viewed with distrust and apprehension by the majority of the population.

The training programmes at both the Kabul Police Academy and the regional training centres provide basic training in the use of firearms but do not offer instruction on how to deal with issues of small arms proliferation. For instance, the respective curricula do not outline how to orchestrate community weapons collections programmes. In light of the glut of small arms in the country and its significance as a security threat, this is a significant omission.

Like the ANA, shortfalls in equipment, notably small arms and light weapons, have greatly circumscribed the ability of the police to perform their duties. For instance, Kabul's Police District 10, chosen as the pilot site for a US-funded 'Model District Program,' which seeks to reform the police service at key districts across the country, only possessed 17 Kalashnikovs and three 9 mm pistols for a total of 378 officers in May 2005.[6]

The failure of the international community to invest adequate resources in the police reform process early in the post-conflict period contributed to such equipment deficits. It was only with US entry into the process that adequate attention was placed on addressing the equipment needs of the police. However, the US procurement programme has been characterized by significant delays in the fielding of weapons, which can be attributed to a number of factors, including the slow delivery of donated weapons and frequent turnover among key CSTC-A procurement personnel (US Department of State and US Department of Defense, 2006, p. 43).

Police that have been issued weapons tend to treat them as personal rather than duty weapons, reinforcing the police's lack of accountability to the state and perpetuating a culture of impunity. In fact, this is true of all equipment provided to the police in the context of the reform process. For instance, one police chief dismissed by the government in 2005 had pilfered all the new equipment provided to his unit through the reform process, including office furniture, vehicles, communications equipment and firearms.[7]

As this anecdote would suggest, equipment provided to specific units, even equipment earmarked for distribution to individual officers, is often treated as the personal possessions of the local police commander. Their control of the assistance tap has enabled these commanders to expand their personal power and influence and, in some cases, engage in the illicit economy. The Ministry of Interior lacks a robust command and control mechanism to monitor and regulate the behaviour of police commanders, particularly in remote areas of the country where the government presence is limited.

With reforms to the police still stalled, the US military expanded its role in the process in 2005 through its newly formed Police Reform Directorate (PRD), a unit of the CSTC-A, supplanting the State Department's Bureau for International Narcotics and Law Enforcement Affairs as the lead US agency. The PRD almost immediately identified the prevailing deficit in police equipment as one of its priority areas. In 2005, it completed an equipment fielding plan that determined the needs and priorities of the force (see Figure 5.1).[8]

To meet urgent operational requirements, the PRD has distributed equipment to the ANP on a priority basis, according to both geographical region and policing branch. The regional order of priority for equipment distribution is as follows: south, east, west, central and north. As for the level of priority accorded to specific police branches, the Border Police is given preference, followed by the Standby Police, Uniformed Police and Highway Police (US Department of State and US Department of Defense, 2006, 45–46).

A June 2005 report of the US Government Accountability Office asserted that the Ministry of Interior possessed 36,500 serviceable rifles and pistols on hand, mainly seized weapons. The report went on to estimate that the police needed an additional 48,500 side arms, 10,000 automatic rifles and 6,250 machine guns to meet its requirements (USGAO, 2005, p. 23). Overall, the ANP had met only 50 per cent of its equipment requirements, as of June 2006.[9] According to current planning, the full equipment needs of the ANP should be met by the first quarter of fiscal year 2008.

Border/ standby police (ABP/ASP)	Equipment	Construction	Mentors	Training
	1 AMD-65 each	BDE	BCPs	9 week
	1 9 mm pistol each	support RES	BDE/BN HQ	(literate)
	1 RPK per 7	BDE	COs	basic course
	1 RPG per 30	BN HQ to		5 week
	1 OCIE set each	support 1		(illiterate)
	1,561 vehicles 1 per 7	CO HQ		basic course
	1 radio per 4 vehicles			2 week
	1 HF manpack per PLT	CO HQ		specialized
	3 VHF hand radios per PLT			training course
	1 radio per HQ			
	1 radio per BCP			
Highway police (AHP)	1 AMD-65 each	BN HQ to	BN HQ	9 week
	1 9 mm pistol each	support 1	COs	(literate)
	1 RPK per 7	CO HQ		basic course
	1 shotgun per 7	CO HQ		5 week
	1 PRG per 30			(illitrates)
	1 OCIE set each			basic course
	460 vehicles 1 per 7			2 week
	2 VHF radios per vehicle			specialized
	1 radio per vehicle			training course
Uniform police (AUP)	1 AMD-65 per 7	REG HQ, REG	MOI	9 week
	1 9 mm pistol each	LOG CTRS	Regional	(literate)
	1 shotgun per 7	Provincial HQ	provincial	basic course
	1 OCIE set each	District HQ	district	5 week
	6,936 vehicles 1 per 7			(illiterate)
	1 radio per vehicle			basic course
	1 radio per district			
	1 VHF hand radio per 3			
	Support contracts	Vehicle maint.	**Ammunition**	AMD-65 120
		phase 1/2	**operational**	9 mm 48
		weapons	**load**	RPK 600
		fuel	**rds/weapon**	RPG 10
		commo. maint.		SHOT 25

Figure 5.1 ANP equipment fielding plan overview (as of November 2006) (source: US Department of State and US Department of Defense, 2006, p. 45).

With CSTC-A assistance, a National Logistics Centre has been established in Kabul, supported by five regional logistical support centres and 34 provincial supply points. This National Logistics System will be responsible for logistics, facilities, communications, procurement and medical support for the ANP. In particular, it will procure, distribute and maintain weapons for the police (Afghanistan Ministry of Interior, 2006). As of the summer of 2006, $149 million of equipment had reached the ANP, the bulk as donations from countries such as Egypt, Hungary, the Czech Republic, Germany and the United States (see Table 5.3) (Afghanistan Ministry of Interior, 2006).

The Kalashnikov assault rifle accounts for the bulk of the Ministry of Interior's arms stocks, something it recognizes to be ill-conducive for

Table 5.3 Sample of weapons donations to the ANP (as of June 2006)

Country	Weapons donated
Egypt	• AK47 (10,000) • Pistols (560) • Assorted ammunition (1,291,000)
Czech Republic	• AK-47 (18,000) • CZ-85 pistols (n/a)
United States	• Smith & Wessen 9 mm pistols with holsters, cleaning kits (12,144), ammunition (n/a)
Germany	• 9 mm Walther P-1 pistols (10,000), ammunition (n/a)
Hungary	• AMD-65 assault rifles (11,605)

Sources: Lowery, 2006; interview with adviser to the Defence Minister, Kabul, 18 May 2005; interview with CSTC-A official in Kabul, 16 May 2005; interview with official from the German Police Project in Kabul, 6 November 2005.

Note
This is not an exhaustive list. It details donations and purchases for which public information is available.

effective community policing. Police across the country characteristically patrol with military equipment such as assault rifles and even rocket-propelled grenades.[10] One of the central aims of the police reform process is to demilitarize the police, which translates into the replacement of the assault rifle, a powerful symbol of Afghanistan's civil war, with the side arm. This will mitigate the intimidating appearance and legacy of the police, thereby encouraging public confidence.

The Ministry of Interior has lobbied extensively in the DIAG Forum and DIAG Joint Secretariat to gain access to weapons collected under the auspices of the DIAG programme; however, the Ministry of Defence, which, as lead agency for the process, controls all of the arms collected, has rebuffed these entreaties.[11] It has justified its rejection of the Ministry of Interior proposal on the basis of its own weapons shortfalls.

With the ANP's logistics and procurement architecture still at an early stage in its development, the CSTC-A continues to control the distribution of the majority of equipment to the force. One of the principal exceptions to this policy was the donation of 18,000 Czech-made assault rifles, which were delivered directly to the Ministry of Interior. Received equipment is stored in a CSTC-A warehouse in Kabul and inventoried by both CSTC-A and Afghan National Logistics Centre officers on US- and Afghan-approved forms before it is distributed according to the priority fielding plan. The CSTC-A provides transportation, with an armed ANP escort, to deliver weapons and ammunition to the designated unit's headquarters, which is at the provincial level for the Uniformed Police, the brigade level for the Border Police and the battalion level for the Standby and Highway Police. These headquarters are responsible for the further distribution of the arms to individual units and policemen.

Once units receive their authorized equipment allowance, as dictated by the fielding plan, they will only receive replacements in the event of defects or maintenance problems. Equipment lost due to other reasons, most notably corruption, will not be replaced. However, US accountability mechanisms end at the headquarters level, making it difficult for the government to enforce this directive and track distributed weapons (US Department of State and US Department of Defense, 2006, pp. 47–49). US mentors attached to ANP units provide *ad hoc* monitoring of equipment, often sending status reports to the CSTC-A, but this is not a part of their mandate, nor do they have the capacity to assume this function in many cases. Furthermore, mentors are not formally required to provide guidance on how to conduct accountability checks of weapons stocks.

However, the CSTC-A is developing a plan in concert with the Ministry of Interior that will require police mentors along with ANP logistics officers to submit logistics reports that detail unit equipment accountability and effectiveness. This initiative should be paralleled by the development of central standardized training for police serving as logistics officers in the field, something which, according to an *Interagency Assessment of Afghanistan Police Training and Readiness* undertaken by the US Department of State and US Department of Defense, was lacking in June 2006. The report aptly affirms that 'training in supply point management, armory procedures, and maintenance management are vital to establishing accountability within the ANP at the end-user level' (US Department of State and US Department of Defense, 2006, p. 49).

The ANP is rife with corruption and clientelism, and a significant proportion of the force reports to regional commanders, rather than the Ministry of Interior. The failure of the training and administrative reform programme to dampen corruption and excoriate the militiamen's mentality from the police service raises concerns about the distribution of guns to rank-and-file policemen.

Exemplifying this dilemma are reports that guns donated to the Ministry of Interior have surfaced on the Afghan black market. According to one source, Czech-made assault rifles were being sold by weapons traders in Kabul within months of their donation to the Ministry of Interior by the government of the Czech Republic.[12] This would indicate that ANP personnel are selling their duty weapons. The Czech government delivered these weapons directly to the Ministry of Interior, i.e., outside the CSTC-A procurement framework. This reveals the inability of the Ministry to handle such large weapons transfers in a manner that meets basic accountability requirements.

Perhaps more worrying than this incident, senior Afghan Ministry of the Interior officials assert that 1,500 assault rifles transferred to the police of Helmand Province in 2006 by the UK PRT could not be accounted for by June 2006. It is believed that the weapons were leaked to militia groupings and insurgent groups in the region.[13] This episode demonstrated that the practice of arming certain police units can be tantamount to arming a regional militia. The only way to mitigate this risk is through the establishment of a more vigorous police vetting system, the adjustment and expansion of the training regime and the intensification of administrative and personnel reforms.

Non-statutory security actors

The existence of large numbers of non-statutory or informal security actors in Afghanistan has acted as a driver of weapons proliferation. These groups are varied, ranging from semi-legitimate actors such as private security companies and militias operating under the umbrella of the formal security sector, to illegal groupings such as insurgent militias. They have fuelled the illicit market in arms and facilitated internal and cross-border arms flows. Attempts to regulate semi-legitimate armed actors and contain their illegal counterparts have been similarly ineffectual.

Private security companies

The influx of international civilian organizations in Afghanistan in the wake of the Taliban's fall coupled with the persistence of high levels of insecurity – a result of general criminality, terrorism and the anti-government insurgency – generated a sustained demand for private security providers. It is indicative of a wider trend of privatization in security that can be detected across the post-conflict reconstruction field over the past decade.

It is difficult to determine the number of private security companies or individual contractors working in Afghanistan, for until the Private Security Company Law is promulgated, no regulatory framework exists to monitor and govern the activities of these actors. Further compounding the difficulty of devising a precise picture of the structure and activities of these groups is the shroud of secrecy under which they operate. PSCs tend to eschew transparency, augmenting suspicion of their activities by local and international actors. This approach can be considered a reaction to a wave of negative media coverage of their activities and the resultant pressure, emanating from many quarters, for the institution of controls on their behaviour, something that many PSCs oppose.

Almost every category of international actor employs PSCs in Afghanistan, including the United Nations, donor governments, private sector companies and NGOs. They have become an omnipresent feature of the Afghan security landscape. Estimates of the number of international private security contractors working in Afghanistan range from 3,000 to 4,000. Contractors are generally divided into two groups: Western expatriates, consisting primarily of nationals from Britain, Australia, New Zealand, South Africa, Canada, Zimbabwe and the United States; and third party nationals, predominantly comprising Gurkhas[14] who previously served in the Indian, British and Nepalese militaries.[15] The Ghurkhas play a crucial role for the PSCs, serving, as one UN official puts it, as a 'middle link between the Afghans and the internationals.'[16]

Western expatriate contractors typically earn between $400 and $650 per day, with salaries rising up to $1,000 per day for special assignments, as in the case of the DynCorp contractors who served in President Karzai's close protection detail.[17] By contrast, third country contractors, referring to those emanating from outside the West such as the Gurkhas, typically earn $45–200 per day, a figure deemed to be commensurate with the cost of living in their home countries.[18] The typical age range for a contractor is 22–56, and contractors possess a minimum of three years of military or police experience.[19]

While the core staff of the PSCs are international, they rely heavily on locally engaged staff. The bulk of man-guarding or static guarding, safe-guarding fixed locations or facilities, is undertaken by Afghan staff. It is even more difficult to provide a precise figure regarding the number of Afghan staff employed by PSCs, as several PSCs sub-contract to regional warlords or small Afghan PSCs.

One of the most conspicuous examples of this practice relates to the Kabul–Kandahar road project, a $250 million USAID-funded project con-tracted to the Louis Berger Group, to rebuild the vital transport artery. The Texas-based company, US Protection and Investigation (USPI), by most accounts the largest PSC operating in Afghanistan, was granted the sub-contract to provide security for the project. According to a 2005 Inter-national Crisis Group report, USPI, working through an intermediary from the Ministry of Interior, employed local militia groups for the task (ICG, 2005, p. 7). Salaries for the militiamen were channelled through local commanders, leaving ample room for graft and corruption.[20] Such practices provide an incentive for the remobilization of militia groups and allow commanders to buttress their patronage-based links with their militi-amen (ICG, 2005, p. 8).[21]

PSCs either import weapons into the country or purchase them from local sources. Some US companies are provided special dispensation to import weapons on US military transports. A significant number of PSCs procure their weapons domestically on the black market. For instance, Global Strategies Group, the company that held the contract to provide security for the US Embassy in 2005, reportedly purchased a significant proportion of its weapons from Kabul weapons bazaars, thereby spurring the local illegal arms trade. The weapons were registered by the US State Department before being issued to their staff.[22]

Many PSC staff utilize their personal weapons on the job, even on so-called 'non-armed contracts.'[23] For instance, while the contract awarded to the Global Strategies Group by the United Nations-supported Joint Elect-oral Management Body (JEMB) for the Afghan presidential election was a

non-armed assignment, the bulk of the Global Strategies Group contractors reportedly carried their own weapons on the job. According to one
contractor, the approach taken by all parties in such situations is 'don't
ask, don't tell.'[24] The vast majority of the Afghan staff operate with personal rather than duty weapons. ANBP officials have called for regulations
to be imposed that would reverse this situation, requiring all weapons utilized by PSC staff to be duty weapons, a policy consistent with the goals of
the demilitarization process.[25] The reaction of the Afghan government
and international community to such exhortations has been muted.

Many Afghan and international actors have argued that PSCs have had
a corrosive impact on the reconstruction process, poisoning relations
between the Afghan population and the international community. One of
the most trenchant criticisms of these groups is that they act above the
law, showing little respect for local norms and customs. There is abundant
anecdotal evidence of PSCs assaulting and insulting Afghan civilians in the
course of their work. Since many Afghans cannot make the distinction
between PSC and international military actors, and, in some cases, even
civilians, such incidents have tarred much of the international community.
Although the draft Law of Private Security Organizations (see Box 5.1)
could provide a framework to regulate their behaviour, until the Ministry
of Interior demonstrates the capacity to enforce it, PSCs will continue to
remain in a state of legal limbo, acting with impunity.

The reality is, however, that with security conditions worsening across
the country, PSCs meet a glaring need for the international community.
They are able to operate in areas where civilian agencies and NGOs, and,
in some cases, even international military forces, will not. They enable
civilian actors to carry out their duties, although with major limitations, in
high-risk areas and situations. The precarious nature of the security situation, coupled with the high sensitivity of donor states to civilian casualties, has made the PSCs a permanent feature of the security landscape. It
demonstrates the necessity for the debate on PSCs to move beyond the
question of how to sideline or marginalize such actors towards dialogue
on how to integrate them into peace-building processes such as small arms
reduction and control.

Militias affiliated with the government

In late May 2006, the Afghan government announced that the president
had approved a plan to mobilize militia forces in the south and east of the
country to meet the widening security gap that existed there due to the
upsurge of insurgent activity. Initial plans for the force stipulated that it
would consist of 2,000 militia fighters across the south alone, approximately 500 in each province. It was reported that commanders had
already been chosen for the Helmand and Uruzgan militias, Sher Mohammad Akhonzada and Jan Mohammad, respectively. Reports of these

appointments were noteworthy, as both individuals are former governors in the two provinces that were removed only months earlier due to international pressure. The UK and Dutch governments conditioned their deployment of PRTs to the two provinces on the removal of the two governors, who allegedly have links to the drug trade and other illicit activities.

Under this scheme, the militiamen would receive a salary of $200 per month, which is almost triple the salary of the average ANP patrolman.[26] According to one well-placed government official, these Auxiliary Police units would fall under the command and control of the provincial governor and police chief. They would only be utilized when the police require reinforcements, at which time they would be employed under temporary contracts. Weapons would not be issued to the militiamen; they would be responsible for bringing their own weapons, which would subsequently be registered by the government. The official went on to say that the majority of the groups that would be employed by the scheme would be akin to Pashtun community self-defence forces. The implication was that predatory criminal militias would not be involved in the scheme.

Further deliberation on the scheme, with greater involvement of international stakeholders, led to the release of a revised version in late 2006. The scope of the original scheme was expanded, calling for the mobilization of 11,500 Auxiliary Police in 21 provinces, with an emphasis on the security-challenged provinces of the south and east. Under this iteration, recruits for the force will receive two weeks of training provided by the CSTC-A and will be vetted by the Afghan government. Weapons will be issued to the force along with a uniform distinct from that of the regular police.[27] They will be subordinate to the Ministry of the Interior and provincial governors, but it is unclear how effective oversight will be provided. Salaries will be consistent with that of the regular police. Over time, it is envisaged that the Auxiliary Police units, with ongoing training, will be integrated into the regular police, although no clear timetable has been offered. The revised plan served to formalize and institutionalize the structure in an effort to reconcile any contradictions with the formal security apparatus; however, ambiguity continues to shroud many elements of it, notably vetting procedures and oversight protocols, foreshadowing significant problems.[28]

Although the development of the Auxiliary Police plan has aroused intense attention and debate, the employment of militias in support of the formal security apparatus is hardly a novel phenomenon. They have been mobilized in the past on an *ad hoc* basis to provide security support to the UN and government for key events such as the presidential and parliamentary elections.[29] In fact, the government plan appears to formalize a trend that had been ongoing for several months, as militia forces had been operating under the auspices of the government in several provinces including Paktya, Khost and Kunar, and provincial officials had begun discussing the prospect in Farah and Ghazni (*Pajhwok Afghan News*, 2006c).[30]

Governors in these provinces had, with the support of the central government, been utilizing funds from their discretionary budgets to raise and sustain militias to support the police.[31]

While the notion of exploiting traditional security structures to fill the prevailing security vacuum is surely compelling, it has the potential to undermine the demilitarization project and exacerbate insecurity. Accordingly, the introduction of the plan has been met with opposition by large sections of the international community and members of the government, particularly those representing the northern ethnic minority groups. The concerns expressed have revolved around three factors. First, the mobilization of militias runs contrary to the government's demilitarization process and seemingly undercuts any prospect of advancing the DIAG programme in the region. It has sent a powerful signal that the government is not committed to the process.

Second, the provision of special dispensation to rearm and remobilize militias in Pashtun areas has been treated with resentment by the northern ethnic factions,[32] the majority of which disarmed, at least partially, under the DDR programme. It has aroused fears of resurgent Pashtun nationalism and exceptionalism and has prompted many to discuss openly the prospect of remilitarization. Many of the northern leaders have derisively referred to the prospective Auxiliary Police as 'Karzai's Taliban.'[33]

Third, the legitimization of the militias, creating a rival security organ, could undercut the ANP and its efforts to establish a monopoly on the use of coercive force.[34]

As stated earlier, the exploitation of militias in post-Taliban Afghanistan is hardly a novel phenomenon and has occurred in a number of different contexts. One of the reasons for the US government's assent to the auxiliary policing plan is its own practice of utilizing militias. The US-led Coalition has developed strategic alliances with various commanders in the southeast of the country to utilize their militias to support counter-insurgency operations. Lacking the manpower to conduct large-scale operations in the expansive and rugged topography of the southeast, the Coalition has relied heavily on local militia proxies. It is believed that 1,500–2,000 militiamen have been in the indirect employ of the Coalition.[35] Individual commanders have reportedly received up to $10,000 per month in cash grants from the Coalition in exchange for their support.[36] The relationship between the US and Padshah Khan Zadran, a warlord from Paktika Province, in 2002 and 2003 exemplified this policy (Sedra, 2002).

In the immediate aftermath of the fall of the Taliban, Zadran was one of the most powerful commanders in eastern Afghanistan, with military reach into four provinces: Paktya, Logar, Paktika and Khost. He also became one of the central Coalition allies in the war on terror. Zadran openly stated in a 2002 interview with the *New York Times* that, out of the 6,000 soldiers under his command, 600 were in the direct pay of the

United States (Fisher, 2002). The United States also reportedly equipped Zadran with weapons and sophisticated communications equipment such as satellite phones. Emboldened by US support, Zadran openly defied the central government, launching rocket attacks on Gardez City and occupying the governor's office of Khost Province in 2002. Despite some bellicose rhetoric, the government was initially incapable of mounting an effective response to Zadran, due primarily to his relationship with the United States. In 2003, the United States withdrew support from Zadran due to a number of factors, including his increasingly public confrontation with the central government, his deliberate provision of fallacious intelligence to Coalition authorities and a number of confrontations between Coalition troops and Zadran's militia. Deprived of Coalition monetary assistance and political cover, Zadran could not sustain his militia nor insulate himself from government pressure, leaving him marginalized. On 1 December 2003, he was captured by the Pakistani military and later handed over to the Afghan authorities.

Such practices are at odds with the goals of the demilitarization process. To resolve the apparent contradiction in US policy, which endorsed the demilitarization of Afghan society while simultaneously facilitating the mobilization of allied groups in strategically important areas, it accorded its militia clients a semi-official status, exempting them from the demilitarization process. In doing so, the US has pledged to oversee their disarmament or absorption into the formal security architecture when their role becomes redundant. Nonetheless, the tactic has altered local power dynamics, giving these militias an edge over their rivals who lack ties to the Coalition.

Contrary to the paramount goal of the Karzai government, the centralization of power and authority in Kabul, the Coalition approach has fostered the creation of rival power centres. This approach is a by-product of the larger US strategy in Afghanistan, which is motivated more by the dictates of the global war on terror than the imperative of achieving a durable peace. US policy, in many ways, is geared to the containment of insecurity – in the form of terrorism, narcotics trafficking and transnational organized crime – rather than the more costly task of addressing its structural causes. It reflects the overarching problem of advancing highly sensitive and resource-intensive peace-building processes, such as small arms control and reduction programmes, when they diverge from the interests of key stakeholders.

Spoiler groups

Understanding trends in regard to small arms and light weapons among Afghanistan's spoiler groups, notably the Taliban, emphasize the importance of launching a robust disarmament programme and constructing an effective weapons management and procurement system within the security sector. The failure to reduce significantly the number of arms in circulation through a countrywide disarmament initiative has served as an enabler for the insurgency. Moreover, the failure to expeditiously establish sound weapons management protocols and erect an Afghan-run procurement system has contributed to the widespread leakage of government-owned weapons into the black market, many of which have found their way into the hands of anti-government groups.

The Secretary-General reported in August 2005 that 'a comparison of mine and improvised explosive device attacks carried out in the south and south-east in May 2004 and May 2005 shows a 40 per cent increase in May 2005' (UNSG, 2005, p. 15). A factor facilitating the rise in IED attacks is the wide availability of explosive materials in the country. As one ANBP official is quoted as saying, the arms caches that litter the country are 'cash 'n carry for bomb makers' (McGeough, 2004). While a great deal of the weaponry available in these caches has been rendered non-operational after years of decay, the explosive materials they contain can still be harvested for use in IEDs. This merely accentuates the importance of the APMASD and DIAG programmes, intended to collect, secure or destroy all such materials.

With warlords and spoiler groups flush with cash generated from the drug trade and other elements of the illicit economy, they have been seeking to upgrade and alter the profile of their weapons holdings. The presence of international military forces, buffeted by US air power, and an increasingly capable ANA has forced warlords and spoiler groups to adjust their tactics. While heavy weapons such as tanks and artillery may have conferred a strategic advantage during the civil war period prior to 2001, when no faction enjoyed a clear preponderance of force, they are now a burden on commanders. In an asymmetric power setting, small arms provide the best means for commanders to insulate and advance their interests.

In the case of commanders allied to the regime, small arms are easily concealed to avoid the perception that they not cooperating with the demilitarization process and fully supporting the political dispensation, while allowing them to carve out a niche in the illicit economy and maintain their regional power bases. Moreover, it gives them an insurance policy in the event of the breakdown of the regime and the resumption of civil conflict. In the case of anti-government spoiler groups, it enables them to wage a modern insurgency campaign against a vastly technologically superior enemy at a minimal cost. Small arms also enable commanders to secure their interests in the illicit economy, notably drug-producing areas and drug-trafficking routes. As many warlords have assumed the guise of narcotics entrepreneurs and as drug production has shifted from a few core provinces in the south and northeast to encompass the entire country, the importance of small arms as a means to protect the trade and their market share in it has expanded.[37]

The achievements of the DDR and HWC programmes, while impressive, should be viewed in this light. Abandoning such heavy weapons and surplus outdated small arms was a convenient way for allies of the government to demonstrate their support for the new political order, accruing the political advantages and legitimacy that it confers, without significantly eroding their power. It is a period of transition in terms of the small arms situation in the country, and the demilitarization process must reflect this. New emphasis must be placed on collecting small arms and light weapons, with a focus on explosive materials, around the country. The reticence to confront this issue, due in large part to the perception that the gun culture in Afghanistan is immovable, must be overcome if the SSR process is to achieve tangible gains and the security situation is to be stabilized.

Notes

1 Interview with senior Japanese Embassy official in Kabul, 12 May 2005.
2 Interview with consultant in the Ministry of Interior, Kabul, 21 May 2005.
3 Interview with international NGO official in Kabul, 10 November 2005.
4 Interview with adviser to the Defence Minister, Kabul, 18 May 2005.
5 This is in addition to the roughly $2 billion already expended on ANA equipment and infrastructure up to 2006.
6 Interview with private security contractor in Kabul, 19 May 2005.
7 Interview with official from the German Police Project in Kabul, 6 November 2005.
8 Interview with official from the German Police Project in Kabul, 6 November 2005.
9 Interview with CSTC-A officials in Kabul, 24 June 2006.
10 Interview with the spokesman of the Ministry of Interior in Kabul, 8 May 2005.
11 Interview with ANBP official in Kabul, 9 November 2005.
12 Interview with private security contractor in Kabul, 14 May 2005.
13 Interview with senior Afghan Interior Ministry official in Kabul, 23 June 2006; interview with Afghan National Police commander in Kabul, 20 June 2006.
14 Gurkhas are soldiers from Nepal.
15 Interview with private security contractor in Kabul, 20 May 2005.
16 Interview with United Nations Office of Project Services (UNOPS) official in Kabul, 23 May 2005.
17 Interview with private security contractor in Kabul, 20 May 2005.
18 Interview with private security contractor in Kabul, 14 May 2005.
19 Interview with private security contractor in Kabul, 14 May 2005.
20 The commanders claimed 10 per cent of each militiamen's salary, a portion of which was subsequently delivered to the Ministry of Interior commander. The majority of those who were employed as guards for the project emanated from the 2nd Corps of the Afghan Military Force (AMF) out of Kandahar. Ranging in size from 3,000–5,000 troops, the majority of the soldiers had not entered the DDR programme, as most spontaneously disarmed following the collapse of the Taliban to act as labourers for the poppy harvest (interview with senior ANBP official in Kabul, 13 June 2006).
21 Interview with senior ANBP official in Kabul, 30 April 2005.
22 Interview with private security contractor in Kabul, 14 May 2005.
23 Interview with private security contractor in Kabul, 14 May 2005.
24 Interview with private security contractor in Kabul, 14 May 2005.

25 Interview with senior ANBP official in Kabul, 30 April 2005.
26 Interview with senior ANBP official in Kabul, 13 June 2006.
27 Early reports indicate that the Auxiliary Police have been provided with uniforms identical to that of the regular police (personal communication with Western donor official, 7 March 2007).
28 Interview with donor official in Waterloo, Canada, 19 December 2006.
29 Interview with senior government representative in Kabul, 12 June 2006.
30 Interview with European Union official in Kabul, 18 June 2006.
31 Interview with UNAMA official in Kabul, 17 June 2006.
32 These include the Tajiks, Uzbeks and Hazarra.
33 Interview with senior ANBP official in Kabul, 13 June 2006.
34 Interview with senior UNAMA official in Kabul, 17 June 2006.
35 Interview with senior ANBP official in Kabul, 13 June 2006.
36 Interview with ANBP official in Kabul, 3 June 2004.
37 Interview with UNODC official in Kabul, 17 June 2006; interview with Ministry of Counter-Narcotics official in Kabul, 16 June 2006.

Conclusion

Mark Sedra

The widespread availability of arms in Afghan society poses a salient risk to the post-Taliban political order. Beyond the obvious public safety and health risk that arms pose to the general population, they have facilitated the growth of the illicit economy – typified by the drug trade – and an increasingly potent anti-government insurgency. Warlords have used their weapons to carve out spheres of influence, assuring their autonomy and preventing the government from extending its writ across the country. Perhaps most worrying, the presence of so many figures with links to armed groups within the government raises the stakes of legitimate political disputes, increasing the probability that they may degenerate into violence that could undermine the integrity of the state. The gun is surely not the cause of instability in Afghanistan, but it is one of the principal facilitators of it. By extension, reducing the salience of the gun, advancing efforts to demilitarize Afghan society, can serve as an enabler of the reconstruction and peace-building process.

The demilitarization of society, the establishment of a legal framework to control arms proliferation and the formation of a coherent policy on weapons procurement represent the three points of what can be conceptualized as a small arms triad in post-conflict contexts. Addressing acute cases of small arms proliferation requires parallel progress at each of these points, something that has not occurred in the Afghan context, where very little attention has been accorded to the small arms issue, despite the massive scale of the problem. Disarmament was only a symbolic element of the DDR process; little consideration was given to the legal dimension of the issue until 2005 and a rational procurement policy for the security forces was slow to develop.

This can partially be attributed to conditions that were inhospitable for action on the issue. The Afghan case aptly illustrates that the potential for small arms reduction and control programming is dependent on the presence of a number of conditions that can be grouped under the headings of security, development and political.

In the security sphere, a base level of security and stability is required to advance small arms collection and control efforts. Steps must be taken to break previous cycles of violence and imbue the population with the confidence to abandon their arms. In a country with such a long legacy of internecine strife, this is enormously difficult and was dependent on two factors: the deployment of a robust peace support mission capable of providing a security buffer for the process, and the successful implementation of a security sector reform process to entrench the rule of law across the country. Neither fully materialized, as the international community failed to extend the International Security Assistance Force (ISAF) across the whole of Afghanistan and the SSR process was advanced in a deliberate and disjointed fashion, with judicial and law enforcement reforms being overshadowed by the training and equipping of the ANA. As a result, an underlying sense of insecurity has pervaded the country, which has impelled both groups and individuals to look to the gun rather than the state to provide for their safety.

In the development sphere, Afghanistan remains one of the most impoverished countries in the world, ranking 173 out of 178 countries on the UNDP's Human Development Index (UNDP, 2004). One of the only stable sources of income for most Afghans comes from the gun. Serving in a warlord or criminal militia provides rare economic security. Weaning them away from this dependency requires the creation of opportunities in the legitimate economy. The reintegration component of the DDR programme has sought to give militiamen the basic tools to operate within the civilian economy, but has not provided opportunities for them to employ those tools. Afghans will continue to turn to the gun as a coping mechanism unless legitimate alternative livelihoods can be provided.

Politically, the major local and international stakeholders in Afghanistan's reconstruction process must demonstrate the necessary political will to address the small arms issue meaningfully. The Afghan government's accommodationist approach to commanders and the ambivalent policy of the US towards the demilitarization have exemplified the absence of that will. A clear consensus among all the main political stakeholders is indispensable, but, in Afghanistan, that only began to emerge, albeit slowly, in 2005. The notion of consensus does not imply that all Afghan commanders will support the process; some will inevitably resist it. Resistance can be overcome, however, if a plurality of political actors tied to the government unites in their support for the process.

In the Afghan case, government obstinacy on the small arms issue has been out of step with public opinion, as the majority of Afghans have consistently rated disarmament as one of their foremost priorities. Accordingly, the notion that an overarching Afghan gun culture will render any community-wide disarmament process unfeasible is spurious. Generating the political will needed to advance a comprehensive small arms reduction and control effort requires a new awareness in the Afghan government of the centrality of the small arms issue in restoring security and stability to the country, as well as a renewed determination to challenge actors, particularly those allied to the state, who defy the rule of law and the sovereignty of the government. International stakeholders, for their part, must be willing to lobby the government more forcefully to adopt a more serious approach to the issue and furnish it with the incentives and disincentives to do so. Civil society also has a crucial role to play in channelling public will for disarmament into genuine political pressure on the Afghan government and international donor community to take decisive action.

The small arms dilemma is a cross-cutting issue that demands a holistic approach. Until it is embedded in the SSR process, development programming and the political reform agenda, a comprehensive countrywide arms collection process and a sustainable arms control regime will be unachievable. Some progress has been made over the past five years to forge the societal conditions necessary to address the small arms dilemma in a meaningful way, but the issue continues to be taboo for many actors. It increasingly appears that this psychological barrier to action will only be broken from below, with pressure from the Afghan population and civil society for the Afghan government and international community to act. With the Afghan state-building project in its fifth year and the window for international engagement gradually closing, it is important that such a movement materializes soon. As long as small arms remain readily available, Afghanistan's transition to democracy and stability will remain incomplete, and the spectre of a return to civil conflict will hang over the country.

Part III

Case studies

Introduction

Michael Bhatia

Part III presents six provincial case studies (Ghor, Paktya, Kandahar City, Jalalabad City, Kunduz/Baghlan and the Hazarajat), based on the analytical framework presented in the previous chapters of this book, in order to demonstrate the diversity of local security conditions and dynamics in Afghanistan. Four of these areas have been the location of significant post-Bonn conflict, as was the case with armed disputes between competing groups in Paktya and Ghor and the riots over the proposed desecration of the Koran by US forces.

The primary source for each chapter is the varied testimonies of local combatants and other interviewed individuals, then supplemented by facts and analysis gathered from secondary academic sources. The case study chapters explore the following issues:

- the nature and structure of local armed groups and their methods of mobilization;
- the history of conflict in each region;
- conceptions of legitimate and illegitimate mobilization;
- the relationship between commanders, communities, combatants and political–military parties;
- the role and impact of the government of Afghanistan in local security/insecurity;
- the status of official armed units in the province (ANA, ANP, NDS, ABP, etc.);
- the status of weapons licensing;
- the activities of Private Security Companies;
- Evidence on the local arms trade and supply/demand of weapons and ammunition.

Case study research was conducted in summer 2004 and spring 2005. Over the past year, with both the expansion of the DIAG programme and the parliamentary elections, as well as the AGF insurgency's reassertion, the political–military situation in certain provinces has changed considerably, with the rotation and replacement of key government appointees.[1]

The inclusion of case studies provides an in-depth account of local histories and dynamics, while presenting opportunities for cross-case comparison. For example, it becomes evident that political–military parties and local strongmen were far more dominant in the northeast than in the southeastern province of Paktya. Meanwhile, tribal militias and community mobilization operate in substantively different terms in Paktya than in Kandahar, with substantively different conceptions of legitimate mobilization and the individual authority of the *qawmi meshran* and local *khans.* Paktya, Kandahar, Ghor and Jalalabad have all experienced events that violently displayed the weaknesses and contradictions of the post-Bonn Afghan government. Paktya and Ghor revealed the troubled relationship between centrally appointed (and often abusive) local commanders and other local armed groups. Jalalabad and Kandahar illustrate the role of the Coalition and private security companies (PSCs) in supporting local armed groups, often to the detriment of security sector reform, central authority and local security and human rights. Weapons licensing remains generally unimplemented in major areas of Afghanistan. The Coalition has both catalysed (as with the British PRT in Mazar and the USAR PRT in Kandahar) and obstructed this process.

A quick statistical comparison of combatant profiles reveals that the average age of first mobilization was under 18 or even under 16 for a significant percentage of combatants. Deviation among provinces was not considerable, with all provinces above 30 per cent for under 16 mobilization. There were significant differences among provinces in terms of prominent non-combat livelihoods, the locations and degree of labour migration and the level of schooling. Certain motives were more common in some regions than in others. For example, in the northeast provinces, descriptions of force were far more common than in any other part of Afghanistan. Compulsion was not discussed at all in Paktya. Elder authority in Paktya was limited to periods of political transition (1992–1995, 2001–2002) and was generally absent in other periods of conflict. In contrast, in Ghor and parts of the Hazarajat, elder authority is common in all periods of conflict.

Note

1 Following the April 2005 riots over the Koran's desecration, Gul Agha Sherzai and din Mohammed were switched as governors of Kandahar and Jalalabad. Later, in the run-up to the parliamentary election, Hazrat Ali stepped down as the Nangarhar Chief of Police in order to run in the parliamentary elections, ultimately securing a seat in the *Meshrano Jirga.*

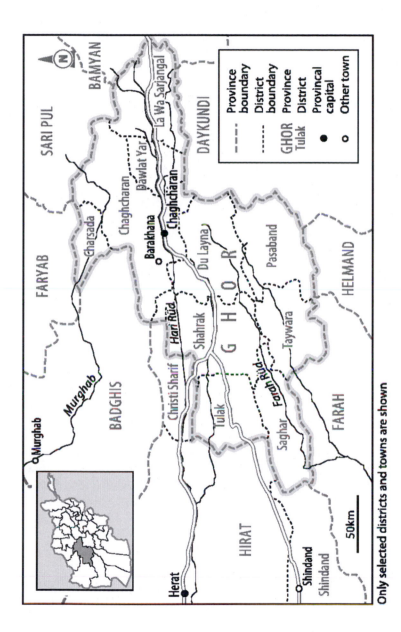

Only selected districts and towns are shown

Map 6.1 Ghor Province.

6 Ghor Province

All against all?

Michael Bhatia

The case of Ghor Province explores the following issues:

- the relationship between communities, commanders and individual combatants;
- the role of elder authority and legitimacy in mobilizing combatants and empowering commanders;
- the regional politics of commander alliances;
- the impact of the post-Bonn creation of the AMF on local weapons flows and combatant mobilization.

As described in Chapter 1 ('the Afghan security dilemma'), the case of Ghor Province demonstrates how the line between the maintenance of local militia for protection, and the role of these groups in threatening other *qawms* (or in engaging in predation) is blurred. This chapter first provides basic information as to the topography, leaders and prominent ethnic groups in Ghor Province. It second sheds new light on the local fighting of summer 2004 between commanders Abdul Salaam Khan and Ahmad Khan Morghabi, illustrating the role of the central government in local violence through the legitimation and empowerment of local commanders. Indeed, Ahmad Khan Morghabi's forces received new equipment as part of Operation Enduring Freedom, while his militia's incorporation into the AMF spurred a graphic increase in demand for small arms in Ghor.

The events of June 2004 also illustrate the shifting position of local militias, and the differences between local and external interpretations of conflict. Third, the history of conflict in Ghor is detailed, with a particular focus on the interaction between Ghor commanders and other regional power brokers in Hirat, Badghis and Faryab. Fourth, the chapter examines the relationships between local strongmen, communities and combatants; detailing how commanders have acquired autonomy from community oversight mechanisms.

Setting the local scene

Located on the western edge of the central highlands, and bordering to the north the provinces of Faryab and Badghis and to the west the province of Hirat, the population of Ghor contains as many as 30 *qawm*s of Aimaq (Dari-speaking) ethnicity.[1] While bordering the predominantly Hazara central highlands, the geo-politics of Ghor Province are largely oriented to the north and west. The total population is estimated to be between 485,000, spread out over 36,479 square kilometres.[2]

Ghor remains one of the most under-researched provinces in Afghanistan. There is a limited NGO presence in the region (e.g., AfghanAID), while the UN has been present largely only in the run-up to the presidential and parliamentary elections through the Joint Electoral Management Body and UNOPS. A 150-strong Lithuanian Provincial Reconstruction Team, which also includes military representatives from the United States, Iceland and Denmark, was deployed to the province in November 2005. A total of 67 per cent of registered voters turned out for the parliamentary elections, which was higher than the regional and national average.

Some districts (particularly the three bordering Helmand and Uruzgan) are involved in poppy production, which is attributed to the lack of a government security presence. However, the crop is not cultivated in any sizeable proportions and performs poorly given the agricultural conditions in the province; the crop is generally utilized to provide households with cash income (Mansfield, 2006).

A researcher affiliated with the Small Arms Survey reported that the province is also serving as a transit point and trade route for small arms from Tajikistan and Uzbekistan to Helmand, Farah, Uruzgan and Kandahar. Some weapons are reported to be going to Pakistan to either Taliban or to narco-traffickers. Taliban remnants are present in southern Pasaband district.

Currently, the two primary commanders in the region are Abdul Salaam of the Reza *qawm*[3] and Haji Ahmad Khan Morghabi of the Morghab *qawm* and valley. The dominant party in Ghor is Jamiat-e-Islami, although Hezb-e-Islami, Ittihad and Harakat-e-Inqelab-e-Islami (Nabi) all had a presence during the Soviet period. Two Hizb-e-Wahdat commanders (Etamadi and Bahr) are believed to control the two eastern districts (La Wa Sarjangal) of the province (ANSO, 2004; UNHCR district profiles). Former Hezb-e-Islami commanders now head the provincial ministries of education, telecommunications and agriculture.

A 2004 ANSO report indicates that there were approximately 3,000 armed men in the province, of which 500 belonged to former governor Dr. Ibrahim Malikzada and 300 to Abdul Salaam, some of which were 'actively engaged in smuggling, drug trafficking, and factional conflicts' (ANSO, 2004). Dr. Ibrahim was elected to the *Wolesi Jirga* in the 2005 parliamentary elections. There were reportedly 300 largely untrained police officers in the province (ANSO, 2004). As in other parts of Afghanistan, commanders were far more willing to hand over their heavy weapons than to provide their soldiers and their small arms to the ANBP, with approximately 70 heavy weapons (mortars, DShKs, and Zigkoyak) collected from the 41st Division.

Reinterpreting the June 2004 violence and the Afghan Military Force (AMF)

Ghor Province gained attention on 17 June 2004, when Commander Abdul Salaam Khan's forces moved into Chaghcharan City (with the support of the police), ousting both the provincial governor, Dr. Ibrahim Malikzada, and the Commander of the 41st Division, Ahmad Morghabi. Dr. Ibrahim was seen to control sections not only of Ghor Province but also of districts in the neighbouring provinces of Farah, Hirat and Helmand. Abdul Salaam's forces withdrew on 23 June, which was followed by the deployment of a 200-strong ANA contingent with a US Army Embedded Training Team. During the incident, 10–18 people were killed, and the local bureau of the Afghan Independent Human Rights Commission (AIHRC) was raided (Jamali, 2004). Malikzada's forces were later involved in an armed attack on the Cheshti district of Hirat Province, neighbouring Ghor, in an attempt to remove the local commander (*Saudi Press Agency*, 2004).

External sources stress the removal of a centrally appointed governor and AMF commander by unaffiliated regional warlords. The BBC and other observers perceive the events of July 2004 as yet another example of a regional challenge to Karzai's emerging government. Interviews with combatants reveal a different interpretation of these events. They stress that the various groups involved supported Abdul Salaam due to the predatory behaviour of the forces that were formerly in place. According to many of the 41st Division combatants interviewed, a Coalition was formed between the Reza and the Miri and 'all the people rose against' Ahmad Morghabi and the 41st division. However, according to one combatant, Abdul Salaam's forces quickly began engaging in their own predatory behaviour, looting and burning shops in the bazaar.[4]

The Karzai government had placed the 41st Division under Commander Ahmad Morghabi, who proceeded to recruit new forces from a variety of different local *qawms*. A substantial portion of the combatants interviewed (and involved in the DDR process in Ghor Province) had only become combatants after the fall of the Taliban. The announcement of the formation of the AMF actually spurred the initial mobilization of some combatants. In Ghor, the ANBP's activities were not only focused on the residual caseload from the past two decades of conflict (1978–2001) but also on a group of newly mobilized soldiers, who had only joined after the Bonn process.

According to some combatants, recruits were promised a monthly salary of over $40 per month and were required to purchase a weapon in order to join the local division. This not only served to inflate the local weapons market but also meant that the commander did not have to submit his own weapons upon DDR but could instead submit weapons that individual soldiers had recently purchased. Due to increased demand, the cost of a Chinese AK increased from $40 to $100–160, with 30 bullets costing $2.[5]

Most combatants assert that those weapons that were not turned in to DDR were confiscated by their commanders and sent to the Morghab valley. Certain combatants sold key household assets (such as livestock) in order to purchase weapons to join the division. A shared and common narrative of this time is apparent in the following accounts:

> When the Taliban left Chaghcharan, Ahmad Morghabi made the division and told us he could give us some money – of course, we are poor people – so we wrote our name and became soldiers. In the beginning, they promised 5,000–6,000 Afs [$100–120] per month as well as cars and clothes, and that after two years I would become a Colonel in a division. He kept on delaying and we only got 800–1,000 Afs [$16–20] in two months. Later, when we made a little bit of noise, he used the force against us also. Ahmad Morghabi had another force of special soldiers, who were family and relatives.[6]

> [I joined] because they told us they'd give us a salary of 2,500–3,000 Afs [$50–60] per month; but when we came, sometimes they only gave 200–300 Afs [$4–6]. From the beginning they promised a lot of money, but then nothing.... They used a lot of force [to make us stay].[7]

> We had a very hard time – because all of our agriculture was destroyed. We had no water, and we had no other job. Some people told us they'd give us more money to be a soldier in this division. They told us we'd get lots of money, but we received very little, they lied to us. We received 2,000 Afs [$40] at first, but later only 500–1,000 Afs [$10–20] occasionally. When we came here, we told them we didn't want to stay, then by force they made us stay.[8]

Approximately 400–500 core people and relatives (the *nazm-e-khas* or special soldiers), armed with both AKs and with RPG 7/9, were able to control another 1,200–1,500 combatants, armed largely with AKs and pistols, by force. Whether to initiate or sustain mobilization, forced conscription is known as *jalb*, where 'if we didn't come, soldiers would come to our home and bring us to the division.'[9] Having achieved the role of division commander, Ahmad Morghabi then utilized his formal appointment as a platform upon which to carry out predatory activities in the province. According to his combatants, not only would the soldiers establish checkpoints and demand a tax from all vehicles travelling from Hirat, but he also forcefully imprisoned both men and women and used local conflicts in order to extort money from villagers (as much as $1,500).[10] To sum up, those combatants who joined the 41st Division of Ahmad Morghabi's after the Bonn conference indicated that they first joined for economic reasons but were forced to remain combatants by Ahmed Khan's *nazm-e-khas*.

Local conflict history

Historically, while Chaghcharan City has been held by whatever regime controlled the central Kabul-based government, the districts outside of the city have maintained varying degrees of autonomy. Provincial political–military dynamics are both shaped and affected by actors and developments in the neighbouring provinces of Badghis, Faryab and Hirat. Commanders receive support from neighbouring province commanders but also deploy their soldiers to fight in surrounding provinces, as they did both for and against Ismail Khan in Hirat and Shindand in 2004.[11]

Jihad

If they were recruited during the jihad period, most combatants received their weapons through a party, whether by travelling to Pakistan or from a commander. However, during the Rabbani regime, the Taliban and after 9/11, many combatants had to purchase their own weapon on the local weapons market. With the formation of the AMF, commanders such as Faizal Ahmed Khan, who received support from Panjsher, would provide weapons to their soldiers, while the soldiers of Salaam Khan generally had to purchase their own weapon and those that joined the 41st Division purchased weapons only to have these confiscated by the division commander Ahmad Morghabi.

Civil war

Substantive local unrest did not expand until after the Soviet invasion, although there was dissent over earlier Khalqi policies regarding marriage and religion. During the jihad period, small groups would travel to Pakistan in order to acquire weapons from the parties or on the open market (Markuls or Pakistan-made AK, known as AK-Dera).

On this occasion, some combatants were exposed either to religious indoctrination or military training by the parties. One combatant noted that 1,000 children (around 12 years of age) were sent to a Hezb-e-Islami training camp in Pakistan in 1985 to receive both religious education and military training, with the expectation of beginning to fight upon reaching age 16.[12] Representatives from Hezb-e-Islami and Jamiat also travelled to the region to spread propaganda through nightletters (pamphlets posted on village walls) and radio broadcasts in order to encourage resistance against the Soviet presence.

As of 1988, the party distribution of full-time mujahideen in all of western Afghanistan was 65 per cent Jamiat, 8 per cent Hezb-e-Islami, 13 per cent Harakat (Rubin, 1996, p. 200). In 1987, Ismail Khan sponsored a cross-party commanders' conference in Saghar district of Ghor in an attempt to create cooperation and unity among 1,200 commanders. While initially successful, this Coalition was later undermined and ignored by the Peshawar-based party leadership (Nojumi, 2002, p. 94; Giustozzi, 2000, p. 241).

A key determinant of party affiliation was the willingness of the party in Peshawar or Quetta to provide the local representatives with weapons. One Aaliyar combatant noted that his group joined Ittihad as 'another party didn't accept us, only this group accepted us ... every time we went they gave us 10 weapons.'[13] Food and other provisions were either donated by families through *zakat* or taken by force.[14]

Those individuals who studied in government-run schools or did not join the mujahideen were often persecuted by their community commanders, with their homes burned and family members kidnapped or beaten, leading some either to migrate to Chaghcharan City or join government security forces (including the *Nezmi-hama* or city police).[15] Living in proximity to the city also compelled many to choose the government. Yet, the benefits of joining the government in terms of both wages and subsidized necessities could be substantial.[16] Still, as demonstrated in the case of Ibrahim Beg of the Miri, commanders principally switched to the side of the government in order to acquire support against their foes in other *qawms* (Giustozzi, 2000, pp. 124–125).

According to one combatant in Ghor, 'originally it did not matter if a person joined a commander from a different qawm ... little by little, there was a change, when each nation selected a new commander in order for each nation to gain power.' The same combatant notes that he 'never understood why we were fighting – only the commanders told us to fight or not to fight, we didn't understand – Salaam and old people told us you must come to our groups.'[17]

Taliban era

The reconciliation programme of the Najibullah government after 1989 led many commanders to hand in their weapons and affiliate with the central government. The transition to the Rabbani mujahideen government involved the formation of a government division in Chaghcharan City and the dominance of the mujahideen in government and security institutions. The Taliban held Chaghcharan centre from 1997–2001, allying with some of these local commanders.

Occupation of central Chaghcharan by the Taliban led to a general collapse of most local resistance movements. According to one combatant, the Taliban's capture of Ghor led more families to emigrate from the province than to engage in active resistance. Another source of grievance was their demands regarding the disarmament of the population – each family was required either to provide a weapon or face imprisonment.

During the Taliban era, the distribution of resources from the central Jamiat party and the Northern Alliance constituted a source of local conflict between commanders, with one commander arguing that: 'money is the only reason commanders change sides.'[18] Previous disputes between Abdul Salaam Khan, Ahmad Morghabi and Ismail Khan were cited to be over the allocation of resources from the Northern Alliance. Another combatant notes: 'In the time of the Russians, we had good solidarity and union with each other, but in the time of President Rabbani and the Taliban, we had such problems with each other.'[19]

Post-9/11 period

The death of Ahmad Shah Massoud and the deployment of American Special Operations Forces (and their limited provision of new weapons) both resurrected the local resistance and re-empowered local armed groups. Indeed, the Morghab valley was an early staging point for Ismail Khan's return to power in Hirat and for American action against the Taliban.

Arms (PKs and short-barrelled 15–16 AKZSU-74 'Krinkovs') were provided by the United States to Ahmad Morghabi, who then distributed these to his core followers. The combatants also received an increase in salary from nothing for several months to 100 Afs ($2) per day.[20] Another combatant noted the arms delivery by parachute to sub-commander Gulamin in Morghab of two cartons of AK ammunition and four cartons of PK ammunition.[21] After 9/11, an Aaliyar commander indicated that he received field telephones and 5–6 billion old Afghanis, which was used to pay salaries and purchase weapons, food and clothing from traders.[22] A Yarpulad combatant noted supply flights from Panjsher, which brought food, clothing, and 500–1,000 Afs ($10–20) per soldier per month to Faizal Akmed Khan.[23]

Substantial insecurity returned to Ghor with the removal of the Taliban, as local commanders began to fight against one another in the midst of a security vacuum. One combatant, who had previously fled to Faryab, asserted that 'all of the Commanders were fighting between each other,' and that this fighting 'was not from the local people, as the commanders were so powerful they didn't listen to or respect the community.'[24] Until the deployment of American Embedded Trainers and the Afghan National Army in summer 2004, 'all the nations were fighting against each other ... to take more power from the government over control of provincial and district positions.'[25]

The various *qawms* are still involved in occasional hostilities against one other (largely Yarpulad versus Miri versus the Reza versus the Morghabi), which has sparked local displacement in several cases, with individuals leaving for Hirat or Faryab. The line between the maintenance of local groups for protection and the role of these groups in threatening other *qawms* (or in engaging in predation) is by no means clear.

Communities, commanders and combatants

As discussed, Ghor Province includes as many as 30 Aimaq/Tajik *qawms*, many of which maintain armed groups under the control of a prominent group member.

As described in Chapter 3, the *qawm* is a collective body, which can highly recommend and/or demand mobilization. The *qawm* is the source of elder and community authority, which served as a particularly prominent motive in Ghor during the jihad, civil war and the Bonn period.

Relationship between commander and community

One Miri combatant who commenced fighting during the jihad notes:

> Each nation of Ghor has special groups, and commanders told people they had to join. All of the different nations, they collected one person from each family, and the *mullah* often also said for us to go, and this was enough.[26]

This confirms the earlier examination of the significance of non-material resources in promoting mobilization, particularly in terms of religious and community support. These resources, however, are situation-specific and dependent on commanders' receptivity to community input.

The relationship between the *qawm* and the commander is both cooperative and in danger of transition, whereby a collective body may become autocratic and individually oriented. There is a constant question as to whether the community of elders is able to establish (and enforce) a division between mobilization for legitimate versus illegitimate purposes. Operating within this framework, commanders are able to engage in certain types of violence with the consent of the broader community (largely local protection and community-endorsed political violence, e.g., against the Soviets or the Taliban) but are unable to engage in types of violence beyond protection with community consent. For example, according to one combatant, among the Miri *qawm*, both the local *mullahs* and the elders indicated that fighting after the Soviet withdrawal was no longer religiously sanctioned. He recalls that: 'The Miri nation said jihad was over and the mullah said if you keep fighting, if you died, it will not be good, and God will not bless you.'[27] Without this consent, the commander

Table 6.1 Combatant profiles of Ghor Province (34 combatants)

Schooling	37% have some education, 50% of which studied in the local mosque or madrassas
Prominent livelihoods	Farmer, shepherd, street labourer, driver, shopkeeper
Labour migration	14.7% to Iran 2.9% to Faryab 5.9% to Hirat Province
Average age of first mobilization:	18.8 years
Recruited under 18	47%
Recruited at or under 16	30%
Purchased own weapon (post-9/11)	62.5%
First mobilized during:	
Jihad period	38%
Civil war	17.6%
Taliban era	17.6%
Post-9/11 period	26.4%
Prominent motives by period:	
Jihad	Jihad, religious/elder authority, grievance, force
Civil war	Grievance, protection, elder authority, economic incentives
Taliban era	Protection, force, economic incentives, grievance
Post-9/11 period	Elder authority, economic incentives, force, protection

is not able to utilize the *qawm*'s authority to invoke the necessity of obedience and the concept of honour.

Still, if the commander's stature and power has increased to the point where he dictates the composition of the *qawmi meshran*, he will be able to utilize this community and elder authority in order to mobilize soldiers. As noted by one Miri combatant, both after the Soviet withdrawal and with the collapse of the Taliban, 'the commanders were so powerful they didn't [have to] listen to or respect the community.'[28] Another Reza combatant notes:

> In the time when they selected Salaam Khan [as the commander], the elders, *maulavi* and *mullah* were more powerful. Now the commander is more powerful. He can change the community, but they cannot change Commander Salaam ... No one can tell him no.[29]

Hence, the commander is able to dictate the composition of the community decision-making bodies, and the community has lost its ability to check and restrict the power of the commander.

Even if the commander does not have this authorization and legitimacy, he may still be permitted to recruit soldiers autonomously and engage in certain types of fighting without community assistance. Thus, even if the commander and the community of elders at times share a symbiotic relationship, this does not prevent the commander from engaging in certain types of entrepreneurial violence. This question is directly relevant in terms of the commander's ability to mobilize his soldiers for action against the new government and in terms of whether local perceptions as to the legitimacy of the new government will limit a commander's autonomy.[30]

Political parties

The emergence of *tanzims* introduced a new actor into community mobilization, and these *tanzims* ultimately emboldened commanders at the cost of communities, undermining the community's role in identifying legitimate forms of mobilization. A commander is selected due to his position as a prominent *khan* (or landholder), the position and influence of his family (uncles or fathers) and/or his level of education and military experience. As revealed in the interviews with combatants, the authority of community elders and religious figures, as well as the prominent social positions of many of the commanders, enhances their ability both to mobilize and retain combatants. An Aaliyar combatant stressed the role of wealth in determining commanders and party affiliation and also the role of *tanzims* for further empowering commanders:

> Aaliyar is a big *qawm*, so some people listened to certain rich people, and other people listened to other rich people. Some rich people joined Harakat, some Ittihad. In our place, it was Haji Mawladad. He's the rich, good person; so we joined ourselves with him and he was Jamiat ... These rich people are popular because they have money, and they became commanders. The money they took from the *tanzims* they collected for themselves and they didn't give us anything.... Now you can see them, they are so rich and we have nothing.[31]

This combatant narrative confirms the impact of party money in empowering local commanders, to the detriment of local communities.

Elder authority

The role of elder authority is seen to be particularly strong among the Reza and Aaliyar *qawms* and less so among the Yarpulad. The Reza *qawm* has over 5,000 families, with some of these families in disputes with one another, which leads members to ally with either Salaam Khan or with other commanders from different *qawms*. Still, the vast majority of Reza combatants indicated that respect for authority was their primary reason for joining Abdul Salaam Khan; arguing, for example, that:

> Salaam Khan is the *sardari-e-qawm* and he selects us, and it is the honour of our *qawm*, and when he says something, no one can say no ... I must respect him.[32]

> We belonged to one nation – Reza – so that was the reason I joined him. The Russians gave us a hard time, they put people in jail, the *mullah* told all of us to go to the jihad, and so we went. The commanders had people write their name in a book in the mosque. I had no information until I was a soldier with Commander Salaam, he had his own business with Jamiat, but we know nothing. He told us we were with the Jamiat party. I never left him as he was from our *qawm*, and we must stay with him.[33]

> Salaam Khan is a big person from our qawm, when he fought, we had to fight. I just belong to Salaam Khan, what he said I will do.[34]

During the jihad, ten Reza families would go to the mosque, where one to three people would be selected by the *mullah* to join the commander. Over the past five years, combatants received a salary of $16–20 or 700 kg of wheat per year (which increased to 140 kg per month (1,680 per year) when Salaam joined the Taliban), which Salaam Khan was able to provide through a tax levied on all community members.[35] Accordingly, a family must provide 25 kg of wheat per year for every cow it possesses; this tax is collected by the soldiers. Upon being selected, soldiers also need to supply their own weapon.

The space between mobilization through respect for elder authority and force can be ambiguous. Over the course of a discussion concerning his first recruitment into the jihad, a combatant switched between discussions of obedience to questions of authority and to overt force:

> The elders of the community, they selected me to go to the fighting. We stayed by force – because we couldn't stay in our home peacefully. This type of force – if I didn't go they would take cows, money, everything in the home. They would hurt us, and put us in prison. From time of Karmal until time of Karzai, this was by force.[36]

Others mixed in descriptions of elder authority as force and also described the varied impact of grievance and economic incentives according to the period of involvement. Referring to the civil war period, two combatants recalled:

> We had conflicts between *qawms*. We must defend ourselves from other people. Also we needed some money, sometimes during the winter, Salaam would give us wood or wheat. In the beginning, it was also a little bit by force, as he belonged to our nation.[37]

The jihad was over but we had nothing else to do, the commanders used force to be able to fight against each other. Then came the Taliban and they were also like the foreigners and for six years we fought again. Also we don't have anything.[38]

These combatants were the only members of the Tajik Reza group in Ghor willing to describe what others viewed as obedience to authority as force.

Lack of dominance of communal ties

Individuals from different *qawms* can also join commanders from other *qawms*, whether due to their need for protection from intra-*qawm* disputes or due to their need for economic assistance. The role of protection in inducing mobilization is evident in the following account:

> [I joined] for security, so someone doesn't give us a hard time, this was why I stayed with Abdul Salaam, so other people who would give me a hard time would understand that I am with Commander Salaam. My older brother died due to a problem with other people [from Dowlat-yar *qawm*]. This family got weapons and so I was scared. I had to join and become a combatant to defend myself from these people.[39]

Members of the Aaliyar *qawm* have their own commanders and have also been allied with Abdul Salaam and with Dr. Ibrahim in the past. Accordingly, it was more common for individuals from different *qawms* to join together during the jihad period until the time of the Najibullah government, when the difficulties between *qawms* became more pronounced. This is not to argue that all of the *qawm* members supported the mujahideen or the government. According to one Yarpulad combatant, that *qawm* was divided whereby 'the group that had more power joined the mujahideen; and those that did not have anything or did not know what to do joined the government.'[40] Consequently, assertions as to the overwhelming dominance of local communal ties distorts a local reality, whereby individuals affiliated themselves with groups either because of familial disputes or to gain access to socioeconomic opportunities available only outside of their village, whether in pursuit of an increase in status or in response to intra-group conflict.

Economic incentives

Other motives for mobilization are also evident in this region. Interviews with Ghor combatants included significant information on the importance and size of economic incentives and on the role of child combatants. Combatants came from a broad range of economic backgrounds, with substantial differences in the amount of land possessed. Clearly, commanders and sub-commanders possessed far more land than the common soldier. Those combatants who joined for economic reasons did not receive the substantial windfalls characteristic of accounts of greed-motivated combatants. One combatant notes that he received approximately $20 per month during the Rabbani time (one million old Afghani) and then $28 per month during the Karzai time, in addition to food at the military base. He indicated that he joined 'because I had nothing else to do, we had a bad situation economically'; he joined 'just to survive, just for a salary, also to help my people.' He split his salary between his family and for his own use.[41]

Recruitment at child age

At least half of the combatants were first mobilized under the age of 18. One combatant was recruited when he was nine, first serving in the kitchen making tea and potatoes and then receiving a weapon between the ages of 13 and 15. He notes:

> I was young, they forced me, I must go. If I didn't go, I must pay, if I don't pay, they can imprison me.... The older people fought more [and had rockets], I didn't fight that often. I had no choice, I had to go, even when I needed to collect wheat. All the time, the commanders used force; if no force, nobody would fight. Maulavi Moussa had special people to use force, maybe 20 people with new AK-47s.[42]

He notes, however, that he volunteered to fight against the Taliban and was not forced, as it was: 'a different situation, sometimes it's about force, and sometimes about our *qawm*, then there was discrimination between Pashto and Dari-speakers.'[43] This singular account reveals the widely varying motives and rich histories of each combatant. Over the course of a conflict, mobilization can be driven by force or independent choice.

Conclusion

The case of Ghor demonstrates the dynamics discussed in the opening chapters of this book. It reveals the interplay between local commanders, regional powers and the central government. It demonstrates how commanders have been able to overpower community elders, reducing the traditional checks on their power by determining the composition of local *shuras*. Local commanders are empowered by external actors – whether *tanzims*, the Karzai government or the Coalition – at the cost of community oversight mechanisms. As demonstrated in Chapter 1, these commanders are able to utilize community mobilization for security and protection for their own ends and for predatory purposes.

The central government legitimized predatory local commanders through the creation of a provincial AMF division, which increased the supply of weapons to the province and led to the mobilization of a new generation of combatants. The state was a direct participant in local violence. By providing a title to Morghabi's local forces, the Karzai government became compromised in the eyes of local combatants and communities. The local AMF commander utilized his acquisition of a national title to acquire combatants, persecute opposing villages and consolidate economic/political power in the province. National legitimacy became another tool for a commander's pursuit of local dominance and increased insecurity and violent conflict. The AMF was constituted less by former combatants than by newly mobilized individuals. The post-Bonn narrative of the conflict between a weak but virtuous central government versus bad local warlords is challenged by the events of July 2004 (Giustozzi, 2004). Indeed, as demonstrated by Ghor, the government is implicated in this local insecurity and warlordism due to its legitimation of local militias.

Notes

1 Currently, the term Tajik is inappropriately applied to most populations that speak Dari as their primary language. To an extent, this can be seen to have affected how Afghans identify themselves to foreigners. In Chaghcharan, when asked as to their ethnicity, most interviewees first cited their *qawm* and then noted that they were Tajik. As seen in Adamec, in the majority of ethnic distribution maps, the population of Ghor Province is represented as predominantly of Taimani or Chahari Aimaq origin (Adamec, 2003, p. 138).
2 Population statistics online, available at: statoids.com/uaf.html and cia.gov/cia/publications/factbook/print/af.html (accessed 4 December 2007).
3 Abdul Salaam owes his position due to the prominence of his family (his uncle was an elder and a representative in Daoud Khan's Parliament and disappeared during the Khalqi government) and also due to his previous military training (he was a conscript in the Afghan Army in 1978 and participated with Ismail Khan in the insurrection in Herat in 1979). He first belonged to Hezb-e-Islami, until the uncle was assassinated by this movement, whereupon he joined the Jamiat-e-Islami Commander Ghulam Serwar, until he left to form his own group within his *qawm* due to Serwar's decision to join Harakat-ul-Mohseni. During the jihad, he fought in both Ghor and with Commanders Akmed Rahimi and Raiz Najibullah in Faryab Province. Abdul Salaam made a brief union with the Taliban, during which time he allied with Commander Zahir Nahibzadar and sent soldiers to fight in Jelghi-Mazar in Badghis Province. Combatants and commanders attribute this decision to a number of different factors, ranging from the Taliban's capture of Abdul Salaam's cousin to the disparities in the provision of resources from the Northern Alliance/United Front. He previously was locally allied to Mullah Serwar, Qazi Mohammed, Ghulam Khan and Iayazuddin (each of which have between 150 and 200 people) as well as to others in Faryab Province. In August 2002, Human Rights Watch reported that the forces of Abdul Salaam attacked a commander in Barakhana, mutilated and tortured his soldiers, intimidated their

families and burned down their homes (HRW, 2004). Interview with Abdul Salaam Khan, Chaghcharan, Ghor, April 2005.

4 Combatant #90, Chaghcharan, Ghor, May 2005.
5 Combatant #90/118/130, Chaghcharan, Ghor, May 2005.
6 Combatant #90, Chaghcharan, Ghor, May 2005.
7 Combatant #89, Chaghcharan, Ghor, May 2005.
8 Commander #81, Chaghcharan, Ghor, May 2005.
9 Combatant #95, Chaghcharan, Ghor, May 2005.
10 Combatant #89, Chaghcharan, Ghor, May 2005.
11 Faizal Akmed Khan and the Yarpulad *qawm* have particularly close ties to Ismail Khan, deploying to support his forces in Herat following the death of his son in summer 2004, in coordination with Morghabi and Kareem Aimaq of Badghis.
12 Combatant #124, Chaghcharan, Ghor, May 2005.
13 Combatant #101, Chaghcharan, Ghor, May 2005.
14 Combatant #93, Chaghcharan, Ghor, April 2005.
15 Combatant #104, Chaghcharan, Ghor, May 2005.
16 Combatant #120, Chaghcharan, Ghor, May 2005.
17 Combatant #105, Chaghcharan, Ghor, April 2005.
18 Commander Akmed Rahimi, Chaghcharan, Ghor, May 2005.
19 Combatant #113, Chaghcharan, Ghor, May 2005.
20 Ismail Khan spent three to four months in the Morghab valley in 2001. There were approximately 1,000 soldiers in the Morghab. Combatant #110, Chaghcharan, Ghor (May 2005).
21 Combatant #122, Chaghcharan, Ghor, May 2005.
22 Price of 10,000 Afghani per weapon, primarily Chinese/Russian Kalashnikovs, and French and Iranian weapons. Others paid 12,000 Afghanis for a 'wykers,' which has a tripod (Combatant #116/99, Chaghcharan, Ghor, May 2005).
23 Combatant #121, Chaghcharan, Ghor, May 2005.
24 Combatant #94, Chaghcharan, Ghor, May 2005.
25 Combatant #100, Chaghcharan, Ghor, April 2005.
26 Combatant #93, Chaghcharan, Ghor, April 2005.
27 Combatant #93, Chaghcharan, Ghor, April 2005.
28 Combatant #94, Chaghcharan, Ghor, May 2005.
29 Combatant #112, Chaghcharan, Ghor, May 2005.
30 Combatant #131, Chaghcharan, Ghor, May 2005.
31 Combatant #117, Chaghcharan, Ghor, May 2005.
32 Combatant #112, Chaghcharan, Ghor, May 2005.
33 Combatant #91, Chaghcharan, Ghor, April 2005.
34 Combatant #128, Chaghcharan, Ghor, April 2005.
35 Combatant #115, Chaghcharan, Ghor, May 2005.
36 Combatant #117, Chaghcharan, Ghor, May 2005.
37 Combatant #98, Chaghcharan, Ghor, May 2005.
38 Combatant #108, Chaghcharan, Ghor, May 2005.
39 Combatant #96, Chaghcharan, Ghor, May 2005.
40 Combatant #104, Chaghcharan, Ghor, May 2005.
41 Combatant #119, Chaghcharan, Ghor, May 2005.
42 Combatant #123, Chaghcharan, Ghor, May 2005.
43 Combatant #123, Chaghcharan, Ghor, May 2005.

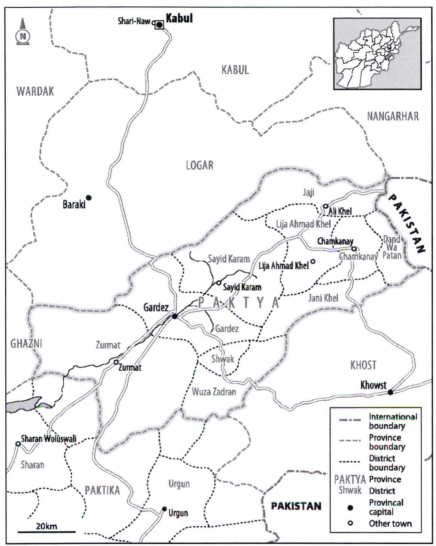

Map 7.1 Paktya Province.

7 Paktya Province

Sources of order and disorder

Michael Bhatia

The case of Paktya Province explores the following issues:

- community conceptions of legitimate and illegitimate mobilization and violence;
- involvement of the central government in promoting insecurity from 2001 to 2002;
- the relationship between communities, commanders and individual combatants;
- the impact of conflict on community structures;
- the renewed establishment of rule-governed tribal police (known internally as either *arbakai, robakee* or *arbakee*);
- early presence of weapons licensing.

The chapter begins by describing the ethnic composition of Paktya and concludes with a description of the political–military contest between Padshah Khan Zadran, on the one hand, and the Gardeze Tajik and Ahmadzais, on the other hand, in 2002. It then points to the role of PSCs and the Coalition in creating new opportunities for mobilization and highlights the prominent role of patronage in the identification of local police and PSC combatants. Second, the chapter illustrates the role of *tanzims* and the Afghan state in undermining the *qawms* and empowering local commanders. After a brief discussion of the combatant motivation in Paktya, the chapter then focuses on the *arbakian*, with the goal of exploring community conceptions of legitimate violence and mobilization.

Ultimately, the case of Paktya further illustrates the shifting relationship between commanders and communities. There are many different types of mobilization and militias in Paktya; some are informal and opportunistic, while others are historically rooted and rule-governed. It is thus necessary to distinguish between types of conflict and the scale of mobilization (see Chapter 2). On the whole, community checks on commander power are far more intact than in other parts of Afghanistan. In many cases, communities remain the central power brokers and simply delegate greater emergency powers to *khans* and commanders in periods of crisis and conflict.[1] Still, particularly among the Moqbal and Tutakheil tribes, commanders and other individuals have acquired both latitude and power.

Setting the local scene

The province of Paktya is located in the southeast of Afghanistan, bordering the Afghan provinces of Khost, Logar, Ghazni, Nangarhar and Paktika. A portion of the province also borders the tribal areas of Pakistan. Geographically, the province is constituted by a fertile central plain surrounded, most prominently to the south and to the east, by a series of mountains. The province has a population of 415,000 spread out over an area of 6,432 square kilometres.[2]

Paktya Province is traditionally viewed to have the most formidable traditional Pashtun tribal structures, particularly among the Jaji, Jadran and Mangal tribes, each of which are further constituted by a series of *kheil* (sub-tribes). These tribes are viewed to be the nang (or honour-bound) Pashtuns, with the most entrenched practice of Pashtunwali (the Pashtun code of behaviour that stipulates both hospitality and revenge). Historically, tensions have existed among the Gardeze Tajik elite occupying key provincial governing institutions, the mountainous 'black' Pashtun tribes (Jaji and Zadran) and other Pashtun tribes residing on the plains (Mangal) (Noelle, 1997, p. 137).

Containing approximately ten sub-tribes, the Ahmadzai branch of the Ghilzai tribe is both prominent within the province (with President Najibullah its most noted former member) but also scattered beyond Paktya (Ghazni, Logar, Kandahar, Kabul and Nangarhar).[3] Serving on both sides of the conflict during the Soviet invasion, Ahmadzai cohesion is weakened by divides between traditional leadership and those who derive their power from the government in power in either Gardez or Kabul. However, this division also served to limit conflict by presenting channels for cross-faction discussion and negotiation during the transition from Communist to mujahideen rule.

Inter-tribal disputes and insecurities often occur over land and the cutting of forests (which includes the substantial role of Pakistan-based traders in cutting forests in periods of insecurity). In September 1959, there was fighting between the Mangal and Zadran over forestry rights, which led 3,000–4,000 Mangal tribesmen to flee to Pakistan. Most recently, a tribal land dispute in the province in 2004 led to the death of 20 individuals (HRW, 2004). In August 2005, land disputes led to armed conflict between the Darawal and Daulatzai tribes of Paktya, involving as many as 60 armed men, with conflict emerging between the Matun tribe and Kuchis in neighbouring Khost Province (*Kabul Times*, 2005).

The province gained prominence in the post-Bonn period due to a dispute between Padshah Khan Zadran and the Gardez tribal *shura* (a union between the Ahmadzais and Gardez Tajiks) over the appointment of Padshah Khan Zadran as governor of the province.[4] Accordingly, this contest for power is generally viewed to have been orchestrated through Kabul by Marshall Fahim (then Minister of Defence) and Yunus Qanouni (then Minister of the Interior). A UN officer labelled the resulting conflict the 'single most dangerous hiccup in the Bonn process.'[5] Zadran fired rockets on Gardez, targeting elders who support the interim governor Taj Mohammed Wardak and killing 25 people (Ahmed-Ullah, 2002). Padshah Khan Zadran successfully used Coalition support as a method of consolidating his own power in both Paktya and Khost, which included the provision of false intelligence to the Coalition, leading the group to bomb a convoy of tribal elders.

As many as 600 of Padshah Khan Zadran's men were said to be employed and trained by US Special Forces and the CIA (Westervelt, 2002). This was lamented by the head of the *arbakian* (tribal police) for the Zadran tribe, who argued that:

> When Padshah Khan Zadran took the money and weapons from the USA, he was able to take some of the *arbakian* soldiers, even though it was not the decision of the *shura*. He brought them twice to fight in Gardez, and both times they lost, as the soldiers were only fighting for money and did not produce a good result.[6]

Other Pashtun tribes similarly complained that the National Directorate of Security (NDS) and ex-Communist officials were providing incorrect information on tribal members to the Coalition, which led to search and seizure operations.[7] In September and October 2003, a substantial transition occurred, when provincial AMF commanders were replaced by General Munir Mangal, a former officer under the Karmal/Najibullah Soviet-backed government (Sly, 2003).

The United States established the first Provincial Reconstruction Team (PRT) in the province in December 2002. Gardez was also the site of a prominent Coalition combat battalion, a future ANA corps, a Police Recruit Training Centre (RTC) and an Italian-designation pilot project for the rule of law. Before this, following the initiation of Operation Enduring Freedom, a series of Coalition fire bases were established throughout the province, both near Zurmat and near the border with Pakistan.

Several NGOs have a long-standing presence in the province, with decades of cooperation with the tribes, although a sizeable number left in 2003 due to the deteriorating security situation. Electoral turnout for the recent parliamentary elections was 64 per cent, which was far above the national average of 49.2 per cent and was high in comparison to the rest of the southeast (54.7 per cent) (JEMB, 2007).

While the Taliban insurgency remains strong in the neighbouring province of Paktika, aside from Zurmat district, Paktya Province has proven to be the most secure of the southeastern Afghan provinces, which has been attributed largely to the strength of local tribes. Still, there are continued reports of outreach by Taliban recruiters to communities through nightletters as well as through a cross-border radio station. The Taliban are also seen to be a factor in intensifying the April 2005 protests over the alleged desecration of the Koran in Guantanamo. The most prominent and charismatic Taliban figures from Paktya Province are Maulavi Haqqani (Zadran, HIK) and Maulavi Nasrullah Mansour.[8]

Whereas up until the arrival of the Taliban, the province was a net importer of arms, the current period marks a reversal. As of 2005, weapons (particularly Chinese and Russian AKs) were reportedly being sold to Pakistan by small traders, where they are purchased for distribution to insurgents operating in Kashmir and Afghanistan.

Local armed actors

Gardez was the location of the AMF's 3rd Corps, which theoretically incorporated the 14th Division, 30th Division, the 822nd Brigade, Border Brigades and approximately 800 soldiers in the Governor's Force in both Paktya and in the neighbouring provinces of Ghazni, Paktika and Khost. As in other areas, there was considerable disparity between the projected and actual size of these units. While the first phase target was for 2,350 combatants, only 900 soldiers were ultimately verified.[9]

While the Taliban successfully disarmed many of the commanders in the region, following the movement's retreat from the region, weapons stockpiles went to the control of local commanders and individuals. Since 2003, commanders outside of the AMF structure voluntarily surrendered weapons to the Coalition with one Mangal commander providing three trucks of rockets, heavy weapons and small arms (DShK). In February 2006, five commanders in the province (Torab Khan, Sardar, Safihullah, Zahirullah and Rozi Khan) surrendered 15 metric tons of ammunition and 38 light and heavy weapons (IRIN, 2006).

The province faces a proliferation of armed security actors, ranging from PSCs and Afghan militia serving alongside the Coalition forces in the region to tribal *arbakian* and formal government security bodies (ANP, NDS, ABP, ANA and a new MOD installation security force).

Gardez is now the base for the second ANA Regional Command. In the neighbouring province of Khost, the Coalition catalysed the formation of the Khost Provincial Corps outside of the AMF structure and utilized it as a supporting unit for Coalition operations. Further, Presidential Guard Units are present to protect the PRT and Khost Civil–Military Operations Centre.[10] The Coalition fire base and the Afghan Border Police (ABP) unit of 59 soldiers and 28 lieutenants (of a mandated strength of 150) rely on the *arbakian* to secure their areas of operation and the border. Of the 50 ABP soldiers, only ten have weapons, some of which are family owned.

Following 9/11, commanders without tribal authority used their own personal and familial networks to create new militias to work alongside American forces. There are currently 140 Afghan soldiers serving with the Coalition's Operational Detachment Alpha in Paktya, 80 of whom come from the town of Ahmadabad. In contrast to other parts of Afghanistan, the soldiers working with the Coalition in Paktya are predominantly young and without previous affiliation to an armed faction or to the *arbakian*. The Coalition deliberately attempts to recruit young adults in order to expose a new generation to US ideals (referred to as 'McDonalds-ization' by one Coalition officer). One of these combatants notes:

> When the Taliban ended, there came a *qawm-e-shura* and they decided to give some people to the foreigners. Then I went by myself. They spoke to all the nation for volunteers who wanted to join to help security of foreigners. They didn't ask my family directly.[11]

Combatants were provided with a short training programme and organized into teams of seven (seven Kalikov, one RPG, one PK) and utilized in Operation Anaconda at Tora Bora. Upon decommissioning, soldiers were allowed to keep their weapon in order 'to protect ourselves from people who accused us of working with the Americans' and received eight clips with 30 bullets.[12] Other soldiers brought weapons from home and exchanged these for newer AKs with five clips of ammunition.[13] Private security companies created new incentives for individuals either to retain or to pick up arms.

A number of different government security bodies are stationed in Gardez City, including the ANA, ANP, NDS and Amniat-e-Milli (also called the Amniat-e-Police). The statutory relationship between these bodies is unclear, with some confusion as to the different roles and responsibilities. The ANA is stationed at critical road junctures, and 104 members of the Amniat-e-Milli are distributed over four stations in Gardez City. The National Directorate of Security in Paktya has as many as 250 personnel, without a standard uniform, which complicates civilian identification of different national security personnel.

All of the ANP interviewed received at least one month of training from the DynCorp-run Regional Training Centre in Gardez. When asked to repeat what they were taught, one police officer indicated minimal response to provocations (self-defence) and that 'we must respect all the human beings'; while another stated that he learned how to do a patrol and search, to respect the commander and to 'take care of discipline and respect our job.'[14] Weapons training included how to load the weapon, attack and defend and how to check for ammunition. Generally, the Paktya ANP are viewed to have behaved reasonably well in response to the April 2005 southeastern riots over the proposed desecration of the Koran at Guantanamo, responding with limited force to the protesters and rioters.

In theory, for the Amniat-e-Milli, each individual is to be provided with their own weapon and with 120 rounds of ammunition. In reality, many of the weapons at these posts are individually owned, although the weapons are still regarded as duty weapons and have to be kept at the post. While the ANP in Gardez are fully equipped, those in neighbouring districts suffer from a lack of ammunition (with each officer in Zurmat receiving only 50 of the 120 rounds promised). The ABP in Jaji have only ten weapons for 50 officers. Salary for an employee of the Ministry of Interior (MoI) is 3,300 Afghanis per month. If the officer is stationed in front of a UN building, he receives an additional supplement of $120 per month.

According to their own testimony, none of the ANP police officers interviewed in Paktya previously belonged to a *tanzim, arbakian* or an armed group prior to the commencement of police service. However, family connections did play a significant role in recruitment. Of the seven policemen interviewed, eight had been given their job due to the presence of a family member within the police or security administration. Several were relatives of the police commander Hai Gul. The family contact is typically a cousin or uncle, with the soldier used as a bodyguard for the police commander.

In two of these cases, insecurity and the looting of their capital assets (whether in terms of their shops or their cars) led these policemen to leave business and become security officials and join the police.[15] This loss of capital forced individuals to use family networks to become police officers.

While this may be seen as a sign of patronage, it appears to operate more as a referral system. Similarly, hiring for the Coalition Afghan militias and for PSC Afghan security staff in Paktya involves some type of referral service. An officer or individual is relied upon to provide a group for security service. For example, a security PSC recruiting in Paktya (seeking to train Afghans to provide security for NGO and embassy installations) indicated that 71 of its recruits were provided by three references, under the belief that the 'culture is based on friends and relatives.'[16]

Coalition search and seizure operations were one of the main factors driving weapons licensing in Paktya. Approximately 200–300 weapons licences have been provided to individuals in the 14 districts of Loya Paktya, with 30 weapons licences provided for individuals living in Gardez City.[17] A laminated licence lists the type of weapon, its registration number, the name of the registered user, his address, his father's name, his signature and an official stamp. Licences are provided to individuals at their request – following a police investigation – if the individual is an *arbakian* member or if the individual lives in a remote area without police protection and is involved in a local dispute. The MoI distributed both weapons and weapons licences to those individuals responsible for election security through the *qawmi meshran*. The Provincial Chief of Police indicated that weapons are confiscated from those individuals without licences and kept in the central police station for the use of the provincial police. The police hold approximately 1,100 AKs in their depot.

Local conflict history

Jihad

The province was severely depopulated during the Soviet invasion. A coordinating resistance *shura* was established with representatives from eight local tribes (Mangal, Zadran, Jaji, Tutakheil and Ahmadzai). A number of different *tanzims* were present, with the most prominent being Harakat and Hezb-e-Islami Khalis, followed by NIFA and Ittihad. Some tribes all went to one tanzim, while others divided membership among different groups, whether to acquire more material assistance or as a consequence of internal divisions. An Isakheil Ahmadzai elder describes how: 'All of Isakhel divided between three *tanzims* and took weapons and material from them. But inside of Afghanistan we were united. We made this decision in order to get the most resources.'[18] According to Ahmadzai elders, those Ahmadzai members with education went to Hezb-e-Islami; those without went either to Ma'az or Harakat. Another elder indicated that the community only recommended joining moderate parties. To a degree, sections of Ahmadzai affiliated with Harakat due to the fact that Mullah Nabi Mohammadi was an Ahmadzai *ulema* from the neighbouring province of Logar. Some combatants, particularly those who were exceptionally personally devoted to a Sufi *pir* (such as Pir Gailani), allied themselves and were mobilized due to extra-local factors. In Jaji, there was a period of inter-factional fighting between Hezb-e-Islami (led by Kashmir Khan of Logar) and Ittihad during both the jihad and the civil war.

While comparatively little information is available on those individuals with Communist affiliation, it appears that individuals without tribal status joined the Khalq and Parcham government. In the 1980s, the Najibullah government was able to establish pro-government militias near Jaji, which involved the distribution of weapons to children and other community members living near government outposts for protection against other *tanzims*.[19] In 1985, an increase of weapons supplies allowed Jalaluddin Haqqani to attack government outposts in Ali Kheil (near Jaji) and in Khost, which was followed by a major Soviet offensive against Jaji and Chamkanay (Isby, 1989, p. 35). In May 1988, government forces were expelled from their base in Chamkanay, Jaji, with the weapons stockpiles distributed 'on a percentage basis' to the local mujahideen (with the captured heavy weapons prohibited from being removed from the district). The tribe then established a joint administration composed of a council of scholars, a tribal council and a military council (AIC, 1988a, p. 11).

The effect of conflict on the various *qawms* has varied considerably. In some cases, conflict did weaken the community of elders. As noted by Haji Sirdar of the Ahmadzai nation:

> The Ahmadzai nation had no leader. The nation needed vehicles, cars and equipment ... From the beginning, the *qawm* was more powerful than these *tanzims*. When the *tanzims* came, people divided into different groups. At that time, the *tanzims* became more powerful than the nations, because the *tanzims* had more weapons, artillery and money. And also we needed the material to defend ourselves. But of course when we came back to our country, we had good respect inside our nation, but in reality we needed material from the *tanzims*.[20]

As noted by the *qawmi mesher* of Jaji,

> From the beginning, the *qawm* had big force and respect. After that, when the *tanzims* came, and the Khalqis/Parchamis, it was so bad. No one listened to the community of elders. All the people were divided by the Communists and the *tanzims*. During the civil war, the *arbakian* was still weak but growing stronger. But now it is strong, and everybody listens.[21]

Commander Daoud Jaji asserts that this 'conflict of ideas' in the *qawm-e-shura* was due to 'money.'[22] As a consequence, one elder of the Mangal tribe describes the community of elders as being caught between the Communist government and the mujahideen, asserting that the Mangals were the 'victims' of both groups, with the Communists taking the elders to prison and with Hezb-e-Islami Hekmatyar killing 120 Mangals.[23] Hezb-e-Islami Hekmatyar also attempted to gain control of the Ahmadzai tribe through the assassination of prominent tribal elders in Peshawar.

Civil war

The shifting distribution of power away from the *qawm* and towards the *tanzim* directly contributed to the instability that occurred during the civil war. The period following the collapse of the Najibullah government is locally described as a period of anarchy and absence of law, characterized by insecurity and disorder, checkpoints and extortion. The primary contenders for power in the province were Hezb-e-Islami Khalis (led by Maulavi Haqqani of the Zadran tribe, who later became the Taliban's Minister for Tribal Affairs) and Harakat (Maulavi Nusrullah Mansour). During the civil war, while Hezb-e-Islami was able to transit through Paktya, the tribes did not participate in or contribute soldiers to the fighting in Kabul. During this period, some of the tribes – including both the

Jaji and the Mangal – mobilized their *arbakian* in order to protect their localities from other *tanzims*. Commander Daoud argues that the Jaji *qawm-e-shura* prevented the various commanders from fighting, although the commander kept his own soldiers mobilized, 'of course, because I didn't want to leave Paktya to the other mujahideen.'[24]

As discussed in Chapter 1, some of those combatants used for the protection of localities were also engaged in predatory activities against others, particularly among the Muqbal and Tutakheil tribes. Predatory approaches migrated from Kabul, as newly empowered commanders were able to gain control of local areas. Some communities of elders were able to regain their power, stabilizing their villages and localities. Other communities were too weakened by displacement, and commanders empowered by the parties remained unchecked by traditional structures.

Indeed, one Pashtun of the Muqbal tribe's account displays just how varied dynamics were within one province alone during the civil war:

> The problem was that we needed to collect some money for home, this was the big issue for us. I don't know for which reason [that I joined to become a soldier]. This was the situation in the civil war, all people belonged to different nations, they gave us a card, this was a visa for life. If you don't have this card, maybe someone can kill me.... Old people had old commanders from their nation, and young people had young commanders. Our commanders liked young people to make criminal activity, for stealing, for crime, for prostitution and for sexual abuse. During that time, we never took off our shoes, we were so crazy about money. We spent our first year in Kabul and our second year in Paktya, so we stole everything in Paktya. At the time, I knew it was not good for me, but we had no other opportunity, it was a crazy time for us.[25]

> In Kabul, when I couldn't find a job, I took the gun. We had no job, so we took the weapon to make money from local people to steal by force ... Many foreigners helped Sayyaf, and he gave more money than other *tanzims*.... I received 1,000 Pakistani rupees per month, plus any additional money taken from people. We fought against other groups for money. For money we could do anything – destroy a bridge or school or kill people. If they gave us money, we would make everything. It cost 10,000 Pakistani rupees to kill someone.... Later in Sayed Karam [when he returned to Paktya], night time or daytime we went to the highway to take money from the people.[26]

The commander (Faiz Mohammed of the Tutakheil *qawm*) was able to acquire so much power that even though 'the *qawm* wanted to do good, [...] the soldiers did not want to.'[27]

Taliban era

Due to this insecure situation, the various tribes initially welcomed the arrival of the Taliban. The movement immediately disarmed many of the more prominent commanders, clearing out weapon depots and acquiring both heavy weapons and small arms. Yet, by 2000, elders were beginning to resist Taliban authority over issues such as taxation, marijuana eradication, disarmament and local conscription. The Taliban were accepted as long as they respected the autonomy and authority of tribal elders – their increased assertiveness undermined that tolerance.[28] Eventually, the strength of the *qawm*s was enough to deter certain Taliban policies. Particularly in Jaji, the Taliban district administrator was overpowered by the local community *shura* (Bhatia *et al.*, 2003).

When they first captured Paktya, the Taliban recruited 200–300 combatants throughout Paktya, demanding that each *qawm* had to provide 50–60 combatants for deployment to Kabul for 20–30 days. The Taliban developed a formal levy system, which certain Pashtuns and their *qawm*s began to chafe under.

> At first the Taliban came and wanted people from us. Then the *qawm* from all Loya Paktya made a lottery to send people for a short time for one month and then we stopped. Three years later, all the Mangal resisted the Taliban – we never wanted to give people and we didn't like their law.[29]

The current district governor of Zurmat noted:

> When the Taliban came here, first they asked for weapons from me and the *qawm*. So I gave all my artillery to the Taliban and then I went home. The Taliban made a new government. When the Taliban reached Kabul and started fighting, they wanted people from all of Paktya, from whatever nation. From each *woleswali* they needed 50–300 people. So the *woleswali* selected people to go. They were chosen by force, if not they [the Taliban] took money to substitute. The Taliban spoke one thing and then did another.[30]

Only one combatant who joined the Taliban was interviewed. He joined independently (without elder selection) in order to receive 400–500 Afghanis per month plus wheat and personal food.[31] In Jaji, where he was based, local Taliban recruits were intermixed with Pashtuns from other provinces and a commander from neighbouring Logar Province.

Post-9/11 period

Transitions in government typically mark new periods of insecurity in Paktya. This again occurred with the Taliban's evacuation. During these periods, the negative actions associated with warlords were described by combatants, to include checkpoints, taxation, abuse and kidnapping. Local insecurity following the collapse of the Taliban prompted one Gardeze to argue that: 'The Taliban were dangerous for the world but they were better for us because they brought security … When the Western forces drove them out, we were left in the middle of local conflicts like before' (Zahid, 2002b). This period was also referred to as a period of anarchy, when 'no one knew who belonged to the government.'[32] Another combatant argued that:

> When the Taliban left, we knew from experience that whenever the government changed, sad news would come, looting and stealing wood from our home. So we didn't want this to happen again and I became a soldier to protect my family against violence.[33]

For this reason, the communities of elders, among both the Gardeze Tajiks and the Ahmadzais, convened village militias and *arbakian* in order to prevent insecurity. Among some of the Tajik *qawms*, the mobilization was fairly miniscule, with only five people sent by the 150-family Tajik Mirek *qawm*. Weapons were taken from the Gardez Bala Hissar, some of which would be handed in during the DDR programme, while others were sold to traders.[34]

In and around Gardez, however, initial mobilization for the purpose of securing the centre in a period of political transition evolved into the use of this standing force for predatory purposes, with the Gardez force converted into an AMF unit. Zaiuddin and Abdullah (with their sub-commanders Momin and Matin) were selected as heads of the division, and Abdullah Mujahid was selected as Chief of Police. AMF Commander Abdullah's bodyguards were his son, brothers and cousins. Those combatants, initially mobilized through elder authority, were then kept on either through force or through the provision of a basic salary and were used upon the discretion of the commander.

Driven now by economic incentives rather than by elder authority for protection, one new combatant recalled that he 'didn't have activities but to give problems to the people. Without reason we took the money, without any law. If something was correct, we told him it was not the law. We took money and gave it to Abdullah.'[35] These forces were accused of confiscating the salary of the 1,000 soldiers in the division, establishing checkpoints, stealing and kidnapping for ransom and child abuse.[36] A combatant indicated that 10–15 checkpoints were established between Shari-Naw and the Pakistani border, with ten people stationed at each, and with combatants receiving between $10 and $80 per month.

There was a broad disparity in the economic incentives provided to combatants. For many, the scale of incentives was not significant for anything but survival, with occasional handouts of 100 Afghani and the provision of food sufficient only due to the lack of other economic opportunities.[37] Eventually, General Atiqullah Lodin, Zaiuddin and Matin were all removed from power. Abdullah was captured by American forces and sent to Guantanamo; Zaiuddin is currently incarcerated in Bagram.

Communities, commanders and combatants: the *arbakian*

A total of 41 combatants were interviewed in Paktya, primarily in the city of Gardez but also in Jaji and Mangal areas. Approximately ten of these were elites, serving either as the *qawmi mesher*, as a *saar*-group commander (small commander of 10–20 men) or as an officer in the current Afghan army. Of the 31 remaining combatants, four served with the Afghan militias created by the Coalition in late 2001, with three of these four combatants undergoing their first mobilization experience. One of the combatants had served with the Taliban in 2001. The combatants came from diverse backgrounds, with differences in education, labour and livelihoods between elites and common soldiers. The average age of first mobilization was higher than in other regions. Nevertheless, almost one-third first began fighting under the age of 16.

Elder authority only played a dominant role in the protection of the local community, particularly during the civil war and following the collapse of the Taliban. In the absence of community mobilization, other motives shaped mobilization, from obedience to a religious authority to family selection and economic incentives. Particularly striking is the complete absence of narratives of force in descriptions of combatant mobilization in this region as are ideological exposure and commitment to a political–military organization. This is not to say that these motives are not present but simply that they did not occur in the admittedly small set of interviews conducted in this province.

The tribal system is considered most entrenched in Paktya Province, although its strength varies considerably among the various tribes. Even though the various qawms and tribal elders remain intact near Gardez (both among the Ahmadzai or the Tajik Gardeze population), proximity to the provincial capital complicates (and potentially weakens) the relationship between the community of elders and the people. While the initially defensive militias organized around Gardez were compromised by their adoption of predatory behaviour, the tribal police continue to be utilized by other tribes (Mangal, Jaji and Zadran) and are seen to fill a critical security gap (due to the under-resourcing and small size of the ANP), with little complaint from either the local community or from the provincial authorities.

A list created by the Tribal Liaison Office in Kabul in September 2005 indicates a total of 61 *arbakian* groups in Paktya Province, ranging in size

Table 7.1 Combatant profiles of Paktya Province (41 combatants)[a]

Schooling	At least 25% had some form of schooling. Individuals with the most schooling were all former Communist officers, who had left the province to attend the Kabul Military Academy.
Prominent livelihoods	Woodcutting, farmer, street labour, driver.
Labour migration	Many resided in Pakistan as refugees or as temporary labour migrants; several travelled to Saudi Arabia and Iran, one combatant to Dubai.
Average age of first mobilization:	18
Recruited under 18	40%
Recruited at or under 16	30%
First mobilized during:	Data based on 24 interviews.
Jihad	45.8%
Civil war	12.5%
Taliban era	8.3%
Post-9/11 period	33.3%
Prominent motives by period:	
Jihad	Family selection, grievance, economic incentives, Jihad, religious authority.
Civil war	Economic incentives, elder authority.
Taliban era	Economic incentives, family selection.
Post-9/11 period	Elder authority, protection, economic incentives, grievance.

Note
a Table based on interviews with combatants in Paktya (May 2005).

from 30 to 400 members. The majority were established in the summer and autumn of 2004 in order to secure the voting centres and voter registration teams. Others were organized in order to protect communal forests, district roads and sources of drinking water.[38] These forces are meant for use only within the tribes' *manteqa* (area) to punish members for infractions (with the most common sanction being the destruction of a house). Both the Jaji and the Mangal also utilize the *arbakian* to prevent infiltration by neo-Taliban into their communities.

Both provincial governor Taniwal and police chief Hai Gul have sought to use tribal *jirgas* in order to solve local land disputes, with the government now providing 50 per cent of the salaries and with UNAMA employing these groups during elections. Facing a deficit of security personnel in the province, the provincial governor has also made attempts to make the *arbakian* an official provincial body, although this has been met with resistance by many community leaders. Still, while the *arbakian* are increasingly receiving government salaries, the tribes remain reluctant to formalize the tribal police, under the belief that 'formalization of the *arbakian* will erode its legitimacy, it will become another militia with cellphones and weapons.'[39] As noted by Talib Zadran, 'if we take a uniform, we become a part of the government, and we don't want this.'[40]

In Jaji, the *arbakian* are recruited according to family selection, while Commander Daoud also previously maintained an AMF border force (16th Border Brigade), which was recruited independently and was composed of 100–150 soldiers. The decision to join 'belongs to the family'; 'each person can go by themselves, nobody can force them.'[41] Among the Zadran *qawm*, 'in one year, every [extended] family must give one son, whether there was or was not a government, this was the soldier from our nation.'[42]

Zadran *arbakai* soldiers were employed to close checkpoints and solve internal disputes. A standing force of 20 is permanently housed at the district headquarters, with 800–1,000 able to be mobilized in a few hours in the face of a crisis. The *arbakian* are commanded by a *mir* (chief), who is selected for six months by the elders and renewed depending upon behaviour.[43] With approximately 400 *arbakian*, the Mangal *qawm* has a rotating system, whereby one person from each family must come for between 20 days and one month and must provide his own weapon.[44] In the Mangal, Jaji and Zadran, while the *arbakian* is permitted to carry his weapon while in the mountains and for the security of community meetings, he is not permitted to carry it in the village or in public areas.

Throughout Paktya, the community of elders does not call for mass mobilization except for local defence or tribal police service. While the *qawmi meshran* would identify individuals for *arbakian* service, sources indicated that the community of elders neither selected nor demanded that individuals participate in the jihad. Instead, it only recommended that an individual join a tanzim (a moderate or traditionalist group rather than a fundamentalist group). Endorsement is considered distinct from selecting individuals directly to participate in armed groups. Thus, for the individual tribal member, some forms of mobilization are mandatory, and others are discretionary. Individual commanders were still able to mobilize individuals, yet they were generally not able to use the call of the *qawm* or to utilize community/elder authority.

As noted by a Mangal member of the Afghan Army during the Communist period:

> The community of elders (*qawmi meshran*) can recommend that people go to different groups, but the decision belongs to the individual. The final decision rests in the individual to choose the government or the *tanzims*. But if there is a major problem, like after the time of the Taliban, when there was no government, the community told us in a *jirga* that we must provide security in our city to prevent looting. In that time, we all made our choice. In that time, the community asked us. They cannot, however, tell us to go to certain *tanzims*. [They can ask us] only with major problems when we sit together.[45]

Yet, while the elite tribal figures from the Jaji and Ahmadzai tribe denied the use of the tribal system, two combatants from the Alikheil sub-branch of the Jaji tribe, who began fighting in 1980 and 1984, respectively, at approximately 13 years of age, indicated that:

> The *qawmi meshran* said we must start the jihad, as the Soviets did not belong to our nation or religion. I didn't know the meaning – I was so young – the important thing was the *qawm*. So when they said, we went. It was not a problem [that all members of family went] – it was the way to paradise and to be a good patriot. So my father said we would all go to Paradise and start the jihad.[46]

> When the Russians came, the *qawmi meshran* said we must start, and we went. In the system of the *qawm*, one person must go from the family.[47]

This indicates that, while the community may not endorse the selection of combatants in their name, individuals may not be able to distinguish between the commander's authority and the authority of the *qawm*. Jalali and Grau's account of the jihad period echoes this with regard to the Zadran tribe (Jalali and Grau, 1994, pp. 151, 168). Still, in general, the ability of the community of elders to mobilize individuals directly is restricted to certain types of fighting and service. In communities with a strong community of elders, their authority will be used almost exclusively for recruiting for *arbakian* service. The focus is on preserving autonomy and internal security, rather than on participating in national level conflict.

Conclusion

In conclusion, the general restraint of the Paktya Pashtun tribes to use the authority of the *qawm* stands in contrast to the experience in Ghor, Kandahar and other communities. In Paktya, *qawm* authority is only used to mobilize the tribal police. In other provinces, combatants who were subject to elder authority quickly transitioned from fighting the jihad to participating in the civil war. In Paktya, some forms of mobilization are mandatory, and others are discretionary. The community can both recommend and demand mobilization, depending on the type of combat and the identity of the opposition. At least among the major tribes (Ahmadzai, Jaji, Mangal and Zadran), the presence of both consultative mechanisms and the tribal police can serve to provide a base level of security. The legitimacy of the community of elders is based on their limited set of tasks and their consultative nature. External groups, whether Afghan *tanzims* or foreign military forces, upset the ability of community elders to limit mobilization to local protection and policing, creating opportunities for mobilization outside of the community.

As in Ghor Province, the case of Paktya demonstrates how extra-provincial actors can negatively sponsor provincial insecurity. The case of Paktya also illustrates the impact of the creation of the AMF in legitimizing predatory commanders. Positively, while there are a wide variety of armed actors in Paktya, the rules governing their use are under negotiation, whether informally within communities or formally at the provincial level. Predation and rights abuses appear most commonly in periods of political transition, when the community of elders is either weakened or subverted by external authorities. Yet, these transitions also provide an opportunity for the community to come together to protect itself from outsiders.

Notes

1 An anonymous academic reviewer of this chapter, though dissenting with my discussion of various forms of violence, did provide some clarity on the typical relationship between commanders and communities.
2 Population statistics online, available at: statoids.com/uaf.html and www.cia.gov/cia/publications/factbook/print/af.html (accessed 4 December 2007).
3 For the Ahmadzai, these include: Ibrahimkheil, Yakheil, Musakheil, Isakheil, Jabarkheil, Marukheil, Aladdinkheil, Zandikheil, Mantakheil. Two additional: Akarkheil, Kabarkheil. The *kheils* of the Jaji tribe include: Ahmedkheil, Hassankheil, Hashemkheil, Alikheil, Adakheil, Fetullah, Lewani, Petala, Alangi, Matakheil and Bahramkheil. The Mangal are divided between the Janikheil *woleswali* in Paktika (includes the *kheils* of Yarikheil, Waradara, Sperkeydara, Balkheil, Miakheil, Stankheil and Shahbi) and the Musakheil *woleswali* in Khost (includes the *kheils* of Haijuri, Ibikheil, Wardari, Mirarkheil, and Khemalkheil). The *kheils* of the Tutakheil tribe include: Khankheil.
4 Taj Mohammed Wardak briefly served as the governor until 2002, when he was replaced by Raz Mohammed Dalili and then by Asadullah Wafa. In January 2005, there was another switch of governors, as Asidullah Wafa was sent to Kunar, and Governor Taniwal was brought from Kunar to Paktya.
5 Interview, Sebastien Trieves, Gardez, Paktya, June 2005.
6 Combatant #174 (Talib Zadran), Gardez, Paktya, May 2005.
7 One tribal member lamented (interview, tribal elder, Gardez, Paktya, May 2005):

> In the time of jihad, the Americans helped us a lot and we had a good friendship. But after, when there came the new government of the jihad, then they [the Americans] forgot us. And the people blamed the Americans for the start of the civil war. And then the Americans came again, and again they made some mistakes, they arrested some innocent people, and they listened to some useless and nonsense people. They arrested the wrong people, because they did not listen to the community or to the traditions. This was a major fault of the Americans. They must listen and take the right information about who to arrest. First, they must talk to the nation. Even myself, sometimes I am worried because I see people taken to prison without reason; and after nine months they [the USA] release them and say they're sorry. And they lose the respect of the people – and the people don't believe them anymore.

8 Prominent Taliban sub-commanders in Paktya/Paktika include: Maulavi Kabir, Saed Razam, Maulavi Doha, Maulavi Bakhter Jan, Mullah Jan, Mohammed Ali

Jalali and Serajoddin Haqqani. Interview with anonymous international official, May 2005.

9   Interview with ANBP official, Gardez, Paktya, May 2004.
10 Research in Khost Province, April 2004.
11 Combatant #180/181, Gardez, Paktya, May 2005.
12 Combatant #168, Gardez, Paktya, May 2005.
13 Combatants #180/181, Gardez, Paktya, May 2005.
14 Interviews with ANP throughout Gardez, Paktya, May 2005.
15 (ANP) combatant #171/172, Gardez, Paktya, May 2005.
16 Interview with American PSC staff, Gardez, Paktya, May 2005.
17 Interview with General Hai Gul, MOI Commander, Paktya Province, May 2005.
18 Combatant #170 (Ghulam Khan), Gardez, Paktya, May 2005.
19 Giustozzi, 2000; combatant #189, Ahmedkheil, Paktya, May 2005. Family received one AK and one clip of ammunition from the Najibullah government, as well as small salary and coupons for food.
20 Combatant #169 (Haji Sirdar), Gardez, Paktya, May 2005.
21 Elder, Jaji, Paktya, May 2005.
22 Combatant #161 (Commander Daoud Jaji), Gardez, Paktya, May 2005.
23 Combatant #177, Sayed Karam, Paktya, May 2005.
24 Combatant #161 (Commander Daoud Jaji), Gardez, Paktya, May 2005.
25 Combatant #185, Gardez, Paktya, May 2005.
26 Combatant #186, Gardez, Paktya, May 2005.
27 Combatant #186, Gardez, Paktya, May 2005.
28 Anonymous reviewer, Small Arms Survey.
29 Combatant #177, Saedkaram, Paktya, May 2005.
30 Combatant #188, Salikheil, Zurmat, May 2005.
31 Combatant #166, Gardez, Paktya, May 2005.
32 Combatant #164, Gardez, Paktya, May 2005.
33 Combatant #160, Gardez, Paktya, May 2005.
34 Combatant #160, Gardez, Paktya, May 2005.
35 Combatant #183, Gardez, Paktya, May 2005.
36 Sly, 2003; Combatant #163, Gardez, Paktya, May 2005.
37 Combatant #162/163, Gardez, Paktya, May 2005.
38 Information courtesy of the Tribal Liaison Office, Kabul.
39 Interview with Afghan NGO official, May 2005.
40 Combatant #174, Paktya, Gardez, May 2005.
41 Combatant #165, Paktya, Gardez, May 2005.
42 Combatant #174, Paktya, Gardez, May 2005.
43 Combatant #174 (Talib Zadran), Gardez, Paktya, May 2005.
44 Combatant #177, Mirzaki, Paktya, May 2005.
45 Combatant #159, Gardez, Paktya, May 2005. A Mangal elder further illustrates the difference between the way you recruit for *arbakian* and the jihad:

   Of course, there's a difference. The *tanzim* was based on the leader (Hezb-e-Islami/Nehaz) – these different commanders did not belong to the nations and were independent. But the *arbakian*, everything knows their qawm.

   It is different here. In other places, you had to be a soldier for the government by force; and you also had to do jihad by force. But in Paktya, it was different, not to be in army by force [no conscription law before the communists], not to be in jihad by force.
          (Combatant #177 (Sultan Mohammed) Gardez, Paktya, May 2005)
46 Combatant #198, Jaji, Paktya, May 2005.
47 Combatant #197, Jaji, Paktya, May 2005.

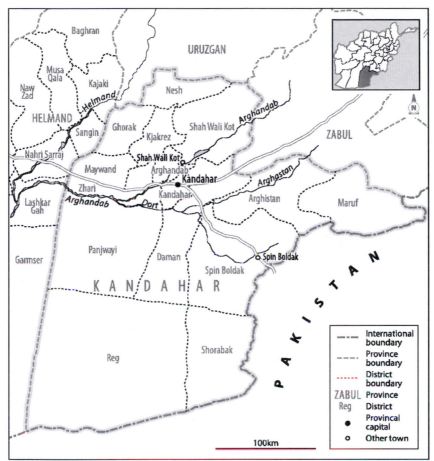

Baghran

URUZGAN

Musa
Qala

Naw
Zad

Kajaki

Nesh

HELMAND

Helmand

Ghorak

Shah Wali Kot

Arghandab

ZABUL

Sangin

Kjakrez

Nahri Sarraj

Shah.Wali Kot

Maywand

Arghandab

Kandahar

Zhari

Kandahar

Arghastan

Lashkar
Gah

Arghandab

Dort

Arghistan

Maruf

Garmser

Panjwayi

Daman

Spin Boldak

Spin Boldak

K A N D A H A R

PAKISTAN

Reg

Shorabak

	International boundary
	Province boundary
	District boundary
ZABUL	Province
Reg	District
●	Provincal capital
○	Other town

100km

Only selected districts and towns are shown

Map 8.1 Kandahar Province.

8 Kandahar City

The political economy of Coalition deployment

Michael Bhatia

From 1979 until 1994, Kandahar experienced a considerable degree of fighting, resulting in the destruction of much of the city centre and the bazaar area. The Taliban are fabled to have emerged as a consequence of a commander's predatory behaviour in Spin Boldak. The city became the seat of the Kandahar *shura*, which was composed of strict rather than moderate Taliban. It played an increasingly dominant role following the 1998 cruise missile attacks by the United States. In contrast to other areas of Afghanistan, traditional religious and tribal authorities were able to maintain (and even expand) their power over the course of the conflict, until the arrival of the Taliban induced many senior tribal figures to migrate from the region (Gul Agha Sherzai, Hamid Karzai, Khan Mohammed, etc.). The city became a national traditional and political hub during the Taliban, diverting power from Kabul. Currently, it is experiencing another boom due to the Coalition presence. The return of fighting in 2006, however, has suppressed its further economic growth.

The case of Kandahar City explores the following issues:

- the role of a provincial *shura* and its relationship with external parties;
- the significance of elder authority in producing combatant mobilization;
- the under-resourcing of the newly constituted and accountable Afghan National Police;
- the political economy of private security provision and the impact on local tribal politics;
- the proliferation of different and competing armed actors, aligned with different tribes;
- a commander's use of PSCs as a method of evading DDR;
- the strength of Kandahar cross-tribal *shura* in resisting the influence of external political–military parties.

The chapter opens by discussing the geo-political features of the province, with a focus on its political significance and tribal composition, which concludes with a brief discussion of recent insurgent activity, poppy production and the arms trade. The second part of the chapter describes the various international and local armed forces operating in Kandahar, the weak effect of the DDR programme and the role of PSCs in relation to the Afghan National Police. The chapter goes on to explore the local history of conflict in Kandahar Province, revealing the role of the cross-tribal *shura* in managing local conflict and in countering the influence of the *tanzims*. Post-9/11 Kandahar saw the collapse of this council, but outright conflict between the tribes has not occurred. These groups now maintain their small fiefdoms, complete with their own armed groups and (until recently) private prisons. The chapter concludes with a further examination of the relationship between communities, commanders and combatants.

Setting the local scene

Located in the southwestern part of Afghanistan and sharing a mountainous border with Pakistan, Kandahar is the heartland of the Durrani-Abdali Pashtuns and the source of the ruling dynasty for both the Kingdom of Kabul (1748–1773) and, now, Afghanistan. The province is bordered by Helmand to the west, Uruzgan to the north and Zabul to the east. Currently, the province's total population is 886,000, spread out over 54,022 square kilometres, with 459,000 residing in Kandahar district.[1]

The city is dominated by four major tribes: the Alikozai, the Barakzai, the Popalzai and the Noorzai.[2] The tribal structures in the region are far larger in comparison to those in the rest of the southeast. Segments of the Alizai, Atsakzai and Alikozai are also present in the northern four districts of Helmand (Musa Qala, Naw Zad, Baghran and Sangin), while the Barakzai and Popalzai tribes are present in Uruzgan (Dorronsoro, 2005, p. 135). A major mujahideen base was located in the Sharafat-Koh mountains in the neighbouring province of Farah, which was divided between Atsakzai, Noorzai, Barakzai and Alizai tribal militias (Jalali and Grau, 1994, p. 286).

Since their first deployment in autumn 2005, the Canadian NATO forces in the province have also been subject to a steady stream of suicide bombings. However, between 2003 and 2005, the Taliban attacked mainly soft targets, whether NGOs or prominent religious and local political figures, which sparked the withdrawal of a number of NGOs, first in November 2003 and again in March 2004.

Amid allegations of fraud, voter turnout in Kandahar was low (53 per cent participation in the presidential election, 25 per cent participation in the parliamentary election) (Wilder, 2005, p. 33). The neighbouring provinces of Uruzgan (25 per cent), Zabul (22 per cent) and Helmand (37 per cent) had similarly low voter turnout (JEMB, 2007). The Aliokzai emerged from the parliamentary elections without any significant representation in Parliament, while both the Barakzai and the Popalzai were able to unite behind and elect prominent tribal members (Wilder, 2005).

Prior to the poppy eradication campaign, the province was also a major location for poppy production. Pockets of production remain in Panjwayi, Maywand and Khakrez districts.[3] With regard to the arms trade and the prevalence of weapons, there are anecdotal discussions of the movement of weapons across the border to and from Baluchistan and widespread attestation of an ammunition scarcity in Kandahar. According to a UN official, it is difficult to acquire both 5.54 and 7.62 mm ammunition in the province due to ammunition purchases and high demand from the PSCs. A PSC official indicated that their own operations were hindered by a lack of 7.62 mm ammunition, though there is no shortage of RPG rounds. While new Czech weapons were provided to the MoI for the elections, the ANP ran out of ammunition in an attack on the Shorabak District Commissioner by 15 insurgents on 12 June 2004 (UNSECOORD, 2004, p. 2). There is also evidence that the insurgents are maintaining large stockpiles of ammunition for future operations against the Coalition and the government, with the Coalition capturing as much as 1 tonne of ammunition in neighbouring Helmand Province (*Pajhwok*, 2006b).

Current international, government and other armed actors

The Coalition presence in the south was inaugurated by the deployment of a Marine Expeditionary Unit to Kandahar Air Field in 2002. Today, Kandahar City is the site of three Coalition military bodies: the Regional Command and Kandahar Air Field forces; the Provincial Reconstruction Team in the city centre and the Special Operations units based out of Camp Gecko. These three entities operate autonomously and were not coordinated as of summer 2005. In August 2005, command of the PRT in Kandahar was shifted from US to Canadian control, and the Kandahar brigade shifted to Canadian command in February 2005. At the same time, extra-US NATO forces have increased from 9,700 to 16,000 (Gall, 2006). A French task force existed in the Spin Boldak area until autumn 2006.

Besides the Coalition forces, the city is also home to a US Regional Training Centre for the district police as well as a sizeable number of PSCs.[4] The PRT initiated the issuance of weapons licences in the province. Later on, this process moved from the PRT to the governor's office. As part of this process, a vetting system has been proposed whereby three to five elders or representatives from different groups decide which individuals should be allowed to carry a weapon. The Kandahar PRT is also the original site of the Tactical Police Assistance Teams (three US Reservists with police experience), who are tasked with assessing police training and behaviour.

Currently, in terms of government security bodies, Kandahar is the location of two ANA battalions. Newly trained ANP were deployed to Kandahar in early 2004. Beyond the Provincial ANP (which were both locally recruited and deployed from Kabul), the province is home to a broad selection of other Afghan armed actors, from the Governor's Reserve Police/*Nazm-e-khas*/Quick Reaction Force to the Afghan units utilized by the Coalition and PSCs.

In addition, the NDS is involved in offensive operations in Kandahar and has clashed with the provincial police forces in the past. Asserting the presence of a security vacuum upon the completion of DDR, Gul Agha Sherzai formed the Governor's Reserve Police (*Nazm-e-khas*) in spring 2004. This force was formalized by his successor, Governor Yusuf Pashtun, and is believed to number between 500 and 800 soldiers exempted from DDR. While the externally deployed ANP is used for UN installation security, the Governor's Reserve Police is hired for UN road missions.[5]

On 31 January 2004, 300 ANP were deployed to Kandahar in one of the first deployments of centrally trained police to a province. Within the unit, high levels of optimism about their training and pride for their symbolic representation of the central government were reported. The arrival of the ANP in Kandahar led to considerable disappointment – they were accommodated in the remains of the Kandahar Hotel, given little ammunition and sent to guard UN compounds, rather than engage in policing. The 260 deployed were also undersupplied in terms of weapons, vehicles and accommodation, which prompted 100 to desert.

Similarly, a second ANP unit provided to the Ministry of Finance to monitor the collection of customs at Spin Boldak also faced the desertion of 30 officers. This unit was viewed to be the 'cream of the crop,' having just completed training at the German Police Academy in Kabul. Yet, their morale was immediately negatively affected by their lack of support and resources, low pay and poor living conditions. Only one weapon was available for every two officers; there was also a shortage of ammunition. Moreover, rather than employing this elite ANP unit to encourage local security, the unit was utilized to provide security for the regional UNAMA office, which was considered to be a 'complete waste of one of the best units they had' and that led to a collapse of discipline and morale. Moreover, their deployment had made the existing security structure (militia and untrained police) uncertain regarding its future status.

As described in Table 8.1, the ANP's pay was below that of most other security forces in the province, as well as below that of the previously employed UN guards and Afghan Border Force, which led to the desertion of half of the deployed ANP. The PRT eventually spent approximately $50,000 to improve the unit's living conditions and provide ammunition to the contingent. This example illustrates the current dilemma, whereby more resources and a better salary are available in private militias than in the emerging legitimate and accountable government security institutions. An informal case study of wages provided to armed guards/men in

Table 8.1 Comparison of wages, Kandahar security forces (mid-June 2004)ᵃ

Type	Wage
ANA	$120 per month + food + lodging
ANP	$76 per month (to be expanded to $120)
JEMB election guard	$4 per day (approximately $100 per month)
ABP	$150 per month (paid by Bearing Point)
AMF (Coalition)	$8–10 per day when on mission
AMF guard for Louis Berger Associates	$150–200 per month + food (approximately $50 goes to commander)
Private guard at bridge	$50 per month, paid by Sub-commander Razak (Gul Agha) to confiscate tin and scrap metal from vehicles
MoI police at RTC	$40 per month (police not paid in 6 months)
AMF guards at airport	$100 per month
AMF highway guards	$16 + food
AMF guard at road reconstruction project (Indian company)	$3 per month ($1 goes to Commander Atta Mohammed); guard belonged to *Nezmi-has*, formerly of Gul Agha Shirzai
Traffic Police	$72 per month (provided by JICA)
AMF (2nd Division)	$16 per month + some food (guarding Kandahar mosque and posts surrounding Coalition Gecko base, receiving $4 monthly supplement)
MoI Police at PRT	$100 per month

Note
a Information based on informal survey of armed actors in Kandahar City conducted in June 2004.

Kandahar reveals both the wide variety of armed actors as well as the existence of clear economic incentives for armed men to become involved in private, rather than government, armed employment (see Table 8.1).

Continuation of armed groups despite DDR

Prior to DDR, Kandahar was the home of the AMF's 2nd Corps and 7th Division. Originally, the size of AMF forces in Kandahar was proposed to be 14,000 and then lowered to 7,500, with UNAMA later noting that even these numbers were inflated, and the size of the force was more likely to be 3,500. The Kandahar AMF structure included the Tribal Road Security Chiefs, which were organized by Gul Agha Sherzai. The Coalition utilized the 503 Brigade (under General Torjan) and also formed an Afghan National Guard to provide further force protection to the Kandahar PRTs.[6] While, theoretically, the AMF was under the control of the Alikozai commander Khan Mohammed, the brigades, divisions and subdivisions within this structure belonged to non-aligned commanders and operated autonomously. Accordingly, the commanders feared an unbalanced DDR process that would threaten the equilibrium among the tribes and therefore delay the programme.[7]

The DDR programme's impact is questionable in Kandahar, where the proliferation of PSCs and opportunities for Coalition employment led many either to avoid the process entirely or to miss out on reintegration assistance. With the demobilization of the AMF, a commander's strength is expressed less in terms of offensive capability against an opposing unit than in terms of the ability to acquire supporting contracts, to maintain armed units and to integrate into official and quasi-official security structures.

Each of the non-state armed groups/PSCs is dominated by a different Kandahari faction: USPI is Popalzai and the Coalition Afghan Security Force (which evolved from fulfilling a patrolling function to now providing base security) is Popalzai and Barakzai. In addition, prior to the presidential elections, UNOPS hired armed security (as many as 500) through commanders and independently, which are then deputized by the Provincial Chief of Police. As with the governor's *nazm-e-khas*, each of these groups provides attractive options for combatants to skip DDR and join local militias.[8]

According to a UN official, due to the broad availability of PSC employment opportunities, 'most of those disarmed and demobilized never went through reintegration,' and, thus, have yet to sever their links to and economic dependency on their commanders.[9] An ANP officer stationed at USPI asserted: 'no one can make me go through DDR, before DDR started they removed us to the ANP.'[10] Commanders thus appear to be using PSCs and other government security forces to hide their militias. In this case, even after demobilization, former combatants continue to search out armed work, which provides short-term economic benefits but undermines the ability to integrate into normal 'unarmed' life in the future.

Practically, this could be partially remedied by an extension of the 'R,' or Reintegration, portion of DDR far into the future so as to give these combatants an opportunity to transition to civilian life. Otherwise, with no other viable employment opportunities, these armed men will continue to move from one 'guard' job to another, maintaining their links to their comrades and commanders.

More troublingly, some of these companies (Louis Berger, the UN, etc.) use commanders to obtain recruits, thus maintaining their position as sources of money and other forms of patronage. Ongoing employment with a PSC – typically acquired by a combatant as a consequence of membership in an AMF unit – prevents a soldier from going through reintegration and job retraining. Short-term economic benefits limit long-term economic stability while combatants remain dependent on commanders for their livelihood and arms retainment.

Without a doubt, security will be required for future elections, reconstruction projects and other activities. As described by a JEMB staff member, there is a conundrum about whether to use 'armed thugs' for election security (which typically employ 'brutal methods of crowd control') versus none at all.[11] However, it is necessary to ensure that the style in which they seek to achieve security does not undermine SSR.

While armed actors are used to dealing with the Taliban threat, it has proven to be very difficult to prevent their use beyond their limited security role, as groups then utilize their position in order to engage in local predatory practices. The worst cases involve the funnelling of resources through AMF commanders so as to gain access to their soldiers, as is the case with many of the road construction companies in Kandahar. Not only does this fortify the commander's role as patron, but it typically results in the commander pocketing a significant percentage of the daily wages (typically one-third to one-quarter of the wage).[12]

Beyond the provision of armed men, commanders also benefit financially by controlling the provision of services (e.g., rental cars) to military contingents. For both USPI and the Governor's Reserve Force, the rental cost for five guards armed with AKs and a vehicle is $600 per day.[13] As noted by one UN official, the recruitment and retention of soldiers through their commander maintains the commander as 'the dominant figure in the food chain.'[14] General Padshah Sherzai and Razik Sherzai lease Kandahar Air Field to the Coalition. The Sherzai family is also reported to control the rock quarrying and cement business around Kandahar (ICG, 2003, p. 15). One ex-combatant indicated that the hiring of PRT kitchen staff is done through Qasem Karzai. Approximately one-half of his $280 monthly wage ($160–180) is confiscated in exchange for his continued employment.[15]

Contemporary security dynamics

The dominant theme in the south of Afghanistan has been the steadily worsening security situation since the collapse of the Taliban and the Bonn Agreement. Kandahar City faces three interwoven sources of insecurity: Taliban insurgents, intra-commander fighting or predation and criminality. The latter two are interlinked, although there are also reports (particularly in Farah Province) of commanders facilitating Taliban attacks (against PSCs and the Coalition) in order to exact greater security funds.

The sources of insecurity differ depending on the subject. Prominent Afghans, the Coalition, villagers and other international actors are targeted by the Taliban. Local Afghans are subject to violence from prominent commanders and Afghan security forces (whether government or quasi-legal PSCs). In summer 2005, one prominent aid official privately noted that the dominant security concern for individuals was their fear of being 'Placed Under Control' (held in detention) by Coalition forces.[16]

With regard to the Taliban, one analyst indicated that there were three types of anti-Coalition group in Kandahar: a national—religious rebellion constituted by disenfranchised Pashtuns, foreign jihadists and factional commanders with Taliban contacts.[17] While the presence of charismatic religious figures is a driving force behind the insurgency in Paktya, the absence of similarly unifying figures in the south hinders the insurgency's viability.[18] Up until 2006, insurgency violence was seen to occur in waves, which was attributed to the inability to sustain operations due to a lack of training and financing and the need to return to Pakistan to regroup.

Over the last six months, the number and assertiveness of attacks have markedly increased, returning to levels largely unseen since 2002. Beyond the dramatic increase in suicide attacks, insurgents are attacking both checkpoints and district centres, with massed forces of 20–100. The border districts (Arghistan, Maruf, Lora Wala, Reg) are critical transit points for Taliban insurgents, with Taliban teams of five to ten moving through these areas. In spring 2006, the Taliban were again able to operate in the districts bordering Kandahar City (Panjwayi/Zhari), establishing checkpoints and controlling districts, carrying out trials and executions and settling local disputes in the absence of a government presence (Gall, 2006).

As such, the Taliban have moved from transitioning through districts (enforcing their presence and right of movement) to holding districts (assassinating dissenting tribal chiefs and *mullahs*) and have potentially begun administering justice and resolving disputes in the districts they hold. The rise of the Taliban insurgency has slowed down government reform efforts as well as produced new government plans for the formation of tribal militias in Helmand and Kandahar by figures implicated in both criminality and poppy production. There is some evidence that individuals from marginalized areas are compelled to join the Taliban due to drought and other livelihood vulnerabilities (*majbur*, adj. meaning compelled or forced to do something having no other option).[19]

While the AMF previously provided roadside, installation and area security in Kandahar, they were also held responsible for 80 per cent of all crime and violence in the province, a percentage proposed by a former Kandahar governor.[20] The AIHRC representative in Kandahar noted that 'most people are complaining about land issues' due to competing title documents and attempts by commanders to acquire public land, with violence also linked to the return of refugees.[21]

As in Paktya, government security officials utilize their positions against their personal rivals. A border police commander of the Atsakzai tribe utilized his position to execute 16 members of the Noorzai tribe, dismissing these individuals as 'Taliban fighters,' and is 'now under investigation for allegedly using the war on terrorism as an excuse to settle a personal blood feud' (Sarwar, 2006). Child protection and kidnapping is seen to be a critical issue, which induced mass protests against the governor and the provincial security forces in April 2005. Deputy Chief of Police Saleem (of Logar) was believed to be implicated in kidnapping both through the use of police and a broader group of Sindhi criminals. Two now demobilized

AMF units (15th Division and 7th Armoured Brigade) were implicated in illegal land seizures and conflict.[22]

Thus, while corps commanders proposed that DDR would lead to a security gap, it cannot be forgotten that the Taliban rose to power in this region precisely because of the abuses and behaviour of these commanders. According to a combatant, 'the main problem here in Kandahar is a problem of commanders'; 'they make the criminality for they command the soldiers ... it is the commander that makes the problems.'[23]

Local conflict history

The history of conflict in Kandahar reveals the potential for both inter-tribal cooperation as well as the graphic consequences of inter-tribal conflict. However, as seen in Sarah Chayes' recent book, *The Punishment of Virtue*, external actors (whether the ISI or the Coalition forces) have exacerbated local divisions rather than sought to heal these local rifts (Chayes, 2006, pp. 58–62).

Jihad

During the jihad, Kandahar, unlike the eastern provinces, was known for the relative absence of major *tanzims*. The armed movements remained predominantly locally oriented and determined by their *qawm*, rather than strongly linked to the political–military parties in Peshawar. Among full-time mujahideen in the south, as of 1988, the party distribution was 19 per cent Jamiat, 20 per cent Hezb-e-Islami, 15 per cent Hezb-e-Islami Khalis, 10 per cent NIFA and 29 per cent Harakat (Rubin, 1996, p. 200). Pashtun Durrani tribes either belonged only nominally to Jamiat (through the affiliation of the Alikozai commander Mullah Naqibullah) or to the traditionalist parties of NIFA (Gailani), Harakat (Nabi) or Mojaddedi (ANLF).[24] Both new elites and Ghilzai groups, however, did align with both Hezb-e-Islami and Hezb-e-Islami Khalis. The Malajat, a southern suburb of Kandahar, was also a common basing area for mujahideen forces (Jalali and Grau, 1994, p. 305). Atsakzai militias received arms from Iran and allied with local Maoist movements and Shi'a Harakat militias, with some Barakzai and Atsakzai disputes emerging after 1985 (Jalali and Grau, 1994, p. 289).

Illustrating the broader definition of the term, *qawm*-based mobilization did not only occur around tribes and localities but also around professional groupings. As described by Dorronsoro, prior to the jihad, Gul Agha Sherzai's father (Haji Abdul Latif) was not the head of the Barakzai *qawm* but of a cross-tribe solidarity group known as the *payluch* (the shoeless ones), a group which 'brought together the young men of the bazaar, often the sons of ... professions lacking prestige,' 'oblig[ing] [them] to observe a code of honour and solidarity between members' (Dorronsoro, 2005, p. 110).

During the jihad, the primary mujahideen coordinating body in Kandahar was religious rather than military. The Islamic court of Baluchistan and southwest Afghanistan was 'the most influential body'; 'many of its judges later [became] officials of the Taliban' (Rubin and Malikyar, 2003, p. 8). Central Islamic courts were complemented by a series of mujahideen courts in the various districts of Kandahar. As described by Jalali and Grau:

> unlike other areas of Afghanistan, there was little infighting among the factions involved in the fighting around Kandahar and the mujahideen ran the fight cooperatively through regular meetings of a coordination council. This cooperation provided tactical flexibility to the mujahideen.
>
> (Jalali and Grau, 1994, p. 308)

This cooperation during the battle for Kandahar involved 'rotat[ing] forces in and out of battle to maintain pressure on the Soviet and DRA garrisons' (Jalali and Grau, 1994, pp. 43, 308).

Kandahar Province witnessed some of the most pronounced tensions between the locally based *shura* and commanders and the externally based political parties. Internal cohesion was consistently threatened by external parties favoured by external constituencies. Attempts by the ISI to impose the rule of Hekmatyar and Sayyaf on the region were met with strong resistance by this *shura*, with the Islamic court of Kandahar releasing a fatwa calling all Wahhabis *kafirs* (infidels).[25] As described by Rubin:

> the tribal system in Qandahar resisted not only protostate structures but also the party system and the ISI ... The large khans had extensive networks of patronage and links to both the market and, in some cases, the international system (some were former diplomats or other officials); they were better placed than khans of the East to provide leadership and other collective goods. The growth of politically organized Islamist fronts was limited by the strength of the khans.
>
> (Rubin, 1996, pp. 243–244)

And, yet, the rise of new power brokers was able to challenge the tribal structure, as seen to a minor extent during the jihad and, far more significantly, during the Taliban regime. These figures were able to leverage outside resources. Yet, their influence may be ultimately fleeting, unless they are able to acquire a dominant position within their tribe. As noted by one combatant:

> Some people when they belong to a party receive power only from the party, because they have no nation. But there are other commanders,

like Mullah Naqib, who have power from the party and from the nation. Sirkati [an Alikozai formerly aligned with Hezb-e-Islami] only has power from the party. Thus, Mullah Naqib is still powerful, while Sirkati's power is over.'[26]

Civil war

However, while serving as a basis for successful and collective organization against outside actors, the *shura* was less capable when it came to handling internal issues. It was not able to prevent the outbreak of factional competition and criminality between these parties and was only able to 'play a regulatory role ... after the outbreak of conflicts, with the aim of reconciliation.'[27] Between 1988 and 1989, Najibullah deployed Dostum's Jawzjani militias to the Kabul garrison, which compromised Najibullah's attempts to ally with local tribes and form self-defence militias (Rubin, 1996, p. 262). In early summer 1991, clashes broke out between Mullah Naqibullah (Jamiat) and Asadullah (Hezb-e-Islami) in the Khakrez and Arghandab districts and between Haji Lalai (NIFA) and Chat Akhunzada in Shah Wali Kot, with the joint tribal *shura* attempting, but ultimately unable, to stop the infighting (AIC, 1991b, p. 38).

Following the Najibullah government's collapse, Kandahar's seven districts, as well as its provincial governing institutions and ministries, were divided among the local tribes (HRRAC, 2003, p. 53). Proposing similarities between the civil war and post-Bonn Kandahar, a combatant provides the following description of the civil war period in Kandahar:

> It was a time of revolution, every commander of a nation captured one place. Mullah Naqib captured the division, so we went there. Many people went there because they wanted to go to make military service. We did not receive a salary – no one ever received a salary for military service, not even during Zahir Shah. But he was the main person from our nation, when the *qawmi mesher* says something, we must do it. Before the Taliban, every district [*rayon*] belonged to a different nation. When the Taliban left this country – the Taliban had no nation and no one knew where they were from – all the nations came back and again gathered their soldiers. I came back because they were the people from our nation. I didn't know what else to do.[28]

Upon assuming control of a ministry or office, whether for governance or security, the tribal authority acquired additional legitimacy through association with the national government. The (Alikozai Pashtun) commanders were now able to present themselves as the legitimate military representatives of the central government due to their control of the army barracks and headquarters. Other groups controlled the police and other ministries, with insecurity occurring in the transition areas between these groups and city districts. Outside of Kandahar City, the road between the city and Spin Boldak was dominated first by the Atsakzai commander Ismat Muslim (1984–1988) and, later, by groups loyal to Hekmatyar.

The Taliban era

During the civil war period, although trade was hindered by multiple checkpoints established by commanders, Kandahar emerged as a transit point for the re-exportation of goods to Pakistan via the Afghanistan Transit Trade Agreement and 'formed the most important part of the commercial road connecting Gulf countries to the Pakistan market' (Nojumi, 2002, p. 117; Rubin, 1996, pp. 244–245). Reputedly, the Taliban emerged as a consequence of this insecurity and other violations and were backed both by the ISI and Pakistan's 'trucking mafia' (Bhatia and Goodhand, 2003, p. 68).

There continues to be two dissenting interpretations of the Taliban movement. Externally, the Taliban are viewed as a movement with origins in Kandahar. Locally, however, those that belonged to the Taliban were viewed to be outside of the province's traditional tribal structure. A typical example of the former interpretation is seen in the following account in the April 2006 issue of the *Jamestown Terrorism Monitor*:

> Throughout the reign of the Taliban (1996–2001) and beyond, the local population has remained loyal to this enigmatic movement. The enduring strength and popularity of the movement is partly rooted in the Taliban's synthesis of rural Islamic values and Durrani Pashtun culture.
>
> (Rahmani, 2006)

According to this interpretation, the Taliban completely manifest Kandahar tribal dynamics and reflect the values as well as hold the sympathies of the local population. Interviews with local tribal members and with local combatants emphasize the second interpretation. While the Kandahar City tribes did cede power willingly to the Taliban in 1994, the traditional tribal elites and structures did not play a significant role in the composition and expansion of the movement.

Alikozai insurrections by Abdul Hakim against the Taliban were prevented by Mullah Naqibullah, although the Taliban targeted Arghandab by attempting to restrict water resources in response to a minor local rebellion. One combatant argues: 'We knew our people and didn't know where they [the Taliban] were from.'[29] The Taliban were seen to be removed from traditional sources of power in Kandahar City and thus were viewed as a product of the dislocation due to the Soviet invasion, mass displacement to Pakistan and the provision of support to figures outside of the traditional tribal structure. The movement is thus seen to be a consequence of delocalization and detribalization of southern Pashtuns (similar, then, to those that supported Hezb-e-Islami Hekmatyar in eastern Afghanistan) (Rashid, 2000, pp. 32–33).

Unfortunately, little evidence was gathered as to the recruitment and conscription practices of the Taliban in the region. However, an Uruzgani combatant (who fought against the Taliban with Ittihad in Kabul and later returned to join the Popalzai insurrection in Uruzgan) noted: 'A special community in the village said that if you have five *jeribs* (1 hectare) of land, you have to send one to two sons.'[30]

Post-9/11 period

Following the collapse of the Taliban, there was a pronounced fear of the re-emergence of tribal rivalries in Kandahar. With the assistance of Hamid Karzai and Gul Agha Sherzai, Coalition Special Operations units contacted either displaced or diminished tribal leaders in order to empower them to invoke and mobilize their tribal militias. Under an arrangement negotiated by now-President Karzai, the Taliban agreed to surrender the city to Mullah Naqibullah of the Alikozai – the very figure who had surrendered the city to the Taliban in 1995. Power was then divided among the prominent tribal figures: Gul Agha Sherzai of the Barakzai served as governor from 2002–2004, Khan Mohammed was selected as the AMF Corps Commander and Muhammad Akrem Khakrezwal was the Provincial Chief of Police. Immediately after the Bonn period, tensions existed not only between the various tribal commanders (Alikozai versus Barakzai) but also between the forces of Gul Agha Sherzai and those of Ismail Khan, with the Pashtun tribes threatening to mobilize in order to end Ismail Khan's persecution of Pashtuns in western Afghanistan and in Shindand district (Rubin and Malikyar, 2003, p. 13).

While prominent figures such as Gul Agha Sherzai may dominate discussions of the city, in fact, authority is diffused between the tribes. Each of the major tribes is able to act as a 'law unto itself,' carrying out illegal detentions and previously maintaining private prisons.[31] In 2004, independent rogue taxation by various ministries was widely evident, with the provincial Minister of Transportation taxing commercial vehicles and the Ministry of Mines taxing crushed rocks ($0.4 per square metre) and tin. According to the provincial governor, the provincial Ministry of Transportation (MoT) was collecting approximately $72,000 per month and then only sending $20,000 to the government.[32] Thus, current provincial political–military dynamics are marked by the diffusion of authority.

Communities, commanders and combatants

A total of 37 interviews were conducted with combatants in Kandahar City, arranged largely through a series of reintegration programmes. The jihad

Table 8.2 Combatant profiles of Kandahar City (37 combatants)

Schooling	14% (2 studied in Kabul, 1 in Quetta, 2 in Kandahar (2nd–6th grade)
Prominent livelihoods	Day labourer, farmer, fruit trade, transport, shopkeeping, poppy harvesting.
Labour migration	21% to Quetta or Peshawar. Significance of internal displacement due to conflict and relocation to Kandahar from Kabul and Uruzgan.
Average age of first mobilization:	18
Recruited under 18	49%
Recruited at or under 16	37%
First mobilized during:	
Jihad	47%
Civil war	17%
Taliban era	0%
Post-9/11 period	36%
Prominent motives by period:	
Jihad	Family, religious and elder authority, grievance, economic incentives, family/group belonging.
Civil war	Elder authority, family belonging, protection, economic incentives.
Taliban era	Economic incentives.
Post-9/11 period	Economic incentives, elder authority, family/group belonging, grievance, protection.

era and the period from 2000–2002 are the two major periods of mobilization – contradicting the view that the DDR programme was oriented towards combatants from previous eras of fighting. Instead, the period following 9/11 witnessed the rapid expansion of militias, with 36 per cent of those interviewed first picking up a weapon during this time. Only one of these combatants admitted to having served with the Taliban, although his period of first mobilization was during the jihad era. Two joined the local militias convened by the Najibullah government. Five of those interviewed served with a PSC.

As was the case in the two preceding case studies (Ghor and Paktya), combatant accounts in Kandahar stressed elder authority as a significant motive for mobilization across all periods of fighting. Both the level of schooling and the level of labour migration were low in comparison to other areas. A substantial number of combatants discussed conflict-driven internal and external displacement. Combatants possessed a broad range of economic livelihoods beyond their status as combatants.

Recruitment at child age

As described in Table 8.1, a substantial portion of the combatants inter-viewed was first recruited under the age of either 18 (50 per cent) or 16 (37 per cent). Some children were first exposed to the armed groups when joining their brothers, fathers or uncles in the base or family home and pro-viding tea or other forms of hospitality to the fighters. Beyond their family ties, they became socialized and began to identify with the armed group. Other children followed a more direct form of progression, first serving as porters, then as intermediaries between the villages and the city and, finally, provided with a weapon to engage in fighting. Generally, from approxi-mately age eight children provided food, bread and a yogurt drink to com-batants and were formally provided with a weapon at the age of 13 or 14.

The following combatant account reveals the stages of involvement:

> When I was five to seven years old, I was inside the base to give food and water to other mujahideen. Because Mullah Naqib was the main person from our nation, we like to respect him and we did this type of activity. After I grew up, and was 14–15 years old, I picked up the gun and I went to be a watchmen and to the frontline in the time of Najib until we went inside the city in the time of the revolution [civil war]. I went because of the tradition in our land, when the main person from our nation tell us, like Mullah Gul Khan or Khan Mohammed or Mohammed Akram, these were our main people. If they tell us some-thing, we must do the same thing, we are the youngest, they are the oldest. All the time they told us to make jihad, to make clean our country from the bad/evil people, and of the need to be free. Our tra-dition is that we must always respect the old people.[33]

Elder authority

As was illustrated by the comparison between Ghor and Paktya, as well as in Chapter 3, the dimensions of elder authority (tribal *khans* and the *qawmi meshran*) vary between communities. Some of the senior tribal figures are able to combine their elder authority with religious authority (whether through their own learning or through the presence of other *mullahs* or *maulavis*), which enhances obedience. Similarly, familial authority will enhance the potential for mobilization if it supports the call and decision of the elder and religious figures. Elder authority generally means that a commander does not need to provide a salary. In certain cases, mobilization for elder authority occasionally went against the eco-nomic interest of the individual combatant, necessitating a broader inter-pretation of economic utility.

When compared to certain Paktya *qawms*, Kandahar's commanders appear to hold more sway over their communities than vice versa.

Community consent does not appear to dictate concepts of legitimate versus illegitimate violent activity. As a consequence, the *qawm*-based military groupings in Kandahar contain strongman-type elements, particularly during periods of peace and when the community is not overtly threatened. Although concepts of elder authority appear linked to the protection of a community or group, the commander determines the type of fighting permitted, with little input from a *shura*. The security of the community elder appears tied to broader honour of the community. The individual, much more so than in Paktya, is considered an embodiment of the group.

The following narratives describe the changing role of elder authority across all four periods of the Afghan conflict. With regard to elder authority during the jihad, an Alikozai combatant proposes:

> Until the Russians left, the main person from our nation said it was necessary to fight, and after the Russians left, they said we had to stop. The *qawm* formed an office, and distributed weapons from Pakistan. The *qawmi meshran* spoke to the nation about the holy jihad. For me my father told me – you can fight until the Russians leave. It was not by force, it was naturally. All the people went by themselves, and I also went by myself.[34]

The role of elder authority continued during the civil war:

> It was the government of different nations – he [Mohammed Akram] was the main person from our nation, so all young people had to join him. Every nation had our own commander; to defend their own nations from each other, as all nations had conflict with each other.[35]

> It was a hard time, he was the main person from our nation, fighting started in the city, and we had to defend him and his place. He is the man from our nation, it is tradition, we must support him. He was Qulu-Urdu commander, he needed soldiers for protection. He is our *qawmi mesher*, he told us to make security for the city.[36]

Similarly, the role of elder authority among the Barakzai in the decision to join the Coalition against the Taliban is seen in the following account:

> We started fighting against Taliban because it was the command of Gul Agha Sherzai. We will not miss this life, as to have a weapon is not good, but that was our obligation. We accept that he is the head of the tribe, and we listen to him, if the government gives good jobs, we will never obey him in the future for fighting, if not we will join them. We didn't like to fight against the Taliban because we had to work but when we fought the Taliban they became our enemy. When we were

doing daily labour we could join a good company, but the commanders are also the head of our tribe and he ordered us to come, otherwise we did not want to fight. In that time, Gul Agha Sherzai just
ordered us, and we made decision to come and fight.[37]

Even with the completion of the DDR process and the initiation of the
DIAG programme (which prohibits all armed groups aside from those
community militias recognized by the government and those utilized by
the Coalition), this authority allows commanders to recollect combatants
quickly:

When the *qawmi mesher* asks, no one can tell him no. These people
from the militias can get everything, can quickly collect a lot of
people, but officially they don't have militia ... He talks with the
nation and after an hour he can collect 1,000 people. Many people
are tired and don't want to go, but still people are scared of these
people. Many people cannot trust them anymore. The money is not
important. People can come without the money. For me, the money's
not important, he's the person from our nation, he told me to come
and I came.[38]

Thus, in contrast to Paktya, elder authority in Kandahar is increasingly
focused on prominent personalities rather than on a community of elders.
Personal distaste and disinterest in mobilizing still could not override feel-
ings of obligation. Obligation and obedience required of the combatant
produces a certain amount of disgruntlement, particularly as it went
against the economic interest of the combatant.

There is some sign that the ability of commanders to acquire combatants through elder authority may be limited in the future. Part of this is
founded on disenchantment with the jihad period (widely considered the
most legitimate period of fighting), as combatants witnessed their commanders accrue wealth. Moreover, combatants perceive the provision of
resources by states and the patronage network to contribute significantly
to the maintenance of militias. This viewpoint is evident in the following
narratives:

Mojaddedi gave money to commanders, but half the money went into
the pocket of the commanders and half of it went to us.... The Commanders have many things, money and lands ... None of them [the
normal combatants] have a bicycle but all of the commanders have
expensive cars ... Now, we are unhappy with our commanders, they
were using us, and we are poor still now.... In the future, these commanders will be armed again if the government does not do anything,
because they have more money, they can buy the weapons from Pakistan. You should DDR these commanders from their money.[39]

[The Commanders] got money from other countries, sitting in Pakistan they would just order us to fight. In that time, countries were giving money to fight. In the future, they will also give money to our commanders for fighting. Our request is that foreigners stop helping the commanders. Commander Hamid Agha has 3,000 cans of ghee (oil) and we do not have one.[40]

There is thus some indication that combatants' ties with their commanders are weakening, with several indicating that they would not obey a commander's order to fight in the future. This stands in contrast to the narratives encountered in Ghor Province, where loyalty to the commander trumped all other concerns and dictated mobilization.

Economic incentives

While the endorsement of elder authority replaces the need to provide a salary, economic incentives were also a prominent motive across all periods of conflict; they were the motive cited by the two combatants who joined the Najibullah government's militia in Kandahar as well as by the combatant who joined the Taliban.[41] Mobilization for economic gain also requires that a combatant have avenues into a particular group, which is typically acquired through either familial or other ties. Even so, combatants will assess their options in relation to the type of fighting or mobilization required. While the Taliban offered a good salary, one combatant was reluctant to join, as mobilization required fighting outside of a locality.[42] Some combatants have left profitable professions due to physical insecurity (as occurred during the civil war) or due to the fact that becoming a combatant was viewed to be more economically stable. One combatant started a fruit trading business after the jihad. As a consequence of checkpoints, accidents, floods and the drought, he lost eight to nine million Pakistani rupees over 11 years and decided to become a combatant in 2002 to earn $16–30 per month.[43] Another combatant recalls:

> They gave me a salary 2,500 Afs [$50] per month, and the commander also gave me more, so it was 4,000 Afs [$80]. As a shopkeeper, you cannot always make 5,000 [$100], you can also lose it. As a soldier, the money was fixed, everything was OK. In contrast, to be a good shopkeeper was not an easy job.[44]

A mechanic who moonlights with USPI in order to raise additional funds recalled: 'Business in the workshop sometimes is good and sometimes is not. We have to rent the shop, and I have six to seven students, it became so expensive and I could not make a lot of money.'[45] Another combatant asserts that he joined USPI because 'my cousin told me that I could get better money than now, so that was why I came.'[46]

These accounts further reveal how combatant mobilization serves as a means of rounding out a soldier's economic portfolio. These combatants are not uniskilled but return to an armed group or PSC in order to attain additional funds or to support another business venture.

In the current period, access to economic opportunities necessitates either familial or tribal links, particularly for employment with prominent PSCs or as a Coalition service provider. As described in Chapter 3, commanders use their family members as bodyguards. These extended family members are also provided with sizeable salaries and better access to economic opportunities. Any individual may be able to join certain armed groups, but the attainment of a substantial wage requires a personal connection.

Becoming a combatant in Kandahar appears to be far more profitable than in other areas of the country – supposedly due to the intersection of the profitable foreign security contracts as well as to poppy harvesting. A combatant who guarded an Indian reconstruction company received 6,000 Pakistani rupees, while a Popalzai who protected a Japanese company earned $150 per month.[47] Moreover, it appears as though entrance into certain reintegration programmes was also privileged. Some of the first combatants interviewed at the Cooperation Centre for Afghanistan (an Afghan NGO) reintegration training centre had never served as combatants but instead were able to be assigned to the AMF through family connections, with the intention of acquiring job training and education benefits.

Protection

Insecurity – whether caused by the growth of the Taliban insurgency or other forms of lawlessness in village areas – also contributes to continued mobilization through displacement. The penetration of villages by insurgents and the execution of proposed collaborators can promote mobilization due to the need for both sustenance and protection. With the resurgence of the Taliban, individuals who participated in the campaign in 2002 are now the subject of reprisal attacks. This is evident in the following accounts:

> When the Taliban finished power, we saw that we were independent, but still there are many Taliban in my district. I am scared of them, so I wrote my name [signed up to the AMF] with the Karzai government, and brought my family from Shah Wali Kot to Kandahar City. And still, I am scared to go back to my district due to the Taliban, who say I take food and money from the Americans. I don't want to see any more Taliban, I don't belong to anyone. I can't go to Shah Wali Kot, I stay in Kandahar.[48]

> We helped these people [the Coalition] and now we have problem with Taliban, and we cannot even go home. Now we don't know what to do. We can't leave the city, they will kill us.[49]

Yet, insecurity was not only a product of Taliban rule. Other village and local conflicts continue to occur. After the Bonn Agreement, a combatant left Uruzgan because the governor was corrupt, describing:

> no law, with conflicts over water and land. The Coalition in Uruzgan will not help to resolve these complaints, and does not prevent lawlessness. I became a soldier because I had no other opportunity – it's so hard to find another job to collect money for your home, for this reason I wrote my name in the *Qulu-urdu*.[50]

Insecurity induced combatant mobilization, in order to acquire both a livelihood and affiliation with an armed group. Inter-familial conflicts can also result in mobilization (again in search of a salary or protection.) One combatant recalls:

> [We have] a problem inside our village with other people – they killed my brother. Even now we cannot go inside our village. Because of this conflict we came to Kandahar City, and we didn't know what to do, so I joined the division, because of the salary, and because the people in our village belonged to another group, so we had to take care and defend ourselves, and become soldiers.[51]

Thus, beyond the role of economic motives and elder authority, absent the stabilization of rural areas and the creation of an accountable government, individuals will become combatants in order to acquire protection or as a consequence of economic insecurity.

Conclusion

The case of Kandahar demonstrates a varying manifestation of tribal militias in Afghanistan. As mentioned, the DIAG process exempts tribal and community militias from its authority. However, the tribal militias in Kandahar can quickly evolve from self-protection to predatory forces. In contrast to Paktya – where the tribes/*qawms* are comparatively small and seek to limit the activities of commanders – the tribes in Kandahar are largely dominated by prominent individuals and families, who, while acting in consultation with their local *jirga/shura*, have also been strengthened considerably due to their commercial relationship with the Coalition forces and their dominance of provincial security institutions.

In Kandahar, commanders serve both as patrons and as heads of their tribes. In Kandahari Pashtun tribes, commanders are situated somewhere between community militias and strongmen. In the process of conflict, combined with the waning role of the state and the provision of resources by external authorities, community checks on the power of key personalities appear to have waned. The tribes are focused more on the heritage, descent and pre-eminence of key families and charismatic religious authorities rather than implementing community consent and review checks. Tribal leaders are thus able to use their tribal authority in order to mobilize combatants for a broad range of other tasks. The vast scale of funds for reconstruction, military service provision and security sent to Kandahar has increased the position of prominent tribal figures, allowing them to expand their power networks and develop further autonomy both from the central state and their constituent communities. As such, they are able to rely on both their authority and incentives to recruit soldiers and maintain their influence.

These commanders are also supported by a network of religious figures who supplement their tribal authority with forms of religious authority. Moreover, commanders acquired an air of national legitimacy when they were designated as officially part of the national government. As such, taking advantage of the combatant's information deficit, they presented recruitment to potential combatants as fulfilling 'national service,' making mobilization into the AMF equivalent to former national conscription laws.[52]

As discussed, in periods of political transition (following the withdrawal of either the Najibullah government or the Taliban) the dominant local tribes (Alikozai, Popalzai, Barakzai) jockey for the control of provincial governance and security institutions. While mobilization around sub-tribe, *qawm* and locality remains, those who lead these groups largely gained their prominence during the jihad (most particularly Gul Agha Sherzai and Mullah Naqibullah) and not due to the pre-conflict prominence of their families. Without a doubt, tribal and community *shuras* play a role in controlling and restraining violence, but they also determine what sorts of activities are permissible under their watch. This extends to all areas, from the permitted presence of Taliban forces to opium production and trafficking and land and water disputes. Their ability to recruit due to their tribal positions indicates that the absence of standing militias does not coincide with the erosion of the ability to mobilize soldiers.

Indeed, the case of Kandahar further illustrates the effects of the post-Bonn era on pre-existing militia structures. Most critically, it shows how the period following 9/11 led to the reinvigoration of tribal-based militias by producing an entirely new generation of combatants. The chapter particularly focuses on and reveals the role of the political economy dimension, describing the expansion by commanders into the economic realm. Table 8.1 demonstrates the economic incentives behind remaining with PSC forces rather than either demobilizing or joining the reforming national police. The vast array of both state and non-state militias in Kandahar – and the short-sighted decision by PSCs and the Coalition to provide funds to commanders for the creation and maintenance of militias – fortifies the link between commanders and their combatants. Moreover, ANP morale suffered when these soldiers compared their status and pay as newly reformed national police with the untrained combatants belonging to the provincial police and the PSCs.

Coalition forces and PSCs often act at cross-purposes and undermine their strategic objectives through their tactical actions. External actors have done so by being particularly blind to the linkage between economics, politics and security, both by hiring out local militias and by providing service contracts to prominent commanders. While this can co-opt commanders for the short term and demonstrate the economic dividends involved in supporting the Coalition, these dividends are still contingent on the commander's maintenance of armed influence. More importantly, the provision of resources to commanders allows them to fortify their links with combatants and to maintain their dominance of tribal communities.

Finally, the rise of the insurgency in Kandahar presents considerable cause for concern. Elder authority was a (if not *the*) prominent motive for Kandahar combatants during three of the four periods of fighting. Tribal elder authority was invoked against the Taliban rather than for the Taliban. Without a charismatic religious authority, the AGF remains dependent on either imposing their will through fear on local communities or taking advantage of temporary overlapping interests. Communities thus far appear unwilling to utilize community authority to demand mobilization. Any evidence to the contrary will mark a disturbing change in the conflict, revealing an emerging societal consensus against the Coalition and Karzai government.

Notes

1 Population statistics online, available at: statoids.com/uaf.html and cia.gov/cia/publications/factbook/print/af.html (accessed 4 December 2007).
2 *Kheils* of Noorzai include: Sultanzai, Mirulzai, Sameze, Torkusi; Barakzai *kheils* include: Pakarzai, Baluzai; Popalzai *kheils* include: Bamizi; Alikozai *kheils* include: Ajazi, Tiri.
3 In 2004, an interviewed combatant asserted that all commanders were involved in poppy production due to their possession of land. Combatants will occasionally contract seasonal labour in the fields. In 2004, the entire 503rd battalion of the AMF was sent by the commanders to harvest poppy. Combatant #3, Kandahar, June 2004.
4 Interview with RTC trainer, Kandahar, June 2004.
5 Of the $4–5 provided to a soldier per day, one-half is believed to be taken by the commander. Information based on informal survey of armed actors in Kandahar Province and meetings with international security officials in June 2004.
6 Interview with ANBP official, Kandahar, June 2005.
7 Interview with ANBP official, Kandahar, June 2004.
8 Interview with JEMB/RTC officer, Kandahar, June 2004.

9 Interview with UN official, Kandahar, May 2005.
10 Combatant #288, Kandahar, June 2005.
11 Interview with Kandahar JEMB official, June 2004.
12 Combatant #286, Kandahar, June 2005.
13 A USPI Afghan hire's weapon is personally owned and is brought home at the end of the day.
14 Interview with UN official, Kandahar, May 2005.
15 Combatant #286, Kandahar, June 2005.
16 Interview with US Government Official, Kabul, April 2005.
17 Interview with Bruno Collier, Kandahar, June 2005.
18 Interview with DfID DA, Matthijs Toot, Cambridge, UK, December 2004.
19 Interview with DfID DA, Matthijs Toot, Cambridge, UK, December 2004.
20 Interview with Governor Yusuf Pashtun, Kandahar, June 2004.
21 Interview with Engineer Noorzai, AIHRC Head, Kandahar, June 2004; Bruno Collier, ANSO, June 2004.
22 Interview with PRT Commander, Kandahar, June 2004.
23 Combatant #3, Kandahar, June 2004.
24 Exploring Mullah Naqibullah's decision to join Jamiat, Dorronsoro proposes:

> None of his social characteristics – a Pushtun small landowner who had not been politically active before the war – appeared to predispose him to join Jamiyat-i Islami. However, in this region Ma'az membership was largely Barakzai, Harakat-e-Inqilab was dominated by Ghilzai from the neighboring provinces of Ghazni and Logar, and Hezb-i Islami was locally Ghilzai. Therefore it was probably more logical for *mullah* Naqibullah to join Jamiyat-i Islami, which was locally 'neutral' in tribal terms and which also possessed substantial resources.
>
> (Dorronsoro, 2005, pp. 167–168)

25 Rubin, 1996, p. 263; Kaplan, 1990–2001, p. 216. In 1990, a commander from Kandahar wrote to the BBC, asserting:

> I would like to tell that we know you [Sayyaf] have a comfortable life in Peshawar. You are unaware of the Afghans who live inside Afghanistan. They see you as a Wahabi [*sic*]. If the ex-King returns, I am certain you [Sayyaf] will be left alone or with a few of your supporters from Paghman and Wardak Province. Today we are obliged to support you because you give us weapons. We want the country to be freed and peace to be restored.
>
> (Hyman, 1990, p. 118)

26 Combatant #272, Kandahar, June 2005.
27 '*Shura* councils were rarely effective, and only more closely-knit systems, where the commanders were more narrowly constrained by some form of organisation, were able to implement cooperation' (Dorronsoro, 2005, p. 210).
28 Combatant #280, Kandahar, June 2005.
29 Combatant #264, Kandahar, June 2005.
30 Combatant #125, Chaghcharan, Ghor, April 2005.
31 Interview with journalist, Kandahar, Afghanistan, June 2004.
32 Interview with Provincial Governor Yusuf Pashtun, Kandahar, June 2004.
33 Combatant #276, Kandahar, June 2005.
34 Combatant #272, Kandahar, June 2005.
35 Combatant #288, Kandahar, June 2005.
36 Combatant #275, Kandahar, June 2005.
37 Combatant #3, Kandahar, June 2004.
38 Combatant #269, Kandahar, June 2005.

39 Combatant #4, Kandahar, June 2004.
40 Combatant #3, Kandahar, June 2004.
41 The combatant who joined the Najibullah government recalled:

> We went by ourselves to take some salary. My brother was also a soldier there, two of my brothers died during time of Najib. Anyone could go there and join themselves. This was the situation in Afghanistan, if you stay, you must choose either Najib or mujahideen side. I had no other activity, I went for the salary. 3000 Afs [$60] is good money because things were cheap, and we received coupons.
>
> (Combatant #278, Kandahar, June 2005)

42 The Taliban:

> offered us a lot. They would offer 2.2 m [old] Afghani per month, but we didn't go. In the time of Najibullah, we were in our own area, I didn't [have to] leave to go fight. In the time of the Taliban, they would take us to kill another brother, the money could not give us satisfaction to do this. The Taliban could give us everything and we would not go.
>
> (Combatant #286, Kandahar, June 2005).

43 Combatant #279, Kandahar, June 2005.
44 Combatant #257, Kandahar, June 2005.
45 Combatant #289, Kandahar, June 2005.
46 Combatant #292, Kandahar, June 2005.
47 Combatant #264, Kandahar, June 2005; Combatant #265, Kandahar, June 2005.
48 Combatant #267, Kandahar, June 2005.
49 Combatant #269, Kandahar, June 2005.
50 Combatant #262, Kandahar, June 2005. *Qulu-urdu* is a local military headquarters.
51 Combatant #282, Kandahar, June 2005.
52 Combatant #258, Kandahar, June 2005.

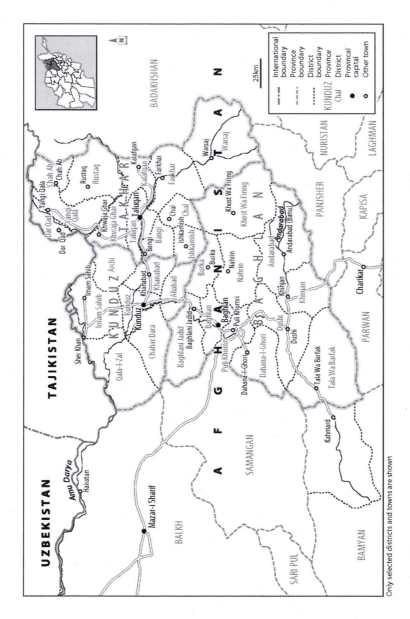

Only selected districts and towns are shown

Map 9.1 Kunduz, Takhar and Baghlan provinces.

9 Kunduz, Takhar and Baghlan

Parties, strongmen and shifting alliances

Michael Bhatia

The cases of Kunduz, Takhar and Baghlan reveal the following issues:

- the high incidence of forced conscription;
- the prominence of families, parties and strongmen rather than community elders;
- the factors driving armed groups to ethnic heterogeneity or homogeneity;
- the increase in the size of a commander's forces as a consequence of the Taliban's arrival.

After setting the local scene in terms of the ethnic composition of and the international presence in the three provinces, this chapter focuses on security during the post-9/11 period, particularly on the role of commanders and their current political positions. Commanders occupy prominent provincial and national positions, even though some (such as Amir Khan Baghlani) are still forcibly retaining combatants. The chapter begins with a brief review of the local conflict history. This chapter particularly highlights the shifting affiliations between commanders, communities and political–military parties, demonstrating how broad ethnic categories possess limited to no explanatory value in describing the nature of militias in northeast Afghanistan. Depending on extra-local alliances and the proximity of threat, armed groups can transform over time from ethnic heterogeneity to homogeneity and vice versa. The chapter concludes with an examination of the prominent combatant motives in the northeast region of the country, noting the high occurrence of forced conscription and search for protection, as well as the relative absence of elder authority in the mobilization process.

Setting the local scene

Kunduz has a population of 820,000 in an area of 8,040 square kilometres. Baghlan has 745,000 inhabitants and Takhar 750,000. The three provinces are located in the northeast of Afghanistan in a fertile plain serving as a

critical cross-road linking Kabul to the former Soviet republics of Tajikistan and Uzbekistan. For historical reasons, a broad range of ethnic
groups were encountered during the interviews in the northeast, including: Pashai, Tajik, Lakaiye Uzbek, Safi, Aimaq, Mongols, Arabs and Farsi-
wans.[1] The Pashtun tribes encountered include both Durrani and
Ghilzais: Noorzai, Arrokai, Alikozai, Barakzai, Akakheil, Turanya, Naser
and Ahmadzai. These Pashtuns and Nuristanis are now removed from the
tribal dynamics that shaped interactions in their villages of origin due to
the persecution of Pashtun civilians after the fall of the Taliban.

Kunduz is home to numerous NGOs, a Dyncorp-run Regional Training
Centre for police and a German-run PRT. The German PRT is constituted
by 443 Germans, 80 other nationalities and 93 Afghan support staff (both
security and other service provision). There are four Danish Military
Observer Teams (total of 24 people) and three German Liaison Monitoring Teams that conduct week-long patrols throughout nearby provinces.

Post-Bonn security and local armed groups

Since the Bonn Agreement, the north has been one of the more secure
areas of Afghanistan, although the predatory behaviour of commanders
(many of whom acquired district and provincial government positions)
has produced local vulnerabilities. Turnout for the parliamentary elections was 54 per cent in Baghlan, 61 per cent in Kunduz and 66 per cent
in Takhar. This is far above the national average of 49.4 per cent but
below the presidential turnout of 70 per cent (Wilder, 2005, p. 33; JEMB,
2007). While revealing the comparative peace in the northeast and the
degree of local support for the electoral process, both political processes
were significantly affected by arms proliferation and local commanders.

In 2002, a series of district profiles conducted throughout the northeast
(Takhar and Kunduz) indicated that village elders were irrelevant,
ignored or considerably weakened. Instead, Jamiat party members dominated most district and provincial positions (UNHCR, 2002c, d, e). Following the Taliban's withdrawal, the long-resident Pashtun populations were
subject to persecution by the triumphant Northern Alliance forces,
prompting as many as 20,000 to flee to the south (Dorronsoro, 2005, p.
343; HRW, 2002).

More recently, in June 2005, grassroots protests broke out in Rustaq district of Takhar against the local commander (Piramkul) over the involvement of his forces in child sexual abuse. During the protests, his forces
killed as many as four protesters. As a consequence, the size of the protest
expanded from 500 to 10,000. This led to the deployment of the ANA, to
Coalition over-flights and to the removal of all district officers. In May
2006, fighting broke out between two commanders in northern Baghlan
(Mohammad Yaqoob and Abdul Ghaffar), involving 70 combatants and
inducing an over-flight by ISAF (Jahesh, 2006).

Anti-Coalition Forces (ACF) operate in northern Kunduz and in parts of Badakshan. They have imported new weapons from Tajikistan and are attempting to capitalize on local unrest from the counter-narcotics campaign.[2] While there have been a number of high-profile attacks on NGO personnel in the northeast, international security officials generally attribute these attacks to government-affiliated local commanders rather than to the AGF.[3]

In 2005, a political analyst warned that commanders, due to the lack of payment provided by the programme, were considering selling weapons to Pakistan rather than turning in weapons under DIAG.[4] However, the rise of the AGF insurgency may lead commanders either to retain stocks or to purchase new weapons. Illegal goods (whether drugs or guns) enter Afghanistan via small border crossings on the Amu Darya, although the flow of arms has decreased since the conclusion of the war. An ABP colonel indicated that smugglers are often captured carrying opium (catches in spring 2005 include: 70 kg, 115 kg and 7 kg) and weapons to protect their goods. The group captured with 70 kg of opium also had one RPG and three AKs.[5]

As in other parts of Afghanistan, Kunduz is constituted by a large number of different government security forces and armed actors, each with a different level of training, oversight, resources and roles and responsibilities. In Kunduz, this is best exemplified by the situation at the Sher Khan border next to the Amu Darya (ancient Oxus) river. At the post, there is a broad array of armed entities and police present, with confusion as to the distribution of roles and responsibilities. They include the Customs Police, the Border Police (ABP), the Highway Police (AHP) and the ANP.

In comparison to the other forces, the ANP is particularly underserved. At the time the interviews were carried out, the ANP had not received a salary for ten months, while the AHP and ABP received salaries every month. Similarly, the ANP had only two weapons for five people, with eight full clips of ammunition.[6] The ABP and ANP members encountered had received 20 days of training at the RTC, while the ABP colonel had had an extended training programme of 45 days. Outside of the Sher Khan border, the MoD is reported to be recruiting soldiers from the now demobilized AMF in order to create a Property Protection Unit, re-employing ex-soldiers as armed guards. The German PRT was assigned soldiers and guards directly through the AMF corps, who were employed there after DDR, with a Chinese construction company also employing ex-soldiers as security guards.

Local commanders with troubled histories have achieved positions of provincial and national prominence. The 2005 governor of Kunduz Province is Engineer Mohammad Omar, who was the only Pashtun in the region who did not defect to the Taliban. Having lost his Pashtun support base, he remains surrounded only by his relatives and some other Tajik and Uzbek affiliates. Haji Salaam (AMF Commander in Kunduz) confiscated the salaries of his affiliated combatants and later became a police commander for the ABP forces in Takhar and Kunduz. Abdul Mutalabek first commanded AMF Brigade 726 and later became provincial police chief in Kunduz. General Daoud Khan rose from being a relatively unknown member of Massoud's inner circle in the Panjsher to the AMF Regional Corps Commander of the Northeast and then the Deputy Minister of Interior. Disqualified from running in the parliamentary elections due to his links to armed groups, Bashir Baghlani was selected as the governor of Farah Province.[7]

In general, the disarmament certification requirements for the parliamentary elections – as well as the detonation of a commander's weapon and ammunition stockpile in May 2005, killing his neighbours as well as his entire family – induced some prominent commanders to surrender some of their weapons surpluses.[8] Those who voluntarily disarmed included Haji Agha Gul (Mayor of Taluqan), Ghulam Hazrat (Deputy Police Chief of Taluqan), Pir Mohammed (Uzbek and former Commander of 762 Brigade), Makhdom Abdullah (head of regional branch of Afghan Red Crescent Society), Arbab Wali, Noor Khan, Mamoor Hassan, Mullah Omar, Ghulam Hazrat and Najibullah (NDS chief). Amir Gul Baghlani (of Baghlan Province) handed over three trucks of arms and ammunition (ANBP, 2006a).

Local conflict history

As of 1988, the party distribution among full-time mujahideen in the north was: 41 per cent Jamiat, 10 per cent Hezb-e-Islami, 12 per cent NIFA and 27 per cent Harakat (Rubin, 1996, p. 200). The presence of detribalized and delocalized southern groups also allowed Ittihad and Hezb-e-Islami to acquire an early foothold in the region. However, until the arrival of the Taliban, the choice of *tanzims* was generally based on local identity and family affiliation rather than broader ethnic identity. To a certain extent, smaller armed groups were organized around family members, particularly in terms of the selection of bodyguards and permanent members, and these bodyguards were utilized to recruit new members from those civilians residing around this base.[9] Both pro-government and mujahideen parties were multi-ethnic. Pashtuns joined Dostum's pre-Junbish militias, and Uzbeks were members of Hezb-e-Islami (as best revealed in Imam Sahib).

Throughout the northeast, aside from during the Taliban-era, the frontlines were generally fluid rather than fixed. Certain villages were divided between multiple commanders.[10] The Kayan military zone in southern Baghlan was created by the Soviets in 1982 (led by Said Mansoor Kayan, Aga Khan and Arbab Haider), and was protected by 10,000 Ismaili militiamen who sided with the Soviets due to conflicts with the resistance attributed to their minority status (AIC, 1988b, pp. 19–20). By 1984, Kunduz, Takhar, Badakhshan and Balkh all fell under Massoud's Supervisory Council of the North (SCN), which was established to coordinate the actions of the various mujahideen commanders (Nojumi, 2002, p. 92). In 1988, fully stocked garrisons in Kunduz, Taluqan and Khanabad were abandoned by government forces (Giustozzi, 2000, p. 108).

Mujahideen infighting induced displacement from Kunduz as early as 1987 (Giustozzi, 2000, p. 126). The Andarabad valley (particularly Nahrin district) in Baghlan and Kunduz was divided between Hezb-e-Islami (Malim Jamal) and Jamiat. The Jamiat deployed a substantial amount of resources to the village, including Zig air-defence weapons, Kalashnikov-type weapons, PK light machine guns and assorted ammunition. Victory over Hezb-e-Islami was followed by Jamiat's integration of these regions into its administrative structures from the Panjsher. In the late Najibullah period, fighting occurred between the government's Uzbek militias (later to become part of Junbish) and Jamiat. Later, while Dostum administered Balkh, Samangan, Jawzjan and Faryab, during the civil war he also had affiliated militias in parts of Takhar and northern Kunduz. Following the collapse of the Najibullah government, the Ismaili commander Sayyad Nader Kayani (son of Said Mansoor Kayan) allied with Junbish and acquired local control of areas in both Kunduz and Baghlan (Nojumi, 2002, p. 114).

Fighting between parties (Jamiat and Hezb-e-Islami) only accelerated during the civil war (1992–1996). A combatant characterized the nature of these disputes as follows:

> We didn't fight all the time. When we take wheat from the road [by the checkpoints], people give a religious tax. Sometimes we wanted more, or they [Hezb-e-Islami] wanted more. If we took too little, we started to fight. If they took too little, they started to fight. After a few days, old people would come and make a peace agreement.[11]

Uzbek commanders of Hezb-e-Islami controlled Imam Sahib, while the Pashtun Ittihad commander Amir Chughai inherited the Kunduz garrison and controlled Kunduz City. Imam-Sahib was a critical area of dispute between the Uzbek Junbish militias and the Uzbek Hezb-e-Islami factions.[12] Beginning in 1993, Dostum's forces fought with both Jamiat and Ittihad over the Sher Khan border area and other parts of Kunduz (Rubin, 1996, p. 276). Recalling the civil war, one combatant revealed the intersection of force and protection and the degree to which life in certain villages was shaped or even dominated by warfare:

> Civil war started, everything was destroyed. My economic situation was not good and so I joined the mujahideen in fighting between Hezb-e-Islami and Dostum, and then left the country for Pakistan. While I

joined for economic reasons, if I didn't join maybe another person would take me by force. If I went with someone else, Commander Arbab would accuse me. Everything was by force, when they took me to be with them. My father didn't say anything, we knew the situation. The mujahideen said it must be either my father or me to join.[13]

During the civil war, the SCN capital of Taluqan was used to train the Islamic Renaissance Party of Tajikistan's forces, while the Ittihad commander Chughai also supported Tajik Islamists.

Taliban era

The Taliban gained control of and then lost the northern regions largely through negotiation with local commanders, allying themselves most prominently with the Hezb-e-Islami commanders of Baghlan Province. Bashir Baghlani defected (with his sub-commander Amir Gul) to the Taliban early on. In July 2000, Bashir was arrested by the Taliban and accused of establishing contact with Jamiat in the Panjsher. Amir Gul assumed control over these forces (UNSG, 2000). Taliban discrimination against non-Pashtun ethnicities induced many to leave multi-ethnic militias:

> During Taliban, 100–150 people left Bashir Khan [Baghlani] to join Rabbani, those who were Farsiwan or Uzbek, Tajiks and Hazaras. [We left] because the Taliban made a lot of discrimination, they said we were Uzbek or Farsiwan, so we left.[14]

Heterogeneous militias quickly became ethnically homogeneous upon joining the Taliban; while anti-Taliban militias became more heterogeneous as former enemies allied against the Taliban movement.

Taliban allies were well supplied, given access to Taliban stockpiles and provided with a broad array of weapons. Taliban forces also increased due to the imposition of local conscription and the provision of economic incentives. With regard to forced conscription, Taliban forces recalled: 'In the time of Taliban, they gave us a hard time, and they took us by force, otherwise we had to pay money.'[15] 'In time of Taliban, you must go by force to join the Taliban to the frontline. If they didn't go you must pay 1.5 million Afghanis per period of 2–4 months.'[16]

Commander Nasiri (formerly of NIFA) allied with the Taliban in Khanabad. At the same time, his forces increased from 500 to 1,000 people. Due to the resources at the Taliban's disposal, dedicated soldiers were provided with higher salaries and a broad variety of armament. Nasiri's *nazm-e-khas* received Datsun trucks and Makarov pistols, while his general forces had Grinov tripod-mounted machine guns, PKs, light machine guns, 5.45 Kalikov automatic rifles and rockets.[17] While they were able to assume dominance over the region rapidly, a number of frontlines quickly developed, both in southern Baghlan against Hizb-e-Wahdat's forces based in Kahmard and also in northern Takhar.

Massoud utilized Taluqan as his headquarters following his retreat from the Shomali plain, with Jamiat incorporated and allied with a broad array of non-Pashtun ethnic groups. The arrival of the Taliban also induced mass displacement from Takhar to Tajikistan. As much as 90 per cent of the population fled. New multi-ethnic militias were formed. Although technically in the neighbouring province of Bamyan, in Sayghan, a Sunni Tajik joined Hizb-Wahdat in order to protect his village. This individual reveals briefly how ethnic identity was less relevant than shared community given the immediacy of local defence.[18]

> We're the people from Bamyan – it doesn't matter if we're Tajik or Hazara, we all belong to Khalili. During Taliban, the time was so hard, as the Taliban destroyed our home, so I had no choice. I must defend my family and my home. He was the only person from our village, so I joined Sadeq.[19]

The threat from the Taliban induced multi-ethnic alliances. Throughout the northeast, commanders were able to increase their forces due to the Taliban's arrival. Fewer combatants attributed their mobilization to force. Rumours of Taliban atrocities, often relayed by the internally displaced, induced mass combatant mobilization for village protection from the Taliban. As recounted by one Mongol combatant from Takhar who joined Jamiat commander Haji Arbabi (who led a multi-ethnic force of Mongols, Arabs, Pashtuns and Tajiks): 'When the Taliban came, we saw they wanted to destroy our home. All of us from the village rose up to take the weapon, including me.'[20] Reflecting this desire for village protection, Commander Mir Alam's forces increased from 20–30 during the civil war to 200–300 during the Taliban regime.[21] Abdullah Guard's forces grew from 80 people during the Rabbani time to 350 under the Taliban.[22]

A number of combatants were interviewed from the forces of Mohammad Bashir Baghlani and Amir Gul Baghlani, who were previously affiliated with the Taliban but who are now serving in Karzai government positions. Bashir Baghlani replaced Engineer Bashir when the latter was killed during the Rabbani period. Amir Gul, in turn, replaced Bashir Baghlani when he was arrested by the Taliban. During the jihad, Bashir Baghlani demanded that each family provide two people to go to the frontline.[23] During the civil war, Bashir Khan fought Arbab Zikria and Ali Mohammed (who was Noorzai) in Jari Khoshk Baghlan (Jari Khoshk).

Amir Gul's forces were drawn from a broad variety of ethnicities ranging from Pashai to Uzbeks. With the arrival of the Taliban, he organized his force around Pashtuns, reacquiring a more ethnically heterogeneous group when he switched to Jamiat during Operation Enduring

Freedom. During the Taliban, Gul's forces operated alongside Afghan soldiers from Kandahar, Herat and Mazar-e-Sharif, as well as international combatants from the Arabian Peninsula, from Punjab and the Northeast Frontier Province in Pakistan.

There are substantial discrepancies in descriptions of the size of Gul's forces. One combatant proposed that Gul had 500–600 soldiers, of which 25 were bodyguards and 15–16 were relatives. The job of the *nazm-e-khas* was to 'take people ... by force to go to the frontline' and to conduct criminal activities, such as stealing or smuggling oil and narcotics to Tajikistan, Takhar and Nahrin.[24] Another combatant asserted that Gul had 1,200 combatants, of whom 200–300 were *nazm-e-khas* and 50 were bodyguards, which 'all the time ... took money from the people' and 'took wood from gardens by force, as well as fruit, sheep and cows.'[25] While the general combatants only received a salary once in four years, the *nazm-e-khas* and bodyguards received funds constantly.

Post-9/11 period

With his defection from the Taliban, Amir Gul Baghlani later became the head of AMF Brigade 733 and was later considered to lead the AHP in Baghlan, which reminds one of the 'fox in the henhouse' analogy, whereby those previously accused of criminal activities become responsible for legal enforcement.[26] Even after the collapse of the Taliban and the completion of DDR, commanders affiliated with Amir Gul continue to conscript individuals forcibly. One combatant recalled: 'People are still scared of him. We don't know who to speak to [to address these problems].... There is so much criminality in Baghlan. Please can you help?'[27] Another commander revealed Amir Gul's continuing armed power and political influence, describing how: 'In Baghlan, he [Amir Gul] has brigade, weapons and bodyguards; he is not working in the government, but is the main person and decides who is appointed to which position.'[28] Thus, under the Karzai government, Amir Gul has maintained his regional fiefdom and thereby continues to determine who is selected for provincial and district government positions. As demonstrated in the introduction, in the description of the role of the state in enhancing the power of local commanders, Amir Gul's power has only expanded in the post-Bonn era, despite his combatants' descriptions of his forced conscription and other criminal activities.

Communities, commanders and combatants

A total of 56 combatants from the provinces of Kunduz, Badakhshan, Takhar and Baghlan were interviewed at the Spin Gar factory in Kunduz City, while undergoing reintegration training. A select number of interviews were completed in two additional districts of Kunduz (Khanabad,

Imam Sahib) and also in Takhar (Taluqan) Province. The interviews did not provide the same quality of information as that acquired in Ghor and Paktya. However, as already described, unique insight was acquired as to the mobilization practices of Bashir Khan and Amir Gul Baghlani.

Of the 56 combatants interviewed, three were members of government forces, and nine served with the Taliban. All of these became Taliban by affiliation. Their broader participation and association with a party or movement was a product of their commander's affiliation. It was not an independent choice. All of those who served with the government forces during the jihad later joined either the mujahideen government or the anti-Taliban resistance, with most citing 'economic incentives' as driving the choice to remain a soldier. This echoes Rubin's statement that 'commanders usually belonged to parties, but the mass of mujahideen owed loyalty to their commanders on the basis of local social networks. A commander who shifted political allegiance took his followers with him' (Rubin, 1996, p. 202).

All combatants in this region indicated that they had received their weapons from their commanders, with no cases of an individual independently purchasing its weapons. Combatants described their use of and

Table 9.1 Combatant profiles of Kunduz, Baghlan and Takhar (56 combatants)

Schooling	25%; majority up to the 4th class, others to 9th or 12th class.
Prominent livelihoods	Farmer, street labour, carpenter, civil servant.
Migration	30%; the majority migrated to Pakistan as conflict displaced; 3.5% to Iran for labour; 1.5% as refugees to Tajikistan during the Taliban era; internal displacement to Takhar.

Average age of first mobilization:
  Recruited under 18
  Recruited at or under 16
	17.1
	59%
	49%

First mobilized during:
  Jihad
  Civil war
  Taliban era
  Post-9/11 period
	
	24%
	42%
	27%
	1%

Prominent motives by period:
  Jihad
 	
  Civil war
  Taliban era
  Post-9/11 period
	
	Grievance, force, protection, family/elder authority, economic incentives.
	Force, protection, family authority.
	Grievance, group belonging, force.
	Economic incentives, group belonging, force, protection.

access to a variety of weapons, including short-barrelled AKs (Kalikovs), Grinov tripod-mounted machine guns, PK light machine guns, Makarov pistols, RPGs and mortars. Combatants were also provided with ammunition (as many as five full clips). One combatant indicated, however, that, while ammunition was plentifully provided during times of war, at other times, combatants were only provided with a small number for the protection of their homes.[29]

Forced conscription

Forced mobilization was the most recurring motive in the northern-region combatant narratives. While particularly prominent during the civil war period and among those who joined in Baghlan, force was a common motive during all periods of mobilization, including the jihad period. The following statement reflects the experience of many combatants:

> It was time of revolution, no one left you alone, when you grew up a little they gave you a weapon. Many commanders, they saw us and took us by force. Many different commanders asked us to go with them. We had to join them – they took us by force [*bazor*]. Everything was by force, they took us by force. I would go to the frontline for 20 days to one month, I would then run away and come home. Then after two to three months, again they took me by force.[30]

Commanders, who generally fit the ideal type of local strongmen, structured their forces to ensure internal control, distributing specialized weapons to their bodyguards and *nazm-e-khas*. For example, a Khanabad commander had 40 people in his group, all of whom received RPGs, while his ten relatives serving in the special brigade received Grinovs and AKs.[31] In another example, 10–15 of the 50–60 people with Ittihad commander Zabit Nurullah were special bodyguards, with whom the commander used to 'make people nervous.'[32]

Elder authority

Descriptions of elder authority were generally absent, although still occasionally evident among certain Tajiks. Even then, however, the mobilization structures were new, and the authority bodies appeared to be far weaker than those in either Ghor or southern Afghanistan.[33] As a result, strongmen's power is acquired individually and not through the support of a broader community of elders. Village members describe mobilization as forcible rather than due to elder authority.

> With them, everything was by force. If I did not go with him, maybe another commander would take me by force. Commander Mahidin

belonged to my *qawm*, and in my village, if I joined another commander, Mahidin would give problems to my family.[34]

Sometimes, however, the line between forced conscription and elder
authority is blurred:

> These commanders are also the man from the *qawm* – they must be
> respected – whether by force or not. You must respect them, if they
> tell you, you cannot run away. He's the member of our *qawm*, if
> there's a conflict in our village, he deals with it.[35]

However, while the commander is from the same village as the combatants, his authority is not due to a reciprocal relationship with a community
of elders. He has risen independently and utilizes family networks rather
than elder authority. Commanders act as strongmen rather than as traditional *khans*.

Protection

Another prominent motive throughout all periods of fighting was mobilization for protection. Mobilization for protection incorporates a broad
degree of situations, from the decision of the family to send an individual
to a group, to an individual joining a commander so as to be protected
from intra-familial conflict over land and other possessions. The dominance of accounts of both force and protection in Kunduz hints at the
trauma inflicted on northern communities by the prolonged conflict:

> I stayed as soldier to defend myself – all the time we have conflict
> inside the village. I went with Commander Jalal to have a weapon, so
> no one could do something wrong with me.[36]

> During the civil war, whoever had the force could defend themselves –
> so I took the gun to defend myself. My father told me [to join the
> commander], as we needed to defend our family.[37]

> Such a horrible situation, you must pick up the weapon. If I went to
> the government, my people died. If I joined the mujahideen, my
> people died. So I just picked up the weapon to defend my family and
> home. In that time we joined in order to have food for our family and
> to be safe for all the family. My father always told us that we must
> defend ourselves and join different commanders depending on the
> situation to be safe.[38]

> Someone tried to take my land by force; so I picked up a weapon to
> repel this. The people who have a weapon, if you don't protect your

land, they will take it from you. I received a gun from Commander
Amiri, who was the *mesher* from our area, who just gave me the weapon
without any requirements. Then I left school only to defend my land.[39]

To join a commander, it was both by force and without force. Situation was so hard, if you didn't go you must pay money. [If you
joined], the commander now understood the family was with him, but
we didn't receive any food or clothing for the family. If we had fighting in the village, the commander protected my family. I stayed with
him so that all the people knew that one person from our family was
there until the situation was normal.[40]

We had no other opportunity. There were many bad times here, different parties and groups. I must participate to protect my family and
myself.[41]

The logic of participation in the village is survival and thus distinct
from the logic of participation in the broader conflict. Affiliation provides
protection, particularly when a village is divided between several
commanders.

Forced conscription as a combatant for the Taliban also made demobilized combatants vulnerable to intra-village attack after the Taliban's
withdrawal. This factor sustained mobilization and led a combatant to join
the AMF in search of protection.

I came back because the Pashtun Taliban had given a hard time to
other nations. Then we must stay with government, in order to
protect ourselves from other nations. They [the other nations] did
not understand that we went by force. It was good to work with the
government, but also we needed to protect our family.[42]

Economic incentives

Notably, in contrast to other regions (most particularly Ghor), only a
small portion (approximately 1 per cent) of those combatants interviewed in the Kunduz region were first mobilized following the Bonn
Agreement, although the vast majority of combatants continued to serve
during this time (and needed to do so in order to receive reintegration
assistance). Those that were first mobilized after the Bonn Agreement
cited economic incentives overwhelmingly as their reason for rejoining
an armed group.[43]

The salaries of those combatants range from 800 to 2,500 Afghani
($16–50) per month, depending on proximity to the commander and their
position. In some areas, commanders were able to acquire recruits by manipulating information as to their prospective salary. One combatant indicated

that the commander promised that 'each soldier would get four million Junbish afghani, and a lot of food and a good job. Everything was a lie.'[44]

Group belonging

Several other combatants cited group belonging. This reveals that, while many had been mobilized through force during the Taliban era and the civil war, these combatants developed friendships and other links to group members that served to sustain their presence in armed groups.[45] Others indicated that the formalization of the militias through the creation of the AMF allowed commanders to present mobilization as a means of fulfilling national service.

> They told us we could come to official military service – didn't give us a weapon, just stayed in the post and watched. They came to our village and took us and told us this was military service. They just told us politely – not by force – that this was military service. And I wanted to finish military service – or they would take me in the future and it was better to go now.[46]

As mentioned earlier, the formalization of local militias through the creation of the AMF allowed commanders to acquire national endorsement and then to use this endorsement to their own advantage. Commanders were thus able to present themselves as national representatives and could acquire recruits through the provision of limited information (e.g., as to salary).

Recruitment at child age

Finally, the three northern provinces had a significantly higher proportion of child combatants than the other cases. Of the interviewed combatants, 59 per cent were recruited under the age of 18 and 49 per cent under the age of 16. However, the use of child combatants varied considerably between groups. A combatant first mobilized at the age of 12 indicated that seven of the 43 people in his group were his age, stating that 'since I've been young, since I've known the difference between my left and right hand, I've been in war.'[47] Another combatant indicated that, while he was recruited into the group at 12 or 13, he was not provided with a weapon until he was 20. Today, he is increasingly disillusioned from his involvement in all periods of the fighting, arguing:

> The rich people took the poor people's sons by force to fight in the jihad against Najib. We were so small. We didn't have weapons. We just brought weapons and clips to the soldiers. It was a stupid time. We didn't understand anything about life. All the people were looking for their own interest, people were lying. We wanted to take care of our family (sisters and mothers), and defend our family from

the criminal people. Now I hate the commanders, and I don't even want to tell them hello.[48]

Now adults, many of the combatants were first recruited as children. This has far-reaching implications for both professional training and psychological trauma, as these combatants do not have the same variety and diversity of livelihood skills as other combatants.

Conclusion

Due to the short period of fieldwork and the large area covered, this chapter is by no means conclusive as to the dynamics in the north. Even this brief research, however, reveals a number of important developments in the northeast demanding further attention. Community elders appeared to play a considerably less significant role than in the Pashtun, Hazara or Ghor populations. Formalized and inclusive community decision-making bodies are weak compared to the strength of parties, families and commanders. Individuals discussed their qawms in broad terms and did not focus on the link between their commanders and their communities. Some villages were united by conflict; others were divided into multiple commanders with affiliations to different political parties. However, when uniting to meet a community threat, commanders are newly empowered and legitimized (and witnessed an increase in the size of their forces) during such periods. When the threat diminishes, the commander retains a small cadre of combatants, and can utilize these to engage in predatory activities and to conscript soldiers forcibly.

In this region, commanders closely embody the ideal type of the strongman, structuring their forces to ensure internal discipline and to acquire conscripts forcefully from their villages. Patterns of community consultation (and demands for community mobilization) appear to be limited, with *shuras* overpowered by commanders. Bodyguards and *nazm-e-khas* as are used to conscript individuals forcibly.

Force is the most common motive for combatant mobilization across all four periods of fighting. Commanders allied with external parties in order to acquire power relative to local competitors. Due to their connection to the Jamiat party, Kunduz commanders had a direct link to the mujahideen government during the civil war and to the first Karzai government (2002–2004). As in all other areas, the creation of the AMF allowed commanders to acquire national legitimacy.

Most importantly, the case of Kunduz, Baghlan and Takhar shows that, although the northeast is profoundly multi-ethnic in composition, ethnic antagonism is not preordained. Depending on the period, armed groups were made up of a wide variety of ethnic groups. Individuals from a broad array of ethnic groups constituted both Junbish and Hezb-e-Islami. Previously warring ethnicities allied in order to protect themselves from an external threat. This displays how ethnicity is generally not a useful explanatory variable for conflict in the northeast of Afghanistan.

Interestingly, a review of the ethnic composition of Amir Gul and Bashir Baghlani's militias reveals a transition from heterogeneity to homogeneous ethnic composition during the Taliban era, due to the fact that, with the commander's affiliation, the forces lost the support of non-Pashtun ethnicities. During Operation Enduring Freedom, group composition returned to ethnic heterogeneity, as a multi-ethnic alliance was formed against the Taliban.

Notes

1 In order to neutralize Ghilzai and Durrani threats to his rule and secure the northern frontier against invasion from Russian Tatarstan, Amir Abdur Rahman Khan engaged in the forced relocation of southeastern Pashtuns and Nuristanis to northern Afghanistan, to Takhar and to Badghis and Faryab Province in the northwest. The growth of the cotton industry (as seen with the Spin Gar factory) also prompted the economically motivated migration to the region by Pashtuns and other ethnic groups (the author thanks the anonymous reviewer for this point).
2 Interview with German PRT, Kunduz, June 2005.
3 Interview with international security officials (ANSO, UNAMA, ISAF), Kunduz and Kabul, 2004–2005.
4 Interview with international political analyst, Kunduz, May 2005.
5 Interview with Afghan Border Police Colonel, Sher Khan border point, Kunduz, May 2005.
6 Another ANP member interviewed had only 15 bullets for his rifle, which is a duty and not a personal weapon.
7 Information gathered from interviews in Kunduz Province, April 2004/May 2005.
8 The blast on 3 May 2005 killed 29 people and wounded 70, although the Commander Jalal Bajgaye survived (*Reuters*, 2005).
9 One combatant joined his uncle, who was a Jamiat commander, and argued: 'We are all in one family – he made a group and we had to join him. My big brothers were also there. My uncle was the commander, they had a lot of people.' (Combatant #235, Khanabad, May 2005).
10 The author thanks the anonymous academic reviewer for this point.
11 Combatant #214, Kunduz, May 2005; for further information on history of Jamiat-HIH clashes in Nahrin and Argandab, see AIC, 1991a.
12 Imam Sahib, originally named Pashtun Kot, was the birthplace of Hekmatyar.
13 Combatant #204, Kunduz, May 2005.
14 Combatant #210, Kunduz, May 2005.
15 Combatant #243, Kunduz, May 2005.
16 Combatant #213, Kunduz May 2005. Another account of forced conscription:

> When we came back [from Pakistan] the Taliban took us by force. If you did not go, they took money. If you did not pay money, they told us you must leave the land, so I became a soldier. During the Karzai time, it was also by force, they didn't give us land or money, they took us again by force.
>
> (Combatant 216, Kunduz, May 2005)

17 Combatant #241, Kunduz, May 2005.
18 Combatant #206, Kunduz, May 2005.
19 Combatant #206, Kunduz, May 2005.
20 Combatant #254, Kunduz, May 2005.
21 Combatant #239, Kunduz, May 2005.
22 Combatant #248, Kunduz, May 2005.
23 Combatant #218, Kunduz, May 2005.
24 Combatant #208, Kunduz, May 2005.
25 Combatant #207, Kunduz, May 2005.
26 Already, under the command of Khalil Andarabi, the local AHP unit has been implicated in drug trafficking.
27 Combatant #208, Kunduz, May 2005.
28 Combatant #213, Kunduz, May 2005.
29 Combatant #248/250, Kunduz, May 2005.
30 Combatant #253, Kunduz, May 2005.
31 Combatant #235, Khanabad, May 2005.
32 Combatant #230, Kunduz, May 2005.
33 One combatant did assert that mobilization was 'not by force, but it was asked from our nation.' (Combatant #228, Kunduz, May 2005).
34 Combatant #205, Kunduz, May 2005.
35 Combatant #227, Kunduz, May 2005.
36 Combatant #217, Kunduz, May 2005.
37 Combatant #219, Kunduz, May 2005.
38 Combatant #238, Kunduz, May 2005.
39 Combatant #244, Kunduz, May 2005.
40 Combatant #248, Kunduz, May 2005.
41 Combatant #235, Khanabad, May 2005.
42 Combatant #213, Kunduz, May 2005.
43 Combatant #212/215, Kunduz, May 2005.
44 Combatant #215, Kunduz, May 2005.
45 'From the beginning it was by force, and then I found some friends, and I stayed because I realize it was better to stay with Jalali then to risk being forced to fight with another commander.' (Combatant #212, Kunduz, May 2005).
46 Combatant #253, Kunduz, May 2005.
47 Combatant #237, Khanabad, May 2005.
48 Combatant #250, Kunduz, May 2005.

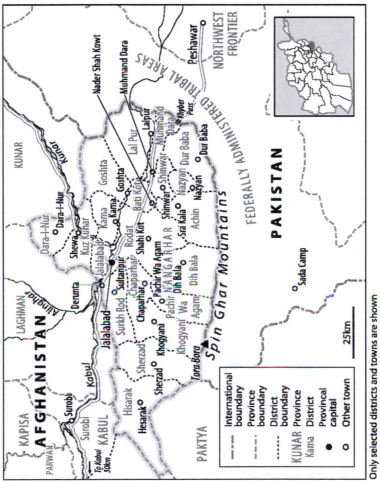

Only selected districts and towns are shown

Map 10.1 Nangarhar Province.

10 Jalalabad

The consequences of Coalition support

Michael Bhatia

The case of Jalalabad explores the following issues:

- the impact of Coalition operations and support on the position of local commanders;
- the proliferation of armed groups and the obstacles to weapons licensing;
- the nature of economic incentives for mobilization.

After describing the geographical and varied ethnic composition of the province, the chapter focuses on recent violence, poppy production and small arms trafficking. Second, it discusses the wide variety of both international and local armed actors present in Jalalabad and the consequences on commander power networks, armed group maintenance and small arms licensing. Particular attention is given to the evolution of Hazrat Ali's militias and the impact of Coalition support. Third, the chapter reviews the history of armed conflict in the region, focusing particularly on the shifting fortunes of the Nangarhar *shura*. The latter's conflict resolution function was considerably more significant than its role in conflict mobilization. Finally, the interviews of the combatants from Jalalabad reveal the prominent role of economic incentives for mobilization. Elder authority is rarely discussed as a factor driving mobilization. Instead, combatants cite economic incentives and force as dominant motives across the periods of mobilization. Moreover, family patronage groups appeared to be more significant than community armed groups in the recruitment and mobilization of combatants.

Setting the local scene

Nangarhar Province has the second highest population density in Afghanistan, with 1,089,000 people concentrated in 7,727 square kilometres. Geographically, Jalalabad is the southeastern gateway to Afghanistan from Pakistan via the Khyber Pass. The province neighbours Laghman to the north, Kunar to the east and Paktya (and the Tora Bora mountains) to the west. Aside from indigenous Afghan Arabs, Tajiks, Safis, Sayeds and Pashais, the province is largely constituted by a series of Pashtun *qawms*, including Khogiani, Shirzad, Shinwari, Saidad, Amerkheil, Akhunzada, Mohmand, Gujar, Samerkheil, Niazi, Qazian, Dustakheil, Ibrahimkheil and Tarakheil.[1]

The Jalalabad offensive of March and April 1989, largely constituted by Hezb-e-Islami forces with assistance from Pakistan's ISI, was expected to produce a quick mujahideen victory following Soviet withdrawal. Instead, it became mired in fighting between mujahideen parties and commanders, revealing the momentous challenges that would face an independent Afghanistan (Nojumi, 2002, p. 96). More recently, 48 per cent of eligible voters participated in the parliamentary elections, which was only marginally above the regional average of 47 per cent and below the national average of 49 per cent (JEMB, 2007). This turnout also represented a significant decline from the regional presidential turnout of 54.8 per cent (Wilder, 2005, p. 33).

In the post-Bonn period, the province gained prominence due to two events. First, only several months after Abdul Haq was murdered while trying to negotiate with tribal *khans* for action against the Taliban, his brother Haji Abdul Qadir was also murdered (with his son-in-law) in Kabul shortly after becoming Vice-President of the interim government of Afghanistan. With the assassination of his two younger but more prominent brothers, the eldest brother, Haji Din Mohammed, was appointed as the provincial governor – a position which he held until June 2005, when he was rotated to Kandahar. Recently, Hazrat Ali (former Chief of Police and competitor of Din Mohammed) was elected to the *Wolesi Jirga*, receiving the largest percentage of votes in the province, although his armed factions are still believed to hold some influence in the region. Second, in May 2005, rioting over the proposed desecration of the Koran by Coalition forces led to the destruction of the Embassy of Pakistan, as well as the Agency Coordinating Body for Afghan Relief, AIHRC and other NGO offices.

The Pechdara valley in neighbouring Kunar Province is viewed to be both a major Taliban centre (complete with foreign combatants) and a poppy-producing area (Shahzad, 2006a). In Kunar, as in Paktya, illegal logging has led to conflict and the formation of local tribal militias to prevent smugglers (*AP*, 2005a; AIC, 1990).

The province has historically been one of the three primary poppy production areas in Afghanistan, and it emerged as a key trading centre during the Taliban period. With regard to poppy production and other illicit activity, Nangarhar received $70 million in anti-narcotics funding over the course of 2005, with a 96 per cent drop in opium production, although this could be better attributed to the high price of wheat and grain the year before (Franco, 2005). In March 2006, 40 heroin-processing factories were destroyed in the Shinwari, Achin, Nazyan and Spin Ghar districts (*Pajhwok*, 2006a).

With regard to the availability of small arms, a wide variety of weapons are readily available in either the local bazaar or in bazaars across the border in Pakistan's Northwest Frontier Province. Old weapons are currently being sent to Pakistan and are then refurbished, modified and sent back to Afghanistan. AKs are converted into short-barrelled imitations of the AKZU. A source indicated that there was some transit of high-quality Russian weapons and ammunition with recent production dates.[2]

Local and international armed groups

There are currently five different Coalition armed forces operating in and around Jalalabad: PRT, Operational Detachment Alpha, Marine Combat Manoeuvre Unit, Special Forces and CIA. Each has different agendas and different approaches to Afghan actors, resulting in 'no coherence within the USA military establishment' in strategy.[3]

Jalalabad is similarly marked by a broad range of local armed actors, each of which is aligned with one of two major factions: Hazrat Ali (former Chief of Police and now *Meshrano Jirga* representative), Din Mohammed (former governor and now governor of Kandahar), Gul Karim (created an armed unit through Ministry for Tribal Affairs), Haji Mohammed Zahir (son of Haji Qadir; controls the Frontier Forces, which also acts as the primary armed support for the former governor Din Mohammed)[4] and Hazrat Ali (possesses various police forces and other armed groups).

Due to the diversity of armed groups and their external supporters, the joint Provincial Security Task Force (composed of the Coalition, the PRT, UNAMA and the various Afghan government representatives) has been unable to create a weapons identification card and registration system.

A Pashai, Hazrat Ali previously possessed between 12,000 and 18,000 soldiers, 6,000 of which are stationed in Jalalabad. These forces were employed by the Coalition during Operation Anaconda (globalsecurity.org; Glasser, 2002). His bodyguards and *nazm-e-khas* are projected to number 200 and are relatives of one of his wives. These forces were utilized to secure roads and homes, capture commanders and collect money from others. Until 2003, Hazrat Ali was accused of running illegal checkpoints on the Kabul–Peshawar road (ICG, 2003, p. 10). According to another source, 'the activities of the special trusted soldiers were to keep road security, to act as bodyguards, to capture other persons and to gather money from other people.'[5] These *nazm-e-khas* soldiers possess Kalikovs, while the majority had normal AKs.[6]

He was able to consolidate power further as the Provincial Chief of Police for Nangarhar by simply putting on many of his militia police uniforms without undergoing any substantial training. Moreover, Hazrat Ali initially provided the guard force for UN facilities – which were eventually replaced by centrally deployed RTC-trained and registered MoI units –

and many of the 500-strong Afghan Security Forces utilized by the Coalition.[7] According to Human Rights Watch,

> One of the major sources of power and authority for Hazrat Ali and his gang is his close relations with the US military and intelligence. He has successfully used this relationship to harm and intimidate his political rivals. He has arrested people and constantly threatens them with sending them to Guantanamo.
>
> (HRW, 2004)

In order to run in the parliamentary elections, Hazrat Ali turned in a large weapons cache in mid-August 2005, but he is still believed to maintain an illegal armed group and arms stockpiles (Outlook, 2005).

Other commanders acquire funds through involvement in the local poppy production (either direct or through taxation), the logging of the forests in Paktya, Kunar and Nuristan and involvement in smuggling and the transport trade. Reporters have indicated the link between commanders employed by the Coalition and the local narcotics and smuggling trade, which has prompted locals to compare unfavourably the current situation with that under the Taliban.[8] UNOPS and USPI subcontract for the protection of their projects to local militias and are often subject to 'verified bribery.'[9] According to a UNOPS representative, commander extortion was still present on the Jalalabad–Kunar road in June 2005, with one commander of 15 soldiers demanding $15,000 for protection per month.[10]

Local conflict history

Jihad

According to Nojumi, Nangarhar and the eastern provinces of Afghanistan 'received the largest portion of military equipment and facilities' and 'held one of the largest military organizations in Afghanistan' (Nojumi, 2002, p. 149). In the neighbouring mountains of Khogyani, Surobi and Achin districts, cave networks were established (predominantly by HIK) complete with stores of light and heavy weapons and SAMs. Government frontier forces and militia posts were also present in most districts.

As of 1988, the party distribution among full-time mujahideen in the east was 9 per cent Jamiat, 15 per cent Hezb-e-Islami Hekmatyar, 28 per cent Hezb-e-Islami Khalis, 30 per cent NIFA and 11 per cent Harakat (Rubin, 1996, p. 200). However, local commanders were able to achieve a degree of autonomy from the party offices in Peshawar and, in the case of Abdul Haq, were even able to open independent offices in Peshawar. Within HIK, Abdul Haq was able to develop 'lines of communication' and cooperate with Massoud's forces in the Panjsher (Nojumi, 2002, p. 106).[11] This autonomy was combined with coordination via an inter-group *shura*.

In certain districts, such as the border district of Surobi (until the arrival of HIH during the civil war), communities remained cohesive, and the community of elders remained the dominant local decision makers, despite the presence of multiple mujahideen groups (AIC, 1986). In other parts of Nangarhar, 'neutral' Afghan villages were subject to punitive attacks by mujahideen factions and accused of supporting the government (Giustozzi, 2000, p. 126). A Jawzjani militia contingent was deployed to secure the Kabul–Jalalabad road in the waning days of the Najibullah government.

Civil war era

Following the Najibullah government's collapse, the mujahideen looted government weapons depots, endowing these local commanders with even greater autonomy from the parties in Pakistan. Haji Qadir was selected by local commanders as the province's governor in 1993. Although the province did not experience the level of factional fighting compared to that in Kabul, Kandahar or the Kunduz region, armed disputes did emerge among the various factions outside of the capital (Nojumi, 2002, p. 115).[12] Early in 1993, conflict briefly broke out between NIFA (which was locally allied with Hezb-e-Islami) and HIK in Jalalabad, with the NIFA commander Shamali assassinated and these forces expelled to Surobi (Rubin, 1996, p. 277).

Until the Taliban's arrival, Hekmatyar's base was in Surobi, just outside of Nangarhar. During the civil war, refugees from Kabul fled to Jalalabad and the Shar Shahi internal displacement camp (Nojumi, 2002, p. 114).

The province also became a key location for the training of foreign fighters and for the export of Afghans to other conflicts. The Darwanta camp near Jalalabad was used to train Arab militants, first by Hekmatyar's Hezb-e-Islami and later by the Taliban (Dorronsoro, 2005, p. 303). Moreover, Hekmatyar also deployed soldiers from Jalalabad to participate in the fighting in Nagorno-Karabakh. One soldier recalled: 'Then the foreign minister of Azerbaijan came to request soldiers, and only Hekmatyar provided soldiers. He first sent 160 Najib officers and then a total of 500.'[13] The combatant was told that he would be going to Turkey and instead was sent to Azerbaijan. He received $700 per month.[14] During this period and prior to the arrival of the Taliban, Bin Laden developed some links to many of the local commanders, who would later support the Coalition operations, including Haji Qadir and Hazrat Ali (Nasir, 2003).

Taliban era

By mid-September 1996, the Taliban had captured Nangarhar with the consent of the *shura*, with Haji Qadir fleeing to Pakistan (Nojumi, 2002,

p. 150). However, the lack of economic incentives provided by the Taliban was one factor that prohibited certain combatants from joining them in the Jalalabad area.[15] Local Taliban included Haji Qari Mujahed and Commander Ali Akhmed of Kunar. Of the 28 members of Ali Akmed's forces, six were bodyguards, each of which received approximately 100 Pakistan rupees (Pkr) (approximately $2) per day (3,000Pkr or $53 per month) with drivers receiving more.[16]

Post-9/11 period

The withdrawal of the Taliban led to a competition for local power among three factions: Hazrat Ali of Hezb-e-Islami Khalis (with links to Defence Minister Fahim), Haji Mohammed Zaman Ghamshareek (of NIFA) and Din Mohammed and the late Haji Qadir (Ali, 2001). Eventually, an Eastern Zone *shura* was formed between the three power leaders. However, according to Dorronsoro, 'the shura of Jalalabad is divided into a number of factions and exercises no authority further than a few kilometers from the town' (Dorronsoro, 2005, p. 332).

While this did not fundamentally resolve the basic competition between the parties, it did provide a forum for the peaceful resolution of disputes and the distribution of ministries between the various power bases. As in Kandahar and in Paktya, while the *shura* and community of elders was basically successful in preventing outright conflict between the various factions (both during the civil war and currently), they are generally unable to prevent the insecurity that results from factional competition. Similarly, as in Kandahar, these factions are now competing (and utilizing the Coalition's provision of resources) in order to consolidate their own power.

Communities, commanders and combatants

A total of 29 combatants were interviewed in Jalalabad while undergoing reintegration job training with a variety of NGOs. Both Taliban members and those who fought with the Soviet-backed government were interviewed. While a significant number had some form of education, particularly in comparison to Kandahar and Ghor, the combatants in Jalalabad appear to be poorly skilled in comparison to those in other areas (perhaps due to their young age of mobilization). Although a significant portion of combatants had left Afghanistan, migration was primarily induced by conflict rather than in search of labour. The jihad period was the most prominent period for initial mobilization, followed by the period succeeding the Bonn process.

In Jalalabad, there were two cases of combatants required to pay bribes in order to receive reintegration training (with a commander's sale of DDR cards for 1,000–2,000Pkr) and to join the ANA.[17] Those combatants who first joined the AMF after the Taliban's defeat were able to join via friends or relatives who already belonged to commanders.

Recruitment during child age was particularly prominent in Jalalabad. While the average age of combatants was 17, 55 per cent of those interviewed were recruited under the age of 18 and 38 per cent under the age of 16. This was driven by necessity. According to one combatant, while there were many children of 16 in one armed group, it was 'not the decision of the commanders, but was because we needed a small salary for ourselves.'[18]

Economic incentives

While economic incentives were a dominant motive for combatants across periods, the actual size of these incentives was not substantial. They generally consisted of pocket money and food. There were two examples where drought prompted individuals to diversify their family's economic portfolios and become soldiers. Approximately 3,000Pkr ($60) was the maximum salary, with others receiving as little as 400,000–500,000 old Afs (worth 400–500 new Afs or $10) and later 2,000Pkr ($40) during the AMF.[19] Even for senior figures the amount delivered was fairly low. A brigade commander under Hazrat Ali was supposed to receive 3,560 Afs per month, but this was only received every three months, with a certain amount further reduced as a bribe.[20] A series of combatants (including

Table 10.1 Combatant profiles of Jalalabad (29 combatants)

Schooling	52%, broad range from elementary to high school.
Prominent livelihoods	Small business, street labour (in Pakistan).
Migration	45%; the majority of which is conflict-induced, some labour migration, 3% went to Iran for construction work.
Average age of first mobilization:	17 years.
Recruited under 18	55%
Recruited at or under 16	38%
First mobilized during:	
Jihad	41%
Civil war	24%
Taliban era	14%
Post-9/11 period	28%
Prominent motives by period:	
Jihad	Family authority, ideology, entitlements, protection, force.
Civil war	Economic incentives, force, protection.
Taliban era	Economic incentives, group belonging, grievance, elder authority.
Post-9/11 period	Economic Incentives, group belonging and protection.

one Taliban) who received only 400 Afs per month noted that even this was significant:

> We had economic and finance problems ... We had no other opportunity. Jalil also had very little money, sometimes he gave it, sometimes not. Sometimes he asked us to join without money. Many people can't understand for 25 years, there were no jobs, they could do nothing. The only way to get money was to kill.... For some small money, they could do anything, but this is not the normal way of life.[21]

> In the future someone will use us and give us some guns, because in this country the biggest problem is the absence of jobs.[22]

> It was the time of the gun, all of the people wanted to join the commanders for the money. I studied in school, and also joined him. Only one day a week, I would go, and so the money was enough. I served as guard. My father was not happy, he was a teacher and didn't like the weapon, so I was just there secretly. I just came for small money and to have something in my pocket. It is not important for me which regime is coming, whether Taliban or Karzai.[23]

Given the high degree of conflict-induced displacement, some combatants first joined an armed group while living as refugees in Pakistan. During the jihad, access to entitlements (a refugee card and the resulting benefits) was one factor driving party affiliation.

> But in Pakistan, we also saw the situation, we needed a refugee card, and so had to join. I took the card for my family to stay in the camps. We didn't get a salary, but sometimes the commander would give us gift of oil and wheat ... If you live in the camp, also one person from the family must sometimes go to the jihad. After it became our job, our profession, and our life, sometime we would go to jihad, it was a part of our life.[24]

For some combatants, joining a commander was the exclusive way to acquire the means to survive or to supplement cash income. As demonstrated by the interview extract above, membership in an armed group can permit a combatant to fund other endeavours (such as schooling) or to acquire supplementary personal income, regardless of parental disapproval.

The dominant role of economic incentives is further displayed by a combatant's willingness to leave one commander and join another based on comparative economic benefit. During the civil war, and, to some extent, over the past five years, combatants also indicated a willingness to 'shop' between commanders, deciding to join a commander based upon the wage and the work involved.

> Many commanders came, if I was disappointed by one, I would join another for more money. The problem was when they disappointed us, and we had no other job options, and if they gave us a little money. We must take food for our family. If the commanders didn't give money, I would switch myself.[25]

Others indicated that pay was partly tied to performance.

> Sometime at the checkpoint we captured opium or other narcotics, commander would be so happy, he'd give us a gift. We went with our car to watch the border, and always captured some narcotics and some thieves and we brought them to the commanders. This is why they gave us some hashish.[26]

This is further demonstrated in the accounts of the pay and resource differentials provided to the *nazm-e-khas* and bodyguards of Hazrat Ali and other local commanders. As in other locations, the provision of a salary (even after the commander received a monthly payment from the central MoD to be delivered to the combatant) was arbitrary, thus fortifying the bond between commander and combatant, rather than between the combatant and the national government. Whether in terms of salary, food or light drugs (hashish), the combatant remains in a dependent relationship with the commander, particularly in periods of drought and insecurity.

As in Kandahar, the discrepancy between the perceived wealth of senior commanders and figureheads versus the actual salary provided to soldiers has induced complaints. The post-Taliban era has accelerated income inequality, both within armed groups and within Afghanistan as a whole. One combatant argued:

> The commanders have everything now, but we [the common soldiers] don't even have a home. They did not make the real jihad or reconstruct the country; they only went to jihad for their own interest of criminality and money. But we are not the same as them.[27]

In sum, the Jalalabad case reveals the broader dimensions of economically induced combatant mobilization, from the provision of basic support and entitlements (due to the absence of other livelihood options) to a combatant shopping between commanders to acquire the best conditions.

Protection

As in other parts of Afghanistan, a recurring cross-case motive for mobilization was the need for affiliation with a commander in order to reduce familial insecurity (even if against relatives):

> There was a conflict in the family, in order to defend myself and my family ... I went to pick up the weapon.[28]

> My father didn't want us to have any weapon – but we had a family conflict with our uncle over land. One of my uncles killed my brother, and also wanted to kill us. So this was the reason we needed a weapon to defend ourselves.[29]

As described, the source of the threat was often within an extended family. The extended family unit would not necessarily bond together in periods of external threat or party infighting but instead would align with different factions so as to require resources and backing for intra-family disputes.

Elder authority

The presence of *qawm*-based community elders allowed elder authority to become an occurring motive. Yet, it was only significant among a select number of communities during the jihad and Taliban period. Elder authority was used to fight against the Soviet presence, as well as both for and against the Taliban, depending on the orientation of the commander.[30] As in Kunduz and Ghor and in contrast to Paktya, local commanders acted far more like strongmen than like traditional community militias. The perceived illegitimacy of commanders led to recurring accounts of forced conscription. As in other areas, a request for mobilization was far more likely to be obeyed if supported by a series of overlapping authorities (both elder, religious and familial). This is evident from the following combatant account:

> This was a decision of the nation/community. So my cousin and everyone rose up against the Russians. All the people asked about the jihad and all the people joined together. Tor Pacha [of HIK] was a popular religious figure in our nation [*pir khana*] when he said we all started holy jihad against the Russians.[31]

Still, accounts of force far overwhelmed those of obedience to elder or religious authority, with Hazrat Ali engaging in forced conscription during the civil war. Even if a relative or family member was a commander, Hazrat Ali 'had power, he had a lot of force, we were scared of him. He talked to our people, and said they must send some young people to him.'[32]

Group belonging

Another combatant recounted how, although initially recruited through force, group belonging and economic incentives can serve to keep a combatant in a group.

> The first time [we were mobilized] by force; we didn't know the situation. After when we stayed there, it was not by force, we stayed by ourselves. They told us our country would be independent and we said let's go. We didn't understand – this was a stupid time. It was not necessary that war was the only way of life. Sometimes they gave us salary or wheat and food for our home. We had no other activity and options. Sometimes the major problem is jobs and to know something. Now we've learned something for our future, and they give us money for our pocket and family. Now we have hope and can never go to war. But before was not the same situation. The situation was useless, and we ourselves were also useless, because we didn't understand anything.[33]

As argued in Chapter 3, the latter account emphasizes the necessity of viewing mobilization as a multi-stage process and as a sequence, rather than as a solitary event. New motives emerge for sustaining mobilization as a consequence of joining an armed group, and new ties of social obligation are formed.

Conclusion

Strikingly, economic incentives were by far the predominant motive for combatants in this region, evident across all four periods of conflict in a manner unseen in other locations. Incentives were significant less in material terms than in the comparative absence of other livelihood opportunities (during periods of conflict and drought) and therefore extended beyond money to include, for example, the need for refugee identification cards in Pakistan. Combatants went so far as to switch between commanders for higher salaries.

Combatant accounts also revealed considerable ambiguity as to the role of community elders in driving mobilization, noting the prominence of commanders rather than either communities or parties.

As in Kandahar, the case of Jalalabad also clearly demonstrates the negative impact of Coalition support for local commanders, as well as the frail nature of the post-Bonn security situation. The provincial security institutions are a hiding place for commanders' militias and are utilized in inter-factional disputes and competitions over looting rights. In contrast to Kandahar and Paktya, community elders do not appear to play a substantive role in monitoring the activities of local commanders. The latter are able to utilize both elder and religious authority to mobilize soldiers. While the joint *shura* has been able to prevent the outbreak of excessive conflict in the city, it has not been able to prevent commanders from engaging in predatory activity (particularly outside of Jalalabad City), reduce conflict and competition between the factional militias or implement other measures for local good governance and conflict resolution.

Notes

1 The Kohgyiani tribe is composed of three *kheils*: Kharguni, Sherzadi and Waziri.
2 Interview with UN official, Jalalabad, June 2005.
3 Interview with UN official, Jalalabad, June 2005.
4 Haji Zahir's forces are equipped with officially licensed HK MP5s from Pakistan. Zahir's Frontier Force has had some standoffs with Coalition over their use in Jalalabad City.

> On December 14th, the Commander of the Frontier Brigade of the Eastern Region, Haji Zaher, surrendered a significant stockpile of ammunition: 400 boxes of ammunition, 1,648 unboxed ammunition – including 690 mortars rounds and other heavy caliber weapon rounds – as well as anti-personnel landmines.
>
> (UNDP, 2005)

5 Combatant #319, Jalalabad, June 2005.
6 Combatant #319, Jalalabad, June 2005.
7 In Kunar, the Afghan Guards supporting the Coalition are equipped with truck-mounted DShKs and light armour. The commander of the Afghan Guards in Laghman is Commander Pashtun (Dawlat Shah).
8 A local Afghan is quoted as saying: 'Everybody says warlords, but who are these warlords? They are commanders, they are government ministers … We didn't like the Taliban but there was security then, there were laws. But now anyone with a gun is the law' (Gannon, 2003). '"They're involved in illegal activities. The battalion commanders, the border police, they're all involved in illegal activities," the police official said, adding that the crimes include extortion, drug trafficking and other smuggling operations' (Barron, 2005).
9 Discussion with international UN contractors, Jalalabad, June 2005.
10 Interview with UNOPS representative, Jalalabad, June 2005.
11 While his brother (Haji Qadir) would later control the Jalalabad *shura*, Abdul Haq operated primarily around Kabul, autonomous from both parties and the ISI.
12 Indeed, outside of Jalalabad, Commander Ayoob and Noor of HIK fought against Jamiat in the areas around Torkham and Khogyani and from Chopiar to Tora Bora. Noor's forces numbered approximately 50–60 during the civil war.
13 Combatant #340, Jalalabad, June 2005.
14 Combatant #340, Jalalabad, June 2005.
15 Combatant #333, Jalalabad, June 2005.
16 Combatant #344, Jalalabad, June 2005.
17 Combatant #344, Jalalabad, June 2005.
18 Combatant #338, Jalalabad, June 2005.
19 Combatant #338, Jalalabad, June 2005.
20 Combatant #327, Jalalabad, June 2005.
21 Combatant #338, Jalalabad, June 2005.
22 Combatant #333, Jalalabad, June 2005.
23 Combatant #318, Jalalabad, June 2005.
24 Combatant #320, Jalalabad, June 2005.
25 Combatant #321, Jalalabad, June 2005.
26 Combatant #332, Jalalabad, June 2005.
27 Combatant #319, Jalalabad, June 2005.
28 Combatant #342, Jalalabad, June 2005.
29 Combatant #317, Jalalabad, June 2005.
30 Combatant #321, Jalalabad, June 2005; Combatant #320, Jalalabad, June 2005.
31 Combatant #335, Jalalabad, June 2005.
32 Combatant #319, Jalalabad, June 2005.
33 Combatant #336, Jalalabad, June 2005.

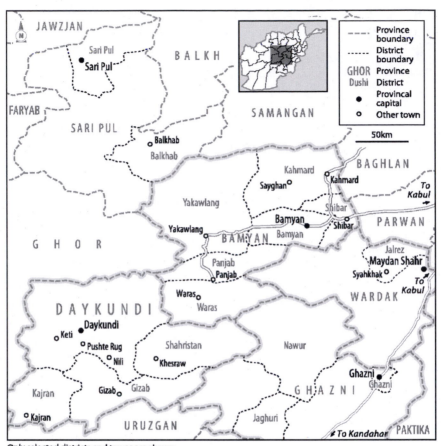

Only selected districts and towns are shown

Map 11.1 Hazarajat Region.

11 Hazarajat

Daykundi, Shahristan, Panjab and Syahkhak

Michael Bhatia

Despite considerable improvements since the days of persecution, starvation and blockades under the Taliban, the Hazarajat continues to face both economic marginalization and relatively minor internal disputes. Nonetheless, the Hazarajat region is generally more secure than the other provinces described in this volume, with the absence of the massive stockpiles of arms common in other areas of Afghanistan. Problematically, outside of central Bamyan, little is known of the communities that constitute the majority of either the province or the region, particularly in its remote western corners.

The case of the Hazarajat reveals:

- a broader conception of self-defence and protection than in the rest of Afghanistan;
- a growing awareness and political mobilization around religious and social persecution;
- strong elder authority focused more on individuals than on communities;
- the presence of specialized, unpaid fighting groups;
- the presence of a specialized group during the jihad known as the *fedayee*;
- the balance between mobilization due to elder authority and accounts of force;
- the differences among perceptions of unity and shared ethnicity.

After describing the geography, ethnic composition and varied Hazara population estimates, this chapter proceeds to examine the post-Bonn security conditions in the region, focusing on the problem areas of Kahmard, Daykundi, Shahristan and Panjab.

Second, it describes the history of conflict in the Hazarajat, focusing on the emergence of the Shura-e-Ittifaq and its fragmentation into smaller parties as well as the formation of another multi-party Hazara alliance under Hezb-e-Wahdat. Contending elites utilized resources from external actors to overpower internal coordinating bodies. Internal unity and cohesion was significantly shaped by the behaviour of external powers. A shared concept of ethnicity ultimately triumphed over Iranian attempts to introduce clerical rule in the region, with the Iranian government under the Taliban shifting to support Hazara unity (while also providing material support to the Northern Alliance). Later, Hazara armed movements suppressed intra-factional competition and united when threatened by an external non-Hazara armed movement (as best exemplified by the Taliban).

Third, this chapter describes the prominent motives for combatant mobilization found in the region, describing the *nazm-e-khas*, the *fedayee*, the conceptualization of protection and self-defence and the dimensions of elder authority while also focusing on economic incentives and labour migration.

Setting the local scene

The Hazarajat occupies the central mountainous spine of Afghanistan. It consists of a series of rivers, rain-fed hilltop grasslands, steep mountains and fertile valleys, small settlements and some sizeable market towns (such as Bamyan, Nili and Yakawlang). As a consequence of the brutal state-building campaign of Amir Abdur Rahman Khan (which received a religious endorsement and was justified in the name of 'jihad'), the Hazara population was massively displaced to major Afghan cities (as well as to India, Pakistan and Iran), with Pashtun *kuchis* (nomads) given grants of land and access to pastures throughout the region (Ghani, 1978; Alden Wily, 2004, pp. 50–58).

Consequently, prior to 1964, there was no single province dominated by Hazaras. Instead, the borders were drawn such that the group was a minority in other provinces (Parwan, Baghlan, Balkh, Kabul, Urozgan, Ghor, Wardak) and a majority in none. Hazara majority districts were also often located far from the provincial centre – a symbol of their entrenched marginalization.[1] Beginning with the creation of Bamyan Province in 1964, new Hazara-dominated provinces were formed. These include Sari Pul Province in 1988 and now Daykundi (incorporating Shahristan, Gizab and Kajran districts) in 2004, the latter of which was previously a remote and chronically underserved area (known as the 'hunger belt') of northern Uruzgan (Constable, 2004, p. A10). More recently, Haji Mohammad Mohaqeq, previously the Minister of Planning and now the speaker of the *Wolesi Jirga*, attempted to create a unified Hazara Province but ultimately failed to secure Karzai's permission (Rubin and Malikyar, 2003).

There is considerable dispute as to the precise size of the Hazara population. A 1990 population estimate projects the total national Hazara population to be two million, constituting 40 per cent of the population in Wardak, 20 per cent in Kabul (or 400,000 of its two million residents) and

80 per cent in Bamyan, Ghor and Ghazni (Emadi, 1997). As described above, the substantial Hazara populations in cities such as Kabul and Mazar is attributable to forced displacement under Amir Abdur Rahman. Other sources place the total population at between four and seven million (Emadi, 1997; Grevemeyer, 1988). In contrast, the Library of Congress proposes that the Hazaras constitute approximately 18 per cent of Afghanistan's total population, which would place the Hazara population at 5.6 million (Blood, 2001). According to the Central Statistics Office, the population of Bamyan is 356,000, of which 11,000 live in urban areas, while Panjab has a population of 66,600.[2]

According to Gregorian (1969), the broad Hazara ethnicity incorporates three different groups (Daykundi, Dai-Zengi (Sengi) and Behsud (Sud)), which are further subdivided into subdivisions (27 in Daykundi, 30 in Dai-Zengi and 34 in Behsud). Those Hazaras living outside of the Hazarajat are known by the following terms: the Koh-e-Baba, the Shaikh Ali, the Badakshan, the Aimaq, the Taimani Hazaras and the Berberis.[3] Differences, competing interests and divisions exist among *sayyeds* (esteemed families and their descendants), landlords and commanders as well as among other 'traditional patterns of power and political allegiance' (HRRAC, 2003, p. 55).

Other Shi'a minorities, including Sadats, Qizilbashes and Sayyeds, reside within the region. Moreover, a substantial Tajik population inhabits the eastern districts of Shibar, Bamyan and Kahmard, with a smaller number of Pashtuns and Tatars residing in Kahmard. The non-Shi'a population has declined considerably, with the displacement of Tajiks from Kahmard, Bamyan and Shibar following the withdrawal of the Taliban (UNHCR, 2002b). The province and region is also home to a substantial percentage of the country's Ismaili Shi'a population (who are also found in neighbouring Baghlan and Badakhshan). Thus, while the Hazarajat and Hizb-e-Wahdat is often viewed as a unified aggregate, this broad label masks substantial internal differences between communities and within this broad group.

Current insecurity and local armed groups

Since the Bonn Agreement, the region (particularly the area surrounding Bamyan) has been known largely for its comparative peace, particularly for international expatriates. Immediately after the Bonn Agreement, districts and provinces in the Hazarajat were governed by those from either the Akbari or Khalili faction of Hizb-e-Wahdat. From 2001–2004, the Panjab was governed by a Hizb-e-Wahdat representative belonging to the Akbari faction who had also served as the Taliban's governor for the district (HRRAC, 2003, p. 54).

Voter turnout for both the presidential and parliamentary elections has been among the highest in the country, with the central highlands the exclusive region to experience an increase (rather than a decrease) in participation between the two elections. Indeed, 72 per cent of registered voters participated in the parliamentary elections, with participation in the neighbouring provinces of Sari Pul, Samangan and Daykundi all well above 60 per cent.

The province is also known for its liberalism and gender equity, which is revealed by the high proportion of women in the Parliament and Karzai government cabinet positions. Moreover, the arms stockpiles discovered in the Hazarajat have been smaller than those found in other regions, which can be attributed to the absence of major government garrisons in these areas during the Soviet and Najibullah period, as well as the exclusion of Shi'a groups from the US–Pakistan arms pipeline. Most arms were either purchased individually by combatant families, captured from smaller DRA outposts or supplied by external governments.

The case of the Hazarajat also illustrates the previously mentioned fact that perceptions of security vary among actors. While aid agencies and Coalition forces have not been subject to armed attack, locals are subject to threats from opposing commanders and to extortion and land disputes, although by no means to the degree common in other regions of Afghanistan (Baghlan, Jalalabad, Kandahar, etc.). The particular problem areas in the Hazara region are Daykundi Province and Kahmard. Although poppy has long been grown in the districts of Sayghan and Kahmard (taking up 40–60 per cent of cultivable land on occasion), poppy production only migrated to other parts of the province in the post-Bonn period (AKDN, undated pamphlet).

The security events and challenges in these different areas of the Hazarajat include:

- Daykundi. According to ANBP, there are a multiplicity of commanders and militias possessing approximately 15,000 weapons in Daykundi district. As described by one elder, 'in Shahristan district there is one commander, in Daykundi, there are 200.'[4] From 9–10 April 2004, clashes were reported between rival commanders allied with (Minister of Commerce) Sayyed Mostafa Kazemi attacking those belonging to Abdul Karim Khalili (later Vice-President) (RFE/RL, 2004). During the October 2005 parliamentary elections, four polling stations in Daykundi could not be opened due to insecurity (Monir and Younus, 2005). One candidate (Haji Mustafa Etemadi) was barred from running in the *Wolesi Jirga* elections due to his maintenance of an illegal armed group. In Daykundi, poppy production crowds out other forms of agriculture, with one elder noting that commanders both promote the growing of poppy and demand one-quarter of a given crop as tax.
- Kahmard. Over the course of summer 2002, there was an armed contest between Rahmatullah and Toofan for control of the district,

which sparked the displacement of both Hazaras and Tatars. Although both are Tajiks by ethnicity, Toofan is affiliated with Hizb-e-Wahdat (UNHCR, 2002b; USCIS, 2004).

- Panjab. There is a long history of conflict between the Hazara and *kuchi* populations over the rain-fed pastoral land on the surrounding hillsides. The district is divided between the two factions of Hizb-e-Wahdat, with commanders executing their political opponents in summer 2002 (UNHCR, 2002a).
- Ghazni. A Harakat-Nabi commander and Ghazni Taliban-era provincial governor, Maulavi Taj Mohammed (also known as 'Qari Baba'), were arrested by Coalition Forces in Ghazni for maintaining an illegal arms cache (Arman-e-Milli, 2005).

In both Kahmard and Daykundi, conflicts often crystallize over land disputes or over the taxation of transiting poppies.[5] Moreover, the limited authority and presence of the central government in Daykundi, Kahmard and other remote parts of the Hazarajat is seen to permit the migration of poppy to these districts. While the security challenges in these regions may be insignificant when compared to those in southern Afghanistan, these accounts do reveal that security is still a substantial concern for community elders and local populations in the Hazarajat.

Currently, the province is home to a New Zealand PRT, which has patrol bases in Shahristan and regularly engages in vehicular patrols to Kahmard, Sayghan and Panjab. However, due to weather conditions, much of the province is off-limits during the winter and early spring. Both Panjab and Daykundi also have UNOPS, WFP and electoral registration offices, although these are not permanently staffed. There is some consideration for deploying an independent PRT to Daykundi. In 2004, soon after the creation of Daykundi Province, a centrally trained ANP Rapid Reaction Force was deployed (constituting 22 soldiers, including two RPGs and two RPDs) to Daykundi, which was used both to protect the provincial government and to arrest criminals.

Within the AMF structure and as part of the Kabul 4th Corps, Bamyan contained three major units: the 35th Division in Panjab, the 34th Division in Bamyan and the 856 Brigade in Kahmard. In addition, sub-units of these groups were stationed in Shahristan and in parts of Daykundi. Within the AMF structure, the 34th was allied with Khalili and the 35th with Akbari. Enmity between Shahristan and Daykundi prevented the units from transiting an opponent's territory, requiring ANBP to travel to the region to complete its mission. Although technically not part of the 4th Corps, Hizb-e-Wahdat and other Shi'a militias were found in Sari Pul (part of the AMF 2nd Corps) and in Ghazni (the Governor's Forces of Division 14). The Coalition, PSCs and the UN utilized some of these local militias for security and for their broader operations, particularly in Ghazni and Daykundi. During the presidential election, JEMB/UNOPS hired electoral security from local AMF commanders (providing $4–5 salary per day and $2 for food). While JEMB initially wanted to hire *shura* members for less money, UNOPS opposed the salary cuts. In Ghazni, Mawin Haidari (and his sub-commander) organized a militia for the Coalition, which was later used to provide protection for the PRT and for the Turkish construction company (through USPI) involved in building the Ghazni portion of the Kabul–Kandahar road.

Regional conflict history

Jihad

The Hazara contribution to the jihad – as well as the political–military dynamics displayed throughout the Hazarajat – is relatively unknown, as most Western journalists and observers (based in Peshawar) focus on Afghanistan's southern regions. Resistance to the Khalqi coup and the Soviet invasion began in winter 1979 in the Hazarajat, which catalysed the formation of the Shura-e Ittifaq following a cross-Hazarajat council. The party autonomously administered much of the region from 1979 until 1982. This marked a return to autonomous self-government, which had ended during the reign of Abdurrahman Khan. Previously, the penetration of state authorities in the region – particularly beyond Bamyan – had been limited. Regional autonomy was only threatened again when the Taliban captured Bamyan in 1998 and was able to penetrate into both Yakawlang and Shahristan. In the past, the Hazara relationship with the Afghan state had been characterized by either neglect or severe ethnic discrimination and persecution, which reached catastrophic proportions under the Taliban with its campaign of blockades and ethnic cleansing.

Immediately following the Soviet invasion, the Hazara population developed a highly centralized political–military and administrative structure. Previously, tribal affiliation had been weakened by substantial emigration. The dominant relationship was between a landowner and his tenants and other dependents. Until the campaigns of Abdurrahman Khan, these figures had also retained their own armed men, were able to exact taxes and were supported by local religious authorities and clerics (Emadi, 1997).

These landowners and the supporting clerics were the foundation of the early resistance movement and *shura* coordination in the Hazarajat, although their position was ultimately usurped by the sons of *mirs*, the educated and by some Iranian-backed religious figures. The *shura* divided the Hazarajat into 36 civilian and eight military districts. Each individual was subject to conscription for one year or taxed in order to fund a replacement recruit. The taxation rate was set at 20 per cent of the harvest, and another voluntary militia was established (Emadi, 1997). Every two families were ordered to purchase and possess one rifle, which was later confiscated by the *shura* (Canfield, 2004, p. 248).

The role of the *shura* as a unified front collapsed in 1981, when the group fragmented due to an internal revolt by the emerging movement Sazman-e-Nasr. The *shura* then moved to Ghazni, where the military commander Jagran continued operations (Rubin, 1996, p. 222). Nasr continued factional fighting with the *shura*, eventually expelling the *shura* from much of central Hazarajat and establishing an Iranian-style administration in its place – although its authority would soon be challenged by the Sepah-e-Pasdaran.[6] Most armed groups had offices in either Iran or Quetta (where many would relocate in order to gain autonomy from the Iranian government) receiving arms, military training and establishing political and propaganda offices.[7] The Iranian regime also provided military training to Hazara refugees for potential use in the Iran–Iraq War (Emadi, 1997). Moreover, Hazaras did not belong exclusively to Shi'a political parties but also had links to the full range of Sunni parties based in Peshawar (Mousavi, 1998, p. 182).

Civil war

Between 1978 and 1985, as many as 50 Shi'a groups and parties emerged, with Iranian influence cited as being the primary factor in the emergence of intense inter-factional conflict in the Hazarajat from 1983–1989 (Mousavi, 1998, p. 180). Since at least 1984, relations between the districts of Shahristan, Daykundi and Waras have been characterized by periods of inter-factional rivalry among local commanders aligned with either the *shura*, Sazman-e-Nasr or with Pasdaran. This continued even after the formation of Hizb-e-Wahdat. By 1982, Harakat and *shura* were in open conflict with Pasdaran and Nasr (Sarabi, 2005, p. 60). According to Greve-meyer and Roy:

> the ideologisation of the resistance movement was very narrowly connected with a social component – namely the struggle against the big landowners, i.e. the traditional secular upper class.
>
> (Grevemeyer, 1988, pp. 215–216)

> The ideologization of the resistance, the transformation of the clergy to political leaders and the rise of religiously-oriented resistance groups organized at a grassroots level have led to a polarization in the Hazara society which have resulted in severe conflicts.
>
> (Roy, 1990, p. 40)

For Monsutti:

> The war meant that the power structures became extremely volatile, as the old *mir* were supplanted by the *seyx* and the *sayyed* lost a lot of their prestige. Gradually, many Hazara leaders questioned the Iranian

connection and Islamist ideology, in favor of ethnicist demands. At regional level, clerics and lay intellectuals appear to have made common cause around a discourse of ethnic liberation.

(Monsutti, 2005, p. 95)

Particularly in its later form, intra-Hazara conflict was between those groups pursuing the autonomy of the Hazarajat and a return to the nineteenth century status quo (as seen with the *shura* and Hizb-e-Wahdat Khalili) and those seeking to institutionalize an Iranian-style government of clerics within the Hazarajat (a goal attributed to the Pasdaran) (Grevemeyer, 1988, p. 216).

The Hizb-e-Wahdat alliance (which incorporated Jabha-e-Mujahed, Nohzat-e-Islami, Harakat, Shora-Islami, Raad, Pasdaran and Nasr) was negotiated between 1988 and 1989 but would ultimately fragment during the civil war and the Taliban's occupation of Bamyan. With the occupation by various mujahideen factions of Kabul, Hizb-e-Wahdat controlled the Kabul University campus and other prominent locations in the west of the city, adding to its numbers by welcoming Hazara members of the Soviet-backed government. Fighting broke out between Hizb-e-Wahdat and Ittihad (and its allies in Jamiat) in the spring and summer of 1992. Hizb-e-Wahdat (Abdul Ali Mazari) then affiliated with Junbish and Hezb-e-Islami until 1996, while Akbari aligned with Jamiat. Mazari's alliance with Junbish and HIH/HIG was attributed to the massacre of Hazara civilians in West Kabul in 1992 in what is known as the Afshar massacre. In 1996, when meeting to negotiate with the approaching Taliban forces, the prominent Hazara leader Abdul Ali Mazari was captured and thrown out of a helicopter (Mousavi, 1998, pp. 195–196).

Taliban era

The division within Hizb-e-Wahdat continued during the Taliban regime. Upon the Taliban's blockade of Bamyan in 1998, Akbari (and his Sepah-e-Pasdaran) allied with the Taliban and installed his local affiliates as the Taliban's appointed governors in parts of the western Hazarajat (including Daykundi and Panjab). This can be attributed to either a desire for power against his Hazara opponents or as an attempt to protect local villages. Those areas where Taliban rule was contested (Yakawlang, Mazar, Bamyan) experienced blockades, mass displacement and the massacre of civilian populations.

The Taliban commander Naim Kuchi sent to Panjab in October 1998 not only disarmed the region but also collected the debts owed by the Hazaras to *kuchi* landlords over the period of the conflict (Alden Wily, 2004, p. 54). The Taliban briefly gained hold of Shahristan for six months in 1988 and were initially welcomed until 'harassment' over arms and the imprisonment of Commander Dawrii of Shahristan sparked a local revolt.[8]

As described in the chapter on Kunduz, other ethnicities (Tajiks, etc.) joined with HW to oppose the Taliban in Kahmard district. In Operation Enduring Freedom, local militias allied with the Coalition forces, although both Junbish and Jamiat received far more support.[9]

Post-9/11 period

The relationship between local commanders and national leadership remains complicated. National level disputes were often superimposed onto pre-existing local issues. Affiliation – whether in terms of a community commander or in terms of a combatant under his command – does not imply endorsement of the armed group's broader programme or agenda. Similarly, at the family level, as occurred in other areas of Afghanistan, inter-factional conflict led families to 'strategically deploy' individuals to different groups in order to manage insecurity (Monsutti, 2005, p. 240).

Communities, commanders and combatants

A total of 40 combatants were interviewed in various parts of the Hazarajat (Shahristan and Nili (Daykundi); Panjab (Bamyan); Ghazni City (Ghazni)

Table 11.1 Combatant profiles of the Hazarajat Region (40 combatants)

Schooling	22%; broad range from intermittent madrassas to full university education.
Prominent livelihoods	Wage labourer, farmer/shepherd, carpet-weaver, teacher.
% of migrants	Substantial in Daykundi/Shahristan, few in Ghazni/Siakhak
Average age of first mobilization:	19.2 years
Recruited under 18	43%
Recruited at or under 16	35%
First mobilized during:	
Jihad	43%
Civil war	17.5%
Taliban era	27.5%
Post-9/11 period	12.5%
Prominent motives by period:	
Jihad	Ideology, grievance, elder authority, economic incentives.
Civil war	Economic incentives, protection, elder authority.
Taliban era	Grievance, elder authority, economic incentives, protection.
Post-9/11 period	Economic incentives, protection, elder authority.

and Syahkhak (Wardak)). A range of Shi'a parties and community dynamics were encountered. There was substantial variation in the motives
encountered in each part of the Hazarajat as well as in the nature of
armed structures.

While few of the combatants encountered in Ghazni or Syahkhak had
migrated for economic opportunities, those in Shahristan and Daykundi
had travelled to Iran on at least one occasion, largely due to the limited
economic opportunities in their area. One combatant had worked for
several years at the coal mines in Quetta. For these combatants, participation in the conflict was based around financial imperatives abroad. One
combatant in Syahkhak noted that, while his elder brothers were working
in Iran, he was selected by his family to join the local armed group in
order to secure the family's land.

For those combatants who purchased their weapon, the primary source
was proposed to be the *kuchi* populations, who brought weapons to the
districts upon their annual return from Pakistan.[10] Those combatants in
Ghazni who supported the Coalition received new weapons but not
ammunition.[11]

Self-defence and protection

With regard to combatant motives, the region was notable for a broader
conception of ethnic self-defence; the nature of elder authority among
the Hazaras and the presence of a specialized group during the jihad,
known as the *fedayee* in Ghazni. Economic incentives were a prominent
motive for joining an armed group across all periods; however, its comparative importance shifted considerably depending on the period.

Reflecting the degree to which the period of conflict has involved a
heightened collective identity, a rhetoric of mobilization for self-defence
and protection was still present throughout the Hazarajat, yet the focus
was predominantly on protecting the broader community of Hazaras
(from other national opponents). Although this would involve the need to
defend a community and homestead, the decision was also framed in
terms of the need to protect and secure the broader Hazara collective
identity. Although it did not prevent the early emergence of inter-
factional fighting, a broader ethnic consciousness was a consequence both
of the conflict and of an education campaign by the Hizb-e-Wahdat. As
described by one combatant, youth groups were formed in high schools in
Bamyan and Yakawlang. Although he first joined the youth group due to
economic imperatives, he notes that the HW:

> were advising the Hazara people to keep defence against other groups
> – because these groups were threatening us.... [And that] we should
> have our rights in Afghanistan, we should have participation in future
> government, and that other ethnicities are capturing our rights. We

were informed that we should have our own rights, and do more for our ethnicity.[12]

Another combatant in Ghazni, who joined Haidari's Hizb-e-Wahdat and the related Coalition militia, described his choice in the following manner:

> We [the Hazaras] must defend our freedom – before we had a very hard time, we were tired from muj and Taliban and other types of fighting. We just made union to keep this situation and have peace in our land. Mawin Haidari came to collect these people with the Coalition force to protect this area.[13]

Far more so than in other areas of Afghanistan, in the Hazarajat, the language of mobilization for self-defence and protection extends beyond the locality. Land refers here less to the village and more to the protection of the collective as a whole from external threats as well as the securing of the group's future position in the government. While it was not the exclusive, nor even the dominant, motive for explaining participation, mobilization for protection was described in a different manner than in other areas.

With regard to specialized units – illustrating again how both strongmen and party militias are constituted by differently motivated individuals – two different groups were encountered in the region. First, Daykundi commanders utilize their *nazm-e-khas* to engage in raids against neighbouring villages and engage in criminality; second, the *fedayee* in the Shura-e-Ittifaq units in Ghazni are a specialized unit provided with more focused military and ideological training. Several elders and *mullahs* interviewed in Daykundi lamented the role of these commanders in promoting local conflict. Accordingly, the commanders utilized 'special soldiers' (locally referred to as *nafar-e-khas* and not as *nazm-e-khas*) in order to maintain the balance of fear among the local population and to create a cycle of violence between communities:

> Commanders are putting the people together to be enemies. For example, a commander goes to one person's house, captures animals and gives these to his special soldiers ... If there is a poor family, a commander captures the daughter or sister by force, and gives her to his special soldiers [to whom he also gives drugs]. These special soldiers do not listen to the elders of the area, they do not listen to their parents, they are the most criminal, they are crazy [*dawana*]. The commanders use these people in each field, in each area.[14]

Through their *nazm-e-khas*, commanders are creating bonds of loyalty with combatants that are distinct from that of their communities. These *nazm-e-khas* are utilized both within and between communities.

Ideological socialization and the fedayee

In Ghazni, combatants described a new specialized fighting group, the *fedayee*, ideologically trained party cadres. The *fedayee* were created by the commander of the Shura-e-Ittifaq, which, after 1982, transformed from a national alliance party to a small party based in Jaghori. As a consequence, it blended aspects of community militias, strongmen and political military parties. Some combatants indicated that the *fedayee* were used for special operations against an opponent but did not play the intra-group enforcement role of the *nazm-e-khas/nafar-e-khas*. Descriptions of this group ranged from noting a specific devotion to the commander to indicating access to specific ideological training, creating a specialized and committed group of combatants. This is evident from the following accounts:

> I never changed my mind [about the conflict], I was right, and I am right now ... Nobody told me to go – not my family, not my community – I saw that all the people in my district went against the occupation; so my religion gave me hope to pick up the weapon against the occupation. I was a *fedayee*, a special group. We were so brave, don't care about ourselves, just fighting without care. The group was so special, everything was special, both teaching and a special organization. They were so brave and intelligent. [We received] special classes on religion with special teachers ... The *fedayee* don't care about themselves or about salary, only about their job.[15]

> What he [the commander] said, we did. We were selected from the nation, and also people from Sayyed Jaghori Mujahedi came and selected and made propaganda to us. *Mullahs* and commanders came to mosque and to a village to make speeches.[16]

> We made jihad for free – no one could give us money. Every *tanzim* had this type of group. [There were] two types of mujahideen: one part took the salary, and another part did jihad for free without salary. Some people whose economic situation was so bad they needed help, and others like us who only made jihad for God.[17]

Elder authority

Although first recruited through elder authority and community selection, the *fedayee*'s mentality and behaviour were further shaped by exposure to ideological training, thus endowing them with greater commitment to the cause and to the commander.

In Shahristan, Daykundi and Ghazni, accounts of elder authority were particularly prominent during the jihad and during the Taliban period and to a lesser extent during the civil war and in the post-Bonn period. As mentioned, in Pashtun communities, the 'ideal type' pre-conflict *khan* and *qawmi mesher*'s authority is limited by the broader community of elders and by local consent (as realized in parts of Paktya). Prior to the reign of Abdurrahman Khan, the landowner in Hazarajat had far greater authority. Both due to this tradition (as well as due to the consequences of the conflict) these commanders (particularly in areas of Daykundi and Shahristan) behave more as strongmen, determining the composition of the community of elders. The relative rarity of accounts of forced conscription throughout this region may be partly attributed to the commander's control of the community of elders, as well as to the broader concept of protection described above.

In Daykundi (in the districts of Keti and Siachob), an interview with a *shura* revealed that elder selection was utilized only during the Soviet and Taliban period and not during the civil fighting. Interviews in Shahristan (relating primarily to the jihad and Taliban period) reveal that Commander Dawrii's attempt to recruit soldiers was supported by elders, religious figures and family members, and that he was ultimately able to send 400 soldiers to the fighting in Bamyan.[18] A formal rotation system was developed to send combatants throughout the Hazarajat, whereby 20–30 people were sent by each community for two to three months.[19] Elders then determined which families would contribute soldiers, with one family out of 20–30 families sending a soldier. This process was described in a number of interviews.

> Some families are too poor, some have no young, and some are afraid. We are under the authority of our elders or orders of our parents, they have more experience than us, we respect and obey them.[20]

> Dawrii first called the elders, then the old men advised communities in different areas to fight. Old men specifically advised us to fight ... I will not leave the commander because of the unity of our people and the security of our area. As for DDR, the decision belongs to our commander and I will wait for his advice. I was selected from my family because I could write, [and the] elder told me to come here. The elders didn't tell him to stay, but my father told me to stay here in order to keep the unity and cooperate with the commander.[21]

> All of us are sent according to our elders, to come here and keep security, there is no salary, nothing for us. When we were fighting against the Taliban, we were fighting just at the advice of our elders, for the security of Shahristan as our elders told us.[22]

> The *mullah* and elder of village told us to start fighting, against Khalqi government, because they are non-Muslim. For this reason we organized together and went to Nawur. We were selected by the elders

and the *mullah*. They selected those people who were younger and had some information on fighting. Selected according to small tribes of Hazara, in a big village like Gehru, there are many small villages, and from each village they would get two to three person. I was young and smart, and had a little information about religious things. During the winters, when I was jobless, I had spent time with the *mullah* asking questions about praying/holy quran. We were happy to go fight, people in the village helped with farm and provided doctors but not money. I only went for one year, then came home, and went back for five months just to cook.[23]

As mentioned, this was also common in Syahkhak, Ghazni, Panjab and Daykundi: 'The commander is of our tribe [*mir*], I came to work with him. My father told me that the commander is our tribe, and that I should work with him and be his guard.'[24] As described elsewhere, elder authority becomes particularly potent when further supported by elder and religious authority. Agreement between elders, religious figures and senior family members will all but guarantee mobilization.

Grievance

While elder authority may have been a catalyst for mobilization, support for a decision may be generated by pre-existing grievances:

First the commanders and the elders [asked me], and my mother also allowed me to fight. Still, if someone gives us a very hard time to our village and our nation – as it happened in the time of the Taliban – it is not necessary that the *qawm* should ask us to go.'[25]

Yet, while a decision to become a soldier may be justified according to respect for elder authority during periods of perceived legitimate fighting, a combatant described a similar demand during the civil war as forced mobilization:

The commanders didn't let us leave the gun – this was by force. It was not always by force, but sometimes we had no other job and people made propaganda or used money to take people in the jihad. The reasons changed – later I left the jihad in the Mojaddedi time – but then the local commander took us by force, and we were the local people, so we could do nothing.[26]

These accounts shed light on two additional dimensions of elder authority: individual grievance and shifting perceptions of legitimate and illegitimate mobilization. Individuals were able to make distinctions between the legitimacy and 'rightness' of different types of fighting, which emphasizes the necessity of differentiating the motives behind different periods of fighting.

As in other areas, commanders took advantage of the combatant's knowledge of previous forms of national and regional military service (the *shura*'s early practice of demanding conscripts from every two families as well as the later creation of the AMF) in order to demand mobilization. National conscription laws were utilized to legitimize local mobilization. In the late Taliban period, a combatant recalled:

> Someone told me it was the law of Sayyed Jaghori Mujahedi [of the Shura-e-Ittifaq] that young people must join. It was not force, but by law. If they command us, we went to fight or stayed in our base. When the Taliban left, no one was here as a soldier, the main person from our area, told us to come temporarily to be soldier and keep security of the city.[27]

> When I became 20 years, they recruited me. We must go to help the mujahideen. My father told me to go, [and that] after 20 years, I must make some service for our country for two years.[28]

Elder authority and community selection thus has multiple dimensions in the Hazarajat, from a formal rotation system to its role of simply activating a combatant already committed to fighting due to grievance. As in other areas, perceptions of legitimacy do play a role, with the above combatant describing participation in the civil war as involving forced conscription.[29] Similarly, the *shura*'s early formal conscription laws (1979–1982) and the Karzai government's creation of the AMF permits the commanders to present themselves as agents of the state.

Economic incentives

Economic incentives were prominent motives during the civil war and the post-Bonn period and were also cited by several combatants during both the jihad and under the Taliban regime. With regard to special groups, while the *nafar-e-khas* would receive access to a substantial portion of loot and other privileges, the *fedayee* were notable for accepting no payment.

The formal taxation system developed by the Shura-e-Ittifaq (20 per cent of the annual harvest) provided the resources for the payment of soldiers. If a combatant did not receive a salary and was recruited through elder authority, the broader community would seek to assist the family by providing some services for free and providing community agricultural labour. The salary varied between 150 Afs ($3) per month to as much as 20–30,000 Afs ($400–600) per year in the 1980s (when one cow cost 15,000 Afs, or $300).[30] All of this is evident from the following accounts:

> There was one jihad, [but we] divided into different groups to get money from different countries. My brothers were trying to participate in jihad and make money at the same time.[31]

> The Taliban were coming, they took our women, they bombarded our place, and we must make a frontline against them. Hassanyar belonged to our area; and he told us that if someone wants to defend his home, he will give a salary. Later, I hated them, so I took the weapon to make sure they did not come back.[32]

> It was lots of money at the time. It was used to attract soldiers. My aim was just jihad, not salary, but when I joined the commander I had the salary also. As a shepherd I earned less than 12,000 Afs per year [$240].[33]

In other cases, mobilization was induced by a sharp change in the economic position of the family, whether due to the conflict or due to the death of a family member:

> When my father died, I didn't know what to do, could not farm, had to come for my family. So I became a soldier for fighting (for 10–12 years), and they gave me a salary of one million old Afghani [10,000 new Afs or $200]; so this was the reason I joined the war, I took this money.[34]

As in Jalalabad, one combatant also appeared to 'shop' among commanders in order to receive the best potential salary.[35] In terms of profitability, however, the best opportunities and salary were available through work with the USA PRT and the PSCs in Ghazni following the Bonn Agreement, when soldiers were paid $100–400 per month and were given an additional field stipend of 500 Afs ($10) per day. While the PSC staff was drawn from existing militias, its ability to acquire these more profitable jobs was based on familial or other connections.[36]

Security dilemma

The situation in Daykundi and western Bamyan Province is a prime illustration of the 'Afghan security dilemma.' Communities support commanders in order to defend themselves against neighbouring commanders. These commanders then use this support to engage in their own predatory activities. Consequently, for many combatants (particularly those serving as local reserves rather than as *nafar-e-khas*) the decision to mobilize was presented in terms of protection from commanders from a neighbouring valley or village:

Sadaqat of Pushti Reg was sending his militants and he wanted illegal taxes by force, demanding 9k Afghani. I was obliged to join, because he was capturing our land, money and animals, and he was trying to destroy our houses.[37]

Similarly in Panjab, a combatant recalled:

There wasn't security, so I took the weapon for my family's security. Someone attacked my family, so I [took the weapon] so I would be able to kill him. We were wealthy. At that time, if someone was wealthy, other militants attacked his family, for this reason, I got a weapon.[38]

Particularly in Daykundi and in the absence of neutral government security bodies, the DDR process is seen to produce vulnerability in these communities.

We have an enemy; he is the second Sadaqat of Pushte Reg village. Now it is very hard for us to live there. There is no security and we are going to be disarmed. The warlords have each kind of weapon, they may attack our houses.[39]

I hope we will not be killed by our opposition. You have cut off our hands.[40]

While these combatants all describe this commander as the source of the problems in the area, other community elders indicate that it is a dual dynamic, whereby the militia used to protect a community also threatens neighbouring communities.[41] Thus, while the rhetoric and reality of mobilization for defence and protection is present, it also does not reveal the entire dynamic. One combatant who was not interviewed in Shahristan approached with the following comment:

I disagree with this commander. I disagree with the Akbari people, and other commanders involving in civil fighting. Most of the people are poor people. They would like to be disarmed. They'd like to work. The commanders were using the young men for their own individual fighting.[42]

As discussed in the introduction, individuals may wish to participate in the fighting against a national threat (e.g., the Taliban), without contributing to the local security dilemma and becoming implicated in local violence and will thus seek to join a group in another region.

Conclusion

The Hazara population is not exclusively based in the Hazarajat but has a presence in most major Afghan cities. There is no singular Hazara-style armed group. Most appear to fall between community militias and local strongmen. Political–military parties were most apparent around Kabul and Ghazni and other major urban centres. A commander's *nazm-e-khas* both protect their own communities and threaten neighbouring communities, reflecting the 'Afghan security dilemma.'

The autonomy acquired (and harshly defended) during the Khalqi government consolidated the gains in Hazara national development that had begun in the 1950s. Despite the infighting within the Hazarajat, the Hazaras emerged from the conflict with mobilized and ethnically conscious elites able to play a role on the national stage. Intra-Hazara dynamics reveal both cooperation and conflict. However, an armed challenge or political competition from a non-Hazara group promotes unity and alliance between these groups and the temporary suspension of competition, although some individuals may affiliate with the outside forces (as occurred with the Taliban).

For a substantial proportion of the combatants, mobilization was explained in terms of a desire to protect the entire Hazara population from other groups, revealing a broad conceptualization of community and self-defence. The prominence of ideology and a broader concept of protection revealed a move away from the protection of a local community to the protection of an entire people. This shift was induced both by attacks by other groups on the Hazarajat as well as by an emerging ethnic consciousness at least partly linked to the propaganda, youth group and ideological training activities of political–military parties.

And, yet, the interviews conduced in the Hazarajat also show how a wide range of other factors exist parallel to broadly applied ethnic and religious rhetoric. As with the Tajiks and the Pashtuns, shared ethnicity does not guarantee constant internal political unity. Moreover, as is the case in the Hazarajat, the manner in which arms and other resources are delivered (in this case by the government of Iran) can encourage either unity or fragmentation. Even in times of relative peace, Hazara politicians and commanders have diffuse alliances and agendas.

Notes

1 The population's marginalization is attributed to their predominantly Shi'a beliefs (Khazeni and Monsutti, 2004).
2 Population statistics online, available at: statoids.com/uaf.html and cia.gov/cia/publications/factbook/print/af.html (accessed 4 December 2007).
3 Gregorian, 1969, p. 34. Other *qawms* of the Hazaras include: Abu Hassan (Nawor); Sepoy; Mirshad Beg, Jirghaye-Birzghaye and Jam.

4 Interview with community elders, Daykundi, July 2004.

5 Interview with David Izadifar, UNAMA-Bamiyan, February 2005.

6 *Pasdaran* has multiple meanings. In Iran, this refers to the special guard of the Iranian government. In Afghanistan, this was both the name of a faction and armed movement and also a pejorative term used to describe a faction viewed to be infiltrated by the Iranians and espousing a radical Shi'a ideology of clerical rule.

7 Combatant #295, Ghazni, June 2005.

8 Combatant #12 (Commander Dawrii), Shahristan, July 2004.

9 Combatant #314, Ghazni, June 2005.

10 Combatant #22, Nili, Daykundi, July 2004; Combatant #11, Shahristan, July 2004. Weapons prices: 15,000 Afghani for a Dektorov (unknown weapon) in 1999; an AK-47 for five sheep. Descriptions of the *kuchi*s as weapons smugglers have to be qualified, however, by the fact that this may be an attempt to stigmatize and label falsely the nomadic population. Pronounced tensions exist between the Sunni Pashtun *kuchi*s and the Shi'a Hazara settled populations throughout Afghanistan.

11 Commander #314, Ghazni, June 2005.

12 Combatant #10, Shahristan, July 2004.

13 Combatant #296, Ghazni, June 2005.

14 Interview with elder, Nili, Daykundi, July 2004.

15 Combatant #301, Ghazni, June 2005.

16 Combatant #297, Ghazni, June 2005.

17 Combatant #305, Ghazni, June 2005.

18 Combatant #12 (Commander Dawrii), Shahristan, July 2004.

19 Combatant #15, Shahristan, July 2004.

20 Combatant #13, Shahristan, July 2004.

21 Combatant #11, Shahristan, July 2004.

22 Combatant #14, Shahristan, July 2004.

23 Combatant #18, Shahristan, July 2004.

24 Combatant #31, Panjab, July 2004.

25 Combatant #315, Ghazni, June 2005.

26 Combatant #311, Syahkhak, Wardak, June 2005.

27 Combatant #293, Ghazni, June 2005.

28 Combatant #306, Syahkhak, Wardak, June 2005.

29 Combatant #311, Syahkhak, Wardak, June 2005.

30 Combatant #29, Panjab, July 2004.

31 Combatant #22, Nili, Daykundi, July 2004.

32 Combatant #302, Ghazni, June 2005.

33 Combatant #29, Panjab, July 2004.

34 Combatant #308, Ghazni, June 2005.

35 Combatant #313, Ghazni, June 2005.

36 Combatant #302, Ghazni, June 2005; Combatant #304, Ghazni, June 2005.

37 Combatant #21, Nili, Daykundi, July 2004.

38 Combatant #32, Panjab, July 2004.

39 Combatant #26, Nili, Daykundi, July 2004.

40 Combatant #27, Nili, Daykundi, July 2004.

41 Interview with community elders, Daykundi, July 2004.

42 Comment by combatant, Shahristan, July 2004.

Bibliography

Adamec, Ludwig. 2003. *Historical Dictionary of Afghanistan*. Oxford: The Scarecrow Press, Inc.

Afghanistan Ministry of Defence. 2004. *National Military Strategy*. Kabul: Islamic Republic of Afghanistan.

—— 2006. *Afghan National Army: The Future of a Nation*. Kabul: Ministry of Defence.

Afghanistan Ministry of Interior. 2006.

Afghan National Police: In Service for the People. Kabul: Afghanistan Ministry of Interior and CSTC-A.

Afghanistan Television (Kabul). 2004. 'Security Officials Discover Arms, Ammunition.' 14 April.

AFP (Agence France Presse). 2006a. 'Stinger missiles in Afghanistan a threat to US.' 20 March.

——. 2006b. 'Rusty Soviet tanks fuel Pakistan's steel industry.' 25 April.

——. 2006c. 'Ten dead in fresh Afghanistan gunbattles.' 18 December.

AFP (Hong Kong). 1999. 'Philippine Muslim Rebels Await Afghan Arms Shipment.' 21 February.

Ahmad, Mahfooz. 2000. 'Resistance Movement in Afghanistan (1979–1981).' Reprinted from Pakistan, Vol. XXXVI (3) in Verinder Grover, ed. *Afghanistan: Government and Politics*. New Delhi, India: Deep & Deep Publications Pvt. Ltd.

Ahmed-Ullah, Noreen. 2002. 'Warlord Gears up for Next Fight Against Governor as U.S. Troops Battle al-Qaida Remnants.' *Chicago Tribune* 30 April. Online, available at: highbeam.com/doc/1G1-120414308.html (accessed 4 December 2007).

AIC (Afghanistan Information Centre) (Peshawar). 1986. 'Situation in Nangarhar Province: Micro-study of a Liberated Area.' *Afghanistan Information Centre Monthly Bulletin*. No. 65. August.

——. 1988a. 'A Trip to Jaji District in Paktia.' *Afghanistan Information Centre Monthly Bulletin*. No. 89. August.

——. 1988b. 'Afghan Delegation Expresses Doubts Over Conduct of United Nations-Sponsored Reconstruction Survey Mission to Afghanistan.' *Afghanistan Information Centre Monthly Bulletin*. No. 92. November.

——. 1989a. 'The Future of Afghanistan: An AIC Questionnaire.' *Afghanistan Information Centre Monthly Bulletin*. No. 94. January.

——. 1989b. 'Problems with Wahhabis.' *Afghanistan Information Centre Monthly Bulletin*. No. 97. April.

——. 1990. 'Deforestation in Kunar.' *Afghanistan Information Centre Monthly Bulletin*. Nos. 116–117. November–December, pp. 23–27.

——. 1991a. 'Afghan National Wealth on Pakistani Black Market.' *Afghanistan Information Centre Monthly Bulletin.* Nos. 123–124. June–July.

——. 1991b. 'Poppy Cultivation in Afghanistan.' *Afghanistan Information Centre Monthly Bulletin.* Nos. 123–124. June–July.

——. 1992a. 'From Peshawar to Kabul and Mazar.' *Afghanistan Information Centre Monthly Bulletin.* Nos. 132–135. March–June.

——. 1992b. 'Situation in Paktia.' *Afghanistan Information Centre Monthly Bulletin.* Nos. 132–135. March–June.

AIHRC (Afghan Independent Human Rights Consortium). 2005. 'A Call for Justice: A National Consultation on Past Human Rights Abuses in Afghanistan.' January. Online, available at: aihrc.org.af/Rep_29_Eng/rep29_1_05call 4justice.pdf (accessed 4 December 2007).

AKDN (Aga Khan Development Network). Undated pamphlet. 'Bamyan – a regional profile.'

Alden Wily, Liz. 2004. 'Looking for Peace on the Pastures: Rural Land Relations in Afghanistan.' *AREU Synthesis Paper.* December.

Ali, Salamat. 1991a. 'Afghanistan: Hungry for Arms: Hardliners are Buoyed by Saudi Weapons.' *Far Eastern Economic Review.* 3 October.

——. 1991b. 'Afghanistan: Cause and Effect: Concern in Pakistan over Mujahideen's Arab Allies.' *Far Eastern Economic Review.* 23 May.

——. 1991c. 'Afghanistan: Trading Alms for Arms.' *Far Eastern Economic Review.* 23 May.

Ali, Zulfiqar. 2001. 'JALALABAD: Chaos in Jalalabad.' *Dawn.* 18 November.

——. 2002. 'War on Terror Brings Modern Arms to Tribal Markets.' *Dawn.* 21 August.

Allan, Nigel. 2001. 'Defining Place and People in Afghanistan.' *Post-Soviet Geography and Economics,* Vol. 42, No. 8, pp. 545–560.

ANBP (Afghanistan New Beginnings Programme). 2004. 'ANBP Weekly Summary Report.' No. 36, 25 July–31 July.

——. 2006a. *Brochure for the Second Tokyo Conference on Consolidation of Peace in Afghanistan.* Kabul: ANBP, 15 June.

——. 2006b. *Ammunition Training Course and Re-arrangement of the Ammunition Depot in Khairabad.* Kabul: ANBP, 2 September. Online, available at: reliefweb.int/rw/rwb.nsf/db900sid/RMO1-6TB3WP?OpenDocument (accessed 4 December 2007).

Anderson, Jon. 1983. 'Khan and Khel: Dialectics of Pakhtun Tribalism.' In Richard Tapper, ed. *The Conflict of Tribe and State in Iran and Afghanistan.* New York: St. Martin's Press, pp. 119–149.

Anis (Kabul). 2005. 'Arms Cache Attributed to Taleban.' *IWPR's Afghan Press Monitor,* No. 132. 14–15 August.

ANSO (Afghanistan Non-governmental Organization Security Office). 2004. 'Western Region Situational Analysis.' 15 March.

AP (Associated Press). 2005a. 'Iran Arms Stockpile Worries U.S.' 25 March.

——. 2005b. 'Afghanistan Election Plot Thwarted.' 31 July.

Apter, David. 1997. 'Political Violence in Analytical Perspective.' In David Apter, ed. *The Legitimization of Violence.* London: Macmillan Press, pp. 1–32.

Arman-e-Milli (Kabul). 2005. 'Former Ghazni governor arrested.' *IWPR's Afghan Press Monitor,* No. 163. 27 September.

ASFIFC (Alan Shawn Feinstein International Famine Center). 2003. *Human Security and Livelihoods of Rural Afghans, 2002–2003.* Tufts University, Medford, MA.

Azoy, Whitney. 2003. 'Masood's Parade: Iconography, Revitalization, and Ethnicity in Afghanistan.' *Expedition Magazine*, Vol. 45, No. 1. Spring.

Babakarkhel, Zubair. 2005. 'Arms Seized after Encounter in Sarobi.' *Pajhwok Afghan News*. 10 August.

Bakhtar News Agency (Kabul). 2004. 'Afghan Security Officials Seize Ammunition Cache.' 7 January.

Baldauf, Scott and Ashraf Khan. 2005. 'New Guns, New Drive for Taliban.' *Christian Science Monitor*. 26 September.

Baldauf, Scott and Faye Bowers. 2005. 'Afghanistan Riddled with Drug Ties.' *Christian Science Monitor*. 13 May.

Barron, Porter. 2005. 'Afghanistan Struggles to Keep Warlords off the Ballot.' *Christian Science Monitor*. 8 September.

Bazzi, Mohamad. 2001. 'Weapons Sales Suffering in Pakistan: Gunsmiths say crackdown is hurting trade.' *Newsday*. 26 December.

BBC Online. 2005. Afghan Munitions Blast 'Kills 28. 2 May. Online, available at: news.bbc.co.uk/1/hi/world/south_asia/4506005.stm (accessed 4 December 2007).

Beall, Jo and Daniel Esser. 2005. 'Shaping Urban Futures: Challenges to Governing and Managing Afghan Cities.' *AREU Issues Paper Series*. March.

Berdal, Mats and David Keen. 1997. 'Violence and Economic Agendas in Civil Wars: Some Policy Implications.' *Millennium: Journal of International Studies*, Vol. 26, No. 3, pp. 798–799.

Berdal, Mats and David Malone (eds.). 2000. *Greed and Grievance. Economic Agendas in Civil Wars*. Boulder, CO and London: Lynne Rienner Publishers.

Bergen, Peter. 2007. 'The Return of Al Qaeda: Where You Bin?' *New Republic*. 29 January.

Bhatia, Michael. 2005. 'Fighting Words: Naming Terrorists, Rebels, Bandits and Other Violent Actors.' *Third World Quarterly*, Vol. 26, No. 1. March.

——. 2007. 'The Future of the Mujahideen: Legacy, Legitimacy and Demobilization.' *International Peacekeeping*. Vol. 14, No. 1. January.

Bhatia, Michael and Jonathan Goodhand (with Haneef Atmar, Suleiman Mohammed and Adam Pain). 2003. 'Profits and Poverty: Aid, Livelihoods and Conflict in Afghanistan.' In Sarah Collinson, ed. *The Application of a Political Economy Approach to Humanitarian Action.*. London: Overseas Development Institute.

Blood, Peter R. (ed.) 2001. *Afghanistan: A Country Study*. Washington: GPO for the Library of Congress. Online, available at: countrystudies.us/Afghanistan/index.htm (accessed 4 December 2007).

Bonn Agreement (Agreement on Provisional Arrangements in Afghanistan Pending the Re-Establishment of Permanent Government Institutions), Bonn, 5 December Online, available at: se2.isn.ch/serviceengine/FileContent?serviceID=23&fileid=8A49DA5A-624D-D320-4E36-82A28924CCDE&Ing=en (accessed 4 December 2007).

Bradsher, Henry. 1999. *Afghan Communism and Soviet Intervention*. Oxford: Oxford University Press.

Buchbinder, David. 2002. 'Guns Offer Past Profit for Afghans: Poor Soldiers are Key Players in a Massive Unregulated Weapons Market.' *Christian Science Monitor*. 6 August.

Cameron-Moore, Simon. 2006. 'Getting Desperate; Afghanistan Mulls forming Militias.' *Reuters*. 11 June.

Canfield, Robert. 2004. 'New Trends Among the Hazaras: From the "Amity of Wolves" to "The Practice of Brotherhood."' *Iranian Studies*, Vol. 37, No. 2. June. pp. 241–262.

Chayes, Sarah. 2006. *The Punishment of Virtue: Inside Afghanistan After the Taliban*. New York: Penguin Press.

Chouvy, P.A. 2004. 'Narco-Terrorism in Afghanistan.' *Terrorism Monitor*, Vol. 2, No. 6. 25 March.

Christensen, Asger. 1988. 'When Muslim Identity has Different Meanings: Religion and Politics in Contemporary Afghanistan.' In Bo Huldt and Erland Jansson, eds. *The Tragedy of Afghanistan: The Social, Cultural and Political Impact of the Soviet Invasion*. London: Croom Helm.

Chrobok, Vera. 2005. 'Demobilising and Reintegrating Afghanistan's Young Soldiers: A Review and Assessment of Program Planning and Implementation.' *BICC Paper* No. 42. Bonn: Bonn International Centre for Conversion.

CIA (Central Intelligence Agency). 2007. Population statistics. Online, available at: cia.gov/cia/publications/factbook/print/af.html (accessed 4 December 2007).

Clapham, Christopher. 1985. *Third World Politics: An Introduction*. Madison, WI: University of Wisconsin Press.

Colletta, Nat J., Markus Kostner and Ingo Wiederhofer. 2004. 'Disarmament, Demobilisation and Reintegration: Lessons and Liabilities in Reconstruction.' In Robert I. Rotberg, ed. *When States Fail: Causes and Consequences*. Princeton, NJ: Princeton University Press, pp. 170–181.

Constable, Pamela. 2004. 'Out of Ruins, Afghan Groups Build Anew.' *Washington Post Foreign Service*. 24 August. P. A10.

Cordesman, Anthony and Abraham R. Wagner. 1991. *The Lessons of Modern War: Volume III: The Afghan and Falklands Conflicts*. Boulder, CO: Westview Press.

Cordovez, Diego and Selig S. Harrison. 1995. *Out of Afghanistan: The Inside Story of the Soviet Withdrawal*. New York: Oxford University Press.

CPIC (Coalition Press Information Center, Combined Forces Command). 2004a. 'Coalition Soldiers Find Weapons Cache.' 6 November.

——. 2004b. 'Pakistan Destroys Militant Training Camps near Afghanistan.' 22 November.

——. 2004c. 'Local Security turns in Cache.' 27 November.

——. 2004d. 'Local Police, Afghan Citizen turn in Weapons Caches.' 29 November.

——. 2004e. 'Weapons Turned In, Found.' 3 December.

——. 2004f. 'Coalition Forces Recover Weapons Caches.' 25 December.

——. 2005a. 'Coalition Forces Recovered Five Weapons Caches Tuesday.' 20 January.

——. 2005b. 'Afghan Police turn in Unusual Cache to Coalition forces.' 12 April.

——. 2005c. 'Two Former Taliban Commanders Reconcile, turn in Cache.' 7 June.

——. 2005d. 'Three Caches Discovered in Eastern Afghanistan.' 9 August.

——. 2005e. 'Afghans turn in Cache to U.S. Forces.' 16 August.

——. 2006a. 'District Official Reports Cache Site to Coalition Forces.' 11 March.

——. 2006b. 'Six Insurgents Killed in Afghanistan as Troops Launch New Operation.' 12 April.

Crile, George. 2003. *Charlie Wilson's War: The Extraordinary Story of the Largest Covert Operation in History*. New York: Atlantic Monthly Press.

Daily Times (Pakistan). 2006. 'Eight Killed in Afghanistan, Taliban Capture 3 Villages.' 1 March.

Davis, Anthony. 1998. 'How the Taliban Became a Military Force.' In William Maley, ed. *Fundamentalism Reborn? Afghanistan and the Taliban.* London: Hurst & Company.

Defenselink. 2004a. 'Afghan Security Situation Continues to Show Improvement.' 19 November.

——. 2004b. 'More Weapons Found, Seized in Afghanistan.' 14 April.

Dennys, Christian. 2005. 'Disarmament, Demobilization and Rearmament? The Effects of Disarmament in Afghanistan.' *Japan Afghan NGO Network (JANN).* June.

Donini, Antonio. 2007. *Local Perceptions of Assistance to Afghanistan.* Vol. 14, No. 1. January, pp. 158–172.

Dorronsoro, Gilles. 2005. *Revolution Unending: Afghanistan: 1979 to the Present.* London: Hurst.

Dupree, Louis. 1980. *Afghanistan.* Princeton, NJ: Princeton University Press.

Edwards, David. 1984. 'Origins of the Anti-Soviet Jihad.' In Grant Farr and John Merriam, eds. *Afghan Resistance: The Politics of Survival.* Lahore: Vanguard Books.

——. 1986. 'Charismatic Leadership and Political Process in Afghanistan.' *Central Asian Survey,* Vol. 5, No. 3/4, pp. 273–299.

Emadi, Hafizullah. 1997. 'The Hazaras and their Role in the Process of Political Transformation in Afghanistan.' *Central Asian Survey,* Vol. 16, No. 3, pp. 363–387.

ESGER. 1996. 'Illegal Border Crossings Becoming more Organized.' 27 June.

Fisher, Ian. 2002. 'Warlord Pushes for Control of Corner of Afghanistan.' *New York Times.* 6 August.

Foley, Conor. 2004. *Land and Property Disputes in Eastern Afghanistan.* Kabul: Norwegian Refugee Council.

Franco, Claudio. 2005. 'Initial Results of Afghan Government Anti-Drug Campaign Are Positive – Report.' *Eurasianet.* 9 September.

——. 2007. 'In Remote Afghan Camp, Taliban Explain How and Why They Fight.' *San Francisco Chronicle Foreign Service.* 21 January.

Friel, Terry. 2006. 'Taliban Insurgency Slows Drugs War – Afghan Minister.' *Reuters.* 16 October.

Frontier Post. 1997. '"Huge Quantity" of Illegal Arms from Afghanistan Seized.' 14 December.

Fullerton, Jon. 1981. 'A Question of Firepower: It's no Longer Homemade Rifles but Sophisticated Captured Weapons that Sustain the Guerrillas.' *Far Eastern Economic Review.* 25 December.

Gall, Carlotta. 2005. 'Islamists and Mujahedeen Secure Victory in Afghan Vote.' *New York Times.* 21 October.

——. 2006. 'Taliban Surging in Afghan Shift From U.S. to NATO.' *New York Times.* 11 June.

Galster, Steven (ed.). 1990. *Afghanistan: The Making of U.S. Policy, 1973–1990.* Vol. 1. Alexandria, VA: Chadwyck Healey/National Security Archive.

Gannon, Kathy. 2003. 'Afghans See U.S.-Backed Warlords As Enemy.' *Associated Press.* 7 September.

GeoMiliTech Consultants Corporation. 1986. 'Proposal to William Casey, Director, Central Intelligence Agency.' *National Security Archive.* 28 July.

Ghani, Ashraf. 1978. 'Islam and State-building in a Tribal Society, Afghanistan: 1880–1901.' *Modern Asian Studies,* Vol. 12, No. 2, pp. 269–284.

Giustozzi, Antonio. 2000. *War, Politics and Society in Afghanistan, 1978–1992.* London: Hurst & Company.

——. 2003. 'Respectable Warlords: The Politics of State-Building in Post-Taliban Afghanistan.' *Crisis States Working Paper*, No. 33. September.

——. 2004. '"Good" State vs. "Bad" Warlords? A Critique of State-Building Strategies in Afghanistan.' *Crisis States Working Paper*, No. 51. October.

——. 2005a. 'The Debate on Warlordism: The Importance of Military Legitimacy,' *LSE Crisis States Programme Discussion Paper*, No. 13, October, p. 8.

——. 2005b. 'The Ethnicisation of an Afghanistan Faction: Junbesh-I Milli from its Origins to the Presidential Elections (2004).' *Crisis States Working Paper*, No. 67. September.

——. 2005c. 'Warlords into Businessmen: The Afghan Transition 2002–2005. Preliminary findings from a research trip, May 2005.' Paper presented at Transforming War Economies Conference. Plymouth, UK. 16–18 June.

Giustozzi, Antonio and Mark Sedra. 2004. 'Army Annex.' In *Securing Afghanistan's Future: Accomplishments and the Strategic Path Forward.* A Government/International Agency Report, prepared for International Conference 31 March–1 April. Asian Development Bank, United Nations Assistance Mission to Afghanistan, United Nations Development Program, World Bank Groups, 24 March.

Glasser, Susan. 2002. 'U.S. Backing Helps Warlord Solidify Power.' *Washington Post Foreign Service.* 18 February, . pA01.

GlobalSecurity.org. Online, available at: globalsecurity.org/military/world/afghanistan/amf.htm; globalsecurity.org/military/world/afghanistan/ddr.htm; globalsecurity.org/military/world/afghanistan/ali.htm (accessed 4 December 2007).

GoA (Government of Afghanistan. 2004). 'Presidential Decree 50: Legal Prosecution of the Violators of the Disarmament and Demobilization Process.' 14 July.

——. 2005a. 'Law of Fire Weapons, Ammunitions and Explosive Materials.' Online, available at: diag.gov.af/weaponlaw.htm (accessed 4 December 2007).

——. 2005b. 'Law of Private Security Organizations' Activity License in Afghanistan.' Draft version.

——. 2006. 'Disbandment of Illegal Armed Groups.' Online, available at: diag.gov.af/ (accessed 4 December 2007).

Goodson, Larry. 1998. 'Periodicity and Intensity in the Afghan War.' *Central Asian Survey*, Vol. 17, No. 3, pp. 471–488.

——. 2001. *Afghanistan's Endless War: State Failure, Regional Politics and the Rise of the Taliban.* Seattle, WA: University of Washington Press.

Government of Japan. 2006. Co-chairs' Summary: The second Tokyo Conference on Consolidation of Peace in Afghanistan (DDR/DIAG). 6 July. Online, available at: mofa.go.jp/region/middle_e/Afghanistan/summary0607.html (accessed 4 December 2007).

Grass, Michael and Brody Mullins. 2003. 'K is for Kandahar.' *Roll Call.* 24. November

Grau, Lester. 2004. 'Something Old, Something New. Guerrillas, Terrorists, and Intelligence Analysis.' *Military Review.* July–August.

Gregorian, Vartan. 1969. *The Emergence of Modern Afghanistan: Politics of Reform and Modernization.* Stanford, CA: Stanford University Press.

Grevemeyer, Jan-Hereen. 1988. 'Ethnicity and National Liberation: The Afghan Hazara Between Resistance and Civil War.' In Fait Ethnique, ed. *Iran est en Afghanistan.* Paris: CNRS.

Griffin, Michael. 2001. *Reaping the Whirlwind: The Rise of the Taliban Movement in Afghanistan.* Sterling, VA: Pluto Press.

Gunaratna, Rohan. 2001. 'Terrorism and Small Arms and Light Weapons.' UN Symposium on Terrorism and Disarmament. 25 October.

Harpviken, Kristian Berg. 1997. 'Transcending Traditionalism: The Emergence of Non-State Military Formations in Afghanistan.' *Journal of Peace Research,* Vol. 34, No. 3, pp. 271–287.

Hersh, Seymour. 2004. *Chain of Command: The Road from 9/11 to Abu Ghraib.* New York: Harper Perennial.

Hilali, A.Z. 2002. 'The costs and benefits of the Afghan War for Pakistan.' *Contemporary South Asia.* Vol. 11, No. 3, pp. 291–310.

Hobsbawm, Eric. 1969/2000. *Bandits.* London: Abacus.

HRRAC (Human Rights Research and Advocacy Consortium). 2003. 'Speaking Out: Afghan Opinions on Rights and Responsibilities.' November.

——. 2004. 'Take the Guns Away: Afghan Voices on Security and Elections.' September.

HRW (Human Rights Watch). 1994. 'India: Arms and Abuses in Indian Punjab and Kashmir.' *HRW Report,* Vol. 6, No. 10. September. Online, available at: hrw/org/campaigns/Kashmir/1994/ (accessed 4 December 2007).

——. 2000. 'Fueling Afghanistan's War.' *Press Backgrounder.* 15 December.

——. 2001. 'Afghanistan: Crisis of Impunity: The Role of Pakistan, Russia, and Iran in Fueling the Civil War.' *HRW Report,* Vol. 13, No. 3. July. Online, available at: hrw.org/reports/2001/afghan2/ (accessed 4 December 2007).

——. 2002. 'Paying for the Taliban's Crimes: Abuses Against Ethnic Pashtuns in Northern Afghanistan.' *HRW Report,* Vol. 14, No. 2. 9 April.

——. 2003. 'Killing You is a Very Easy Thing For Us.' July.

——. 2004. 'The Rule of the Gun: Human Rights Abuses and Political Repression in the Run-up to Afghanistan's Presidential Election.' *Briefing Paper.* September.

——. 2006. 'Lessons in Terror: Attacks on Education in Afghanistan.' *HRW Report,* Vol. 18, No. 6. July. Online, available at: hrw.org/reports/2006/afghanistan0706/ (accessed 4 December 2007).

Hyman, Anthony. 1990. 'Reading Afghan Public Opinion: Voices from the Camps.' *Central Asian Survey,* Vol. 9, No. 4, pp. 113–123.

Ibrahimi, Sayed Yaqub. 2004. 'Afghan Gun Culture Costs Lives.' *Institute for War and Peace Reporting Afghan Recovery Report.* No. 149, 25 November. Online, available at: iwpr.net/?p=arr&s=f&o=15257&apc_state=heniarr2004 (accessed 4 December 2007).

——. 2006a. 'Taleban Find Unexpected Arms Source.' *Institute for War and Peace Reporting Afghan Recovery Report.* No. 206, 12 March. Online, available at: iwpr.net/?p=arr&s=f&o=260271&apc_state=henh (accessed 4 December 2007).

——. 2006b. 'Afghan Disarmament a Never-Ending Process.' *Institute for War and Peace Reporting Afghan Recovery Report.* No. 215, 12 May. Online, available at: iwpr.net/?p=arr&s=f&o=261808&apc_state=heniarr200605 (accessed 4 December 2007).

ICG (International Crisis Group). 2003. 'Afghanistan: The Problem of Pashtun Alienation.' *ICG Asia Report.* No. 62. 5 August. Online, available at: crisisgroup.org/home/index.cfm?id=1641&1=1 (accessed 4 December 2007).

——. 2005. *Afghanistan: Getting Disarmament Back on Track.* Kabul: ICG.

——.2006. 'Afghanistan's New Legislature: Making Democracy Work.' *ICG Asia Report.* No. 116. 15 May. Online, available at: crisisgroup.org/library/documents/asia/south_asia116_afghanistan_new_legislature_making_democracy_work.pdf (accessed 4 December 2007).

IISS (International Institute for Strategic Studies). 1976. *Military Balance 1975–1976.* Oxford, UK: Oxford University Press, p. 52.

——. 1978. *Military Balance 1977–1978.* Oxford, UK: Oxford University Press, pp. 55–56.

——. 1979. *Military Balance 1978–1979.* Oxford, UK: Oxford University Press, pp. 58–59.

——. 1980. *Military Balance 1979–1980.* Oxford, UK: Oxford University Press, pp. 62–63.

——. 1981. *Military Balance 1980–1981.* Oxford, UK: Oxford University Press, p. 65.

——. 1982. *Military Balance 1981–1982.* Oxford, UK: Oxford University Press, p. 77.

——. 1983. *Military Balance 1982–1983.* Oxford, UK: Oxford University Press, p. 83.

——. 1984. *Military Balance 1983–1984.* Oxford, UK: Oxford University Press, p. 87.

——. 1985. *Military Balance 1984–1985.* Oxford, UK: Oxford University Press, pp. 95–96.

——. 1986. *Military Balance 1985–1986.* Oxford, UK: Oxford University Press, pp. 118–119.

——. 1987. *Military Balance 1986–1987.* Oxford, UK: Oxford University Press, pp. 149–150.

——. 1988. *Military Balance 1987–1988.* Oxford, UK: Oxford University Press, pp. 151–152.

——. 1989. *Military Balance 1988–1989.* Oxford, UK: Oxford University Press, pp. 155–156.

——. 1990. *Military Balance 1989–1990.* Oxford, UK: Oxford University Press, pp. 152–153.

——. 1991. *Military Balance 1990–1991.* Oxford, UK: Oxford University Press, pp. 155–156.

——. 1992. *Military Balance 1991–1992.* Oxford, UK: Oxford University Press, pp. 156–157.

——. 1993. *Military Balance 1992–1993.* Oxford, UK: Oxford University Press, pp. 136–137.

——. 1994. *Military Balance 1993–1994.* Oxford, UK: Oxford University Press, pp. 136–137.

——. 1995. *Military Balance 1994–1995.* Oxford, UK: Oxford University Press, pp. 151–152.

——. 1996. *Military Balance 1995–1996.* Oxford, UK: Oxford University Press, pp. 155–156.

——. 1997. *Military Balance 1996–1997.* Oxford, UK: Oxford University Press, pp. 157–158.

——. 1998. *Military Balance 1997–1998.* Oxford, UK: Oxford University Press, pp. 151–152.

——. 1999. *Military Balance 1998–1999.* Oxford, UK: Oxford University Press, pp. 153–154.

——. 2000. *Military Balance 1999–2000.* Oxford, UK: Oxford University Press, pp. 159–160.

——. 2001. *Military Balance 2000–2001.* Oxford, UK: Oxford University Press, pp. 166–167.

——. 2002. *Military Balance 2002.* Oxford, UK: Oxford University Press, p. 127, 159–161.

——. 2003. *Military Balance 2003.* Oxford, UK: Oxford University Press, p. 134.

——. 2004. *Military Balance 2004.* Oxford, UK: Oxford University Press, p. 149.

——. 2006. *Military Balance 2006.* Oxford, UK: Oxford University Press, pp. 228–229; 233.

Iqbal, Nadeem. 2003. 'Arms Gift Signals Pakistan's Afghan aims.' *Asia Times Online,* 22 February. Online, available at: atimes.com/atimes/South_Asia/ EB22Df01.html (accessed 4 December 2007).

IRIN (Integrated Regional Information Network). 2005a. 'Afghanistan: UN to Deal With Ammunition Stockpiles.' 2 January.

——. 2005b. 'Afghanistan: Low Government Presence Threatens Disbandment of Illegal Armed Groups.' 27 September.

——. 2005c. 'Rights Body Warns of Warlords' Success in Elections.' 18 October.

——. 2006. 'Afghanistan: Five Ex-commanders Surrender Arms to DIAG.' 21 February.

——. 2007. 'Afghanistan: Taliban Impose Rule, Hefty Taxes in Musa Qala District.' 2 July.

Isby, David. 1989. *War in a Distant Country: Afghanistan: Invasion and Resistance.* London: Arms and Armour.

Islamic Republic of Afghanistan. 2005a. *Millennium Development Goals Islamic Republic of Afghanistan Country Report 2005: Vision 2020.* Kabul: Islamic Republic of Afghanistan and the United Nations Development Programme (UNDP).

——. 2005b. 11 Province Main Phase DIAG Proposal. 5 November (unpublished).

——. 2005c. Guidelines for DIAG Development Activities. Unpublished.

——. 2005d. 'Guidelines for the Implementation of DIAG Main Phase: From the D&R Commission to Provincial Committees.' 20 September. Online, available at: diag.gov.af/ (accessed 4 December 2007).

——. 2005e. *Electoral Law.* Kabul: Islamic Republic of Afghanistan. Online, available at: jemb.org/eng/Legal%20Framework/Basic%20Legislation/Electoral%20law/English%20Decree.pdf (accessed 4 December 2007).

——. 2005f. DIAG JPCC Planning Documents, Draft 5. 12 May (unpublished).

——. 2006a. *Strategy for Disbandment of Illegal Armed Groups in Afghanistan.* Kabul: Islamic Republic of Afghanistan, January. Online, available at: diag.gov.af/ (accessed 4 December 2007).

——. 2006b. *Afghanistan National Development Strategy – Summary Report.* Kabul: Islamic Republic of Afghanistan.

ITAR-TASS (Moscow). 1996. 'Arms, Drugs Discovered at Afghan Border Crossing.' 3 February.

——. 2001. 'Drugs and Weapons Cache Found on Tajik–Afghan Border.' 28 March.

IWPR (Institute for War and Peace Reporting). 2002. 'Taleban Buying Up Smuggled Guns.' *IWPR ARR,* No. 34. 1 November.

Jackson, Paul. 2003. 'Warlords as Alternative Forms of Governance.' *Small Wars & Insurgencies,* Vol. 14, No. 2. June. pp. 131–150.

Jahesh, Sher Mohammad. 2006. 'Commanders' Clash Leaves One Dead in Baghlan.' *Pajhwok Afghan News.* 24 May.

Jalali, Ahmed and Lester Grau. 1994. *The Other Side of the Mountain: Mujahideen Tactics in the Soviet–Afghan War.* Quantico, VA: U.S. Marine Corps Studies and Analysis.

Jalali, Ali A. 2006. 'The Future of Afghanistan.' *Parameters.* Spring, pp. 4–19. Online, available at: Carlisle.army.mil/usawc/Parameters/06spring/jalli.htm (accessed 12 December 2007).

Jamali, A. 2004. 'The Fall of Ghor: An Ominous Development for Karzai.' *Jamestown Terrorism Monitor,* Vol. 1, No. 37. 23 June. Online, available at: Jamestown.org/publications_details.php?volume_id=401&issue_id=2996&article_id=2368148 (accessed 12 December 2007).

Jawad, Rana. 2005. 'Pakistan Recovers Truckloads of Arms from 'Biggest' Al-Qa'ida Base.' *Agence France Press.* 15 September.

JEMB (Joint Electoral Management Body). 2007. *Estimated Turnout By Province.* Online, available at: results.jemb.org/home.asp (accessed 16 August 2007).

Kabul Times. 2005. 'Land Dispute Leaves One Dead in Paktia.' *IWPR's Afghan Press Monitor,* No. 132. 14–15 August.

Kaplan, Robert. *1990–2001. Soldiers of God: With Islamic Warriors in Afghanistan and Pakistan.* New York: Vintage.

Kartha, Tara. 1999. *Tools of Terror: Light Weapons and India's Security.* New Delhi: Institute for Defence Studies and Analysis.

Karzai, Hamid. 2003. 'Consolidation of Peace in Afghanistan – Change of Order "From Guns to Plows.".' Statement at the Tokyo Conference. 22 February.

Katzman, Kenneth. 2006. 'Afghanistan: Elections, Constitution, and Government.' *Congressional Research Service (CRS) Report for Congress.* 2 November.

Kenzhetaev, Marat. 2007. 'Arms Deliveries to Afghanistan in the 1990s.' *Moscow Defense Brief,* Vol. 2, No. 8. Online, available at: mdb.cast.ru/mbd/6-2001/ns/ada/ (accessed 4 December 2007).

KHAAR. 2001. 'Fata Dealers Sell Arms to Anti-Taliban Forces.' 9 June.

Khan, Farooq. 2003. 'Arms Licence Ban Blocks Billions in Govt Revenue: Citizen's Right to Self-Protection Curtailed.' 20 January.

Khazeni, Arash and Alessandro Monsutti. 2004. 'Hazara.' In Ehsan Yarshater, ed. *Encyclopaedia Iranica,* Vol. 12. New York: Encyclopaedia Iranica Foundation.

Kingma, Kees. 2002. 'Demobilization, Reintegration and Peacebuilding in Africa.' *International Peacekeeping.* Vol. 9, No. 2, pp. 181–201.

Lake, David and Donald Rothchild. 1996. 'Containing Fear: the Origin and Management of Ethnic Conflict.' *International Security,* Vol. 21, No. 2. Autumn, pp. 45–71.

Langer, Gary. 2005. 'Poll: Four Years After the Fall of the Taliban, Afghans Optimistic About the Future.' *ABC News.* 8 December.

Lister, Sarah and Adam Pain. 2004. 'Trading in Power: The Politics of "Free" Markets in Afghanistan.' *Afghanistan Research and Evaluation Unit Briefing Paper.* Kabul: Afghan Research and Evaluation Unit. Online, available at: areu.org.af/?option=com_docman&Itermid+&task=doc_download&gid=367 (accessed 4 December 2007).

Lopes Cardozo, Barbara, Oleg O. Bilukha, Carol A. Gotway Crawford, Irshad Shaikh, Mitchell I. Wolfe, Michael L. Gerber and Mark Anderson. 2004. 'Mental Health, Social Functioning, and Disability in Postwar Afghanistan.' *Journal of the American Medical Association.* Vol. 292, No. 5, pp. 575–584.

Lowery, Mason T. 2006. 'Germany Donates 10,000 Pistols to Afghanistan.' *DefendAmerica*, 26 January. Online, available at: defendamerica.mil/articles/jan2006/a012606ms1.html (accessed 4 December 2007).

Lumpe, Lora. 1999. 'The Leader of the Pack: The United States Leads the World in Weapons Sales and Giveaways.' *Bulletin of the Atomic Scientists*, Vol. 55, No. 1. January–February.

McGeough, Paul. 2004. 'Warriors' Redundancy Scheme.' *Sydney Morning Herald*. 27 October.

——. 2005. 'Women Try to Bridge Afghanistan's Political Gulf.' *Age* (Australia). 3 September.

Maley, William. 1987. 'Political Legitimation in Contemporary Afghanistan.' *Asian Survey*, Vol. 27, No. 6. June, pp. 705–725.

——. 1991. 'Social Dynamics and the Disutility of Terror: Afghanistan, 1978–1989.' In Timothy Bushnell, Vladimir Shlapentokh, Christopher K. Vanderpool and Jeyaratnam Sundram, eds. *State Organized Terror: The Case of Violent Internal Repression.* Boulder, CO: Westview Press.

——. 1998/2001. 'Introduction: Interpreting the Taliban.' In William Maley, ed. *Fundamentalism Reborn? Afghanistan and the Taliban.* London: Hurst & Company.

Manila Philippine Daily Inquirer. 2001. 'Philippine Military Chief: Abu Sayyaf Arms Sourced From Pakistan, Afghanistan.' 28 August.

Mansfield, David. 2006. 'Water Management, Livestock and the Opium Economy: Opium Poppy Cultivation in Nangarhar and Ghor.' *AREU Case Study Series.* December.

Mansfield, David and Adam Pain. 2005. 'Opium Poppy Eradication: How to Raise Risk When There is Nothing to Lose?' *AREU Briefing Paper.* August.

Miller, Greg. 2006. 'U.S. Official Says Taliban is on the Rise.' *Los Angeles Times.* 1 March.

Monir, Makia and Borhan Younus. 2005. 'Some Polling Stations Yet to Receive Ballot Papers.' *Pajhwok Afghan News.* 17 September.

Monsutti, Alessandro. 2005. *War and Migration: Social Networks and Economic Strategies of the Hazaras of Afghanistan.* New York: Routledge.

Morarjee, Rachel. 2006. 'Doubts Intensify over Afghanistan's Future.' *Christian Science Monitor.* 11 September.

Mosnews.com. 2006. 'Russia to Supply Ammunition to Afghanistan at U.S. Request – Report.' 22 May.

Motlagh, Jason. 2006a. 'Time is on the Taliban's side.' *Asia Times.* 1 December.

——. 2006b. '16 Taliban Killed, Two Commanders Seized in Afghanistan.' *Asia Times.* 1 December.

Mousavi, Sayyed. 1998. *The Hazaras of Afghanistan: An Historical, Cultural, Economic and Political Study.* Surrey, UK: Curzon Press.

Muggah, Robert. 2004. 'Stop the Guns Targeting Aid Workers.' *Globe and Mail*, Toronto, Canada. 11 August.

Musah, Abdel-Fatau and Niobe Thompson. 1999. 'South Asia: Drugs, Guns and Regional Conflict.' In Abdel-Fatau Musah and Niobe Thompson, eds. *Over a Barrel: Light Weapons and Human Rights in the Commonwealth.* London/New Delhi: Commonwealth Human Rights Initiative.

Nasir, Anwar, 1987. 'Pakistan: The War Within: Zia's support for Afghan rebels fuels internal violence.' *Far Eastern Economic Review*, Vol. 24. September.

Nasir, Sohail Abdul. 2003. 'Afghanistan: The more it Changes.' *Bulletin of the Atomic Scientists*, Vol. 59, No. 2. March/April, pp. 40–48.

Nation (Islamabad). 1994. 'Article Surveys Market for Light Weapons.' 13 September.

NATO (North Atlantic Treaty Organization). 2007. 'NATO Support to Afghan National Army (ANA).' June. Online, available at: nato.int/issues/afghanistan/factsheets/ana-support.html (accessed 20 August 2007).

News (Islamabad). 2001. 'Former Afghan Mujahideen Assure to Support Campaign Against Arms.' 20 June.

Newsome, Bruce. 2003. 'The Myth of Intrinsic Combat Motivation.' *Journal of Strategic Studies*, Vol. 26, No. 4. December, pp. 24–46.

New York Times. 1998. 'Rebels in Sri Lanka Fight with Aid of Global Market in Light Arms.' 7 March.

——. 2006. 'Insurgents Bomb Bazaar, Injure Three.' 1 June.

NISAT (Norwegian Initiative on Small Arms Transfers). 'Afghanistan Country Profile.' Online, available at: nisat.org/default.asp?page=database_info/search.asp (accessed 4 December 2007).

Noelle, Christine. 1997. *State and Tribe in Nineteenth-Century Afghanistan: The Reign of Amir Dost Muhammad Khan (1826–1863)*. Surrey, UK: Curzon Press.

Nojumi, Neamatollah. 2002. *The Rise of the Taliban in Afghanistan: Mass Mobilization, Civil War, and the Future of the Region*. New York, NY: Palgrave.

Orazmukhamedov, K. 2002. *Jihad Turkmenistani-style*. 4 March. Online, available at: nisat.org (accessed 4 December 2007).

Outlook (Kabul). 2005. 'Candidates Again Urged to Turn in Weapons.' *IWPR's Afghan Press Monitor*, No. 163. 27 September. Online, available at: iwpr.net/archive/apm/apm_132.html (accessed 4 December 2007).

Oxfam. 2006a. *The Call for Tough Arms Control: Voices from Afghanistan*. Kabul: Oxfam, January.

——. 2006b. 'Small Arms in Afghanistan: What are the Options for a Civil Society Response?' Report of the Oxfam seminar held on 26 June 2006. Kabul: Oxfam.

——. 2006c. 'Civil Society Response to Small Arms.' Call for Concept Notes. Kabul: Oxfam.

Özerdem, Alpaslan. 2002. 'Disarmament, Demobilization and Reintegration of Former Combatants in Afghanistan: Lessons Learned from a Cross-cultural Perspective.' *Third World Quarterly*, Vol. 23, No. 5. pp. 961–975.

Pajhwok Afghan News (Kabul). 2006a. 'Dozens of Heroin Labs Destroyed in Nangarhar.' 20 March.

——. 2006b. 'One Tonne of Machinegun Bullets Seized in Herat.' 25 March.

——. 2006c. 'Afghan President Approves Formation of Tribal Militias.' 27 May.

Paracha, Abdul Sami. 2002. 'Kalashnikov Rifle's Price Doubles.' *Dawn*. 1 September.

PIPA (Program on International Policy Attitudes). 2006. 'New Poll: Afghan Public Overwhelmingly Rejects al-Qaeda, Taliban.' Press Release. January.

Pirseyedi, Bobi. 2000. *The Small Arms Problem in Central Asia: Features and Implications*. Geneva: United Nations Institute for Disarmament Research.

Post-Conflict Reforms Website. 2006. 'Heavy Weapons Cantonment.' Online, available at: ddrafg.com/heavyweapons.htm (accessed 15 March 2007).

Poulton, Richard. 2004. 'New Ideas for DDR in Afghanistan – Trying to Reduce Disappointments for Afghans and Donors.' Paper prepared for the UNIDIR

Conference on 'Increasing the Cost-Effectiveness of Weapons Collection by Involving Local Communities in Decision-Making.' Geneva, 14–15 September.

Radio Afghanistan Network. 1996a. 'Afghan Security Commission begins to Collect Weapons from Kabul.' Online, available at: nisat.org (accessed 4 December 2007).

——. 1996b. 'Weapons Cache Seized by Security Forces.' 27 October.

——. 1996c. 'Taleban Seizes Weapons Cache in Kabul.' 24 November.

——. 1996d. 'Taleban Seizes Weapons, Ammunition in Khost.' 27 November.

Radio Australia. 2004. 'Afghan Army Seizes Large Weapons Cache.' 26 July. Online, available at: nisat.org (accessed 4 December 2007).

Rahmani, Waliullah. 2006. 'Kandahar Province and the New Wave of Violence.' *Terrorism Monitor*, Vol. 4, No. 8. 20 April, pp. 1–3. Online, available at: Jamestown.org/terrorism/news/uploads/TM_004_008.pdf (accessed 4 December 2007).

Rashid, Ahmed. 2000. *Taliban: Militant Islam, Oil and Fundamentalism in Central Asia*. New Haven: Yale University Press.

——. 2006. 'Don't Think al-Qaeda is on the Back Foot, it will be on the March in 2007.' *Sunday Telegraph*. 31 December.

——. 2007. 'Letter from Afghanistan: Are the Taliban Winning?' *Current History*. January.

Reuters. 2004. 'Afghans say Capture 24 Taliban; Clashes Increase.' 18 November.

——. 2005. 'Afghans Hunt for Survivors of Blast.' 3 May.

RFE/RL (Radio Free Europe/Radio Free Liberty). 2004. 'Fighting Between Rival Commanders in Central Afghanistan.' April.

Rossi, Simonetta and Antonio Giustozzi. 2006. 'Disarmament, Demobilisation and Reintegration of Ex-Combatants in Afghanistan: Constraints and Limited Capabilities.' *Working Paper* No. 2, Series No. 2. London: LSE Crisis States Research Centre.

Roy, Olivier. 1986. *Islam and Resistance in Afghanistan*. Cambridge, UK: Cambridge University Press.

——. 1989a. 'Afghanistan – War as a Factor of Entry into Politics.' *Central Asian Survey*, Vol. 8, No. 4, pp. 43–62.

——. 1989b. 'Afghanistan: Back to tribalism or on to Lebanon?' *Third World Quarterly*, Vol. 11, No. 4, pp. 70–82.

——. 1990. *Islam and Resistance in Afghanistan*. 2nd edn. Cambridge, UK: Cambridge University Press.

Rubin, Barnett. 1995. *The Search for Peace in Afghanistan: From Buffer State to Failed State*. New Haven, CT: Yale University Press.

——. 1996. *The Fragmentation of Afghanistan: State Formation and Collapse in the International System*. New Haven, CT: Yale University Press.

——. 2003. *Identifying Options and Entry Points for Disarmament, Demobilization and Reintegration in Afghanistan*. New York: Center on International Cooperation, New York University.

——. 2007. 'Saving Afghanistan.' *Foreign Affairs*, Vol. 86, No. 1. January/February. Online, available at: Online, available at: foreignaffairs.org/20070101faessay86105/Barnett-r-rubin/saving-afghanistan.html&cid=1111719041&ei=ogh3ReuLI5uaHIrZkYUJ (accessed 12 December 2007).

Rubin, Barnett and Helen Malikyar. 2003. 'The Politics of Center–Periphery Relations in Afghanistan.' New York: Center on International Cooperation, New

York University. Online, available at: cic.nyu.edu/archive/pdf/WBCPAfgh.pdf (accessed 4 December 2007).

Rubin, Barnett, Ashraf Ghani, William Maley, Ahmed Rashid and Olivier Roy. 2001. 'Afghanistan: Reconstruction and Peace-building in a Regional Framework.' *KOFF Peacebuilding Reports.* January.

Samander, Rahimullah. 2003. 'Senior Police Official Ousted.' *IWPR Afghanistan Recovery Report,* No. 63. June 2003.

Sarabi, Humayun. 2005. 'Politics and Modern History of Hazara: Sectarian Politics.' Master of Arts in Law and Diplomacy Thesis for the Fletcher School of Law and Diplomacy, Tufts University, Medford, MA. Autumn 2005.

Sarwar, Sultan. 2006. 'Afghanistan: Reports Claim "War On Terror" Used To Hide Blood-Feud Killings.' RFE/RL. 31 March.

Saudi Press Agency. 2004. 'Three Killed in Western Afghanistan Turf War.' 8 August.

Scholte, Willem F., Miranda Olff, Peter Ventevogel, Giel-Jan de Vries, Eveline Jansveld, Barbara Lopes Cardozo and Carol A. Gotway Crawford. 2004. 'Mental Health Symptoms Following War and Repression in Eastern Afghanistan.' Vol. 292, No. 5, pp. 585–593.

Sedra, Mark. 2002. 'Challenging the Warlord Culture: Security Sector Reform in Post-Taliban Afghanistan.' *BICC Paper* 25. Bonn: Bonn International Centre for Conversion.

——. 2004a. *Securing Afghanistan's Future: Accomplishments and Strategic Pathway Forward – Disarmament, Demobilization and Reintegration of Ex-Combatants Technical Annex.* Kabul: Islamic Transitional State of Afghanistan.

——. 2004b. 'Civil Military Relations in Afghanistan: The Provincial Reconstruction Team Debate.' Paper presented at the Consultation on Strategic Policy Options for Canada in Afghanistan. Organized by Foreign Affairs Canada in partnership with the Asia-Pacific Foundation. Held in Aylmer, Quebec, Canada on 9 November.

——. 2006. 'Security Sector Reform in Afghanistan: The Slide Toward Expediency.' *International Peacekeeping.* Vol. 13, No. 1, March, pp. 94–110.

——. 2007. 'Small Arms and the State in Afghanistan: Demilitarisation, Arms Control and Procurement.' Unpublished background paper prepared for the Small Arms Survey. January.

Sedra, Mark and Peter Middlebrook. 2005. 'Beyond Bonn: Revisioning the International Compact for Afghanistan.' Silver City, NM and Washington, DC: Foreign Policy in Focus, November.

Sengupta, Kim. 2006. 'Pakistanis Accused of Aiding Taliban with Missile Parts.' *Independent* (UK). 15 March.

Shahrani, Nazif. 1984. 'Introduction: Marxist "Revolution" and Islamic Resistance in Afghanistan.' In Nazif Shahrani and Robert Canfield, eds. *Revolutions and Rebellions in Afghanistan: Anthropological Perspectives.* Berkeley, CA: University of California Press.

Shahzad, Syed Saleem. 2005. 'Armed and Dangerous: Taliban Gear Up.' *Asia Times Online.* 22 December.

——. 2006a. 'In Search of the Taliban's Missing Link.' *Asia Times.* September.

——. 2006b. 'Osama Back in the US Crosshairs.' *Asia Times Online.* 16 May.

——. 2006c. 'Taliban's New Commander Ready for a Fight.' *Asia Times Online.* 20 May.

Shaw, Geoff and David Spencer. 2003. 'Fighting in Afghanistan: Lessons from the

Soviet Intervention, 1979–89.' *Defense & Security Analysis*, Vol. 19, No. 2, pp. 177–188.

Shinwari, Ibrahim. 2002. 'Ammunition Prices in Tribal Areas Register Increase.' *Dawn*. 31 October.

Sly, Liz. 2003. 'Afghan Town of Gardez Drives away its Warlords.' *Chicago Tribune*. 9 October.

Small Arms Survey. 2003. *Small Arms Survey 2003: Development Denied*. Oxford: Oxford University Press.

Smith, Chris. 1993. 'The Diffusion of Small Arms and Light Weapons in Pakistan and Northern India.' *London Defence Studies*, No. 20. Centre for Defence Studies. September.

Statoids. Population statistics. Online, available at: statoids.com/uaf.html.

Stiger, Elca and Alessandro Monsutti. 2005. 'Transnational Networks: Recognising a Regional Reality.' *AREU Briefing Paper*. April.

Stobdan, Peter. 1997. 'Changing Matrix of Afghan Conflict.' *Strategic Analysis* (Islamabad), Vol. 19, Nos. 10–11, p. 252.

Sullivan, Kevin. 1998. 'Pakistanis Arming the World's Guerrillas.' *Washington Post Foreign Service*. 9 July.

Tarzi, Amin. 2005. 'Afghanistan: Disarming the Militias – Which Militias and Which Arms?' RFE/RL. 27 April.

Terzieff, Juliette. 2002. 'Pakistani Tribes, Gun Trade go Hand in Hand: Merchants Supply nearby Afghanistan.' *San Francisco Chronicle*. 18 March.

Thier, J. Alexander. 2003. *Security and State-Building in Afghanistan*. New York: Asia Foundation.

Tilly, Charles. 1985. 'War Making and State Making as Organized Crime.' In Peter B. Evans, Dietrich Rueschemeyer and Theda Skocpol, eds. *Bringing the State Back In*. Cambridge: Cambridge University Press, pp. 169–191.

Tran, Trini. 2006. 'U.S. giving Afghans $2B Worth of Weaponry.' *Associated Press*. 3 July.

ul Haque, Ihtasham. 2004. 'US will Buy Small Arms from Pakistan: Military Requirements of Iraq and Afghanistan.' *Dawn*. 15 July.

UNDP (United Nations Development Programme). 2004. *Afghanistan National Human Development Report 2004*. Kabul: UNDP.

——. 2005. 'Afghanistan: Haji Zaher, Commander of the Frontier Brigade in the Eastern region, Voluntarily Surrenders Stockpile of Ammunition.' 15 December.

UNEP (United Nations Environmental Programme). 2003. *Post-Conflict Environment Assessment: Afghanistan*. Online, available at: unep.org/publications/search/pub_details_s.asp?ID=109 (accessed 4 December 2007).

UNHCR (United Nations High Commission for Refugees). 2002a. 'Panjab District Profile.' 17 September. Online, available at: aims.org.af/ (accessed 4 December 2007).

——. 2002b. 'Kahmard District Profile.' 18 September. Online, available at: Online, available at: aims.org.af/afg/dist_profiles/unhcr_district_profiles/northern/baghlan/kahmard/kahmard.pdf (accessed 4 December 2007).

——. 2002c. 'Imam-Sahib District Profile.' 12 September. Online, available at: Online, available at: aims.org.af/afg/dist_profiles/unhcr_district_profiles/northern/kunduz/iman_sahib_sahib.pdf (accessed 4 December 2007).

——. 2002d. 'Khanabad District Profile.' 4 August. Online, available at: Online, available at: aims.org.af/afg/dist_profiles/unhcr_district_profiles/northern/ kunduz/khan_abad.pdf (accessed 4 December 2007).

——. 2002e. 'Kunduz District Profile.' 12 September. Online, available at: Online, available at: aims.org.af/afg/dist_profiles/unhcr_district_profiles/northern/ kunduz/kunduz.pdf (accessed 4 December 2007).

UNICEF. 2004. 'Child Soldier Demobilization Shows Results in Afghanistan.' 16 December. Online, available at: unicef.org/media/media_24531.html (accessed 4 December 2007).

United States Department of Defense. 2001. 'Afghanistan: Country Handbook.' DOD-2630-AFG-001-02. October.

United States Department of State. 2006a. 'Afghanistan: 2005 Country Reports on Human Rights Practices.' 8 March. Online, available at: state.gov/g/drl/ris/ hrrpt/2005/61704.htm (accessed 4 December 2007).

——. 2006b. 'NATO Troops to Destroy Cache of 15,000 Land Mines in Afghanistan.' 21 March. Online, available at: Online, available at: globalsecurity.org/military/library/news/2006/03/mil-060321-usia01.htm (accessed 4 December 2007).

United States Department of State and United States Department of Defense. 2006. *Interagency Assessment of Afghanistan Police Training and Readiness*. Washington, DC: United States Department of State and United States Department of Defense Offices of Inspector Generals, November.

UNSECOORD (UN Security Coordinator). 2004. *Afghanistan Country Security Situation Report*. 14 to 20 June 2004.

UNSG (United Nations Secretary General). 2000. 'The Situation in Afghanistan and its International Peace and Security: Report of the Secretary-General.' A/55/393-S/2000/875, 18 September.

——. 2004. 'The Situation in Afghanistan and its Implications for International Peace and Security: Report of the Secretary-General.' A/58/742-S/2004/230, 19 March.

——. 2005. 'The Situation in Afghanistan and its Implications for Peace and Security.' A/60/224-S/2005/525, 12 August.

——. 2006. 'The Situation in Afghanistan and its Implications for International Peace and Security: Report of the Secretary-General.' A/60/712-S/2006/145, 7 March.

USCIS (US Citizenship and Immigration Services). 2004. *Afghanistan: Information on Taliban Activity After the Fall of the Taliban Regime in November 2001*. 5 January.

USGAD (United States Government Accountability Office). 2005. *Afghanistan Security: Efforts to Establish Army and Police Have Made Progress, But Future Plans Need to Be Better Defined*. Washington, DC: GAO, June.

Utas, Mats. 2005. 'Agency of Victims: Young Women in the Liberian Civil War.' In Alcinda Honwana and Filip De Boeck, eds. *Makers and Breakers: Children and Youth in Postcolonial Africa*. Oxford: James Currey.

van Niekerk, Phillip and André Verlöy. 2002. *Africa's 'Merchant of Death' Sold Arms to the Taliban*. 31 January. Online, available at: public-i.org/report.aspx?aid=25 (accessed 4 December 2007).

Wali, Abdel. 2002. 'Disarmament Drive.' *International War and Peace Reporting Afghanistan Recovery Report*. No. 20, 22 July.

Walsh, Declan. 2006a. 'UN Report Accuses Afghan MPs of Torture and Massacres.' *Guardian*. 12 June.

——. 2006b. 'Jihad Equipment is not for Personal Use.' *Guardian* (UK). 11 December.

Watson, Paul. 2006. 'In Afghanistan, Money Tips the Scales of Justice.' *Los Angeles Times*. 18 December.

Westervelt, Eric. 2002. 'Analysis: Afghanistan's Government Prepares to use Military Force to Control Warlord Padsha Khan Zadran.' National Public Radio. 16 August. Online, available at: highbeam.com/doc/1P1-55304111.html (accessed 4 December 2007).

Wilder, Andrew. 2005. 'A House Divided? Analysing the 2005 Afghan Elections.' *AREU Issues Paper*. December.

Xinhuan. 2005. 'Bosnian Serb Republic to Donate Weapons to Afghanistan.' 17 December. Online, available at: Online, available at: english.peopledaily.com.cn/200512/18/eng20051218_228897.html (accessed 4 December 2007).

——. 2006a. 'Afghan Officers Arrested for Smuggling Weapons to Taliban.' 23 September 2006. Online, available at: Online, available at: english.peopledaily.com.cn/200609/22/eng20060922_305146.html (accessed 4 December 2007).

——. 2006b. '2 Killed, 60 Injured in Ammunition Cache Blast in Afghanistan.' 24 March.

Yousaf, Mohammad and Mark Adkin. 1992. *Afghanistan – The Bear Trap: The Defeat of a Superpower*. Barnsley, UK: Leo Cooper.

Yusufzai, Rahimullah. 2000. 'Resistance in Afghanistan: The Panjshir Model.' Reprinted from *Regional* Studies, Islamabad, Vol. III, No. 3, in Verinder Grover, ed. *Afghanistan: Government and Politics*. New Delhi, India: Deep & Deep Publications Pvt. Ltd.

Zahid, Sultan Aziz. 2002a. 'Chaos Outside the Capital.' *KnightRidder/Tribune News Service*. April.

——. 2002b. 'Khost in Turmoil.' *IWPRs ARR*, No. 21, 2 August.

Zubrzycki, John. 1996. 'Afghan Refugees Transform An Old Silk-Road Stop.' *Christian Science Monitor*, Vol. 26, September. Online, available at: csmonitor.com/1996/0926/092696.intl.letterfrom.1.html (accessed 12 December 2007).

Index